Praise for *Lords of the Deccan*

'Rarely has the history of peninsular India, of this period, been told as anything more than a dry and ceaseless monotony of battles between obscure and unimaginable rulers. Anirudh Kanisetti's *Lords of the Deccan* has lifted the history of south India out of the dusty archives of Indian archaeology and epigraphy. Meticulously researched and narrated with a style that is at once lively and judicious, *Lords of the Deccan* synthesizes a wide array of innovations in recent scholarship with the older tradition of political history. Kanisetti harnesses his impressive skills as a storyteller to breathe new life into his subject, deftly interweaving the careers of individual kings, the structures and networks of noble families, and the great transformations in religious, cultural and literary life into a single coherent and riveting account of south India in this crucial period, which saw the region enter historical centre-stage and take on many contours still palpable today.'

– Daud Ali

'*Lords of the Deccan* is the completely thrilling and game-changing debut of a major new talent. Anirudh Kanisetti is a superb writer and a talented storyteller as well as an impressively judicious and subtle historian. He breathes life into the rajas, scholars and soldiers of two nearly forgotten medieval dynasties and resurrects for us a whole extraordinary world with flair, nuance, clarity and sophistication.'

– William Dalrymple

'*Lords of the Deccan* is an assured and supremely entertaining account of a clamorous, tumultuous and little-known period of Indian history – the early medieval Deccan period. Navigating these unchartered waters with considerable confidence and panache, Anirudh Kanisetti brings to vivid light both the savagery and the song of these riotous five hundred years. He does so, moreover, by dismantling the opaque language of historiography for the lay-reader and giving them the tools to truly understand the dialect of power – the temple building, the ode-writing, the painting and even the very manipulation of language and religion. With *Lords of the Deccan*, Kanisetti has claimed for himself a place of pride in the cartography of Indian history writing.'

– Ira Mukhoty

Lords of the Deccan

Lords of the Deccan

Southern India from the Chalukyas
to the Cholas

Anirudh Kanisetti

juggernaut

JUGGERNAUT BOOKS
C-I-128, First Floor, Sangam Vihar, Near Holi Chowk,
New Delhi 110080, India

First published by Juggernaut Books 2022

10 9 8 7 6 5

P-ISBN: 9789391165055
E-ISBN: 9789391165024

Typeset in Adobe Caslon Pro by R. Ajith Kumar, Noida

Printed at Thomson Press India Ltd

ಅಹೋ! ಕಥಮ್ ಏತದ್ ಮಯಾ ಕೃತಮ್!

And to the generations who have shaped the world before us.

Contents

x   Contents

Introduction

Every monsoon, rain clouds bathe the cool, dark surfaces of an ancient temple in Ellora, Maharashtra. Peals of thunder echo in its cavernous halls, like the bells that once greeted throngs of devotees.

There's something dazzlingly different about this gigantic temple. You see, it isn't a building of the kind you and I might be used to. It wasn't assembled bottom up from the ground, brick by brick, stone by stone.

It was *excavated*.

It is called the Kailashanatha, the Lord of Kailasha, because generations of awestruck visitors have seen it as a manifestation of the mountain upon which the god Shiva lives. To fashion it, thousands of sculptors carved up an enormous basalt cliff face, removing two *million* cubic feet of rock (enough to fill two Olympic-sized swimming pools). They did so in barely twenty years in the ninth century CE, with a plan breathtaking in its scale and attention to detail, leaving behind a monolith the size of a football field and about half the height of the Leaning Tower of Pisa. A monolith in the shape of a spectacular south Indian temple, with the weight of its superstructure cascading down in wider and wider tiers, decked with sculptures of frolicking deities. The Kailashanatha is a *single sculpture* so large that it approaches the size of modern buildings. As a monolithic structure, it is unlikely to be matched in size and beauty for the rest of human history.

This extraordinary edifice was made by people who thought themselves every bit as modern as you or I. They were a vibrant, warlike, sophisticated people. They were ruled by men who claimed the majestic title of Sri-Prithivi-Vallabha, the Beloved of Sri (the goddess of fortune) and Prithivi (the goddess of Earth). Their empire dominated the ancient Deccan plateau at the heart of India, especially the states of Maharashtra and Karnataka, today an area almost as large as Germany and many times more populous. At their peak, these Vallabha emperors received the prostrations of hosts of vassal kings from Madhya Pradesh, Chhattisgarh, Odisha, Andhra, Telangana and Tamil Nadu, and dominated most of India south of the Narmada river. One Arab merchant, visiting this medieval superpower in the ninth–tenth centuries, mentioned the lord of the Deccan in the same breath as the Abbasid caliph, the emperor of China, and the Byzantine emperor.[1] Another visited the glittering capital of the Deccan, Manyakheta, and left us with an account of its wonders:

> … in that city there are for the ordinary people one million elephants which carry the merchandise … In this temple there are about twenty thousand idols made of a variety of precious metals, and carved stones mounted with artistically-worked precious jewels … [There] is an idol whose height is twelve cubits and is placed on a throne of gold in the centre of a golden cupola, the whole of which is set with jewels like white pearl, ruby, sapphire, blue and emerald stone.[2]

Both these accounts – even allowing for some exaggeration – leave no doubt that in the eyes of the medieval world the Deccan was the wealthiest and most powerful of all the kingdoms of the Indian subcontinent.

This book is a story about this time when the Deccan ruled India: an epic journey through five hundred years of a history that has long been forgotten.

☙

Our tale begins in the sixth century CE, a few decades after the collapse of the Western Roman Empire in Europe, only a few years after the disintegration of the Gupta empire of northern India. In the dry and arid heartland of the Deccan, cattle raids, banditry and abduction were ubiquitous. Here, an obscure clan of *chalke* (crowbar)-wielding agriculturists or pastoralists[3] learned the difficult lessons of war and diplomacy, and began to battle their way up the shifting hierarchies of India's kingdoms. Within the space of three generations, they declared themselves a new imperial dynasty – the Chalukyas – established a mighty citadel in the sandstone cliffs of Vatapi in northern Karnataka, and exploded on to the historical stage by defeating the dominant ruler of north India. That collision, which occurred in 618 CE on the shores of the Narmada river, is where this book begins. It will set the stage for a half-millennium of Deccan dominance.

In the first part of this book we will watch these Chalukyas, masters of medieval Indian geopolitics, at work. They understood very well that there was little wealth to be scratched out of the arid lands of the Deccan. Soon after their emergence on the medieval Indian stage, they went to war north, south, east and west, ruthlessly raiding their wealthier neighbours and breaking into the networks of the Indian Ocean trade. We will watch how an empire was made, attempting to peek, through the dust of centuries, into the minds and hearts of the men and women at its centre. We will accompany them in these wars, gaining a singular look into the machinations of medieval Indian power, and the glories and tragedies associated with it. We'll see how this power shaped and was shaped by the turbulent religious and social tides of medieval India, observing these upstart Chalukyas – constantly looking for new propaganda to rally their unruly vassal chiefs and subjects – ally with the rising tides of *bhakti* devotion to Shiva the Destroyer; patronize the use of Sanskrit literary texts in south India; and embark on a wave of monumental building projects, establishing some of the oldest surviving temples in the subcontinent.

By the mid-eighth century, this project of dynastic aggrandizement had elevated the Chalukyas to the heart of a sprawling network of vassal kings, governors, trading ports and pilgrimage sites that dominated the Deccan plateau and much of India's western coast. A cadet Chalukya line ruled a kingdom of their own in Andhra, on India's east coast. This vast agglomeration of people could mobilize resources of such a scale that a Chalukya vassal, acting on his own initiative, was able to smash the Umayyad Caliphate's attempt to conquer Gujarat in 737 CE, defeating a seemingly invincible army that had seized Sind and parts of Gujarat, and even reached the outskirts of Ujjain in modern-day Madhya Pradesh.

In the second part of this book, as the world changes, we will watch the Vallabha emperors of the Deccan – a title now held by a clan called the Rashtrakutas – lead the plateau to a splendid apogee. During their time, the Abbasid Caliphate in the west and the Tang dynasty of China to the east oversaw an age of flourishing trade with the Indian subcontinent. The cities of the arid plateau and the ports of western India, under Rashtrakuta control, began to trade in everything from indigo and perfumes to exotic poisons, fruits, animals and spices. The Rashtrakutas took advantage, inviting Arab merchants to serve as the governors of harbours humming with activity, ordering fine Sanskrit verses to be composed in their honour, and importing the finest horses in the world to serve in their armies. We will follow them as they project this power into the rest of the subcontinent. They will lead armies of marauding south Indians into the Gangetic plains, nearly a millennium before the rise of the Marathas. They will manipulate the politics of Madhya Pradesh, Andhra Pradesh and Tamil Nadu from their seats of power in Maharashtra and Karnataka, moving pawns around a vast geopolitical chessboard. We will watch them compile great grammatical treatises in Kannada, and hear how their poets mounted the first serious challenge to literary Sanskrit, once India's dominant language of power and prestige. We will watch them commission the dazzling

Kailashanatha temple and the splendid imperial city of Manyakheta, projects that cost tens if not hundreds of millions of dollars in that day's currency. And we will see how, like their predecessors, they used religion as royal propaganda, patronizing a unique form of Jainism that once ruled south India as the equal of Hinduism.

However, the rest of India did not sit idly by as the Deccan threw its weight around the subcontinent. In the third and final part of this book, we will see how the rise of new challengers to its dominance left the medieval Deccan world in burning ruins. We will watch the military disasters that led to the collapse of the Rashtrakutas – easily some of the most calamitous upsets in Indian history – and observe how, in the bloody anarchy that followed, the Chalukyas returned to once again restore order to the Deccan. Their return came not a minute too soon. In the deep south, a new power rose to challenge them: the imperial Cholas, perhaps the most famous of all south Indian dynasties today. Over the course of twenty years, we will accompany the terrified courts of the Deccan as they watched the Cholas burn and conquer kingdoms through India's east coast and attack Indonesia, an unheard-of feat for any medieval Indian polity. And we will see how those bloodthirsty conquerors finally met their match in the gritty, determined Chalukya Vallabhas of the Deccan. We will witness the clash of these two south Indian superpowers, the culmination of centuries of social and political evolution in the Deccan and the Tamil country. Both commanded armies numbering in the tens of thousands, both ruled enormous, sophisticated courts in bejewelled temple-studded capitals. Both hated each other with a burning passion that razed cities to the ground, tore families apart, killed kings and left kingdoms in ruins.

In the midst of this chaos, a new generation of Chalukyas and Cholas tried, at last, to put an end to the violence. Betraying his father and brother, a new Vallabha, wiser and warier than his predecessors, backstabbed his way to power with the help of a Chola ally. But just when it seemed that – at long last – peace would return to the land, one of the most shocking political upsets of south Indian history unfolded in the Tamil country, ending any hope of peace and reconciliation between the two great geopolitical regions. As vassals of the Chalukyas rose to challenge their dominance across the Deccan, we will leave the plateau on the brink of a century of renewed war, that would only end with Delhi's invasions of the south and the rise of Vijayanagara and the Deccan Sultanates.

⁓

Most Indians today are unaware that the Deccan has such a dramatic and world-changing past. Our understanding of the history of this vast, diverse subcontinent is based on an obsession with 'imperial moments' – often fleeting moments in history when north India is able to impose its dominance over other regions. In our school textbooks – which retain a disproportionate influence in shaping our identities and sense of the past – we leap five hundred years from the Mauryas of the second century BCE to the Guptas of the third century CE. We then jump six hundred years from the end of the Gupta empire directly to the arrival of the Turkic sultans in north India in the twelfth century, and thence move neatly to the Mughals, the British and then Independence. Somehow, in this subcontinent that is as large as, more populous than and exponentially more diverse than western Europe, we are used to ignoring the histories of entire peoples, eras and regions when thinking about how India became India.

This is a ludicrous way to contemplate the subcontinent's history. Ignoring the history of the Deccan in recounting the history of India is like ignoring the history of France or Germany in telling the history of Europe.

This book aims to do something about that. It is the story of India between two north Indian 'imperial moments', the half millennium or so after the end of the Gupta empire and before the establishment of the Delhi Sultanate. In order to do so, it roots itself unabashedly in the Deccan. Yet it does not seek to replace a north Indian 'imperial moment' with a south Indian one, but instead seeks to develop a more complicated and interconnected narrative of the history of this enormous and diverse land between the Himalayas and the Indian Ocean.

Our modern obsession with 'imperial moments' makes it difficult to appreciate the scale and uniqueness of the subcontinent's history. By now, every region of India has its legends of great and glorious monarchs who 'made contributions' to a medieval or ancient culture implicitly connected to a contemporary political identity. This view reduces our past to a stale series of moralistic stories and figures who serve black-and-white conceptions of linguistic, regional or religious glory. In this view, Indian kings were not living, breathing human beings like you or I, but flawless paragons, images based on little more than tiresome sermonizing as to what constitutes 'greatness'.

On the other hand, a new trend in popular history attempts to paint them as sexy influencers similar to what one would find in HBO's *Game of Thrones*; another makes them out to be enlightened crusaders for human rights a thousand years before the concept existed. These caricatures are boring substitutes for the vibrant and diverse lives that our ancestors actually lived.

This book takes a somewhat different approach to thinking about and writing about the past.

Imagine that somehow, in the year 3020, all that remains of India from 2020 are ads issued by the Union government in newspapers in Uttar Pradesh; Instagram posts from posh art galleries in New Delhi; and recordings of grand galas attended by the who's who of society, industry and the art world in Mumbai. Future historians decide to engage with this evidence from their past in three ways. One group diligently collects the government's ads into a neat chronology, declaring it the most effective government that ever existed, the most flawless and intellectual political leadership ever, an exemplar in pandemic management, economic recovery and social harmony for all who came after. Another pores over the Instagram posts and waxes eloquent about the amazing art that filled the museums and dreams, starry-eyed, of the generous patrons who must have showered money upon the talented artists who created them. Another fashions gorgeously produced sensory experiences that hardly anyone can afford to purchase, filled with tear-inducing nostalgia about the lavish events and luxurious clothing of this long-forgotten golden age. Crowds of people shake their heads sadly and yearn to go back to those days.

Under such circumstances, it would be easy to ignore the humdrum struggles of the millions of other people who lived in India in the 2020s and didn't get to leave behind the fragments of evidence that our imaginary thirty-first century historians are so enamoured with. It would be easy to forget about Kolkata, Chennai, Bengaluru, Hyderabad.

This – fragmentary evidence fit into feel-good nationalist sermons or feel-cool romantic narratives – is the state of popular writing about medieval India today. A thousand years on, we have forgotten how to imagine a past India as searing and *real* as the India we inhabit today.

So how will this book be any different? We cannot magically conjure up more evidence than actually exists from more than a thousand years ago. Not a lot survives from the time this book explores, partially due to the lack of systematic archaeological study. As far as actual evidence goes, we're mostly stuck with royal land grants full of kingly boasts of generosity, religiosity, and administrative, sexual, artistic and military prowess. We have imposing temples covered with sculptures. We have literary and sculptural portraits of glittering court life. Like our imagined 2020–3020 scenario, a thousand years on, all the evidence we have from this distant time was shaped by a tiny and supremely well-off social elite and their self-promotion. If we are to have a realistic understanding of our history, we need to interpret this keeping in mind that these are mere fragments of a vast and complicated world similar to ours, inhabited by individuals who shared the same fundamental human impulses – including the urge to pretend they were less imperfect than they actually were.

And so the kings and queens you will meet in this book are neither flawless paragons nor sexy influencers. Instead, they are much like people you might see around you today. This book will help you understand their activities – war, politics, intrigue, patronage – as they were intended and as they were perceived at the time, from battlefield savagery to temple building to literature and sculpture. The book has no heroes or villains, no 'superior' or 'inferior' regions or cultures or morals. Instead, it is a tale of the grand forces of nature and randomness, and the tiny humans who dare to make history out of it all. It will explore the complexity of power and people in medieval India, so similar to our India. We will discern a close alliance of religion and politics; ruthless violence against dissenters and rivals; relentless narcissism and ambition; stark inequality; monumental architecture; seductive glamour; and ravishing, unparalleled, immortal art. It is not a dull, comforting history, but a vivid, fascinating past far closer to the reality we inhabit.

❧

The five hundred years of history through which we'll journey are among the most misunderstood in our modern understanding of the past. Of late, it has become fashionable to accept a colonial-era tripartite division of India's history: a 'Hindu' period, a golden age, called 'ancient'; a 'Muslim' period, a dark age, called 'medieval'; a 'British' period, enlightened, modern. The archaeological and academic consensus does not support this simplistic division. Since the early twentieth century at least, generations of scholars have excoriated it as a deliberate fabrication intended to portray the British as 'rescuing' a Hindu India from 'Mahomedan' tyranny. This image comes across very clearly in works such as Robert Sewell's *A Forgotten Empire: Vijayanagara – A Contribution to the History of India*, which remain popular today for lack of accessible modern writing about the period.

Just like the stereotypes of the rich and powerful which we saw above, this tripartite division obscures a past that is far more complicated than we might think. Historical India is a unique and fascinating world, with features far more profound than the religion a bunch of royals happened to follow. Drawing on more systematic and objective appraisals of the evidence, the scholarly consensus now recognizes an 'ancient' period stretching from the third century BCE to the fifth–sixth centuries CE, involving a deep connection to Central Asia coupled with religious and political efflorescence. This era gradually transitioned into an 'early medieval' period during the seventh to twelfth centuries, associated with radically new ways of organizing polities and societies in the subcontinent, as international trade grew and religions became vastly more complex and politically involved. This was followed by a 'late medieval' period from the thirteenth to the sixteenth centuries involving deeper cultural, political and religious engagement with the Persianate world. The epoch transitioned into one of increasingly powerful and globalized states in the 'early modern' period from the sixteenth to the nineteenth centuries, finally bringing us to the 'modern' period of the subcontinent's history with the onset of colonialism.

Over the time this book covers – the early medieval period, roughly the seventh–twelfth centuries CE – the courts and battlefields of India witnessed events contemporaneous with the most dramatic changes in global history: the birth of Islam in Arabia, the Abbasid 'Golden Age' in Iraq, the formation of the Holy Roman Empire in Germany, the Great Schism between Catholic and Orthodox Christianity, the Song dynasty's economic revolution in China, the rise of neo-Confucianism, high chivalric courtly culture, and the Norman conquest of England. Through this time, India saw supremely important and influential developments in religion, art, architecture, literature and political economy. The major geopolitical regions of this subcontinent – the mountains of the Himalayas, the Gangetic plains, the coasts of Odisha and the Tamil country, the arid pastures of Rajasthan, the Malwa plateau, and of course the Deccan – saw new forms of political, social and religious organization, and developed increasingly complex interrelationships within themselves and with each other. These new ways of doing things would shape the subcontinent into a form we can recognize today.

Hundreds of new cities and towns grew during the medieval period, and rose to prominence. Many of them still survive in some form today: the cities of Dhara, Kalyana, Vatapi, Thanjavur, Kanchi, Old Goa, Banavasi, Mamallapuram, Khajuraho, Warangal, Halebidu and Kannauj. Salons and courts reverberated with the recitation of marvellous literature. Artisans made sumptuous textiles, paintings and jewellery. Their products adorned the bodies of cultured aristocrats and talented dancers participating in rich, diverse and sophisticated material cultures. Thousands of elaborate sculptures and temples were assembled in increasingly complex and awe-inspiring forms. They were paid for by the wealth that perfumed lords and ladies wrung from a growing population of emaciated agriculturists.

All this was nourished by trade and cultural exchange with the rest of the world: and the drama, depth and spectacle of medieval India is easily on par with the global events mentioned above. India had its own William the Conqueror equivalents who invaded ancient island kingdoms and made them their own; its own religious movements whose waves of devotion transformed the lives of millions; its own charismatic, ruthless emperors who remade entire countries in their images; its own powerful, uncompromising religious sects drawing on centuries-old philosophical traditions, whose struggles for power and influence led to the making and breaking of kingdoms. Yet their relationship with the rest of the world – or even their relationship with the rest of Indian history – is poorly understood, at least in the domain of popular history.

This book seeks to remedy this gap in our conception of our past, because no story of these transformations that shook India and the world can be told without giving the medieval Deccan the centrality it deserves.

༄

The erasure of the Deccan from our historical consciousness is one of the strangest reversals of fortunes in Indian history, especially given what its contemporaries thought of it.

Think about the last major Indian empire before this period, that of the Guptas. The Guptas are increasingly present in popular 'historical' fiction in India, always a good metric of the recognizability of a historical dynasty to a general audience (not coincidentally, Maratha, Mughal, Rajput and Chola fiction are also high up on the bestseller list). The Guptas are often thought of as *the* Indian Golden Age, the pinnacle of India's religious history before the coming of the Turks, as well as the apogee of Indian architecture and martial power and art and poetry. Yet on every one of these counts they pale in comparison with their successors in medieval India in general, and the medieval Deccan in particular.

At their peak, almost the entirety of India south of the Narmada would pay the Vallabhas tribute and acknowledge their overlordship – a record matched by no Deccan or south Indian polity before or since. In comparison, Gupta influence was predominantly felt in Uttar Pradesh and Bihar, though they exercised some control in Madhya Pradesh and Gujarat and may have received tribute from as far away as regions in modern-day Pakistan in the northwest of the subcontinent. These north Indian kings only ever managed to attack southern India once, under the reign of the ruthless Samudragupta. Compare him to the *five* Deccan Vallabhas who attacked north India, one (Indra III) reaching as far as Kannauj. One (Vijayaditya I) may have made it as far as the Ganga before being captured, another (Dhruva I) smashed two of north India's most powerful armies near the confluence of the Ganga and Yamuna. At least two (Krishna III and Someshvara I) sacked, burned and subjugated Madhya Pradesh before turning their attentions elsewhere. To the medieval Deccan mind, the Gangetic plains were little more than a stage for the display of their intimidating military might before the shocked eyes of the subcontinent's other kings.

And who were these other kings? Barely a century after the collapse of the Guptas, their political legacy in north India almost completely vanished, to be replaced by other dynasties – the Maukharis, the Pushyabhutis, the Palas, the Pratiharas and, later, the Chandellas, the Paramaras, the Gahadavalas, the Chahamanas and many others – some of whom we will meet through the course of this book. Many of these medieval dynasties arguably left a far deeper imprint on India's literary and aesthetic culture than the Guptas ever did.

Yet all of them pale before the extraordinary power and influence of the emperors of the Deccan, who shaped the fate of many modern-day Indian states, some of which exceed the size and population of European countries. The Kakatiyas of Telangana and the Hoysalas of Karnataka, both of whom still occupy a hallowed place in regional memory, were vassals of the Deccan Vallabhas; they broke free in the chaos that engulfed the Deccan in the thirteenth century, before the invasions of the Delhi Sultanate. The Kadambas and the Shilaharas, their vassals in Goa, founded the great port of Gopakapattinam, which would eventually draw the avarice of the Portuguese and form the nucleus of what is now Old Goa. The bloodthirsty campaigns of the Vallabhas even, inadvertently, led to the emergence of the famous imperial Cholas of the eleventh century. How ironic that when south

India is remembered at all in popular Indian history it is only the Cholas who feature in it, totally overshadowing the Chalukyas and the Rashtrakutas, their accidental preceptors and deadliest rivals.

All this is just the tip of the iceberg, a simplistic comparison of the military and political aspects of power that loom so tall in our modern historical consciousness. You'll see here, as we explore the other aspects of medieval Indian power, that the lords of the Deccan really *made* India.

Hinduism as we know it in southern India might not have existed if not for them. Think of temple visits, for example: when the Deccan began its long trek to imperial power, the idea of enshrining Hindu gods in temples was still new, and primarily a north Indian one. As part of their propaganda projects, Chalukya kings lavished patronage on this new 'Puranic' form of Hinduism, creating a religious practice focused on pilgrimages and on ritual worship at temples built by kings. This decision was hugely significant in the fractious religious landscape of medieval south India, where religious sects professing many different rituals and routes to salvation competed for influence, land, patrons and devotees. The patronage of the Chalukyas, and kings like them, would swing the balance of power decidedly in favour of the many religious practices that we now call Hindu. But in the Deccan, this 'Hinduism' coexisted with an innovative form of Jainism that drew on a similar set of practices: organized monasteries, temples, public rituals, pilgrimage. South Indian Jainism, patronized by the Chalukyas' successors to Deccan overlordship, the Rashtrakutas, was a unique, warlike form of this ostensibly peaceful religion, and was very popular with the Deccan's glamorous military aristocracy. The staggering plurality and contestation that marks medieval Deccan religion is an important counterpoint to our popular notion of India as an eternally or unchangingly Hindu country.

As with religion, so with many other aspects of medieval India. The Deccan, as the subcontinent's dominant power, straddled axes of exchange stretching from Kashmir to Kanyakumari, from Sind to Bengal. Ideas and migrants poured in, drawn by the Vallabhas' wealth, and they mingled with the peoples of the heart of the subcontinent, arriving at uniquely Deccan forms that would in turn spread out to influence the rest of India.

For example, the earliest Deccan temples – some of which are the oldest still-standing temples in the subcontinent today – freely took elements from both north and south India. But Deccanis soon began to innovate entirely new plans of their own. As the Deccan grew ever more socially and politically complex and more influential, we begin to see Deccani temple design elements as far away as Madhya Pradesh, and vice versa. As part of a broader medieval Indian trend towards more elaborate temples based on iterations of simple patterns, the Deccan began to build spectacular star-shaped shrines that have never been equalled since.

The Chalukya emperors also adapted and reworked north Indian Sanskrit political propaganda to suit the Deccan, sparking off generations of imitations and a feverish era of Sanskrit literary production across southern India. Over the centuries, as south India's cities and courts grew ever larger and wealthier, its aesthetics and its grand religious and poetic ideas, enriched the vibrant intellectual culture of Sanskrit, adding to the corpus of thousands of texts on everything from grammar to architecture to political theory. The successors of the Chalukyas, the Rashtrakuta emperors, turned this dynamic on its head: they took a south Indian Sanskrit grammatical treatise and used it to create a grammar for Kannada, the language of the people of Karnataka, the heart of their empire. In doing so, they set off an explosion of regional literature that lasted off and on for a thousand years – the first time any vernacular language successfully challenged Sanskrit's dominance of court culture. If not for their activities, it is doubtful that many south Indian languages (with the exception of Tamil) would have the hallowed literary tradition they now do.

And so on, and so on. Through this book, we will delve into the lives of the men who ruled the Deccan and the complex ways in which this region changed over half a millennium. We will explore how art, literature, religion and architecture were influenced by these stories, holding these fragments of history up as a mirror to a dazzlingly complicated past. And we'll maybe begin to fill in that all-important gap in our concept of what Indianness should mean to us and to the rest of the world.

Though modern Indians have forgotten the Deccan, early modern Indians – in particular, the people of the Deccan Sultanates and Vijayanagara – looked to its ancient emperors for inspiration. The awe-inspiring temples they built across the land impressed many an Adil Shahi sultan, who built palaces in the Chalukya capital of Kalyana and commissioned texts drawing on the culture of their courts, attempting to connect themselves to the Chalukyas' prestige. The rival kings of Vijayanagara used the Chalukya dynastic crest, the boar, as their imperial standard; a Vijayanagari dynasty explicitly claimed the title of 'Chalukya Chakravarti' (Chalukya emperor) for some of its members, and attempted to directly or indirectly control Kalyana; and the empire even reassembled a full-fledged Chalukya temple tank in the royal centre of the city as a sign of its great antecedents.

All this goes to show that the lords of the Deccan were supremely influential people in Indian history. They are worth understanding on their own terms, as the proud rulers of a proud empire untouched by twentieth-century ideas of how a single 'Indian' history should look. But I should clarify again that this book is not a panegyric to them, and that medieval India was a dark, violent and unequal place. The medieval lords of the Deccan were not saintly devotees or noble conquerors or brilliant masterminds. They were human beings doing the best they could, responding to personal disasters, trying to get rich and be happy and find companionship and see beauty in a difficult world. Changing the course of human history was just an unplanned side effect of all that.

A few brief words on the research that went into this book: It began through a quest to understand the history of Andhra and Karnataka, the states where I was born and live in respectively. I was driven to write it by the strange lack of any accessible modern writing on this period.

I am a researcher, writer and digital public humanities scholar, and still a historian-in-training. I would not have been able to write this book without the efforts of generations of academics who have unravelled various aspects of Deccan history. I've read them as comprehensively and critically as I can in order to assemble their insights here in an attempt to bring the medieval Deccan to life in a way that resonates with modern readers. The works of Daud Ali, Durga Prasad Dikshit, A.S. Altekar, G. Yazdani, Adam Hardy, Sheldon Pollock, Shonaleeka Kaul and Whitney Cox were integral to this project. I used studies of inscriptional evidence and medieval texts by Cynthia Talbot, Ronald Inden, Richard H. Davis, K.A. Nilakanta Sastri, Noboru Karashima and Y. Subbarayulu; studies of the interactions between India and the eastern Indian Ocean by Tansen Sen, Hermann Kulke and Kenneth R. Hall; translations of medieval Kannada texts by R.V.S. Sundaram; works on the political economy of medieval south India by Jayashri Mishra, R. Champakalakshmi, R.N. Nandi, Aruna Pariti and Meera Abraham; and my own critical study of inscriptions from the period, as collected in the *Epigraphia Indica*, *Epigraphia Carnatica* and *Indian Antiquary*.

A limitation of my research has been my lack of knowledge of Sanskrit and Old Kannada, which has forced me to rely on translations. Scholars have also tended to focus on textual evidence to understand this period, partially due to the lack of systematic archaeological excavations – an issue highlighted by Jason Hawkes and Derek Kennet. As a partial remedy, I have attempted to use materials from art history to trace out social, political and economic trends. I offer challenging reinterpretations of existing evidence and complicate the romantic portrayals and misconceptions we have of medieval India, and I explain the reasoning and the evidence for doing so in detail in my notes.

Some of what I have chosen to depict may be difficult to establish definitively, given the highly fragmentary state of the evidence. In particular, it is extremely difficult to reconstruct the lived experiences of people from the period, which has forced me to indulge in reasonable speculation. In general, I try to phrase these speculations as tentatively as possible, usually in the form of questions. Explanations and evidence supporting these speculations can be found in the notes. In general, they are based on comparative study from other parts of the medieval world as well as inferences from Sanskrit literature and inscriptions from across southern India. I do not claim that my narrative is definitive or the last word on the subject: this is, first and foremost, a work of popular history.

But I have kept you here for too long. Can you hear a great drum beating, the sounds of a forest in panic as animals flee from the approach of thousands of people? The Vallabha calls for our attention. A terrible battle is about to unfold, and we must witness it. In our ears are the faint echoes of trumpets, horns and the roar of armies. Our time here in the twenty-first century is drawing to a close. Let us rush to medieval India, a world that is in some ways forgotten, but in many more ways a world that is all around us.

Part I

Dawn: The Rise of the Chalukyas

1

Harsha's Laughter

Winter, 618 CE[1]

There must have been thousands – perhaps *tens* of thousands – of men in the forests of the Vindhya hills near the southern bank of the Narmada river. Mingled with their shrieks and shouts, the throbbing of their leather drums, and the blaring of horns and trumpets were the rumbling and trumpeting of hundreds of war elephants, the neighing of horses, the bellowing of bulls. The men had come here to kill and be killed.

On the northern bank of the Narmada was *another* enormous gathering of men. There must have been hints of strange perfumes and unfamiliar flowers in the air, the sounds of instruments from a distant land.

Two great armies were on the verge of irrevocably transforming the world that millions of South Asians inhabited. Two brash young emperors had come here, to the foothills of the Vindhya mountains dividing the southern peninsula of the Indian subcontinent. They were about to set in motion a chain of events leading to one of the most epic stories the subcontinent would ever see – and later forget.

The older[2] of the two emperors, twenty-seven-year-old Harsha (Joy) was the overlord of the thousands of settlements and hundreds of petty kings of the lush plains of north India. He was there, on the banks of the Narmada river, to tear through the Vindhyas and punish[3] the other, Pulakeshin II (Great Lion[4]) of the Chalukya dynasty. Perhaps he thought he would swat away this challenger once and for all, as he had brushed away so many others through a lifetime of cunning diplomacy and brutal wars. Meanwhile, Pulakeshin was the unlikely overlord of an unlikely power – the dry, rocky plateau of the Deccan in south-central India, sparsely populated, torn by war and raids. His reasons for gathering his allies and vassals and coming here were more complicated.

The stakes were high. Harsha was the most powerful warlord north India had seen in centuries, the King of Kings of one of the world's most expansive, economically productive and culturally sophisticated regions. Harsha's 'camp' was really a moving miniature city complete with stables, armouries, stores, workers, attendants and soldiers.[5] At its centre, in a field demarcated with tents and fencing, surrounded by troops and attendants,[6] Harsha appeared before his overawed vassals in a silk dhoti, a diaphanous upper garment embroidered with gold stars loosely tied at his waist, his chest and head piled with pearls and rubies and flowers.[7] Before embarking on this campaign, this potentate of fabulous wealth had probably spent a small fortune in a public sacrifice, giving away gold and cows to delighted priests who promised him all sorts of success in return.[8]

Pulakeshin, on the other hand, had less of an aura of fame and glory. His life up to this point had been one of Hamlet-esque drama as he struggled to keep his father's throne from rivals within his family and without. Being from the Deccan, he was almost certainly duskier and shorter than his rival. The chiefs of this arid land, Pulakeshin included, could hardly match the spectacular finery in which the flashy lords of the north paraded around in 618 CE. Indeed, when he had first seized his crown barely ten years earlier,[9] Pulakeshin's existence would barely have been acknowledged by Harsha.

But that was no longer a problem. This Deccani upstart had challenged the older north Indian for control over a wealthy and profitable territory on the subcontinent's west coast: Lata, modern-day southern Gujarat. Whoever controlled it was guaranteed access to the thriving ports of the Indian Ocean. With this move, far more than merely being acknowledged, he had made Harsha and his army come to *him*.

About a quarter-century earlier, where sandy rivers snake through the basalt rock and sandstone of the Deccan, was born the wailing child who would one day challenge north India's most powerful warlord.

As the newborn screamed, the queen's most senior attendants, members of prominent aristocratic families,[10] rushed to bring the good news to the eagerly waiting father. On the way, they may have stopped briefly to thank the nude lotus-headed goddess Lajja Gauri, patroness of mothers and childbirth.[11] The thrilled king ordered the baby's horoscope cast by the expert astrologers of his court.[12] Drums and trumpets were sounded,[13] and messengers and heralds sent out to proclaim the good news in the marketplaces of small towns and under sacred trees in tiny hamlets. While the humble inhabitants of these settlements might not have had much to say about the matter, the wealthy and who's who of the royal family's fortress town, Vatapi (wind-swelled) – modern-day Badami in Karnataka – sent rare and expensive gifts for the child, to ingratiate themselves with the king and queen. The kingdom that Vatapi controlled over was a network of chiefs and petty rulers, traders and townsmen stretching for a few hundred kilometres around this town in the Malaprabha river valley, in modern-day northern Karnataka.[14]

Even as priests chanted sacred verses in celebratory sacrifices, spooning ghee into flames, much singing and dancing must have broken out within the palace's maze of courtyards and rooms.[15] The little prince received the name Ereya, and probably participated in a series of loud rituals, appearing before crowds on the auspicious occasions of his first haircut, first birthday, and so on. Such public rituals were a key source of political power in sixth-century India: they conferred the prestige and legitimacy crucial to establishing an individual's position in a socio-political pecking order. So these early rituals of Ereya's life – with their chanting priests and offerings of clarified butter – established his high status, and declared to the world that he would head his family's political network in the future.

The other luminaries of that network – the men and women of the palace, court officials and the families of assorted Deccani vassal chiefs – also attended these ceremonies; their participation and interactions served to renew and clarify their position within the pecking order to the court and public.[16] With their families and attendants carrying gifts of perfumes and semi-precious stones[17] in baskets, their modest processions of bullock carts and palanquin bearers wound their way through the bustling streets of Vatapi. Meanwhile, the town's denizens decorated their homes with leaves, flowers and fresh thatch, even as dancers, acrobats and storytellers poured through the streets.

We can only imagine what these aristocrats thought as they watched the royal couple and their new child. They knew that if the status quo were to remain, their descendants would inherit their political position unchanged. Their sons would be Ereya's vassals, just as they were his father's.[18] Their daughters would be his wives and wives' attendants.[19] Their families would pay tribute and appear at the baby's ever-expanding repertoire of public rituals as he grew into a king. These vassals were all men (and very occasionally women) with their own mini-courts, their own mini-armies and their own mini-administrations, with an array of rights and obligations.[20] They worked within a tangled web of allegiances to advance their own interests. The most powerful of the lot, such as those close to the royal clan, must have been pleased enough with this state of affairs, which generally allowed them lives of leisure.[21] There were, however, any number of opportunities for change, for those who dared seize them. After all, the royal family itself had set an example mere decades ago.

⤴

In the early sixth century, when Ereya's family were little more than a group of agriculturists or pastoralists, the Deccan was ripe for military adventures and conquest. There were several petty chiefdoms and only one or two powerful kingdoms around. The Kadambas of Banavasi, nestled away among the imposing hills of the Western Ghats, were one of the latter category; they were generally deferred to as the overlords of parts of southwest Karnataka. But their authority outside of their territorial cores was weak and disputed by dozens of squabbling leaders. In the Deccan, warfare was a fact of life. Raiding and pillaging were fairly common.

The existence of so many petty chiefdoms, none able to secure a decisive edge over their rivals, had up to this point prevented the emergence of long-lasting Deccan superpowers.[22] Local groups and leaders were generally left to their own devices provided they merely submitted some sort of tribute to other, more powerful chiefs, who in turn paid tribute to a distant dynasty, such as the Kadambas. Often even that was not forthcoming or demanded: the vast and unruly lands of the plateau hardly merited the expense it required to attack and keep control over them.

But that was all about to change.

We do not know exactly how Ereya's grandfather's early career panned out, merely that he was not born into the splendid circumstances his grandson was. We don't even know the origins of his family name:

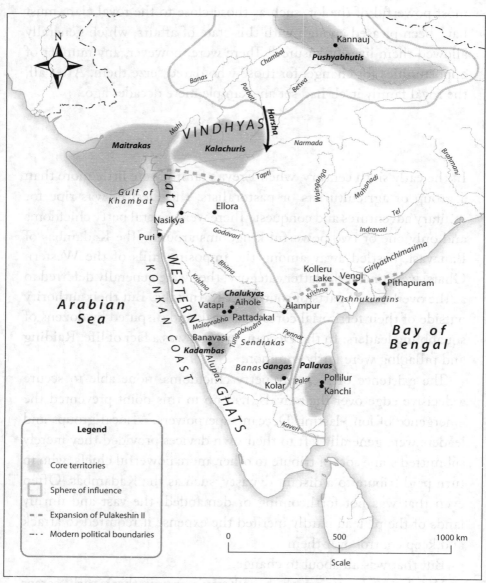

Southern India, early seventh century CE.

there seems to have been some connection to the crowbar, *chalke*, pointing to very humble origins,[23] likely as a leader of an agricultural group in the valley of the Malaprabha river, in the northern part of the modern state of Karnataka. But as the mighty Gupta empire of northern India began to fade away, to be replaced by smaller and more dynamic regional kingdoms in the Punjab, Malwa and Bengal–Bihar, a new kingdom was soon to rise in the Deccan.

Crowbars were heated and hammered into spears, as the cultivators and pastoralists who lived around the valley of the Malaprabha gradually began to heed the orders of this ambitious chief of the Chalke clan. In the early years of this man's career, the agriculturists who followed him were probably clad in little more than a loincloth, armed with just a spear, bow or a crudely shaped sickle as they attacked villages first, then towns, then more powerful warlords, seeking to conquer fertile land and seize loot. With each successful raid they grew progressively wealthier and more scarred, decorated with the weapons and jewellery of fallen foes. They traded the red dirt of the farm for the scented body paints of the wealthy, hired attendants to oil them, bathe them, cook for them. Perhaps they married cultured ladies from the families of small-town aristocrats, perhaps they kidnapped women from the poorest of villages and enslaved them.

A new 'aristocracy' must have slowly formed around the rising Chalke chief, slowly growing in size and confidence, negotiating marriage ties and political alliances as a new kingdom emerged in this land, protected from rivals by the imposing sandstone cliffs of the Malaprabha valley. Ereya's grandfather seems to have gone about it all with a combination of ability, ruthlessness and good luck. Agricultural produce and looted treasures soon swelled the Chalkes' coffers and those of their officials and commanders. They were now wealthy members of the landed, leisured elite. Experts in the performance of rituals, dealers in luxury goods, priests and poets and musicians and dancers and artists rushed to the Chalke court from the older kingdoms of south India and the northern Deccan. These foreign specialists brought with them an aura of legend and ancient tradition, and were a great way to impress Ereya's grandfather's new subjects.

As his horizons began to expand, the Chalke chief decided to make his intentions and his power clear to other, distant rivals. The Malaprabha river valley was no longer enough to contain his ambitions. He wished to declare himself a truly sovereign monarch, equal in rank to well-established and more prestigious kings, such as the aforementioned Kadambas of Banavasi, the dominant rulers of southwest Karnataka. His sovereignty over the swathes of territory he controlled in northern Karnataka needed to be sanctioned by religion to be recognized by his subjects, vassals and rival kings. It was time for the chief to become something more – for that humble name to transform into one that would bedazzle the subcontinent for the next five hundred years and beyond. The humble Chalke clan would be transformed into the Chalukya dynasty.

And so, a spectacular sacrifice was organized to elevate him to royal sovereignty, to higher caste and class status, a ritual badge that would catapult the Chalke chief over those petty rulers and chiefs surrounding him. It was time for him and his descendants to rise to the institution of Indian kingship. He chose to declare this message by performing the *ashvamedha*, the horse sacrifice, an undertaking of such complexity and expense that it was reserved only for the most powerful of rulers.[24] In doing so, the chief offers us a glimpse into how medieval Indian lords used religion and religious rituals to make potent political claims.

The Ashvamedha, its origins long forgotten,[25] had been handed down orally through hundreds of generations. Bits and pieces were constantly being added to and removed from it based on the sacrificers' interest, knowledge and inclination.[26] It had never before been performed in this part of the Deccan, and to undertake it, the Chalke chief must have secured the services of foreign priests at great expense.

It consisted of two parts. The first, quite dramatically depicted in epics such as the Ramayana and Mahabharata, involved setting loose a white stallion with black spots[27] to wander at will for a year, followed by an army. During this time the Chalke chief and his court would gather at his town of Aryapura (modern-day Aihole), not far from Vatapi, which the chief and his sons had been decorating with palaces and shrines funded by the loot from their military campaigns. Here, the court was supposed to pay for four ritual offerings daily[28] as well as recitations of legend and poetry[29] at the site demarcated to sacrifice the horse later.

The horse, meanwhile, roamed the land, trailed by its accompanying army, eating and sleeping and galloping as it saw fit (with the sole restriction of not being allowed to mate, thus preserving its generative powers for the sacrifice).[30] In theory, if it entered the territory of any other independent ruler, he had the opportunity to capture the stallion – gaining a great deal of prestige – but only if he also defeated the army following it. However, if the other ruler didn't stop the horse from wandering around in his territory, he accepted its owner's suzerainty over him. More realistically, the sacrificial horse was probably deliberately guided to territories that its owner had already subjugated, or wished to conquer.

The horse's travels paralleled a king's enjoyment of his kingdom's expanse. The land over which it moved symbolized the territory that the king controlled, and that of other lesser kings who had ritually agreed that their right to rule their land stemmed from his. These subordinate rulers thus served to establish the polity's pecking order and the king's pre-eminent position within it as the king of other kings – *raja-dhi-raja*. But in the second part of the ritual, when the animal returned to the owner's court – in this case the Chalke court at Aryapura – at the end of the year, events took a more macabre turn, at least as the ritual books describe it.[31]

A large grid was demarcated with paint, powders and rope, and consecrated through the lighting of a fire and the pouring of water.[32] Within it, primary and secondary fire altars were set up according to exact specifications as to their shape and position – and even the number, size and shape of the baked clay bricks used to make them.[33] Clay pots shaped like animal and human heads[34] were prepared to contain the many ingredients required for the sacrifice. These would be fed to the flames with pincers, ladles and spoons shaped like nostrils and collarbones and arms, metaphorically representing the body of the sacrificer,[35] the Chalke chief. Most importantly, dozens if not hundreds of priests with specific roles – the chanters, the repeaters, the chief officiants, their assistants – were assembled for this great and difficult undertaking. Fortunes must have been spent to bring foreign specialists from far and wide to conduct the sacrifice and impress the novelty and grandiosity of the ritual upon the chief's subjects.

When the stallion returned, the sacrifice began. The royal creature was rubbed with ghee by the king's wives, who would also braid its mane and drape its body with 101 golden beads.[36] It was then strangled and its corpse covered with a sheet. Other animals – 609 according to one source[37] – were also sacrificed along with it, everything from buffaloes to dogs. The screams of animals were drowned out by the great drone of the chanting of the Vedas.

After 'mourning' the dead horse and fanning it with the yak-tail fan reserved for kings,[38] the chief queen would lie under the sheet[39] while the rest of the king's women joked obscenely (but ritually) with the officiating priests and hundreds of female attendants circled them, 'their hair unbound, singing, dancing and slapping their thighs',[40] all acts of public taboo breaking that would never have been allowed otherwise. Under the supervision of priests, all of these 'transgressive' acts were symbolic of the harnessed powers of fertility, rebirth and renewal.[41]

After this wild night, in the cold light of the next day, the horse's corpse was marked with lines of golden needles[42] along which the priests sliced it into pieces and cooked the best cuts. Its ribs were separated,[43] its flesh roasted and its blood apparently poured into the sacrificial fires from a dismembered hoof.[44] After it was eaten by the attendees of the sacrifice, the power of the stallion was believed to have entered the royal bloodline.

The performance of such a ritual was loaded with other meanings as well. At a metaphysical level, the grid upon which the sacrifice was performed, the vessels used, the ritual slaughter and the verses chanted were believed to have connected and transformed both the world of mortals and the world of the gods.[45] The world was thus reordered; sovereignty was established, success and victory were ensured.

This is what some ritual manuals, which were over a thousand years old even by the sixth century CE, had to say about the Ashvamedha. We have no idea whether the Chalke chief did all that the manuals demanded; all we know for sure is that he performed some version of this sacrifice, and made sure that everyone knew it.[46] And going by the inscriptions he issued, the Chalke chief intended his horse sacrifice to be a declaration of independence and imperial ambitions.[47] There can be no doubt it accomplished that successfully: his birth name was completely forgotten, and all the sources we have call him by the new, royal title he adopted. Henceforth he would be accompanied everywhere by bearers of yak-tail fans, shaded from the harsh Deccan sun by the bejewelled parasol reserved for sovereign monarchs: independent kings who bowed to none but the gods. From now to his death, Ereya's grandfather would be Maharaja 'Great Lion',[48] Pulakeshin I Chalukya.

But though Pulakeshin had now attained the rank of an independent monarch, he seems to have thought that the term 'maharaja' was a little too generic, a little too common. He thus chose a new title that set him apart from all his contemporaries, and suited his improbable rise to power. He declared himself 'Sri-Prithivi-Vallabha',[49] Fortunate Lord of the Earth, or Fortune's Favourite, Earth's Beloved – the consort of both Sri, the goddess of fortune, and Prithivi, goddess of Earth,

The Chalukya insignia as depicted at the Lad Khan temple at Aihole, dated to around the reign of Pulakeshin I in the mid-sixth century. It consists of a boar and a conch, generally associated with the god Vishnu; a wheel above is probably meant to represent the wheel of dharma. To the right is a mirror.

thus the equal of the god Vishnu himself. It was a title that would become so closely tied to the Deccan that for the next five hundred years its emperors would be referred to as Sri-Vallabha, Vallabha-Raja or just Vallabha, Fortune's Favourite, Beloved King or Beloved One, in popular parlance as well as their own propaganda.[50]

Chalukya propaganda thus portrayed Pulakeshin I and his heirs as practically Vishnu on Earth – a claim first made by the Gupta emperors in north India about two hundred years earlier.[51] To call themselves Sri-Prithivi-Vallabha, Fortune's Favourite, Earth's Beloved, was a means of identifying themselves with Vishnu, who in his mythology 'embodied the virtues of kingship' by 'preserving the Earth and the prosperity of the righteous'.[52] In these legends, Vishnu earns the right to marry both Sri/Lakshmi, the goddess of fortune, and Prithivi, the goddess of Earth. Just as Vishnu was their husband and lord, with the right to command them as he saw fit, so, too, was the Chalukya king.

Through the rest of his reign, this new Chalukya king, Pulakeshin I, would continue to bolster the clan's standing through the performance of a series of splendid ancient royal sacrifices[53] – the Hayamedha, Agnistoma, Agnicayana, Vajapeya, Bahusuvarna, Paundarika and Hiranyagarbha[54] – all complex and expensive undertakings in their own right, but clearly worth it for the prestige and legitimacy they conferred. He also ordered the erection of temples, establishing his privileged relationship with their divine inhabitants.[55] Though these activities were centuries old in other parts of the subcontinent, and were even known in parts of the Deccan that had been home to kingdoms, they were unknown in the Malaprabha river valley. By performing all of these, Pulakeshin I sought to distance and elevate himself above his subjects, claiming his authority over them came from the gods themselves, a relationship established and strengthened through these rituals and titles.

Through all this, a profound transformation in his societal and ritual status unfurled, giving him access to new sources of political power. As a newly minted high-caste lord, whose farmer and pastoralist ancestors would never have had the status or wealth for any projects of this sort, Pulakeshin I now made sure his contemporaries saw him as nothing less than the ideal Indian king of theory and legend, building a sophisticated propaganda system all his successors would follow.

Pulakeshin I, we are told, 'delighted in *dharma*',[56] a 'very specific ordering of people, places and things'[57] that was integral to the Puranic

Hinduism he was seeking to embrace, a socio-political and religious institution codified in Sanskrit texts, centred around temples and dependent on an organized system of social and economic relations. Many aspects of this – not just the aforementioned religious practices – were relatively new to the denizens of the Malaprabha river valley. Their religious life up to this point still revolved around megaliths and folk deities of the sacred springs they depended upon for agriculture and lush forage for their animals. The concepts of regular tax, feudal lordship, a highly stratified society, caste and Sanskrit education were relatively new to the vast majority of its inhabitants. Their lord Pulakeshin I, however, claimed to have studied Manu, the most prominent of Brahmin dharma thinkers, assorted *Puranas* narrating the legends of the gods, *and* the entirety of the Mahabharata and Ramayana epics.[58] How a petty agricultural chief-turned-king managed to do all this is unclear; these claims were probably meant to establish him as cultured enough to belong to the aristocratic classes and castes that had once looked down upon him, from whose ranks he now looked down upon his subjects.

As a natural part of his ascension, the Chalukya king also claimed the title 'Brahmanya', Friend to Brahmins.[59] Brahmins were one of the few groups with access to elite forms of education in the medieval Indian world, including the cosmopolitan Sanskrit language, ritual knowledge, and the business of running a state.[60] For nearly a millennium they had dominated India's oral and written knowledge systems. From around the first century CE, they had increasingly diversified from their usual religious roles into other occupations useful to fledgling states like that of the Chalukyas. One land grant from around this time describes them as skilled in everything from fortress construction to battle tactics to administration and performing sacrifices.[61] And so Pulakeshin invited them to settle in Chalukya territory en masse, granting groups of families land in new Brahmin settlements (*agraharas*) or endowing them with the revenue of smaller villages in return for working in his towns and religious establishments. This was an important addition to the relatively simple socio-political arrangements that had prevailed in the Malaprabha river valley before the rise of the Chalukyas.

Henceforth, Pulakeshin's children and grandchildren would be educated by and surrounded by families who claimed or had inherited a similarly high-caste identity. This new-found status was also useful in other ways. Chalukya clan members were now eligible for marriage with the oldest and most prestigious families from within their domains or beyond; they could be assured of potent ritual services and excellent education; and they could feel part of a prestigious and well-connected group of people who sat atop the hierarchy of hundreds of peoples, including tribes, sub-castes, not-castes and not-yet-castes who toiled over the land.[62] Medieval Indian kings were neither the hapless dupes of Brahmins nor the protectors of powerless pious folk they are often made out to be in popular culture. First and foremost, they were for themselves and their own.

Pulakeshin I, his sons, vassals and allies watered battlefields with blood, constructed new irrigation systems, and fed their loot and agrarian produce into sacrificial flames and new temples. Religion acted as an engine of sorts, converting material power into prestige that justified their radical reorganization of land and people, thus laying the foundations for even more material power. By around 543 CE,[63] the clan had set up their primary capital at the great fortified citadel of Vatapi (modern-day Badami), commanding the entrance to the Malaprabha valley, the core of their influence and power. Situated on top of breathtaking cliffs that could only be accessed through difficult and well-guarded paths, this was a site of considerable strategic and religious significance. Not only was it an impenetrable base of operations, but the area had also been a site of active religious practice for thousands of years. To this day it is dotted by massive sacred stones, remnants of an Iron Age culture of ancestor veneration long since forgotten or incorporated into Hinduism and other Indian religions.

Over the course of a single lifetime, the Chalukya dynasty thus introduced a series of radical political, social and religious changes that had hitherto not been seen in the Deccan. The foundations were laid for the emergence of a new superpower.

⤳

Pulakeshin I's grandson, the prince Ereya, must have grown up hearing tales of his lineage with pride and wonder. He and other young aristocrats – some siblings, some cousins, some the children of senior court officials – wandered between thorny trees and huge boulders of the Malaprabha valley. Courtiers and attendants were on call for whatever the young prince might want to know. Perhaps they told him of the ancient megalithic shrines of the valley, left by those long gone, carved out of massive sheets of rock.[64] Once venerated by long-forgotton ancestors, they were still held sacred by the Chalukyas' subjects, who worshipped them alongside the newly introduced gods in the family's shrines: Shiva, Vishnu, the Seven Mothers. Perhaps he was also taught about the Kadambas, who used to control a mighty kingdom to the south, not far from the western coast,[65] who were now on the verge of total defeat at his father's hands.

His mother's brothers, the Sendraka chiefs, may have visited; they were former vassals of the Kadambas, who had abandoned their overlords due to the military successes of the Chalukyas. They had married their sister to Ereya's father, Kirti-Varman I, the son and successor of Pulakeshin I, as a symbol of their allegiance. Perhaps Ereya also saw embassies from Chalukya allies such as the Gangas, the lords of Kolar near modern-day Bengaluru, whose lands bordered the Tamil-speaking kingdoms of the south-eastern coast.[66] Maybe there were even representations from the distant lords of the northern Deccan, the Kalachuris. One of their princesses was Ereya's grandmother by marriage, a later wife of his grandfather Pulakeshin I and the mother of his uncle, the dashing general Mangalesha.

It was a fairly charmed existence, no doubt, especially compared to the hand-to-mouth existence of the cultivators and pastoralists who were the subjects of his father. Ereya would never have to worry about access to food, shelter or sex. Sitting in his family's fort on top of Vatapi's spectacular sandstone cliffs, the boy could easily have convinced himself that the world as far as he could see was his. He might, at best, have to share it with his brothers. One of them had been born with a crooked back. The other was still just a baby.

Had the young prince's life continued this way, he would gradually have been entrusted to more senior teachers, studying war, politics, art, languages (especially Sanskrit, that ultimate symbol of royal sophistication) and religion alongside a cadre of other princes and boys of similarly elite backgrounds.[67] Sanskrit and formal religious education – indicative of the status they had earned through their conquests and performance of prestigious sacrifices – were still a novelty for his family.

Ereya would have learned to command and fight, got married, had some children, worked as a governor or general, and eventually been consecrated king. His father was still very much in his prime, having developed Chalukya influence to the point where it was a major regional power. Their core territory stretched over a vast radius (for the time) of about 240 kilometres,[68] and from there the Vallabha led armies to defeat and subjugate the lords of the southern Deccan (modern-day Karnataka) – smashing the Kadambas and, as mentioned, marrying a princess of the Sendrakas, former vassals of the Kadambas. This was a major upset by the standards of the day: the Kadambas were famed patrons of architecture and learning, and had been connected to pan-Indian developments since well before the Chalukyas even existed. They had been the first southern Indian kings to use courtly Sanskrit and systematically perform public rituals in the early fifth century CE.

The Vallabha also sent raids west, across the hilly rainforests of the Western Ghats, as far as the Konkan coast[69] (in modern-day Maharashtra). Some of his defeated rivals were reinstated as his vassals, others lost their territories to Chalukya clan members or new lineages of vassal kings related to the Vallabha through marriage. Under Ereya's father's rule, Vatapi grew and bloomed, and new cave temples were excavated into the sandstone cliffs – an innovation likely adopted from the eastern or north-western Deccan. Religious and artistic patronage thrived alongside vicious politics as families competed for the royal largesse.

But then, the king died suddenly in 597 CE, when Ereya was barely an adolescent.[70]

This was a critical moment in the story of the Chalukyas. These former peasants had risen to a position where they were the envy of the Deccan's powerful chiefs. At a moment when these terrified lords had been falling over themselves to submit to, ally with or marry into the Chalukya clan, this new-found dominance was suddenly thrown into question. The Kadambas, arguably the oldest and most powerful kingdom in the southern Deccan, had only just been defeated in war and forced to submit. The Chalukyas seemed to have regarded them with a mix of envy and hatred, and spent much blood and money attempting to grind down their power – even, at one point after defeating them, ordering buildings raised over the foundations of destroyed Kadamba edifices.[71] Less of a challenge were the Mauryas of the Konkan and other chiefs such as the Nalas, also subdued in war.[72] Other alliances (especially those sealed with marriages to the dead king, such as the Sendrakas[73]) were now in question, as were other diplomatic treaties and political arrangements the Chalukyas could no longer credibly uphold. A child king was not going to be able to demand the submission of grizzled old warlords with swords older than he was.

The Chalukyas of Vatapi

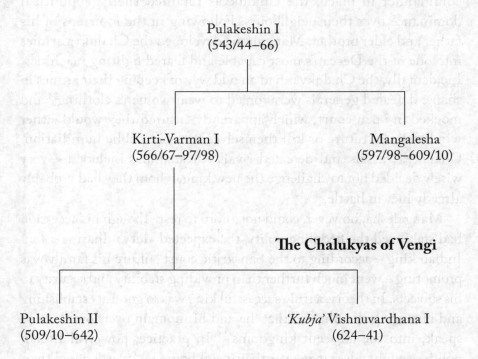

Pulakeshin I
(543/44–66)

Kirti-Varman I
(566/67–97/98)

Mangalesha
(597/98–609/10)

The Chalukyas of Vengi

Pulakeshin II
(509/10–642)

'Kubja' Vishnuvardhana I
(624–41)

Under these circumstances, the dead king's younger half-brother, a man of considerable dash and verve, now seized the throne as Maharaja Mangalesha. Ereya, his siblings and their mother(s) were incorporated into Mangalesha's new court – demoted and moved to less impressive quarters in the palace, but otherwise unharmed. With the prospect of a child ruler gone, and with a capable and energetic commander in place, the Chalukyas retained their geopolitical dominance over their neighbours. Following in the footsteps of his father and elder brother, Mangalesha developed the Chalukya armies into one of the Deccan's most capable and feared fighting machines. Incidentally, the Chalukyas had an odd way of keeping their armies in shape: defeated generals were forced to wear women's clothing[74] and mocked in open court, which apparently ensured they would either win battles in future or kill themselves to avoid public humiliation. Chalukya vassals and defeated rivals – Kadambas included – very wisely decided not to challenge the new king, whom they had probably already met in battle.

Mangalesha, however, could not afford to rest. Though his accession had stabilized the fledgling polity, the expected 'duty' (dharma) of an Indian king – according to the Sanskritic court culture his family was promoting – went much further than providing stability and security to his subjects. In theory, a truly successful king was so good at establishing and nurturing the dharma that 'he and his domain overflowed, so to speak, into the adjacent kingdoms'.[75] In practice, powerful Indian polities sought advantage over their neighbours by 'overflowing' their armies through their borders. This confluence of ideology, war and the personal avarice of kings is aptly summarized in a quote from the *Manusmriti*, used by the scholar Richard Davis in his study of violent looting in medieval India: 'Chariots, horses, parasols, money, grain, cattle, women, all kinds of goods, and base metals all belong to the one who wins them.'[76] Similar declarations from other texts were probably familiar to aristocrats like Mangalesha, should they require religious sanction for self-aggrandizement through war.

The dynasties of the northern Deccan, the seat of the plateau's oldest kingdoms, are unlikely to have expected a serious attack from the Malaprabha valley, which had been little more than a backwater until recently. The most powerful dynasty there, the Kalachuris, had married one of their daughters to the first Chalukya king, Pulakeshin I, perhaps assuming this great honour would be enough to keep these upstarts quiet. On the contrary, this lady – Mangalesha's mother – seems to have actually encouraged her son[77] to attack her brother, the Kalachuri king.

The new Vallabha now led a marauding raid into his uncle's territory. The Kalachuri army of cavalry, infantry and elephantry was routed and driven off the battlefield by Mangalesha's attack.[78] The Chalukyas then sacked the Kalachuri camp, capturing much treasure. The defeat was wholly unexpected: the women of the Kalachuri king's household had accompanied the army to the battlefield to witness their anticipated victory. Mangalesha captured the women, his panegyrists declaring that 'Mangalesha enjoyed the Kalachuri ladies along with their prosperity'.[79] These women, likely from noble families with their own rank within the Kalachuri political network, were forcibly incorporated into Mangalesha's court and suffered (at the very least) depression and homesickness,[80] and probably humiliation, emotional and physical abuse, or sexual assault at the hands of his courtiers and attendants. The Kalachuri king himself retreated, living to fight another day. This raid had been a humiliation, but it had hardly shaken the Kalachuris' grip over the northern Deccan.

Mangalesha returned to Vatapi in triumph, lavishing his supporters with loot. Even gods that were seen as friendly enough to him got a cut.[81] Now, lured by the potential of all this treasure, an array of service providers began to migrate to the Malaprabha river valley.[82] Sculptors came to work for the Chalukyas, some of them from Kadamba and even Kalachuri territory, bringing their distinct styles with them. On the Vallabha's order, splendid new cave temples were now cut into the soft sandstone cliffs of Vatapi, dedicated to the god Vishnu the Preserver, the archetypal deity of kings.

The inauguration of Mangalesha's new projects, coming soon after Pulakeshin I's series of prestigious and painstaking royal sacrifices, is a clear sign that sixth-century Deccanis were attuned to the subcontinent's latest innovations and trends (such as the use of Brahmin settlements and religious propaganda to support royal power) and could harness them to suit their own context. Sacrifices and religion and temples hardly seem 'innovative' to us today, but as far as the Chalukyas were concerned, they were introducing the most modern of foreign ideas to their homeland to tighten their grip on wealth and power.

What young Ereya thought of all this is unknown. The Chalukya kingdom was doing well, its leader was clearly able and well liked, it was safeguarded from its enemies, its vassals did not challenge it. Growing up in the town of Vatapi as the king's nephew must have been a pleasant experience, and he could have relied on urbane company and an excellent education. Had he not pressed his claims to the throne, Ereya may have been guaranteed a comfortable career, perhaps as a general or governor, and could eventually have retired into peaceful obscurity as the leader of his own minor branch of the Chalukya family. But kingship was irresistible to any ambitious and capable prince.[83]

Trouble began to brew as he came of age. Ereya was certainly well connected on his mother's side – she was a Sendraka, a family who were once vassals of the Kadambas of Banavasi – and had powerful friends in his own right. It is possible that he was betrothed or married to a princess of the Gangas of southern Karnataka, and he probably knew many senior Chalukya officers, generals, vassal lords and allied chiefs personally. Perhaps the danger of his position began to dawn on him as Mangalesha's sons, his cousins, grew up and began to challenge his seniority among that generation of Chalukya princes. Perhaps the king saw a popular nephew who could be set up as a power centre opposed to him and his sons.[84] We will never know what bitterness and acrimony erupted in the court.

What we do know is that Ereya was forced to flee Vatapi,[85] perhaps with little more than a few companions. He now desperately began to rally support for a coup[86] against his uncle before Mangalesha's loyalists could seize and defeat his ragtag group of companions. As always, the lords of the Deccan gleefully pounced on this opportunity for personal advancement,[87] including the Bana family (based near modern-day Kolar[88]) and the Alupa family (based near modern-day Shivamogga[89]). A coalition of these minor chiefs soon began to gather around the prince. The prospect of installing a young, pliable ruler who was beholden to them for his throne must have been tantalizing, despite the risk of retaliation from the reigning Vallabha, Mangalesha.

Meanwhile, others attempted to independently break away from Chalukya authority, including – dangerously – both the Kadambas and the Gangas.[90] Even closer to home, a vassal ruler in the Konkan, who had been appointed by the Chalukyas after some preliminary campaigns in the region, began to put on the airs of an independent sovereign. Mangalesha had to move immediately to nip this idea in the bud. The rebel had fortified some islands off the coast, apparently confident that they were impregnable. The Vallabha, like some sort of Indian Caesar,[91] built a bridge of boats, crossed the tossing seas, and slaughtered the inhabitants.[92]

Ereya, meanwhile, moved from chiefdom to chiefdom. His entourage trekked through the Deccan, through vast fields burning under the unrelenting sun, through forests shrill with the call of crickets, winding over hills and between cliffs, feeling the blistering summer heat and the rains of the monsoon on their skin as they watched the sun rise and set on unfamiliar vistas. The rebel prince needed to travel everywhere he could think of in order to find potential supporters: visiting settlements of mud and thatch and manors of wood, negotiating future rewards in return for immediate military or political support. Everything from loot to territory to offices, titles and marriage alliances were likely on offer. It must have been a difficult and stressful endeavour, and the Chalukya prince probably spent more than a few nights sleeping under the starry skies surrounded by a small company of guards, hearing the distant roars of tigers in the dark. But slowly Ereya's camp grew. He learned to fight and command, to flatter and persuade, to threaten and crush, to loot and reward as he grew into royalty the hard way. Soon, Ereya was in open rebellion, warring with his uncle and cousins, seeing on battlefield after battlefield the bloody, broken corpses of soldiers he may have recognized from Vatapi, handing out jewellery and weapons to his new vassals, as men flocked to his banner. A final confrontation with Mangalesha inched ever closer.

In 609 CE, Pulakeshin I's son and grandson clashed near a village called Nadanuru. A few confused hours of dust and turmoil later, the victor summoned Nadanuru's elders to attend on him. Under a makeshift roof of wood and cloth, he offered them an auspicious gift of land and the revenue of all taxes collected in the vicinity: perhaps the first grant he had ever had the authority to make.[93] The sacrifice of a horse's life had once made Ereya's grandfather Pulakeshin I in the eyes of the world. The sacrifice of his uncle's life had made the young prince Pulakeshin II in the eyes of the world.

⁓

If Pulakeshin's neighbours and new vassals had thought the young king would be less assertive or militarily capable than Mangalesha, they were soon proven spectacularly wrong. Pulakeshin II would respond to every challenge with deviousness, resolve and a firm grasp of both politics and geopolitics.

Almost immediately after his accession, with his authority over the Chalukya core territories – let alone its extended network of current and former vassals – still in question, two adventurers from the northern Deccan attempted to dethrone him.[94] Pulakeshin's response (according to an inscription by his court poet, found today on a temple atop Meguti hill in Aryapura/Aihole, near Badami) was straight from a political manual, involving a mixture of conciliation, gifts, dissension and force – the four strategies Indian princes were taught to apply to potential problems. The young king bribed one of the attackers to join his side, with his 'host of elephants',[95] rewarding him with high honours and titles. Reinforced, Pulakeshin then pounced on the other and routed him.

Of course, the entire inscription may have been composed to portray Pulakeshin II as conforming to theoretical notions of a king in Sanskrit literature, just as his grandfather Pulakeshin I claimed to have studied the Vedas. But this careful curation of his royal image, coupled with bold and decisive action to protect his power, was a sign of things to come. Pulakeshin II now turned his attention to the huge challenge of restoring his clan's shattered political network. A message needed to be sent and his new followers rewarded with spoils. And so his eyes alighted on his family's ancient foe, the Kadambas. After two generations of war, the realization seemed to have dawned that the Deccan was not big enough for both of them.

Denizens of the fortress of Banavasi, the Kadamba capital, were generally accustomed to watching white geese swim in the Varada, a tributary of the Tungabhadra river which served as the town's moat.[96] But all those beautiful birds were put to flight by the roar of the besieging Chalukya army, which surrounded Banavasi's earthen ramparts, cut off food supplies, and possibly even blockaded the river with boats. Flocks of serene white geese were replaced by a turbulent ocean of tents, banners, a host of loincloth-clad infantry, with their gleaming spears and painted shields, and the looming silhouettes of war elephants. The invading army was so large, the Chalukyas tell us, that Banavasi, a fortress on land, looked like it was a fortress on the sea.[97] Engulfed by the Pulakeshin tsunami, the main Kadamba line abruptly (and likely bloodily) vanishes from the historical record. Their lands were seized and handed to Pulakeshin's mother's family – the Sendrakas – as well as other clans, as a reward for their support in his war for the throne and to ensure their future loyalty.[98] Clearly, those who sided with the Chalukyas would be rewarded splendidly sooner or later. Those who did not would be crushed.

The Gangas were among the first to recognize this fact. Pulakeshin II of the Chalukyas of Vatapi was evidently a son-in-law any king could be proud of. Possibly through a renewal of an engagement brokered during his father's reign, a Ganga princess was married off to him.[99] To her family, the marriage was an investment in a potentially rosy collective future. After all, any children she might have could be expected to help the Gangas should they ever come to the throne, or act as a powerful pro-Ganga lobby at court if they did not.

A whole host of other dynasties followed in the Gangas' footsteps, tying their fortunes to the re-emerging Chalukyas through the exchange of daughters and promises of fealty and tribute. Pulakeshin would also have taken care to cultivate or replace his uncle's senior commanders and officers, granting them titles and wealth to ensure they stayed loyal. The court was probably reorganized so that the new Vallabha's partisans dominated, and the bases of Chalukya power were once again secured. A true pan-Deccan superpower was emerging. Pulakeshin II was no longer content to call himself Maharaja: he and his successors would be *Maharajadhirajas*, Great Kings of Kings, emperors.[100]

Pulakeshin II now set his eyes on the grand prize that was the northern Deccan – that heartland of empires past and present, watered by the great river Godavari and its tributaries, its shoreline connected to the rich trading ports of the north and west. This was not a new target for Chalukya attention: both his father and uncle had raided and conquered bits of it, especially along the Konkan coast, but their authority was fading (Pulakeshin's own rebellion against Mangalesha had encouraged a Chalukya vassal in the region to make a bid for independence, as we saw earlier). Pulakeshin II would now go about this project much more seriously and systematically, setting himself on a path that would, one day, lead to his meeting Harsha on the banks of the Narmada river.

India's west coast had been a major trading region of the southern peninsula for centuries. But it had waned somewhat in importance since the heyday of the Roman Empire in the first and second centuries CE, when fleets of hundreds of ships would arrive every year from the Roman province of Egypt to buy Indian luxuries. Now, less than a hundred years after the collapse of the Western Roman Empire, the Eastern Roman or Byzantine Empire was beginning to try to restore trading links to India and China, and the Sassanian dynasty of Persia began to expand its own presence in the Indian Ocean.[101] The Chalukyas seemed to have realized that the coasts were becoming increasingly wealthy and could not be left in hands that were not absolutely loyal to them.[102] Control over lucrative trading ports was a grand prize to hand out to loyalists, a guaranteed source of trade income, and most importantly, a source of plush luxury goods that were crucial for maintaining a court of sufficient splendour for a potentate of Pulakeshin's rank.

The great island city of Puri, 'the Lakshmi of the Western Ocean',[103] once stood near the Elephanta island off modern-day Mumbai. It was a serious threat to Chalukya authority in the Konkan, and it would need to be taught to heed the might of the lord of the Deccan. Pulakeshin found a way to attack the fortified island, perhaps hiring merchant ships to transport his infantry from the mainland to the island, or conscripting fisherfolk to build galleys[104] for his attack. Soon after, his ships' hulls sliced through the choppy waters of the

Arabian Sea in squadrons, 'like arrays of rutting elephants',[105] perhaps making an amphibious landing close to the city walls, or breaking into the harbour at an unexpected time, surprising its sleeping guards. It was undoubtedly a bloody and difficult fight – but, like the fall of Banavasi, the dramatic collapse of this seemingly impregnable citadel sent a message. The Konkan would henceforth be ruled by Pulakeshin's maternal uncle, a Sendraka prince,[106] a family that had time and again proven its usefulness to this nephew. As a Sendraka from faraway southern Karnataka, this uncle had no power base of his own in coastal Maharashtra and thus had all the more reason to stay loyal to Pulakeshin if he wanted to survive.

The coast secured, the young emperor now turned his attentions to the interior of the northern Deccan, dotted by ancient Buddhist monasteries (such as Karle, near modern-day Lonavala), dating back to the origins of urban settlements and flourishing trade in the region nearly half a millennium ago.[107] Through this land snaked the ancient highway connecting the markets of northern and southern India, called the Dakshina-patha – the Southern Path. (The modern term 'Deccan' comes from *dakshina/dakkhina*, south.) Nashik, the seat of the Deccan's earliest empire,[108] the Satavahanas, was developed into a de facto second Chalukya capital.[109]

However, in order to truly rule the northern Deccan, Pulakeshin could not be satisfied with merely defeating the powerful Kalachuris and sacking their treasures, as Mangalesha had done. He systematically integrated this foreign land into the Chalukya imperial network, using the tools of politics and economics, far more long-lasting than ephemeral and costly military activities. Pulakeshin handed land to his collaborators there, the terms of the grant (a matter of public record) incorporating local religious formulae.[110] This suggests that he took care to respect local traditions and cults, participating in the region's seasonal festivals while also performing the annual royal rituals of the Sanskritic world, increasingly becoming recognizable across the subcontinent due to the activities of kings such as Pulakeshin. Chalukya prestige and patronage continued to bring ever more artisans and religious teachers from the northern Deccan to the Malaprabha valley,[111] binding the two socio-political networks closer together.

This policy of integration did not take long to bear fruit. Pulakeshin II's influence soon spread far and wide, and players far away from the nucleus of his power were bending over backwards to please him. For instance, as far as 320 kilometres further inland from Nashik, the centre of Chalukya power in the northern Deccan, were the volcanic basalt cliffs of Ellora, a flourishing pilgrimage centre. Here, 'some individual or group with importance' took it upon themselves to commission a cave temple celebrating Pulakeshin and the Chalukyas,[112] its sculptures unmistakably similar to those at Vatapi. For an actor so distant from the Malaprabha valley to invest the time and money needed to execute such a work is a sign of how profitable joining this new polity could be, suggesting an unprecedented northward expansion of the Chalukya clan's influence.

These dramatic developments were watched with great alarm in western India, particularly in the region around the Gulf of Khambat (earlier Cambay), the southern part of modern-day Gujarat, the kingdom of Lata. The Latas would certainly have heard about Pulakeshin's imperial ambitions through groups of itinerant traders and workers, if not directly through diplomacy or spying. Their territory was dotted with excellent port facilities, and was a major entrepot for maritime traffic travelling via the Persian Gulf. It was an even more lucrative prize than the Konkan. Pulakeshin, a man who 'treated his neighbours with contempt',[113] seems to have seen the area as within his rightful geopolitical sphere of influence, and its rulers sent him tribute, perhaps hoping it could buy them peace with the powerful lord of the Deccan. This would be the spark that lit the powder keg, for Pulakeshin was not the only Indian emperor with an interest in controlling Gujarat.

⌒

Harsha, Great King of Kings of north India, was an unconventional sort of emperor. His family, like the Chalukyas, came from a humble background, though he was a descendant of merchant townsmen[114] rather than cultivators or pastoralists. Unlike the Chalukyas, this clan's military capabilities had been forged in the heat of north Indian wars, which meant they had not only fought Alchon Huns from Central Asia but had also been entangled in the dramatic political developments of the previous century attending the final collapse of the Gupta empire – a saga of espionage, conspiracy, betrayal and war.[115] Suffice it to say here that by 606 CE, Harsha, supposedly only fifteen years old, ended up on the throne of Kannauj, north India's most wealthy and prestigious city at the time,[116] after the sudden death of both his elder brother and his brother-in-law.[117]

By 618, at which time Pulakeshin II had subjugated most of the Deccan and was throwing his weight around Gujarat, Harsha had successfully forced most of north India to submit to his imperial formation, spreading his influence across its thousands of thriving settlements ruled by hundreds of vassal dynasties. Over this time, his army is supposed to have grown from 5000 to 60,000 war elephants, from 2000 to 100,000 cavalry,[118] and incorporated innumerable masses of infantry. Even if this is an exaggeration, Harsha was clearly seen by his overawed contemporaries as one of the subcontinent's dominant rulers, if not *the* dominant ruler. In comparison, Pulakeshin's territories had far fewer large towns and productive agricultural regions; few chiefdoms and kingdoms could afford to build massive irrigation works in the Deccan yet. The arid plateau also had many more pastoralists and herders than the lush plains of the north, and was in general more sparsely populated. We do not know how much military might Pulakeshin could summon, but it is doubtful that he could have matched Harsha's.

Having expanded his influence as far as Bengal, commanding the ports of India's east coast, Harsha now wanted to control its west coast as well, potentially linking his territories to flourishing coastal trade routes in both directions. This threat may have been the trigger for the Latas to send tribute to Pulakeshin in the first place. If so, it was a dangerous gambit: as one scholar puts it, 'the sovereign of the Deccan must have considered to be his natural birthright ... unlimited access to the ocean ports of the Gulf of Cambay [Khambat]'.[119] Apparently deciding that tribute was not enough, the Chalukya emperor now attacked and conquered a part of Lata (southern Gujarat) and installed a relative of his as ruler.[120]

Up to this point, Harsha must have watched with growing surprise and interest as his audacious rival survived every challenge thrown at him, but the invasion of Lata must have been the last straw. It was the winter of 618 CE,[121] little more than eight years since Pulakeshin II had come to the throne. There would be no better chance for Harsha, who had been emperor for twelve years, to put him in his place. After consulting astrologers and calculating the outcomes of the campaign, planning out the route to be followed, rallying his armies and vassals, and arranging for supplies along the way, the order was given.

'At the close of the third watch, when all creatures slept,' Harsha's court poet tells us, 'the marching-drum was beaten with a boom deep as the gaping roar of the sky-elephants. Then, after a moment's pause, eight sharp strokes were given upon the drum, making up the number of leagues in the day's march.'[122]

In the dead of night, Harsha's camp – like those of many Indian monarchs, a capital city constantly on the move through his vast empire – roared into activity, trumpets and horns blaring, officers ordering their troops about, war elephants brought out of their stables, hosts of cavalry horses shaking their manes as they were roused from slumber. Tents were uprooted and packed, their pegs packed into bags, fastened along with water bags, awnings and screens on the backs of transport elephants and camels.[123] Foragers scurried around gathering heaps of fodder for the army's animals, while the poorer families of the area hurried to steal the grain left behind, bemoaning their tiny grass huts uprooted by the enormous temporary city.[124] Through the night, an enormous din of sound and clouds of dust were raised, and by the next morning, the mass of thousands of people and animals was ready to move. At its forefront were Harsha's vassals, seated on beautiful female elephants, 'riders holding up bows striped with gold leaf, swords grasped by servants, *chowries* [yak-tail fans] waved by betel-bearers, sheafs of javelins in cases under the charge of those who sat in the back, and saddles curving with scimitars and bristling with golden arrows'.[125]

Before them, on the tallest and most beautiful elephant at hand, shaded from the red sun of the dawn by the enormous white parasol reserved only for emperors, appeared Harsha-Vardhana Pushyabhuti. After first acknowledging the bowing 'company of feudatory kings' according to their rank with gestures and compliments[126] as per Indian courtly protocol,[127] he would have carried out a review of the army. And then these hundreds of thousands of feet and hooves began their march south.

In the Deccan, Pulakeshin was doing the same, his hereditary guard drilling with sharp spears every morning as troops from his vassals and allies, as well as tribes of pastoralists and forest dwellers, began to trickle in. These tribal warriors were generally outside the system of king and vassal lord but could be enticed to join military campaigns. Far from being 'primitive' in any way, Adivasi tribes were keen observers of cultural and political trends, and often played pivotal roles in the affairs of sedentary states. They saw the settled peoples of the subcontinent as a useful source of prestige, tribute and luxury goods,[128] and sometimes worked for them as mercenary troops and

Wikimedia Commons

'The Emperor Harsha pays homage to Buddha, 645 AD'. A painting by Allan Stewart in Hutchinson's *Story of the Nations*, published 1915. Harsha is the figure on the right, under an imperial parasol; he holds another parasol over a statue of the Buddha, wearing a crown and robes. An attendant to the left fans the Buddha with a yak tail. Some details, such as the turbans on the footmen, are anachronistic.

scouts. Harsha was already one of the subcontinent's most famous monarchs; to face him in battle was a great opportunity for loot and glory, and Pulakeshin would need the skills of these fearsome warriors to even the odds.

Though little is known about precisely how ancient and medieval Indians fought battles, contemporary manuals describe huge, heavy formations and counter-formations (*vyuhas*) organized according to complex rules.[129] North India, with access to vast amounts of infantry, elephantry and cavalry, was especially suited to this sort of fighting. The Deccan could not muster or feed the same numbers of infantry, nor did it have access to the overland routes of the horse trade, emerging as they did from Central Asia. If Pulakeshin had fought Harsha in north India, his army would easily have been surrounded and crushed. But in 618, to punish Pulakeshin for his audacious move on southern Gujarat, Harsha had to cross the Narmada river

A Chalukya imperial parasol and yak-tail fans, as depicted in the Lad Khan temple at Aihole, dated to the reign of Pulakeshin I in the mid-sixth century. Dwarf musicians blow conch shells below.

into the Deccan – which tilted the odds in Pulakeshin's favour.
With his control over the northern Deccan solidified by his policy
of economic and political integration, Pulakeshin could now easily
scout out Harsha's route of attack and contest the northern emperor's
attempts to cross the great river. Even if Harsha's probably larger army
were to cross the Narmada, this unwieldy force of infantry, cavalry
and elephants had to enter the thickly forested Vindhya foothills in
order to capture or defeat Pulakeshin – potentially negating their
advantage in numbers.

In addition to local intelligence and favourable terrain, Pulakeshin
had access to the tanks of the ancient world.[130] elephants. These deadly
creatures possessed the mass and sheer shock value needed to break
almost any immobile enemy formation sent against them. Indian kings
could deploy elephants in a variety of ways depending on the kind of
logistical capabilities and strategic requirements they were working
with. The cheapest, most plentiful and most poorly trained beasts
were rarely allowed into the front lines. Instead, they carried teams of
common soliders 'armed with knives, daggers, pots of oil, stones and
other weapons and missiles'[131] and acted as mobile archery platforms.
Aristocrats, who could afford larger elephants and trained staff, carried
gilded bows with assistants to hand them extra missiles, as well as an
expert mahout to guide the animal and goad it into attacking. Their
better-equipped elephant corps, wearing howdahs, tusk spikes and
warpaint, could be used both at range and in close-quarter duels,
when the animals' riders would swap their bows for javelins and long
elephant lances.[132] Should a war elephant be unleashed on an enemy
formation, it would be deployed with foot soldiers to guard its legs
and protect its rear whenever it took a breath from the slaughter.[133]
In a pinch, these immense creatures – specially captured, trained
and fed to fight – could even be armoured, gathered into squadrons
and used as heavy cavalry, as well as to screen formations of infantry
and horsemen.

In the Vindhya foothills,[134] though, none of those elaborate manoeuvres were possible. But the elephants still played a significant role.

In the lush green foliage of a Deccani winter, dozens of Chalukya elephants must have cleared a path through the moist undergrowth, soon churned into mud by miles of marching soldiers. Thousands of bare feet squelched in the mud and trampled down the grass and insects. As the sun bathed the Vindhyas, Chalukya scouts – perhaps allied forest tribes – may have fanned through the seemingly endless forests, using sounds and drums to signal the approach of the enemy. Harsha's army was probably carefully tracked and avoided until the very last moment. Ambushes and sneak attacks may have been planned to stretch their supply lines and worsen morale. Thickets might conceal ambushers with bows and spears, while hills and ravines might hide elephants to trample incautious groups of infantry. When Harsha's army, like the Mughals centuries later, was disoriented and exhausted in the unfamiliar Deccan, Chalukya forces may have aimed to lure them into a brutal, decisive confrontation.

Pulakeshin's troops were ideally adapted to close-quarter combat. His elephants, in the hundreds, were fed huge quantities of alcohol before battle, spikes fitted to their tusks, great bells hung around their necks, howdahs tied to their backs. The animals were then bunched together into close formations for massed charges, brave mahouts desperately trying to guide them with the fearsome *ankusha*, a sharp elephant goad dug into their eyes and temporal glands. To the hypnotic beating of battle drums, the elephants were followed by bands of elite hereditary warriors wearing loincloths and minimal armour, also drunk on alcohol.[135]

Harsha's court poet describes his infantry as wearing topknots and spotted red coats, ears adorned with ivory rings.[136] The north Indian emperor commanded them from the back of his elephant Darpasata, a massive animal whose head was adorned with a 'crested crown of gold'.[137] But beyond this, there is little we know for certain of the confrontation between the two young emperors. Pulakeshin's inscriptions, and those of other medieval royals, paint pictures of horrifying battlefield violence. They describe elephants colliding, tusks gleaming with blood. The hulking beasts would attempt to force each other to topple, their senses dulled by alcohol, as their riders stabbed each other with lances. The screams of men trampled underfoot and gored by tusks, the squeals of fallen elephants whose bellies were pierced by the cruel spears of the Chalukya infantry, must have filled the forest.

But eventually – perhaps after months or weeks, or perhaps after a few disastrous ambushes and confrontations – Harsha seems to have realized that he would have to cut his losses. Forcing the Deccan to accept his suzerainty was not worth sacrificing an entire army. Perhaps he intended to renew the conflict another time, but that time would never come, as rebellions and easier pickings called his attention east and kept him there till the end of his reign.

Pulakeshin II, unlikely lord of the Deccan, had defeated the subcontinent's superpower.

And so, as Harsha ordered his retreat, as the Vindhyas reverberated with the sound of retreating drums and the piercing blast of victory trumpets, Pulakeshin was left to giddily proclaim his astonishing victory.[138] As a Chalukya court poet put it, Emperor Harsha, whose name meant Joy, had lost his laughter in the Deccan. All of a sudden,

The signature of Harsha, taken from an inscription. It reads *svahasto mama maharajadhiraja sri harshaya*, 'By my own hand, Emperor Harsha'. From Vincent Arthur Smith's *The Early History of India*, published 1924.

it was clear not only to Pulakeshin's vassals, not only to his family, but to the entire subcontinent, that the Deccan had arrived. As kings and emperors reeled from the news, Pulakeshin claimed the splendid title of Parameshvara,[139] Paramount Lord. Lata and the northern Deccan were his. He now turned his attention to the rest of India south of the Narmada.

2

Pulakeshin's Blood

Spring, 619 CE

Fresh from the victory over Harsha, Pulakeshin II and the Chalukyas set out to dominate as much of southern India as they could. This wasn't an easy task: rivals and traitors and nemeses were everywhere. And far away in the deepest south, a storm of songs and devotion was being unleashed. The name of an enigmatic, erotic, violent god was on everyone's lips: Shiva, the Auspicious One, the Destroyer.

❧

In the early centuries CE, the coastal belt of Andhra, to the east of the Chalukya dominions of the seventh century, had been host to hundreds of Buddhist monasteries, stupas and pilgrimage sites. Dozens of now-forgotten Buddhist schools – Aparamahavinaseliya, Bahusrutiya, Ahirasamghika, Mahisasaka and more – had vied for the patronage of local communities and wealthy merchants. Buddhist monasteries ran massive religious and commercial establishments, and were perhaps at least as influential in the daily lives of the Andhra people as the then-fledgling apparatus of monarchical rulership. From Andhra, Buddhist artisans, pilgrims, monks and merchants had exchanged ideas with the Tamil country (also known as Tamilakam), the northern Deccan, the Gangetic plains, and even Gandhara and thence with Central Asia and China. Buddhism's position as the most prestigious and powerful of South Asian religions had then seemed unassailable.

But by the second half of the first millennium CE, as the Chalukyas were rising in the Deccan, the influence of this ancient religion was waning. Buddhism was becoming increasingly dependent on patronage from military aristocrats to survive. But few kings or queens of Andhra's ruling dynasties now declared a Buddhist affiliation, preferring newly prominent gods and goddesses, such as the Saptamatrika or Seven Mothers, the avatars of Vishnu, and especially the family of Shiva. This new preference, as we've glimpsed through the activities of the Chalukyas in the Malaprabha river valley, was based on careful political calculation and deliberate institution building as much as on personal devotion. We shall return to this theme soon. For now, it's sufficient to say that by the early 600s CE, the petty dynasties of Andhra were constantly at war with each other and with the Tamils to their south.

Meanwhile, on the shores of the Narmada, Pulakeshin II was realizing that his victory over Harsha was not as decisive as he had expected. Harsha, whatever his deficiencies as a military strategist, was by far the shrewder and more experienced diplomat. To Pulakeshin's northeast, Harsha allied with their common neighbours[1] to stymie any expansion in that direction and retain them as buffer states between the two emperors' competing spheres of influence. Meanwhile, to Pulakeshin's northwest, the rulers of northern Gujarat began to lean towards Harsha under a diplomatic barrage. The Chalukya was far too cunning to try to subjugate them outright and thus be drawn into a conflict on a terrain of Harsha's choosing. Nor was he foolhardy enough to repeat Harsha's strategy and attempt to cross the Narmada.

And so Pulakeshin II's eyes alighted on the east: the coastal plains of Andhra. Its ports were connected to the trade circuits of the eastern

Indian Ocean, guaranteeing luxury goods and tariffs. Its lands were fertile, good prizes for his loyal followers, and its rulers were weakened by wars with their southern neighbours, the Tamil dynasty known as the Pallavas.[2] When the lords of Vengi – the fertile heartland of Andhra, that bounteous delta between the rivers Krishna and Godavari – received word of the Chalukya emperor's march downriver from the Deccan plateau to the Andhra plains, they must have summoned their vassals and ordered the mustering of troops.

By winter 618–spring 619 CE[3] (mere months after his victory against Harsha) Pulakeshin's elephants were hammering at the gates of the fortified city of Pithapuram, capital of one of Vengi's major dynasties. Soon after, he faced another local king on the shores of the Kolleru lake, famous today for its waterfowl. A brutal slaughter was inflicted on this army, supposedly leaving the shores of the lake littered with corpses and turning its waters red for days.[4] An uneasy peace was settled, with the Andhra kings accepting Chalukya overlordship. However, many other challengers – including the tribes of the Eastern Ghats – still threatened their authority there.

Nevertheless, the Chalukyas now had a foothold on both shores of the peninsula, east and west. The Konkan had been secured by the conquest of southern Gujarat and the appointment of viceroys directly related to Pulakeshin in those regions. A similar strategy would need to be followed in order to secure the conquest of Vengi. During his return to Vatapi, Pulakeshin set this programme in motion. At Alampur, the sacred conjunction of the Krishna and Tungabhadra rivers about 200 km from modern-day Hyderabad,[5] he paused to divide up parts of conquered Vengi among his vassals.[6] They were granted the right to rule over the land and make war against its natives to expand their holdings. He then continued onwards to his clifftop fort to celebrate with his sons and queens. Showered with flowers and amidst the roaring acclaim of his subjects, Pulakeshin visited the cave temples of Vatapi to thank his clan's gods.

Chalukya domains were now more expansive than they had ever been: most of the Deccan, from the upper reaches of the Kaveri river to the Narmada, owed them direct or indirect allegiance. Southern Gujarat and the Konkan coast were controlled by Chalukya viceroys, and Chalukya-affiliated warlords ruled over swathes of Andhra on the east coast. Despite Pulakeshin II's by-now legendary military reputation, the ruling of such a wide and diverse domain required bold ways of stating, justifying and enforcing political power.

One way he did this was by embarking on the construction of temples. In doing so, Pulakeshin II demonstrates to us why elites across the Indian subcontinent were abandoning Buddhism and moving towards Puranic Hinduism (associated with encyclopaedic texts called *Puranas*, quite distinct from Vedic Hinduism).[7] After all, there are few more effective ways to cloak avarice and political ambitions than by using the garb of devotion.

⁓

Today, it is difficult to imagine Hinduism without temples, or even to imagine temples as being more than places for worship. That was not the case during the time of the early Chalukyas. Then, the idea of building permanent shrines to 'Hindu' gods was somewhat of an innovation. Buddhists, on the other hand, were used to worshipping idols and congregating around permanent religious institutions such as monasteries or stupas, and folk religion in the subcontinent always had a strong idol-based aspect to its worship of yakshas and other fertility deities. But orthodox Hinduism, even up to the early centuries CE, had still relied primarily on Vedic rituals – expensive and difficult undertakings for kings, and rather ephemeral in how they displayed royal power and political messages. These rituals were performed in temporary altars, built specifically to perform a sacrifice and destroyed after.

But by the fourth century, aided by the patronage of the Gupta emperors of northern India, Hindu cults adopted permanent iconic representations of gods and introduced radical theological innovations in a bid to increase popularity and capture patronage. In the Vedic worldview, the gods, who always remained invisible presences through the rituals, needed periodic sacrifices from mortals to help them defeat anti-gods and bring rains. In the new, temple-based, Puranic Hinduism, gods such as Shiva and Vishnu were embodied as idols and were declared Supreme. They no longer needed sacrifices to help them order the cosmos, but went about their business according to a plan that mortals could not hope to understand. Mortals could also bring them to Earth as permanent residents in temples, not just as temporary visitors to sacrifices. There, they could propitiate these mighty deities with new rituals that were presented as reworked versions of Vedic sacrifices: periodic, daily offering of animals, food, flowers and so on. This innovation proved popular with rich and poor alike. Royals across northern India soon started to build shrines to Hindu gods, while continuing their patronage of existing Buddhist and Jain institutions.

However, temples did not spread only for devotional reasons. Major temples and the deities they enshrined were associated with legends contained in the *Puranas*, and were believed to have potent boons to offer devotees and donors. They attracted pilgrims and, more importantly, commercial activity, creating hubs where India's flourishing religious cults could preach, squabble, sing, celebrate and make money. The popularity of temple-based Hinduism also led to the gradual creation of new religious communities, more amenable to supporting the activities of warlike aristocrats who claimed a special relationship with the gods[8] – all of which were in stark contrast to what Buddhists in south India were willing or able to offer, as will be seen later. Building a temple could also help royals curry favour with existing groups of worshippers, monastic communities, pilgrims and so on. The crowds of devotees that visited temples would frequently hear

of the land grants and military exploits of kings, and associate them
with the inscrutable world-ordering activities of deities, in contrast
to the moralistic tales of Buddhas and Bodhisattvas that they might
hear in a stupa. As one scholar puts it, the rise of ever more elaborate
temples and the growth of royal power inevitably went hand in hand.[9]

This was why it was so important for medieval kings to build
temples, though we may often misinterpret these activities as stemming
purely from devotion. Early Chalukya temples, in particular, show us
how medieval kings used these buildings as a crucial aspect of their
power. Chalukya temples are replete with subtle and not-so-subtle
political messages.

Pulakeshin I's earliest attested activities were Vedic sacrifices,
meant to establish his status amongst other elites conversant with their
meaning – kings, Brahmins, generals, poets, astrologers – rather than
the average Deccani. By the end of his reign, he had begun to seek
more permanent means to express his power to the mass of his subjects.
His imperial title, Sri-Prithivi-Vallabha, had already established his
relationship to Vishnu. But he also used the soft sandstone of the cliffs
of Vatapi to state his personal relationship to the other great god of
temple-based Hinduism – Shiva – whose cults were already popular
in the northern Deccan.

Pulakeshin I's sculptors were ordered to make sculptures totally
unique to the Chalukyas, expressing royal support for these new
religious practices. One such image, a spectacular eighteen-armed
image of a dancing Shiva[10] still welcomes visitors to the cliffs of
Vatapi (modern-day Badami). The god's arms swirl around him like
a blooming lotus, his left foot poised an instant away from striking
the ground.

Pulakeshin I's two warlike sons (Mangalesha and Pulakeshin II's
father) also engaged in a spurt of cave temple building in Vatapi and
other Chalukya towns in the Malaprabha valley, such as Aryapura
(modern-day Aihole). Ancient sacred springs and wells and dolmen

burial sites, where the indigenous peoples of the land had congregated for centuries to celebrate nature's rhythms, were now incorporated into the sites of flashy new temples.[11] Of course, the Chalukyas by no means confined their patronage to Hindu gods; the religious composition of early medieval India was very much in flux, and they built Buddhist and Jain temples to appeal to those audiences as well.[12]

Today, the constructions of the early Chalukya kings are among the oldest known temples in southern India, and they tell us a fair bit about the political clashes and competitive religious environment of the sixth century. For example, the Kadambas of Banavasi, their deadly rivals, associated themselves with the Saptamatrikas, goddesses of victory and liberation with roots in ancient cults. Pulakeshin I's sons went out of their way to use images of these Seven Mothers in their cave temples,[13] competing with the Kadambas to claim the favour of these popular deities.

Mangalesha commissioned an image of the original Sri-Prithivi-Vallabha, Varaha, the man–boar form of Vishnu, who had earned the love of the goddess Earth by rescuing her from a demon at the time of the Great Deluge. The sculpture, evidently meant to establish a visual parallel with the king, can be seen in Cave 3 in modern-day Badami. To this day it retains traces of its original lustrous blue paint. Mangalesha's campaigns against the Kadambas and Kalachuris, it seems to say, are analogous to Vishnu's rescue of Earth from darkness. This Chalukya king's association with Varaha would go on to become one of the subcontinent's most iconic visual motifs: his nephew Pulakeshin II would use the boar as his battle standard, and it would continue to be used intermittently for nearly one thousand years after, even during the time of the Deccan empires of Bijapur and Vijayanagara.[14]

Pulakeshin II inherited some of his uncle Mangalesha's skill at visual propaganda, introducing innovations of his own to Chalukya political messaging. He, however, wanted to make a new sort of temple – not the dark, concealed cave temples that the Deccan was familiar with, but elegant new structures that embraced open air, space, and

Sarah Welch / Wikimedia Commons

Varaha in Badami Cave 3, depicted rescuing the goddess Earth, Prithivi, from the waters, symbolized by a Naga below him. Gods witness the scene from above.

light. His sculptors and *sthapatis* ('establishers', or master architects) oversaw the removal of great blocks of sandstone from the cliffs of Vatapi. These were then assembled into some of the oldest surviving free-standing temples in southern India. Their clean lines were adorned with subtle sculptural motifs – artistic representations of gods, myths and miniature shrines. Built to support their own weight through careful balancing and positioning of joints, Pulakeshin II's temples have endured nearly 1400 years of erosion.

Santosh Badiger / Wikimedia Commons

The 'Upper Shivalaya', a temple dated to the reign of Pulakeshin II. The temple is assembled from jointed blocks of stone with some architectural decoration on its spire: future Chalukya temples would use much more elaborate ornamentation.

Their design borrows from both north and south to make something new, something uniquely *Deccan*. The shape of Pulakeshin II's temples, using the distinctive south Indian tiered superstructure ascending in ever-smaller layers from a wide base, seems to reflect a south-centric worldview. And yet, there are many northern influences, which would only have been included by sculptor guilds at Pulakeshin II's express wish, in order to impress audiences in Vatapi. For example, in sculptural panels on the walls, Shiva can be seen standing straight and calm in the *samabhanga* posture with a snake in his right hand and a trident in his left, all of which are 'common North Indian attributes'.[15] These influences came by way of the northern Deccan, a region that was now firmly in Chalukya hands, though it had been a foreign country just a generation ago. Religions and goods from there were now becoming more popular in the Chalukya home territories, as these once-poor lands grew into prosperous towns and were integrated into the subcontinent's webs of trade and religious exchange. Pulakeshin's splendid new buildings must have been a great hit with the increasingly religious and cosmopolitan people of the Malaprabha valley, a shrewd investment of the loot he had gained from his military campaigns. Pulakeshin II's temples thus tell us a great deal about the complex ways in which medieval Indian elites went about the business of solidifying and perpetuating their power. Given what temple-based Hinduism could offer to the wealthiest and most powerful people, the decline of monastic Buddhism at this time makes much more sense.

Pulakeshin II also brought innovations to other aspects of Chalukya power. Temples helped structure social activity in urban centres, with their consistent daily and seasonal rhythms where the people of the Malaprabha river valley could congregate. But their audience was limited to a radius of a few dozen miles, at most. For faraway subjects and vassals, more concise religio-political messages were needed.

Pulakeshin II now proved himself the equal of his grandfather in propaganda, inventing a legendary backstory for the Chalukyas, erasing their humble *chalke*-wielding past. This was interwoven with land grant formulae once used by the Kadambas, ensuring that the aura of glory that surrounded that old dynasty would now accrue to his clan.

According to Pulakeshin, the Chalukya were a clan 'nourished by the breasts of the Seven Mothers ... who have acquired an uninterrupted continuity of prosperity through the protection of Karttikeya [the war god], who have had all kings made subject to them at the sight of the boar-crest which they have acquired through the favour of the divine Narayana [Vishnu]'.[16] He declared that they were a race of heroes sprung from a pot, a *chuluka*, filled with water from the Ganga by an ancestor who defended the gods from demons.[17] In another version, the Chalukya progenitor was Brahma the Creator himself.[18] In another, there is no pot, but there was a hero whose name is Chalukya.[19] Finally, Pulakeshin also adopted for himself a bevy of titles designed to inspire awe among his vassals and rivals, including Satyashraya, Refuge of Truth – this would be the title by which he was remembered by his successors for centuries after.

The point of all this intense activity in architecture, iconography and political propaganda was manifold. It established that the Chalukyas had rescued the Deccan from all the darkness and anarchy that came before, just as Varaha had rescued the Earth. It established that they were no ordinary mortals, but the favourites of the most popular gods – even the gods of their erstwhile rivals. It established that they ruled over north as well as south, that their power extended into areas that had never bowed to the might of the Deccan before. And, most importantly, it laid the popular and institutional foundations for many more generations of Chalukyas to build temples, make land grants and reorder the Deccan as their ancestors had.

As Pulakeshin went about the business of creating an empire, world-changing events were afoot elsewhere in the 620s. A devastating war had broken out between two of the world's superpowers: the Eastern Roman Empire and the Sassanian Empire of Persia. The Sassanian Empire was left a shadow of its former self, tottering on the brink of anarchy. Large swathes of the Levant and modern-day Turkey and Iraq were in ruins, disrupting trade to the little town of Mecca in the Arabian Peninsula. In 622, a middle-aged former merchant,

Muhammad, fled from there to Yathrib (modern-day Medina) with his followers. He brought with him a new religion: Islam, 'Submission to God'.

This, of course, was of no importance to Pulakeshin II, who still had challenges to overcome in Vengi, while the ambitious Tamil kings were cooking up trouble to the south. Dealing with the first task was the responsibility of Pulakeshin's most trusted lieutenant, his younger brother Vishnuvardhana. This Chalukya was a far wittier and more cynical individual than Pulakeshin. He invariably called himself Kubja-Vishnuvardhana in his own inscriptions, the word *kubja* meaning 'hunchback' – this in an era when court residents delighted in boasting about their physical features and attractiveness.[20] Indeed, he sometimes called himself Vishamasiddhi, Overcomer of Obstacles,[21] a reference both to his military abilities and physical handicap.

The brothers were extremely close. Pulakeshin had, after all, defeated their uncle Mangalesha and fought for their right to primacy in the Deccan almost single-handedly. Vishnuvardhana, in return, worked alongside him as a governor and general at the head of the Chalukyas of Vatapi. He very likely earlier participated in the brutal sacking of Banavasi, the Kadamba capital, and Puri, the great port on the Konkan coast. He is known to have served as Yuvaraja, heir apparent and designated regent, on multiple occasions, and may have held that title when Pulakeshin was away campaigning against Harsha and Vengi in the years 618–19. Given that his elder brother had already spent years developing and consolidating his own personal power, Vishnuvardhana is unlikely to have seen himself as a candidate for the throne of Vatapi. Instead, he seems to have calculated, like the other chiefs of the Deccan, that his talents would be more profitably employed in attempting to seize glory under Pulakeshin's shadow. The easiest way to do that, of course, was through conquest.

By the mid-620s, when Pulakeshin was busy with his construction projects and strengthening his grip over the Deccan at large,

'Footed Bowl with Scenes from the Gauttila Jataka'. Probably made in Vengi in the fifth or sixth century CE, this bowl offers a rare glimpse of the courtly culture of early medieval south India around the time of the Chalukyas' expansion. Note the royal couple sitting on a throne left of centre, with chowrie-bearers behind; they are watching a dancer accompanied by a lyre player. Parasol bearers and a bodyguard can be seen behind.

Vishnuvardhana was in the process of completely subduing Vengi,[22] which was proving remarkably recalcitrant to Chalukya authority. The dynasty Pulakeshin had so bloodily defeated at the Kolleru lake was still around; they were nominally Chalukya vassals, but caused no end of trouble to the brothers as the pair tried to enforce their authority on the other fiercely independent powers of Andhra. An even more serious challenge came from the Adivasi forest peoples of the country.

Vishnuvardhana's inscriptions refer to them as the Durjayas (Difficult to Conquer),[23] occupying a land called 'Giripaschimasima'[24] – 'the place west of the hills' – though we have no idea what the people of this powerful tribal coalition called themselves. It would seem that the Chalukya armies could conquer cities and agrarian land easily enough, but were far less effective in hilly and forested

terrain, especially without friendly tribes to help them (as there may
have been in their campaign against Harsha). These Durjayas must
have had their own charismatic chiefs, their own complex religious
rites, their own sense of identity and time and place nestled away in
mist-wreathed hills and forests bubbling with the sounds of streams,
animals and distant drums. A history of India from their perspective
and that of other tribes like them, confronted by aggressive agrarian
kingdoms, might look very different.

Of course, the relationship between tribal peoples and sedentary
states was not always either amicable or antagonistic, but lay on a
spectrum. Interactions were guided by many factors, including the
relative balance of power between both sides. In some areas, Durjaya
chiefs accepted land grants from the Chalukyas, as did members of
other tribes such as the Matsyas, and a group that still exists today:
the Boyas. Indeed, there is evidence that some Boya priests were
granted Brahmin status and received land grants from Chalukya
hands,[25] hinting that royal Hinduism in the seventh century was
highly effective at appropriating or incorporating local religious ideas
in practice, and vice versa. Boya chieftains could use the prestige and
legitimacy that Hinduism conferred to solidify their authority, and
may thus have deliberately integrated with this new complex of ideas
that the Chalukyas patronized – just as the Chalukyas themselves had
performed sacrifices and built temples to strengthen their grip on power
in the Malaprabha river valley a few generations ago. As we can see,
the interplay of religious and cultural legitimacy, political calculations
and ownership of land in medieval India helped Puranic Hinduism
spread far and wide as the premier religion of kings and lords.

Vishnuvardhana also began to build his own, independent base in
Vengi, consisting of other ambitious local warriors, imported Brahmins
and Deccani warlords, and elements of the old ruling classes directly
loyal to him. All these diverse agents were rewarded with revenue rights
to villages and other financial and symbolic rewards in return for their

military, cultural and political support to his new regime.[26] He, like his elder brother Pulakeshin II, also tapped into the other strategies available to Indian lords of means and discernment, hiring publicists and panegyrists to establish his own personal connection to the gods.

In addition to Vishnuvardhana's campaigns, denizens of Vengi had previously been subjected to brutal Chalukya aggression at the hands of Pulakeshin II during the bloody battle of the Kolleru lake. But obviously not a hint of this comes across in the younger Chalukya's inscriptions. Vishnuvardhana instead portrayed himself as virtuously rescuing the world from the darkness of unjust kings and immoral people, which according to mythology was an ever-present feature of the Kali age that had begun after the Mahabharata war. He, like his brother Pulakeshin II and uncle Mangalesha, intended to be remembered as a royal saviour, which meant that Vishnu legends were trotted out and liberally applied to him as well. For example, Kubja-Vishnuvardhana could also be interpreted as 'Increaser of the Glory of Dwarf-Vishnu' – the avatar of Vishnu called Vamana, the dwarf who rescued the Earth from the anti-gods.

Vamana was not the only deity pressed into the service of this new Chalukya's royal brand. Vishnuvardhana seems to have had a fairly active sex life, and took for himself the titles of Kamadeva – the god of love – while adopting as his personal emblem Kama's symbol, the *makara*, a fantastic creature that was a synthesis of an elephant, a crocodile, a snake and a peacock; he thereby equated himself with the embodiment of male attractiveness and sexuality.[27] For someone with a physical handicap to make this claim is indicative, one would like to believe, of a certain dry humour.

So far we have seen the medieval India propaganda machine in action at the hands of many of the early Chalukya lords: Pulakeshin I, his son Mangalesha and Mangalesha's nephews Pulakeshin II and Vishnuvardhana. This may have given the impression that Chalukya propaganda was always effective and lapped up by the people they dominated – but that's primarily because most sources surviving from the period are Chalukya land grants and architecture, a great example of how history ends up being written by the victors.

But just as not all modern voters are foolhardy enough to take political ads at face value, the denizens of Vengi had a similarly complicated relationship with Chalukya proclamations. In Vengi – which, as mentioned, was once a major Buddhist centre – these voices came from the sangha itself, providing us with a rare perspective from the 'losing side', those medieval Indians who found themselves on the wrong side of new equations of royal power, religion and economics. This is a voice of privilege to be sure, but nevertheless hints at a far more turbulent process of conquest and acculturation than kings might like us to believe.

According to Chandrakirti, an elderly monk from Vengi, contemporary kings (probably the Chalukyas) were little more than 'trained monkeys and dogs that must look to their [Brahmin] masters for instruction before they act'.[28] What about the idea that these kings were associates of the divine just because they built a temple or two? Nonsense – any king who did not use his position to benefit the people and reduce the suffering of living things, but was instead driven by lust for wealth and women, was more likely to be reborn as a donkey or a worm[29] than rise to heaven.[30] What's more, argued the monk, these new rulers couldn't even be trusted to ensure law and order. After all, the exemplar of all thieves was the looting, conquering king who dug holes in the walls of cities and forts just as thieves dug holes in the walls of houses.[31]

But, vocal as Vengi's Buddhists were, neither of the Chalukya brothers paid them any attention. They didn't need to: a Chinese monk who visited Andhra in the seventh century remarked on the fact that barely twenty Buddhist monasteries remained, whereas there were hundreds of flourishing Shaivite temples,[32] crowded with devotees.

The presence of all these temples offers us another chance to question the centrality of kings in our understanding of medieval India. We've seen how temple building was a way for royals to ingratiate themselves with new religious communities or create new ones. But kings were not omnipotent: none of their activities could have seriously changed the religious landscape of India if not for the fact that other, far more powerful forces were at play, remaking the religious world of thousands of people. The Chalukyas and their ilk were merely benefiting from and amplifying a great tsunami of religious change that was beginning to engulf southern India. The temples of kings are the most visible remains of this period, but they are merely reflections of the small and conceited thing that is royal power, often responding to or taking advantage of something far vaster than itself.

This was the explosive flowering of bhakti – an intense, almost mad devotion to a god. In particular, devotion to the god of the matted hair and the tiger skin: Shiva, Destroyer, Auspicious One.

∽

Although it might seem that Indians have always been mostly Hindus, and that Hindu kings are the most important characters in the story of the subcontinent, that is not so evident in the early medieval south. Indeed, the rise in the popularity of Hindu gods, temples and kings in south India, and specifically in Tamilakam, the Tamil country, was a sudden and somewhat improbable phenomenon. History is shaped not just by individuals but by fundamental transformations in how societies of hundreds of thousands of people see and structure themselves. This dynamic can be seen through first-hand accounts from Tamilakam in the seventh century.

While the Deccan and Andhra both had significant Buddhist and Jain presences, as we've seen above, Tamilakam, with its prosperous kingdoms and ports, was the real bastion of their power. Many of that land's great epics had been written by influential Buddhists and

Jains – both ordained monks and members of the lay community. Buddhist and Jain monasteries competed with each other and with sects dedicated to 'Hindu' gods for social and royal largesse. By the sixth and seventh centuries, Buddhists and Jains in the region participated in surprisingly similar forms of worship, digging cave temples into cliff sides and using idols as a focus of devotion;[33] they freely borrowed ideas from each other in an attempt to remain as popular and relevant as possible.[34]

This balance was upset with the rise of poet-saints proposing a radical new theology focused on absolute devotion to Shiva – one that, coincidentally, complemented the new temple-based Hinduism that royals were promoting. In doing so, they became among the most pivotal figures in Indian and global religious history. Their theology, bhakti, presented people with an alternative and viable path to spiritual salvation and social status that did not require the expense of Vedic sacrifices, or the extremities of worldly renunciation that the Buddhists and Jains demanded. It was a path open to all, ascetic or householder. All that was required was absolute love and surrender to Shiva, the Auspicious One. The lack of emphasis on renunciation or expensive rituals, coupled with an easy-to-understand emotional philosophy, made bhakti wildly popular in comparison to Vedic Hinduism.

The bhakti saints wrote beautiful, memorable music and led crowds of devotees in song, travelling from village to village proclaiming the power and love of Shiva. From holy site to holy site they went, followed by cheering and singing crowds, converting householders and rival monks alike.

'How shines before my eyes his brilliant trident!' sang the crowds. 'How gleams the crescent moon atop his lengthy locks! How heavy the scent of *konrai* garland! How bright the glow of conch-shell and *thodu*! Like thunderbolt the sound when elephant skin he tears – Look how he wraps it round like a mantle!'[35]

We can scarcely imagine the profound spiritual experience it must have been, in a world torn by war and famine and misery, to join these dancing, ecstatic crowds, surrounded by bodies throbbing to the beats of the *damaru* drum, hearing praises of Shiva's power, Shiva's love, Shiva's mercy. It seems, understandably, to have inspired almost fanatical devotion. You could ask Shiva for anything – one saint even asked him to rescue him from the predicament of having cheated on his wife – and you could say anything to him.[36] You didn't have to know the rituals, the chants. You could refuse to go on pilgrimages, ignore the flashy new temples that kings were building, search within. Or you could do those too, if you wanted. Shiva, according to the saints, accepted all, and was merciful to all.

'We are slaves to no man!' exulted one saint. '... we belong forever to Shankara [Shiva] ... The Lord of the warlike bull has taken us. Why need we listen to the words of men who parade themselves in silk and gold?'[37]

Buddhists and Jains refused to give up silently when faced with a deadly threat to their lives and livelihoods. One bhakti saint, a former Jain, led a vitriolic campaign against his former colleagues, calling them 'arrogant and fat ... stinking and debased ... lacking in both virtue and clothing', and singing of how Shiva drove them away, 'bearing as weapons fire and a white axe'.[38] Jains responded in kind, denouncing Hindu deities as dissolute characters unworthy of worship,[39] who would only lead their followers further away from enlightenment and into the entanglements of the mortal world – a reference to the bhaktas' claim that one could be saved by Shiva's grace even as a householder. Buddhists and Jains held a dominant position in many towns and courts, challenging the bhaktas to perform public miracles to prove that Shiva actually did intervene in the world to help his devotees. Of course, according to later Shaiva legend, Shiva did exactly that, granting the saints the power to light lamps filled with water instead of oil, cure kings of disease, and survive lime kilns and mad war elephants with aplomb.[40]

Though Shaiva saints might have had a good deal of contempt for

Richard Mortel / Wikimedia Commons

A twelfth-century bronze from Tamilakam, depicting the Shaiva bhakti saint Appar. Appar, a former Jain monk, became one of the most influential bhakti poets of the seventh century. Since the bronze was made half a millennium after his death, it might not be an accurate depiction of his facial features.

kings – 'men who parade[d] themselves in silk and gold' – their poetic activities were profoundly useful to royals. New temples soon emerged, capitalizing on the devotional fervour kindled by the saints. Surely, royal propaganda implied, if people could have absolute faith in the gods, then they should have absolute faith in kings, the beloveds of the gods. The Chalukyas watched attentively as this wave began to spread into the Deccan from the south, alongside the Shaiva cults of the northern Deccan already prominent in their territories, and the flourishing new religious communities now gathering around their own Shiva temples in the Malaprabha valley. They had astutely chosen the winner from among the whirlpool of India's religions. Buddhism would never again rise to the position it had once held in southern India. Despite the searing critiques Buddhism made of the Chalukyas, it seems to have been ignored by royals and commoners alike, and we hear less and less of resistance against the power of temples and kings. Gradually, the people of Vengi and the Deccan, their lands and minds conquered, seemed to have reconciled themselves to the rule of their warlike new overlords and the gods who supposedly supported them.

The eventual fate of Pulakeshin II was decided by a Tamil king who had been directly touched by the message of Shiva's saints. This man is one of the most uniquely complex of all Indian kings. A keen observer of the society over which he ruled, his sardonic wit and sharp sense of self make this aesthete, playwright and poet real like few other medieval kings – especially in comparison to Pulakeshin, whose inscriptions, stage-managed by court poets, present him as more of an archetype of the perfect Indian conqueror than an actual human being with flaws, misgivings or even a point of view. In contrast, this poet-king made it a point to compose his own inscriptions, and even wrote multiple plays, of which two have survived.[41]

His name was Mahendra-Varman, and he belonged to an old dynasty called the Pallavas, rulers of the northernmost part of Tamilakam, bordering both Vengi and the territories of the Gangas in the southern Deccan.[42] By the 600s, the Pallavas had catapulted themselves to a position of pre-eminence in Tamilakam by campaigning against the Buddhist/Jain-affiliated dynasties from their capital city of Kanchipuram, which still thrives today. Despite this, their approach towards the cut-throat religious competition within their territory had generally been fairly balanced. But Mahendra-Varman, supposedly because of the teachings of one of the seniormost of the bhakti saints, explicitly converted from Jainism to Shaivism. While personal convictions were certainly part of this decision, its political usefulness must have also played a role.

This complexity of motivation is on clear display in one of Mahendra's surviving plays, *Matta-Vilasa Prahasana* (Farce of the Drunkard's Games). The *Matta-Vilasa* in the title, meaning 'Drunken Sporter', is a reference to Mahendra himself, who made no secret of his love for alcohol, and even used the epithet in cave temples he commissioned.[43]

The farce is about an alcoholic *kapalin* (skull bearer), an ascetic member of a Shaiva cult whose activities involve wandering around Kanchi with a skull that doubles as a begging bowl for offerings of meat and liquor. One day, the hungover *kapalin* and his equally hungover girlfriend/apprentice discover they have lost their skull bowl. Their suspicion alights on a smug-looking Buddhist monk who is hurrying about, quite satisfied with the rich food and lodgings afforded to his order and secretly wishing that his monastic vows did not prevent him from indulging in wine and women (an interesting contrast to the *kapalin* who lives an otherwise austere life with, however, plenty of alcohol and sex). The two drunkards attempt unsuccessfully to grab him and rough him up, and end up flailing around and making fools of themselves.

Their scuffle is then enlivened by a Pashupata, member of yet another Shaivite school, who has a crush on the *kapalin*'s girlfriend and attempts, poorly, to adjudicate the dispute. This, of course, fails. Someone suggests they go to the judges of Kanchi, but the rest reject it because of how corrupt they are – a candid admission of the royal author's limitations as Kanchi's ruler, and a notable departure from other medieval kings who are generally quite self-satisfied in their boasts of providing perfect law and order. The absurdity is unexpectedly resolved by a madman – possibly a metaphor for Shiva himself in his form as Bhola, the simple-minded[44] – who has found the skull bowl in the possession of a stray dog.

There is much tomfoolery and physical humour in the farce, but the dialogue is razor-sharp and showcases Mahendra's keen observation of the dogmas and absurdities of each of these schools. His characters might not be particularly deep, but they reveal a great deal about how a royal Shaivite viewed the religious innovation, plurality and absurdity of the times. As a Jain who had converted to Shaivism, he pokes only gentle fun at his original faith and reserves most of his wit for the 'heretic' Shaivite schools, and of course the Buddhists, all of whom he evidently disapproves of.[45] The farce appears to have been enough of a hit with the literati that it continued to be performed on and off for centuries, copied out again and again to come down to us today and give us a rare glimpse into the mind of a medieval Indian king.

In the 620s, Chalukya campaigns in Vengi were reaching a crucial stage, and Palakeshin II and Vishnuvardhana could countenance no threats from the south. The Pallavas had been battling the rulers of Andhra for control of this region for decades,[46] and the only way for the Chalukyas to stop their ambitions of northward expansion was through force. Vengi, fractured between many petty dynasties and fading Buddhist monasteries, had been easy for the Chalukyas to swallow whole. But nothing of the sort could be achieved in the religiously and politically vibrant Tamil country. Pulakeshin II seems to have instead aimed to secure Mahendra Pallava's submission[47] and inflict a decisive enough defeat on the Tamils to ensure his grip over Vengi.

At the battle of Pollilur[48] – close to where, twelve centuries later, Tipu Sultan and Hyder Ali would inaugurate modern military rocketry by smashing a British army with gunpowder – the Chalukyas under their boar banner crushed the Pallava forces and drove them behind the walls of Kanchi.[49] The Pallava guards must have watched with apprehension as the dust clouds of the approaching Chalukya army, hot on their heels, blotted out the sun. Hundreds of colourful flags and umbrellas dotted the vast force as the sun glinted off thousands of spears. On an especially large elephant near the centre was Pulakeshin II, wearing a garment of silk and a golden coronet, glistening with sweat in the sweltering heat despite the great imperial parasol an attendant held over him.[50] The fearsome boar banner was held high on a standard nearby, waving in the breeze. Around the emperor were his highest generals and nobles, also mounted on elephants, surrounded by elite hereditary troops holding the fluttering banners of aristocratic households.

Hearing the roars and drums of the Chalukya army, the trumpeting of elephants, and quite possibly the taunts of Pulakeshin, Mahendra apparently realized his kingdom was not, at this time, ready for the challenge. And so he did what every classical Indian text on statecraft would recommend: follow a policy of appeasement.[51] In return for tribute and perhaps a promise that Mahendra would not contest Chalukya control over Vengi, Pulakeshin was convinced to leave Kanchi and its denizens untouched. And so he returned to Vatapi, confident in his status as the dominant ruler of southern India.

ᴄ

The Pallava Mahendra-Varman had every intention of trashing his agreement as soon as he could. He, personally, had neither the inclination nor the ability to invade either the Deccan or Vengi. But he was no pacifist, and understood that the geopolitics of medieval India were a wild jungle, governed by the principle of *matsya-nyaya*, the Law of the Fishes, where the big ate the small, where one either ate or was eaten. The peace with Pulakeshin was only a lull. Though his middle age seems to have been spent exploring the arts, Mahendra had overseen many major Pallava victories over his Tamil neighbours in his early career as king.[52] He now spent his remaining years bolstering

Pallava ties with the other Tamil kingdoms as well as strengthening his forces and preparing them for revenge.

Despite its recent humiliation at Chalukya hands, the Pallava army was still led by some of the subcontinent's most feared commanders. Among them was Mahendra's son and heir Narasimha-Varman, who would prove to be the Chalukyas' nemesis. Narasimha came to the throne around 630, when Chalukya campaigns in Andhra were coming, at last, to a delicate conclusion.[53]

In 631, Vishnuvardhana Chalukya's new regime in Vengi had finally secured control over the blood-soaked coastal plains. His power stretched from the modern-day Visakhapatnam district in the north to Guntur in the south.[54] Pulakeshin II himself was invited to visit on a royal tour, and served as a witness to a land grant made by his younger brother. In a tacit acknowledgement of Vishnuvardhana's growing might, the grant declared that his descendants, not Pulakeshin's, would inherit the kingdom of Vengi.[55] Pulakeshin probably saw these new Chalukyas of Vengi as vassals – which was convenient for his ambitious younger brother, the hunchback who was now, against all odds, a king. The Pallavas thus had powerful Chalukya-affiliated neighbours to their north (Vishnuvardhana) and west (the Gangas).

It is unclear precisely what happened next: perhaps Pulakeshin sought to put down any hopes of Pallava resurgence; perhaps he was encouraged to do so by the Gangas, his in-laws, who bore a particular grudge against the Pallavas,[56] or perhaps Narasimha, confident in his preparations, somehow goaded the elderly Chalukya emperor into an attack.

On Pulakeshin's previous campaign in Tamilakam, he had managed to ensure the neutrality of the other Tamil kingdoms, possibly through his time-honoured strategy of bribery. By now, however, Narasimha appears to have managed to convince the other Tamil kings that Pulakeshin was a far greater threat to them than the Pallavas in the near run.[57] A coalition of three kings – perhaps the Chola, Pandya and Pallava – now awaited his entry into their lands. Pulakeshin, oblivious and overconfident, marched from the arid plateau of the Deccan into the rice fields of Tamilakam.[58] Within a matter of weeks, he was 20 miles from Kanchi, at a village called Manimangala, which still survives.

And there, in a massive upset, Narasimha defeated him.

Pulakeshin retreated, licking his wounds. He gave battle again. And Narasimha defeated him again.

How could Pulakeshin II, Defeater of Harsha, not prevail? Surely all that was required was another attempt.

And, again, Narasimha defeated him. The Chalukya army, under the hitherto victorious boar crest of Vishnu, fled the billowing Pallava bull banner, the resplendent white mount of Shiva. The Deccanis were driven from the Pallava lands. It was a disastrous blow to the prestige of Pulakeshin and the Chalukyas.

Pulakeshin's victories of the 610s and 620s had been nothing but one brilliant success after another. He may very well have believed in his own invincibility after all those years of watching the Malaprabha river valley grow prosperous, jeering at fleeing foes, and luxuriating in his new-found wealth. And now, fortune had deserted him. In slow motion, Pulakeshin's domains descended into turbulence and chaos in the 630s, as the chiefs of the Deccan began to once again question Chalukya authority.

Pulakeshin had boasted endlessly of his victory over Harsha in 618 and had gone about building an image of invulnerability through his brutal wars to keep his vassals in line and cow his neighbours into submission. Now the Pallava Narasimha gleefully gave this man, the hero of the Deccan, a taste of his own medicine and milked his victories for his own propaganda. A later Pallava inscription describes him as: 'Narasimhavarman ... who wrote the syllables (of the word) victory ... on Pulakeshin's (fleeing) back, which he saw in the battles of Pariyala, Manimangala, Suramara, etc.'[59]

With his position and prestige so badly shaken, Pulakeshin must have cast about desperately to reassure his vassals and to search for allies. One of them, perhaps, was his own brother – who, rather than come to Pulakeshin's aid, declared himself Maharaja Vishnuvardhana, Great King, an independent royal title, not that of a vassal, in 641 CE.[60] Perhaps this was a betrayal, or perhaps it was a prearranged deal, struck to ensure that Vishnuvardhana did not contest his nephews' right to succeed to the throne of the ageing, exhausted Pulakeshin.[61] That would prove to be moot, because that throne faced a much more dangerous threat than fratricide: the very next year, 642 CE, Narasimha's elephants were at the gates of Vatapi.[62] It was time for the Pallavas' revenge, time to put an end to these upstart Chalukyas.

How did Pulakeshin II, once Ereya, the climber of rocks, once the rebel who murdered his uncle, once a city-seizing emperor, face his death? Did he sally forth from the walls knowing he would not return alive? Did he wait quietly in his palace, watching the enemy elephants break through the gates of the citadel, their soldiers pouring through the city? Was he forced to watch his great victory pillar, established to commemorate the victories over Harsha and Vengi, being uprooted by a team of elephants, to be carried like a tree trunk to Kanchi?[63] Or perhaps he had died a sad death well before Narasimha Pallava's arrival.[64] As with so many things about early medieval India, we don't know for sure, and we never will. His own descendants never mention the exact circumstances of his death, as though it was taboo to speak of such a great conqueror like he was a mortal.

Though the defeater of Harsha was himself defeated, that legend would never die. For the rest of the Chalukyas the bloody cycle of vengeance had only just been set in motion.

3

Vikramaditya's Revenge

Summer, 642 CE

The Pallava army gorged themselves on the city of Vatapi, fat with the wealth of generations of Chalukyas. The palace was sacked, the men killed and women seized,[1] and its temples looted. According to a later oral legend, the 'Vatapi Ganapati' idol, today the subject of one of the most famous hymns in Carnatic music,[2] was among the spoils, carried away to the Uthrapathiswaraswamy temple near modern-day Nagapattinam[3] in Pallava territory.

The survivors of the sack of Vatapi – all those immigrant preachers, architects, traders, officials, cooks, sweepers and peddlers – must have fled with what little they could carry, and would not return for years. The Pallava king ordered a message to be left for any Chalukya prince who dared return. In a temple in the capital, he had engraved in the characteristically beautiful, almost floral Pallava script that his occupation of his enemy's capital was a 'fierce retribution' that befell Pulakeshin II for having twice threatened Kanchi.[4] On a boulder near the city, he issued another large inscription, later defaced but still preserving the words 'Vatapi' and 'Maha-Malla' (Great Wrestler), one of Narasimha's many titles.[5] The Pallava king also adopted the title of Vatapi-Konda, Conqueror of Vatapi, which would pass into his dynasty's legends, just as 'Defeater of Harsha' had passed into the legends of the Chalukyas.

Through the rest of his reign, Narasimha would never let the Chalukyas forget their humiliation at his hands. He chose to do this in a way that shows us that the Pallavas too were masters of using myth to support propaganda. In both the Ramayana and Mahabharata, the sage Agastya is tricked into eating a demon called Vatapi, who would magically transform himself into a meaty curry to entice weary travellers to eat him, after which he would turn himself back into his demon form, blowing them apart from inside. Agastya, however, immediately digested Vatapi and expelled the remains as gas. This amusing story was recognizable to well-educated courtly audiences, and Narasimha made the most of it. He boasted that he was the 'equal of Agastya, the crusher of Vatapi, who frequently conquered Vallabha-Raja (Pulakeshin II)'.[6]

With the central hub of the Chalukya political network annihilated, and without the wealth and income of the city of Vatapi to sustain them, the court's factions, vassals and families now splintered and went their own ways. Pulakeshin II had married women from many of the Deccan's most prominent dynasties to bind them to him, but that now meant that a host of his sons saw themselves as rightful successors to their father's throne.[7] Though the inscriptional record is unclear, it appears that a number of them wielded varying degrees of influence in different parts of the Deccan, their home bases probably selected with reference to the bastions of their mothers' families. Further complicating the picture were the machinations of the other lords of the Deccan, who had little interest in bowing once again to a powerful Chalukya ruler. Pulakeshin II's empire building, it would seem, was for naught: all the propaganda in the world could not engender lasting loyalty.

Indeed, former Chalukya vassals were wasting no time in proclaiming their independence, with varying degrees of confidence. The viceroy of southern Gujarat adopted the title of 'raja' but did not claim to be a sovereign ruler until he could be sure no victorious Chalukya would punish him for his insolence. So too did the Sendrakas, Pulakeshin's mother's family, who seem to have thought they might as well take their chances with temporary independence.[8] It would appear to have been quite a sensible move: the eldest of Pulakeshin's sons set up base near Kurnool, Andhra Pradesh, and declared himself the Chalukya emperor, Sri-Prithivi-Vallabha, only to die within a year,[9] either assassinated or killed on the battlefield. His son and successor was no luckier.[10] Neither was a younger son of Pulakeshin's, whom we know only through the inscriptions of his wife, the first of a series of formidable Deccan queens that we will meet: a lady known as Vijaya-Mahadevi, who stepped in as regent for their infant son. Vijaya-Mahadevi may have originally been a courtesan, and she was not shy about it. The name 'Boddivoddi', with the 'standard suffix' (*voddi/poti*) for a courtesan, appears in a land grant that the queen issued, and it has been argued that the construction of her sentences suggests that Vijaya-Mahadevi and Boddivoddi are one and the same.[11]

Chalukya queens – as Mangalesha's mother, who encouraged him to attack her birth family, the Kalachuris, shows – did play a role in determining their clan's policies. But Vijaya-Mahadevi's position as queen is especially remarkable. Even aside from her origins as a courtesan, this queen, as a regent for her son, issued land grants, hinting at something unique at play: a woman rising to an unprecedented degree of prominence and control in seventh-century Deccan. Earlier generations of queens were generally only allowed to make grants and donations with the approval of, and in the name of, their sons or husbands, and would appear in public only on ceremonial occasions, usually in a subservient role to the men of the family. But Vijaya-Mahadevi issued land grants in her own name. This implies she was appearing before crowds, attended by some of the insignia of kingship, indulging in behaviours that were usually within the domain of royal men alone. She was claiming the divine right to redistribute land that had hitherto been the exclusive preserve of the Chalukya kings.

In contrast, Vijaya-Mahadevi's rivals and predecessors among Chalukya royal women had been confined to the court, though it should be noted that they had considerable agency within the court itself.[12] Royal women were in many ways as educated and qualified

Arvind Venkatraman / Wikimedia Commons

A fragment of a mural from Pallava cave temples at Panamalai, dated to the eighth century CE. It depicts a female figure, perhaps a queen. She originally stood under a green parasol dotted with white; only its staff and golden fringe is visible behind her here. Painted with considerable detail with the confidence and dexterity of a master, the figure's jewellery hints at the refined material culture that early medieval queens participated in.

as their male counterparts, learning everything from politics to poetry, warfare to administration. Though often treated as tokens of exchange to seal political relationships,[13] it would be unjust to these remarkable women to see them as only devoted mothers and wives. As the men of the clan spilled blood on battlefields, they too fought for favour and prestige and glory in the corridors and courtyards of the *antahpuram*, the Inner City,[14] the women's quarters of the palace. Princesses in medieval India brought with them their own dowries and personal retinues, were often well connected both within and outside the court, and could receive stipends from the state treasury.[15]

Within their Inner City were hierarchies, ranks and etiquette.[16] Seniority and rank among queens were determined by politics 'directly continuous' with those of the main assembly halls[17] where the ruler received the submissions of his vassals: their ranks were generally dependent on those of their husbands, but the politics of the women in the Inner City could also determine royal favours, appointments and titles, and thus indirectly influence the outside world. A princess who successfully rose through the ranks of the Inner City could, and very often did, serve as her birth family's primary lobbyist at court. Women's interests were intimately tied to those of their marital families as well, and in the event of a military disaster or unfavourable succession, their bodies and freedom were even more at risk of capture and assault than those of chiefs fleeing on war elephants. Only a truly foolhardy king would dare ignore what the royal women thought of his political or strategic decisions. Sanskrit literature is replete with instances of these ladies conspiring to brutally murder, mutilate or exile male members of the family.

The circumstances under which Vijaya-Mahadevi came to meet a Chalukya prince, married him and was declared chief queen are unknown, but it would certainly seem that she was a person of great ambition, ability and charm.[18] As a courtesan, in stark contrast to royal ladies who usually appeared in public spaces only during ceremonial events, she would have often been seen in theatres and music and poetry recitals, traditionally the domain of men.

Whatever the circumstances under which her career began, Vijaya-Mahadevi took to her role as chief queen with aplomb over the course of the 640s. As the widow of a king, she had to manage and manipulate both the men of the court and the women of the Inner City, in addition to adhering to the ritual and social expectations that came with royal power. As a former courtesan appearing in public as a queen, she was transgressing orthodox expectations of women in public spaces. Her success in doing so indicates that seventh-century Deccan societies had attitudes different from those espoused by Sanskrit literature, and were less hostile to powerful women than contemporary north Indian courts were.

One member of Vijaya-Mahadevi's new circle was her brother-in-law Vikramaditya,[19] 'Sun of Power'. He was Pulakeshin II's son by a Ganga princess, and he had been waiting in the wings for a long time. It is unclear what he was up to in the immediate aftermath of his father's death, but later in the 640s he appears to have not been important enough to seize the throne by himself, and thus supported Vijaya-Mahadevi and her son, the emperor. But by the 650s, the death of his elder brothers meant he was the most prominent adult male Chalukya still standing. And unlike Vijaya-Mahadevi, he had a powerful dynastic backer: his mother's family, the Gangas of southern Karnataka. The Gangas now found themselves in the happy position where the next Chalukya emperor might be half-Ganga. Vikramaditya also married a Ganga princess,[20] further cementing the alliance. (Dravidian kinship allows for marriage between cousins.) With the support[21] of the Gangas and the friendship of Vijaya-Mahadevi, the regent for the infant Vallabha, Vikramaditya set out to restore the Chalukya political network, and began the bloody process of once again subjugating recalcitrant chiefs to re-establish Chalukya supremacy – ostensibly in the name of the infant emperor.

What Vijaya-Mahadevi thought of her brother-in-law's growing power is unknown. Perhaps she had plans and contingencies to make sure he did not threaten her son's (and thus her) hold on the throne. Meanwhile, Vikramaditya's new wife, the highborn Ganga-Mahadevi, must have had no intention of playing second fiddle to a former courtesan in the Chalukya Inner City. For now, though, their interests were in ostensible alignment. The Chalukya territories were slowly reclaimed and Vatapi recaptured. The inscription that Narasimha Pallava left on a boulder outside, boasting of his humiliation of the Chalukyas, was erased almost a decade after it had been made.

And so this round of wars between the Deccan and Tamilakam came to an exhausting end. But there would be many more to come. The geopolitics of south India practically mandated a rivalry between the Deccan and Tamilakam – with Vengi in modern-day coastal Andhra often the prize at stake, for its capture could give the Deccan access to the eastern seaports and the Tamil land a near monopoly over eastern trade.[22]

Vikramaditya Chalukya, his reputation made, with his family's former vassals once again swearing their loyalty, now sought revenge against his father's murderer, Narasimha Pallava. But he had to first bloody his hands with the lives of his kin.[23] For when the middle-aged prince triumphantly declared himself Vikramaditya I, Sri-Prithivi-Vallabha, to a circle of vassals in 655 CE, no mention was made of Vijaya-Mahadevi and her infant son. They are never heard of again – but it will not be the last time we hear from a powerful Chalukya queen.

⁓

As the shattered Chalukyas regrouped, Vikramaditya I's court decided that two major changes were in order, setting in motion the last steps in the Chalukyas' transition from local chiefs to kings in the classical Indian mould.

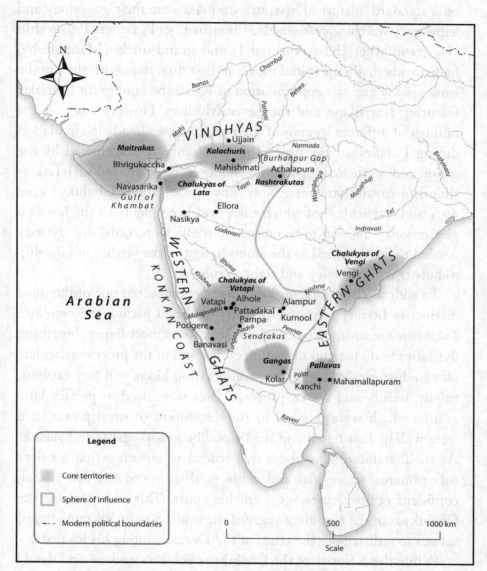

Southern India, mid-seventh to mid-eighth century CE.

First, Chalukya power and political discourse needed to be set on a standard 'historical' narrative to make sure their genealogy and legitimacy were unquestionable. Vikramaditya I's father (Pulakeshin II), grandfather (Kirti-Varman I) and grand-uncle (Mangalesha) had already made the initial moves in that direction, with the Varaha iconography and the appropriation of Kadamba land grant formulae featuring Karttikeya and the Seven Mothers. However, as noted, a number of different legends of their origin were already in circulation during Pulakeshin II's time. This problem was exacerbated by the gossip and myth-making that inevitably accreted around such larger-than-life royal characters. Now, any stories about Chalukya civil wars and fratricide – of which there had been plenty in the last two generations – needed to be erased from official records. The dynasty needed to be presented as the embodiment of the virtues of kingship to bolster its legitimacy and right to rule.

To address this problem, Vikramaditya embraced one of the most distinctive literary forms of the early medieval period: the *prashasti*. *Prashastis* are royal eulogies which seek to connect living, breathing dynasties to divine and heroic ancestors, and in the process articulate official 'histories' of royal lives, enumerating kings' military exploits, valour, beauty and sexual prowess. They were used to preface land grants, which were integral to the devolution of royal power, and were widely distributed and read aloud by kings' agents and vassals. As such, standardizing them was crucial to ensuring that a ruler's subordinates, successors and subjects all received the same loud, confident political message from his court. This was vital for the Chalukyas in the turbulent years of the mid-650s, as Vikramaditya I set out to redistribute the lands of the Deccan among his loyalists.

While the majority of the Chalukyas' subjects spoke – and would continue to speak – a wide variety of regional dialects of Old Kannada, Vikramaditya's *prashastis* and land grants were in Sanskrit.[24] Part of this was due to Sanskrit's association with legend and divinity, which it had possessed since the days of the Vedas. But in the early centuries CE, politicians and poets had also begun to experiment with its copious grammars and lexicons, inaugurating a flourishing literary culture. By the seventh century, new myths, epics, religious stories, dramas and poems bloomed across the subcontinent, and Sanskrit had become established as the premier language of intellectualism, literature and power, creating a universalizing, cosmopolitan world for the upper classes. This cosmopolitan use of Sanskrit had been introduced to the Malaprabha valley by the early Chalukya kings, and we have seen how they used Sanskrit titles and terms, as well as myths and religious ideas expressed in Sanskrit, to justify their rule.

It was to this pan-subcontinental 'Sanskrit Cosmopolis', as Sheldon Pollock calls it, that Vikramaditya's *prashastis* were primarily addressed, not to his subjects. Narasimha Pallava, through his Vatapi analogy, had humiliated the Chalukyas before this elite audience; Vikramaditya now sought to restore his reputation before them. Through their new *prashastis*, the Chalukyas declared they were warlike and virtuous heroes in search of fame and glory like their ancestors had supposedly been from time immemorial;[25] they thus granted themselves the hallowed sanction of dharma, myth and history – which, in medieval India, were often inseparable. Chalukya *prashastis* were declaimed or sung in the appropriate heroic metres; the land grants they prefaced were accepted with folded hands and touched to the forehead of the grantee. The audience – officials, courtly layabouts, queens, princes, priests, and administrators across the Deccan – would henceforth all hear the same standard history, be reminded of the same ideas, and all increasingly think of the Chalukyas as a permanent Deccan institution.

For more than half a millennium, those who claimed the Chalukya name would all begin their *prashastis* with the same splendid formula. This now-forgotten sound was declaimed for centuries from the top to the bottom of the Deccan, etched into the minds of generations of its poets and panegyrists and priests and officials and kings. It must have been one of medieval India's most recognizable jingles:

jayatyāviṣkṛtaṁ viṣṇorvarāhaṁ kṣobhitārṇavaṁ
dakṣiṇonnatadaṁṣṭrāgraviśrāntabhuvanaṁ vapuḥ

Victory to the Boar Incarnation of Vishnu, shaking the ocean as it comes into view
With the Earth resting at peace on the tip of its upraised right tusk[26]

This image vividly embodies not only the Chalukya identification with Varaha, but also the idea of Indian kingship as fundamentally leading to the salvation of the king's subjects.[27] Despite their brutal wars and perfumed courts distanced the toiling masses, the Chalukya kings wanted to be thought of as saviours. The Earth was 'resting at peace' because of their successful performance of royal dharma, commencing with their imaginary ancestors from the very beginning of time; there is no longer any hint of their humble origins. The *prashasti* continues, detailing a rewritten Chalukya genealogy in extravagant Sanskrit. The new official account mentions Pulakeshin I, performer of Vedic sacrifices, learned in dharmic texts; praises his elder son, the father of Pulakeshin II and the conqueror of the Kadambas; sings the praises of Pulakeshin II, defeater of Harsha; and then describes Vikramaditya himself, Sri-Prithivi-Vallabha, the son of Ganga and Chalukya. Of all the ideas the Chalukyas had played around with in their previous propaganda, and of all their acrimonious family history, this was all that made the final cut. No mention is made of Mangalesha, Vijaya-Mahadevi or Vikramaditya I's elder brothers.

Prashastis were written in an ornate and impressive language, showcasing how deeply the Chalukyas were now involved in the subcontinent-spanning world of Sanskrit. But a *prashasti* also erased much of the complicated lives and motivations of the people it mentioned. Unfortunately, *prashastis* make up the vast majority of texts that survive from medieval India, giving us a lopsided view of a possibly far more complex and interesting past.

Five years after his coronation, on 30 April 660 CE,[28] Vikramaditya I made the second of his two great changes to Chalukya kingship, reorienting the family's religious support base towards Shaivism, better reflecting the reality of Deccan power equations. The influence of Shiva-worshipping teachers and institutions had been spreading across the northern Deccan over the last centuries, shifting large sections of the population away from their ancestor- and nature-worshipping ways. In 660, Vikramaditya underwent a formal Shaiva religious ceremony at Marruru, near Alampur, a flourishing pilgrimage centre at the holy spot of the confluence of the Krishna and Tungabhadra rivers[29] – the very spot where his father Pulakeshin II had paused in the early 620s to divide the spoils of Vengi among his followers. The guru who performed this *shiva-mandala-diksha* (Initiation into Shiva's Circle) was granted the revenue of an entire village for his services. Hinting at how systematically Shaivas worked to expand their footprint, this priest then distributed plots of land in the village to other Shaiva priests.[30]

Thanks to activities like these, the age of Shiva had well and truly begun in the Deccan by the late seventh century. Once again, we see how the activities of royals were often only responses to much grander forces, and how courts constituted only one among many powerful organizations that shaped India's history. Dozens of cults dedicated to Shiva flourished across the Deccan plateau. But whereas Tamil Shaivism was assisted by the spread of the bhakti movement, in the Deccan, this transformation was due to the efforts of organized sects such as the Pashupatas – one of whom had appeared in Mahendra Pallava's *Farce of the Drunkard's Games* – and the Kalamukhas or 'Black Faces', who smeared their foreheads with a black streak.[31] These oddball ascetics delighted in breaking taboos and flouting the orthodox views of the *Dharmashastra*. Pashupatas, for example, engaged in 'various forms of antisocial behaviour' including going about 'making lewd gestures to young women', especially those of good families, which would earn them abuses and beatings.[32] This act would magically transfer their sins to the abusers, and transfer to them whatever religious merit the abusers happened to have accrued through more traditional means – such as following their dharma,[33] going on pilgrimages, making charitable donations and so on. Pashupatas also made a habit of hanging around cremation grounds and smearing their bodies with ash – which signified the 'death of the body and of sexual desires'.[34] They were often major presences in some towns, living off petty charity and monastic institutions attached to temples and paid for by royal endowments.

The Pashupatas had spread over centuries from western India into the Gangetic plains and the northern Deccan, establishing massive monasteries overseen by charismatic teachers preaching their doctrine, supposedly first recited by a corpse reanimated by Shiva. So active and energetic were they in spreading the word of Shiva that there were Pashupata preachers in Cambodia in the sixth century CE,[35] travelling alongside merchants and Buddhist monks to East Asia and challenging the modern notion that 'Indian' religions were not interested in proselytizing. Medieval monks, like kings, were not averse to wealth, fame and power.

But Pashupatas were only one of many flourishing, squabbling Shaiva cults that spread into the Deccan in the early centuries of the first millennium. The Kadambas, those early nemeses of the Chalukyas, had donated extensively to monasteries, temples and ascetic groups that worshipped Shiva in myriad forms and ways.[36] These organized Shaiva sects had a very different approach to their god compared to the bhakti saints: they were far more comfortable with royal patronage for one, and were big believers in scripture[37] and ritual. They also used the revenues granted to them to set up feeding houses,[38] conduct religious processions and intercede with the gods on behalf of the laity for humdrum matters such as harvests and births. Such intercessions may have been considered abhorrent by the bhakti saints, but were apparently popular with worshippers. As their influence grew, the most prominent Shaiva monastic gurus would command the attention of elites and lay worshippers across the borders of kingdoms, and control resources that would put most petty kings to shame.[39] Some were even posthumously worshipped in the form of a Shiva linga.[40] The institutions that these gurus led would eventually rise to dominate south India's daily lived practice of Shaivism.

Early Chalukya kings, reflecting the societies they ruled over, had incorporated many subtle Shaiva influences. This is why they had claimed in their inscriptions to be supported by Shiva's son, the war god Skanda/Karttikeya, while simultaneously portraying themselves as incarnations of Vishnu. In 660, Vikramaditya I decided that a direct royal association with Shaiva institutions offered a better means of strengthening Chalukya authority in a time of crisis, never mind that the Pallavas were also Shaivas. Restoring the Chalukya political network meant that accommodations had to be reached with powerful players – and who were more powerful than the Shaiva sects?

Soon after his initiation at Marruru, Vikramaditya likely underwent a second royal consecration, perhaps in a field in Vatapi. This time, the ceremony probably took place under the auspices of a Pashupata guru or representative of some other Shaiva group, rather than the Vedic Brahmin chaplains who oversaw the royal consecration of his great-grandfather Pulakeshin I – another sign of how much the Deccan had been transformed. Pashupata rituals were also different from the bloody Ashvamedha that had consecrated Pulakeshin I. One version of their consecration ritual required that the king and his consort be seated on 'a platform covered with the skins of a fighting bull and a cat',[41] after which they had to 'offer worship to Shiva, the Fire, the [royal] weapons, the [royal] banner'.[42] Next, they were to consume the 'five products of the cow'[43] – a fermented mixture of milk, ghee, curds and a little dung and urine – along with 'rice porridge [prepared on the sacred fire]'[44] and clean their teeth with a twig. Rather than seeking to reorder the universe through the sacrifice, as Vedic religion claimed to do, the Pashupata ritual was based on tantric ideas that magical formulae and ritual actions infused the practitioner directly with power, an idea that kings must have found quite gratifying. It reflects the growing influence of tantrism in Indian religions.

The next day, after the recitation of sixteen sacred mantras, consecrated water was poured on Vikramaditya's head – this was the *rajyabhisheka* ritual that would continue to be practised by Indian royals for centuries after. Water may also have been sprinkled on the front rows of his elite troops, waiting in the light of the early morning, topknots oiled, swords sharpened, shields of wood and bamboo freshly painted with boars and lions and elephants and flowers.[45] Preceded by the resplendent Chalukya boar banner, now 'blessed' by Shiva, the king may have led a 'full military parade',[46] undoubtedly mounted on his beloved piebald horse Chitrakantha, imported at great expense through a port on the west coast that the Chalukyas controlled once again. Vikramaditya must have wound through the streets of the city where he had grown up in the shadow of his dead brothers and father, accompanied by the sounds of drums and the triumphant roars of his subjects as they showered him with parched rice from the roofs of their mansions. Artisans and poets were returning to Vatapi, vassal lords came once again to pay obeisance to Fortune's Favourite. But Vikramaditya would not forget why they had stopped their tribute in the first place.

From his citadel atop the sandstone cliffs, the Vallabha looked south, to the Tamil country.

෧

Narasimha Pallava's lion throne at Mamallapuram, as attributed by the art historian Michael Rabe. The king may have sat here as he directed his architectural projects at the city.

Narasimha Pallava had not been idle the last few decades. He was, like his father, a man of great aesthetic sense, and the treasure he had seized from Vatapi was poured into an ambitious construction project: a new Pallava royal city. Though its construction may have been begun by his father Mahendra, it would be most enduringly associated with Narasimha, and is remembered by one of his titles: Maha-Malla-Puram, 'City of the Great Wrestler' (modern-day Mamallapuram). It was built on the shore to connect the Pallava court directly to the profits of the Indian Ocean trade, and it would be decorated by dozens of unique monolithic shrines carved from entire boulders, many of which still survive today. This was a natural step upwards from carving temples out of caves, and may have been intended to outdo Pulakeshin II's freestanding temples at Vatapi, assembled from blocks of cut stone. This 'architectural arms race' is an indication of political struggle: temples were (and are) not built purely from outpourings of devotion.

What a city Mahamallapuram was. Narasimha's treasury there, cut into the bedrock and sectioned off with bricks for different categories of valuables, is still visible today. So is a proud monolithic lion-shaped throne gazing balefully to the north, where his Chalukya rivals lived. On it, Narasimha Pallava lolled about, a silk cap covering his oiled hair gathered in a knot,[47] taking in the 'cooling off-shore breezes from the East ... or a commanding view of irrigated paddy and orchards, stretching off ... beyond to [his capital] Kancipuram'.[48]

In Mahamallapuram, Narasimha Pallava also embarked on a remarkable creative experiment, which shows us once again the close interaction of art, politics and myth in the framework of medieval Indian power. This experiment was the massive narrative sculpture known as the Great Penance (or The Descent of the Ganga), carved from a single block of sandstone and profusely bedecked with animals, gods, sages, serpents and sophisticated visual double entendres that put even the Chalukya kings, with their sculptural and poetic allusions to Vishnu, to shame. Indeed, putting the Chalukyas to shame was probably one of Narasimha's motivations in commissioning this masterpiece, though his primary goal was, of course, his own glorification and, by extension, the glorification of the Pallavas. For a project on this scale, there was, luckily, a medieval Tamil Michelangelo at hand: the great artisan Mandhatar, 'who surpassed the Greeks in his artistry'.[49]

At the centre of this great sculpture, an emaciated sage, every muscle and bone standing out, balances on one foot with his sunken eyes fixed on the heavens. Next to him, the merciful god Shiva extends his hands in blessing, attended by portly laughing dwarves. Half-bird, half-human beings called *kinnaras* sound a great din with horns, drums and cymbals. Animals join the host: deer, lions, geese, monkeys, cats, mice, elephants. Each of them is carved with

The 'Great Penance' or 'Descent of the Ganga' sculpture at Mamallapuram. Possibly a visual allegory of Narasimha Pallava's lineage and relationship with the gods.

remarkable realism and attention to detail, and almost all of them gaze with great wonder at the centre of the sculpture. All around them, a great host of gods mobilizes to attend this event, the ones further away looking intently and benevolently at the audience, gesturing towards the sage.

There is an immense cleft at the centre of the rock, which once flowed with crystal-clear water through which shimmered the carved nagas – water serpents, fertility divinities with the upper half of a human and the lower half of a great snake, believed to live in rivers. And next to this vertical river is that starving sage, whom the audience will know is Bhagiratha, the sage who prayed to Shiva that the Heavenly Ganga be allowed to descend upon his densely matted hair and thus come to Earth.[50] Of course, as the bhakti saints and the Shaiva sects promised, the merciful Shiva had appeared to him and granted his boon, and as proof, the holy Ganga still flowed through the lands of the plains over 2,000 kilometres to the north.

But to a sophisticated audience trained in art, mythology and literature, many other interpretations of the sculpture were evident. The starving ascetic, for example, could be not only Bhagiratha, but also Arjuna, a great hero of the Mahabharata. The ascetic is receiving from Lord Shiva the mighty weapon known as Pashupata, symbolized by a dwarf with a demonic face painted on his belly. Arjuna was famed as a great wrestler, but so was King Narasimha-Varman, the Maha-Malla. The sculpture can thus also be read as a eulogy to the Pallava king, a declaration that he, like this great hero, had earned Shiva's special favour.

Moving away from the centre, the huge composition is full of delightful nuggets for interpretation. Near the bottom of the panel, where the waterfall once spread into a pool, stand two figures, grinning at the water; one of them holds a pot, a *kumbha*. Now it just so happens that the sage Agastya – who destroyed Vatapi – was born from a pot.

(The story of Agastya's birth: The gods were performing a great sacrifice. Among the chief officiants were Mitra and Varuna. The gorgeous apsara – divine nymph – called Urvasi joined the crowd. So alluring was her walk, so tempting her smoky eyes and luscious curves, that these two gods were not only aroused but actually ejaculated on the spot. Their semen poured into a pot, from which was born Agastya, henceforth known as *kumbha-yoni*, water pot womb.[51])

Who else had destroyed a Vatapi as Agastya had? Narasimha, king of the Pallavas.

And at the bottom of the sculpture, three sages were carved, allusions to King Narasimha, his father King Mahendra, and his grandfather King Simhavishnu,[52] but also to Asvatthama, an ancestor of the Pallavas according to their own imaginary *prashasti* genealogies, his teacher-father Drona (one of the commanders of the Kaurava army in the Mahabharata), and *his* teacher Agastya the Pitcher-Born.[53] These sages, representing three generations of Pallava kings of great importance to the dynasty's self-image, are without heads today. The reason for this will soon become apparent.

Such an elaborate programme of connection between a living dynasty and the myths of heroes and sages had hitherto only appeared in Sanskrit *prashastis*. The Great Penance, brought to life at Mahamallapuram by Narasimha Pallava and the master artist Mandhatar, is thus a sophisticated *prashasti* in stone. In the race to gain prestige by patronizing the greatest artists and to express political ideas through religion and art, the Pallavas had outdone the Chalukyas – and they had built this after defeating and looting *their* capital. It was a marvellous embodiment of the dynasty's humiliation and the glory of the Pallavas.

Vikramaditya Chalukya must have heard of this, sooner or later. Traders constantly moved between India's east and west coasts as well as overland, as did poets, artists and intellectuals. He learned of the monolithic sandstone boar that Narasimha Pallava had had carved and immersed in a temple pond, symbolizing his devotion to Varaha, and also his capture of the Chalukya boar standard.[54] Perhaps architects and sculptors spoke with admiration of the wave of new temples that Narasimha was having made – freestanding monoliths carved out of great boulders, almost as if he was thumbing his nose at Pulakeshin II's temples, assembled from many smaller pieces of sandstone at Vatapi. Carved with marvellous reliefs with dozens of characters – representing the manifestations of the Great Goddess, Vishnu, Shiva or the wily Mahendra Pallava – their domes adorned with beautifully spaced and carved miniature temples, they were like nothing south India had yet seen.

Artistic masterpiece or not, Vikramaditya decided it was time for the Chalukyas to have their revenge on Mahamallapuram.

～

Vikramaditya I had come to the throne in his middle age, and he would bring no less than three generations of royal Chalukyas to the project of crushing the Pallava enemy.

During the tragic regency of Vijaya-Mahadevi, this Chalukya had already built up a reputation as a king killer. Her inscriptions refer to Vikramaditya, her heroic brother-in-law, destroying kings in many battles, achieving victories in all directions, and restoring the 'glory and fortune' of his ancestors.[55] Even if this is exaggeration, meant for Vijaya-Mahadevi to gain some support by flattering her increasingly powerful and ambitious relative, Vikramaditya certainly seems to have had a long, brutal military career; in his *prashastis* he refers to himself as possessing armour into which 'many blows had been plunged'.[56] In his first wars against rebellious chiefs in erstwhile Chalukya territory, he built up the experience he would need to take on Narasimha Pallava.

This endeavour was marked by the same patience that characterized his early years. Vikramaditya was nothing if not dogged and willing to pay the price for the pursuit of his ambitions. He had waited nearly a decade for his brothers to finish each other off before making his bid for power, allying with Vijaya-Mahadevi and disposing of her and her son when he no longer needed them. He now waited for more than a decade after his coronation, working out the political and religious bases of his power, before challenging the Pallavas again. In addition to his experiments with *prashastis* and supporting the Shaivas, he, like his father Pulakeshin II, spent time consolidating Chalukya interactions with the rich revenue streams of the western coast, also importing Arab horses at great expense to maintain elite cavalry squadrons.[57] In Lata in southern Gujarat, Vikramaditya, again like his father, allowed a trusted younger brother to set up a cadet branch[58] (though these Chalukyas of Lata would eventually turn out to be only marginally more loyal than the Chalukyas of Vengi,[59] who had so memorably declared themselves independent just when Pulakeshin II desperately needed their assistance against the Pallavas in 641/2). In the meantime, the Pallava king Narasimha, his new city built but his success perhaps soured by a restored Chalukya kingdom always just beyond his reach, died. His successor Mahendra-Varman II attempted to attack the Gangas of southern Karnataka as a prelude to attacking the Chalukyas, but was defeated and killed.[60]

Portion of the Great Penance sculpture at Mamallapuram, showing the three beheaded royal sages. These are the only images that have been damaged in the entire work, suggesting that they were deliberately targeted.

In 674, Vikramaditya finally decided his time had come[61] and led a marauding Deccan army once more into Tamilakam. Over the next few years, he set out to brutally avenge Narasimha's conquest of Vatapi, claiming for himself the title of *Ranarasika*, 'Lustful for Battle', and *Rajamalla*, 'Wrestler of Kings, because he has destroyed the family of the *Mahamalla* [Narasimha Pallava]'.[62] In this campaign, the king was also likely attended by Shaiva priests, who offered religious services including pre-battle consecrations to ensure victory.[63]

After a gap of nearly half a century, the Chalukya boar banner once again arrived at Kanchi, forcing the young Pallava king – Narasimha's grandson – to flee, abandoning his people to Vikramaditya's mercy. Not that the Chalukya ruler was in a particularly forgiving mood. His inscriptions explain that Kanchi's 'unfathomable' moat was filled in, its 'insurmountable' rampart scaled by his troops, and the city brutally sacked. He refers to the event in language that is shockingly different in tenor to the almost comedic way in which the Pallavas treated their seizure of Vatapi. For Vikramaditya, drawing on the Chalukya tradition of referring to kings as 'lovers' of the Earth, describes with almost macabre glee how he had '*forcibly* wooed the lady of the Southern Quarter and taken possession of Kanchi, the city which was her girdle'.[64] Success in war was a sign of virility and masculinity for medieval Indian kings.

Next in his sights was Mahamallapuram, that ode to Pallava power and a lasting homage to their humiliation of the Chalukyas. Once the city had been looted and its population either cowed or scattered, we can imagine the Chalukya king riding calmly down its wide avenues, mounted on Chitrakantha, his famous piebald steed. He was probably surrounded by a detachment of elite bodyguards on similarly splendid

The Varaha sculpture in a tank at Mamallapuram. Uniquely, it is not accompanied by the Earth goddess and would have been mostly submerged. Art historian Michael Rabe has suggested that the Chalukyas attempted to shatter it.

imported horses. If Chalukya sculptures are any indication, the king himself wore a lower garment of fine silk, and was bare-chested and bedecked in only a few necklaces to take in the warm sea breeze.

How did Vikramaditya react as he took in the sight of all the temples built with stolen Chalukya gold? All we know for certain is that he visited Narasimha Pallava's temple complex, where he was shown the particular images which referred to the Pallava kings Narasimha, Mahendra and Simhavishnu. Perhaps a grin of ghoulish satisfaction crossed his face as he ordered the images beheaded.[65]

Strange as it may seem to us today, the effacement of Pallava art does indeed seem to have been one of the objectives of the Chalukyas in their campaign in Tamilakam in the 670s. It shows us that for medieval Indian rulers, art was a profound religious and political statement, worth investing in architects, sculptors and stonemasons to create, but also worth the expense and risk of gathering warriors, fighting battles and seizing cities to destroy. Today, the monolithic temples at Mamallapuram still bear the scars of Vikramaditya I's raid – by one count, 264 finials were chiselled off.[66] The Varaha that Narasimha had immersed in a tank to commemorate his capture of the Chalukya boar standard was shattered by the blows of heavy hammers.[67] The Chalukya king may have planned to engage in similar iconoclasm on the rest of the Great Penance relief and other portraits of Pallava kings in the Mahamallapuram temple complex. Luckily for posterity, he seems to have been called away before he was able to do so.

Far from being cowed by this onslaught, not only was the young Pallava king gathering an army to repulse the Chalukyas, but his allies – the other kings of Tamilakam – were rallying in support. Vikramaditya would not make the mistake his father Pulakeshin II had made in ignoring the other Tamil kingdoms, and embarked hurriedly on an expedition against them.[68]

As Vikramaditya rampaged through Tamilakam, the Chalukya political network in the Deccan was back to full bloom, aided by the new prominence of the Gangas. At home, his son Vinayaditya and grandson Vijayaditya consolidated the Chalukya royal line through marriage ties and war, 'rooting out all thorns from the body politic'.[69] Vikramaditya's brother-in-law and cousin, the Ganga king, also chalked up a series of successes against the Pallavas.[70]

Eventually, old age, the vast and indomitable Tamil country, and the sandstone heads of dead Pallava kings convinced Vikramaditya he had satisfied the call of 'honour', and he retired back to Vatapi. His decision was probably spurred by a sudden reversal in Peruvalallanur, where his army of 'several lakhs'[71] was supposedly put to flight by a smaller Pallava force.[72] It seems more likely, given the way the rest of the campaign unfolded, that the Pallavas managed to inflict some casualties on the Chalukya rearguard as it withdrew from their lands. Whatever the truth of the matter, it was now clear to all of south India that the Chalukyas were back, that they were not to be crossed, and that they were not going to lose their hard-won supremacy any time soon.

4

Great Goddess

Winter, 682 CE

By the time Vikramaditya I, that bloodthirsty restorer of the family fortunes, died in 682 CE,[1] the Chalukyas had come a long, long way from their humble beginnings as local chiefs living in terror of the Kadambas and Kalachuris. Now, the once mighty Kadamba capital province was merely one component of a vast pan-Deccan political network dominated by their rivals, the Chalukyas. This Chalukya 'circle' of kings and sub-kings stretched from the seashores of southern Gujarat across the dry plateaus of Maharashtra, the thick thorny forests of the Deccan plateau, and the rushing rivers of Karnataka all the way to the very borders of the Tamil country. Slowly growing towns and cities interacted with each other in gradually denser networks. And the largest hub of that network, the sun of this solar system, was the court of the new Chalukya Vallabha, Vinayaditya, moving around the Deccan as Harsha had once moved around northern India – at the heart of an immense military encampment that served as a mobile capital, always ready to deal with the slightest hint of insubordination. The Deccan was beginning to grow into the status of a true superpower comparable to the ancient north Indian empires.

The Chalukyas were certainly the dominant power of the Deccan, but the land was simply too expansive, turbulent and multi-centric, requiring the constant mobilization of economic, political and religious resources to control. Contrary to our notions of vast and powerful centralized empires that paint swathes of modern maps, in reality, a map of medieval India was more like a patchwork of petty chiefdoms separated by wide stretches of sparsely inhabited wilderness, with a few major dynasties exerting various degrees of control over geopolitically important areas. In particular, the Chalukya vassal chiefs of the Deccan were well capable of going their own way or just ignoring Chalukya commands in practice while paying them lip service in public. By the time Vikramaditya's aged son Vinayaditya was finally crowned as Fortune's Favourite, wars and rebellions were already erupting to his east and north.[2] Other means had to be found to widen and deepen Chalukya connections to elites beyond the landed aristocrats with their private armies. The solution lay in expanding royal influence through the most iconic sites of the medieval period, which to this day are so integral to India's self-image: places of pilgrimage.

To ensure that the peoples of the Deccan continued to acknowledge his family's supremacy, the roving Chalukya Vallabha visited sacred river fords[3] or *tirthas*. At these sacred sites where one bank neared the other, the world of the gods neared the world of mortals, and devotees could cleanse themselves of their sins. Once there, the Vallabha – often at the urging of a lady of the *antahpuram*, an indication once again of the intertangled politics of the court – would donate lands to a Brahmin or religious institution, who would then be expected to serve Chalukya interests. *Tirthas* always attracted large crowds, especially during seasonal festivals, when local cultivators and pastoralists might gather to participate in community ceremonies, watch religious orders parade their regalia, dance, listen to chanting monks, and bathe in the sacred waters. As their religious, political and economic weight increased due to royal endowments such as Vinayaditya's, many of these pilgrimage centres gradually took on a life of their own. In 689/90, the Vallabha issued a copperplate inscription 'from his victorious camp at Pampa *tirtha* on the Tungabhadra river'.[4] This seventh-century sacred site of the fierce goddess Pampa would grow into Hampi/Vijayanagara by the sixteenth century, one of the largest cities on Earth and the seat of a gunpowder-wielding Deccan empire whose aristocrats used a modified version of the Chalukya boar crest. We will soon visit another such *tirtha*, Ellora, in the eighth century.

From the Chalukya perspective, in the seventh century, their temples in the sacred sites of the Malaprabha river valley reminded their direct subjects of Chalukya power and devotion to popular gods. Similarly, having a Chalukya loyalist at the Pampa *tirtha* to remind the crowds of their distant obligation to the Chalukya monarch, irrespective of the actual degree of Chalukya control over the *tirtha*, simply made good political sense. This simple politico-religious calculation, made repeatedly over the centuries by the Chalukyas and their vassals and rivals, helped create the web of pilgrimage sites and sacred cities that are so integral to modern Hinduism, particularly in the Deccan.

Towards the end of the seventh century, with the Pallavas to the south beaten into a simmering peace, and with territories in modern Karnataka returning to their fold, the Chalukyas needed to once again secure their grip on Maharashtra and the northern Deccan. Unfortunately, recruits for their endless wars were increasingly hard to come by. Their subjects in the Malaprabha heartland were introduced to a new tax on childless couples[5] (which, the scholar Carol Bolon argues may have led to a surge in the popularity of fertility cults dedicated to the lotus-headed Lajja Gauri, who still remains popular in the area). But there were still no recruits to be had, which led to the Chalukya ruler mobilizing military power by arranging one of the most significant marital alliances of the early medieval period – which will introduce us to an extraordinary Deccan queen.

Since Mangalesha Chalukya's raids in the late sixth century, the

Kalachuri family had re-emerged as a major power in the northern Deccan. These later Kalachuris called themselves Haihayas after a legendary family from the Mahabharata, and their relationship to those of the sixth century is somewhat unclear. After campaigning to secure their submission, the new Chalukya ruler decided not to extend the Chalukya network there as directly as his grandfather Pulakeshin II had. He decided, instead, to bind his fortune with the Kalachuris by marrying his grandson, the young prince Vikramaditya, to *two* of the family's princesses.[6]

Imagine what sights these girls,[7] the sisters Loka-Mahadevi and Trailokya-Mahadevi, saw as their gorgeously bedecked palanquins were carried from the northern Deccan to the Malaprabha valley. The babble of Maharashtri Prakrit they had grown up with was replaced by Old Kannada and the accented Sanskrit of north Karnataka. They saw the Chalukya boar banner fluttering over the mud walls of Vatapi, and entered the halls of the palace to the sound of drums and trumpets. What did they see then, as they were escorted to the mural-decorated Inner City whose corridors the courtesan-queen Vijaya-Mahadevi had once walked, where they would die some day, far from the place they had called home? What mix of trepidation and anticipation did they feel when they were welcomed by a crowd of royal women with eyes as cold and glittering as their jewels? How did it feel as they were slowly subsumed into the politics of this strange court in a strange land? We cannot know, but it will not be long before we hear from them again.

The Vallabha Vinayaditya, meanwhile, was busy with grand designs. Apparently mobilizing the military support of his new Kalachuri in-laws, he sent the crown prince Vijayaditya (the father of his grandson Prince Vikramaditya, thus the father-in-law of the two Kalachuri princesses) to lead a raid on north India in the 690s.[8] The region had been in utter chaos after the death of Harsha, raided and attacked by powerful new kingdoms based in Kashmir, Tibet and Nepal. The

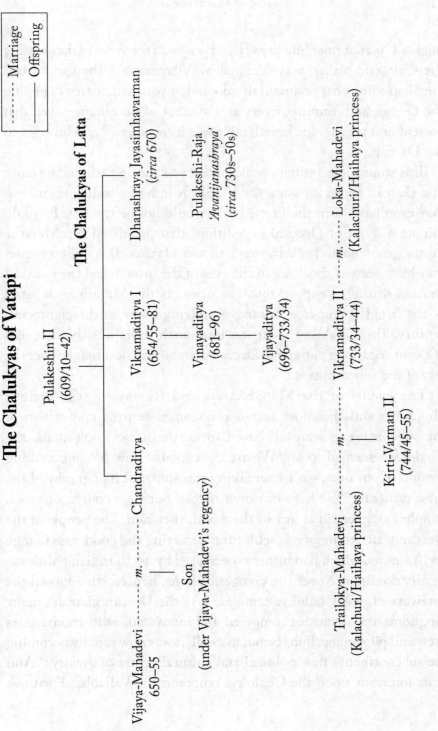

The Chalukyas of Vatapi

Pulakeshin II
(609/10–42)

Vijaya-Mahadevi ----- m. ----- Chandraditya
650–55

Son
(under Vijaya-Mahadevi's regency)

Vikramaditya I
(654/55–81)

Vinayaditya
(681–96)

Vijayaditya
(696–733/34)

Vikramaditya II ----- m. ----- Loka-Mahadevi
(733/34–44)   (Kalachuri/Haihaya princess)

                              Trailokya-Mahadevi
                              (Kalachuri/Haihaya princess)

Kirti-Varman II
(744/45–55)

The Chalukyas of Lata

Dharashraya Jayasimhavarman
(circa 670)

Pulakeshi-Raja
Avanijanashraya',
(circa 730s–50s)

----- Marriage
——— Offspring

Note: Exact regnal years for the Chalukyas of Lata have not survived in the inscriptional record.

mighty Gujarati ruler Siladitya III, who was on the verge of dominating the Gangetic plains, was defeated by Vijayaditya.[9] The vanquished king had somewhat prematurely adopted imperial standards depicting the Ganga and Yamuna rivers as a symbol of dominance over that ancient and prestigious heartland; these were seized[10] and brought to the Deccan.

This stupendous military achievement was the first attested instance of a Deccan power crossing the Vindhyas in half a millennium[11] – it may even have been the first – but it would not be the last. It would initiate a series of Deccani expeditions that pre-dated the Maratha campaigns in north India by over a thousand years. This military upset may have been as shocking in the eyes of the urbane and the political Indians of the seventh–eighth centuries, as the Marathas' defiance of the Mughal emperor Aurangzeb Alamgir was in the eighteenth century. This Chalukya incursion into north India was the first sign of a centuries-long pattern of Deccan geopolitical dominance over the rest of the subcontinent.

The events of the Mahabharata and Ramayana, the earliest kingdoms and the most sacred pilgrimage centres and *tirthas* of the subcontinent, were all based in north India. Look at us, the Chalukyas seemed to say. We are the captains now. We are making a world of our own, we are remaking the 'imperial topography of the subcontinent'.[12] We have our own *tirthas*, our own courts, our own temples, as splendid as any in the world, they said. The people of the Deccan watched in awe as sculptures depicting the goddesses Ganga and Yamuna, which had hitherto been used by north Indian polities to signify dominance over the Gangetic plains, henceforth adorned the gateways of new Chalukya temples.[13] As the Deccan plateau's many kingdoms and dynasties competed and innovated, as its monasteries grew and pilgrimage hubs began to swell, it was now rapidly becoming the subcontinent's new political and cultural centre of gravity.[14] And at its forefront stood the Chalukya emperor: the Vallabha, Fortune's

Favourite. No longer would a simple boar banner suffice: henceforth Chalukya emperors were preceded by the *pali-dhvaja*, a 'compound flagstaff' or 'flag in rows'[15] that bound to the Varaha standard the banners of defeated and vassalized kings, a powerful visual reminder of the vast, diffused political network they controlled.

Over the next two generations, with no other Deccan power left to challenge Chalukya military supremacy, tribute and agricultural revenues poured into the Malaprabha valley, the Chalukya home base. The soil of the valley was poor and best used for millet farming,[16] with other agricultural produce brought in from other Chalukya territories or traded along well-established routes.[17] At one end, protecting the entrance to the valley, was the citadel of Vatapi, commanding views for dozens of kilometres from its fortified heights. Within the valley were the towns of Mahakuta, Aryapura/Ayyavole (modern-day Aihole) and Kisuvolal (modern-day Pattadakal), which had been centres of religious significance for centuries, thanks to their position near rivers or springs.[18] They were now increasingly decorated with temples dedicated to Puranic deities. New money and people poured into the Chalukya heartland, drawn by the military pre-eminence of the court, and the valley was further transformed by these forces. This brings us to another institution that shaped medieval India: the merchant guild.

Perhaps the most important medieval Indian merchant guilds were the Ainurruvar, the Five Hundred Swamis (Lords) of the great *agrahara* at Aihole, a group of five hundred affluent upper-caste men. They were *chaturvedi* (learned in the four Vedas) Brahmins, probably with close ties to the court, and in the seventh–eighth centuries, they worked together to take over commercial activity in the Malaprabha river valley.[19] It is significant that it was not the merchant *setti* castes but the better-connected, landowning Brahmin castes that found themselves best positioned to exploit the new economic opportunities emerging as the Malaprabha valley's cities and towns grew and the demand for food and luxury items swelled.

Over the decades, the Five Hundred Lords gradually brought under their control disparate wandering and local merchants and traders, allocating 'brokerage and monopoly to individuals or groups of traders on certain items'.[20] As the association grew, their moniker soon lost its literality and became the go-to name for them. The Five Hundred brought together many locally powerful groups.[21] As the guild expanded from the Malaprabha valley through the fertile lands between the Krishna and Tungabhadra rivers, 'small and workable federations' were established under its general aegis, sometimes over commercial units spread over as many as four modern districts.[22] Within the overarching 'umbrella' that was the Chalukya political network, more complex economic arrangements than had hitherto existed in the Deccan now began to emerge.

The Five Hundred and their like were powerful agents of the Deccan's transformation, and their activities unfolded alongside another significant trend. Much has been made of the role of kings in shaping India's religious landscape, but just as much credit is due to the networks of wealthy people connected to the court. As courts and the people associated with them – aristocrats, poets, merchants, priests, administrators, military men – became wealthier, a second spurt of temple-building activity[23] exploded across the Malaprabha river valley. By the early eighth century, elite Chalukya subjects could call upon the talents of many guilds of professional *sthapatis* who were drawn there to develop temples dedicated to a wider array of popular deities. Just as with the projects of the early Chalukya monarchs, these elites were not paying for these expensive undertakings purely out of piety. Rather, they competed to display their wealth, sophistication and proximity to the Chalukya court through temple patronage. The more one was able to donate, the higher one's status in the pecking order. Inscriptions (usually prefaced by flowery praises of the Vallabha) proclaimed how much they had donated, making it clear to all who could read – or hear the inscriptions read out – who the great magnates of the court were.

The fortunes that were lavished on these buildings attracted workers from all over the Deccan. These included a surprising number of people from the Telugu country,[24] who apparently found the Chalukyas of Vatapi to be far more generous patrons than the Chalukyas of Vengi. As they worked, climbing up scaffolds to quarry the best-quality stone for temples, these people whom history would otherwise have forgotten carved their names into the cliffs, and marked out the number of days they worked so as to be paid on time. Names like Ayicchasvami, Kottimanchi, Buru, Bithamarga and Dronamma appear,[25] unmistakably Indian but so different from modern Indian names. The sandstone cliffs of the Malaprabha valley, which stand silent now, must have buzzed with activity in the day. We can guess that their lives were far more difficult and full of hard physical labour than those of their aristocratic employers, but little more. It is a shame that we know so little about the lives of those not wealthy enough to leave behind a monument.

What we can see, though, are the great works of art they created on behalf of the elites who ruled over them.

Temples, and the hierarchies they articulated, were designed to be visible to the people of the Malaprabha valley, positioned in pleasant environs to attract a cosmopolitan crowd. Though the earliest temples had been set up on pre-existing sacred sites, they now began to appear on arterial roads and highways on the outskirts of cities.[26] Here, more land was available and they would be accessible to city folk, as well as to people from the villages who grew food for them. They were surrounded by large gardens and orchards, or near lakes and reservoirs, to draw crowds and impress upon them the generosity and piety of the temple's patrons.[27] These crowds, in turn, attracted shopkeepers selling everything from foodstuff to textiles, creating commercial hubs directly or indirectly regulated by merchants or by the king, thus becoming integrated into the new economic and political hierarchies of the Malaprabha valley.

We take all of this – the wealthy patronizing temples, shrines acting as social and commercial centres – for granted in the practice of modern Hinduism. But it is worth reiterating that in the medieval Deccan, this was all overwhelmingly *new*. To a significant extent, it is through the activities of the elites who rose to power alongside the Chalukya clan that temples became as ubiquitous as they are today. But even as their patronage of temples in the Malaprabha valley proclaimed their loyalty to the Chalukyas, these lords and ladies were gradually growing in confidence, power and popularity. It would not be long before they mounted serious challenges to the Deccan's premier dynasty.

⁀

When Prince Vikramaditya Chalukya, husband of the Kalachuri sister-wives, was appointed Yuvaraja sometime around 710 CE, it seemed as though Chalukya power had reached a glorious apogee. His father Vijayaditya, his grandfather Vinayaditya, and his namesake and great-grandfather Vikramaditya I had expanded the dynasty's control and enforced relationships weighed in favour of the Chalukyas across most of the Deccan. And the Pallavas had made no serious attempts to renew their ancestral conflict.

At long last, the Malaprabha river valley, after generations of its people had been sacrificed to the ravenous flames of empire, was beginning to recover – indeed *flourish*. Vikramaditya's father, the Vallabha Vijayaditya, returned to his home after a life spent mostly on the battlefield. He then proceeded to fall head over heels in love with a young courtesan,[28] and spent his last decades relatively at peace. New temple spires were rising around him, urban centres were growing. Tours of the territory were undertaken to visit the dozens of in-laws and married-off adult daughters that made up the courts and *antahpurams* of the emperor and his circle. It appears to have been a relaxed period after the chaos of the preceding years.

At least that is how things seemed on the surface. Just as the world outside the court had many other power centres, such as temples and merchants, the court itself was a viper pit of politics and intrigue with many competing centres of power.

The Chalukya imperial formation, with its unfurling economic and religious networks and hubs, had catapulted many more people into the leagues of the powerful. This was both their ultimate success and the seed of their own destruction. New actors – merchants, ascetics, landlords, aristocrats – were now competing with the Chalukyas for primacy in many new battlefields: temple and artistic patronage, diplomacy, wealth. This created fresh political pressures, requiring the royal family to invest in increasingly lavish displays of public power in order to maintain their primacy in all these fields. Consider even their grandest royal temples, such as the towering Lokapaleshvara temple (now called the Galaganatha) at Pattadakal.[29] It is built in the north Indian style, with an imposing curvilinear spire, rather than the tiered south Indian style. The architecture is apparently meant to commemorate Vijayaditya's raid of north India, and the god's name – 'Lord of the Directions' – was evidently meant to signify that the Chalukyas dominated territory in all the cardinal directions. It was a project of such scale that it practically established Pattadakal as the dynasty's 'new religious centre', or at least as a 'major temple site'.[30] But why did it have to be built on such a scale and at such expense? Because this sandstone superstructure, confidently proclaiming the might of the Chalukyas, is actually meant to conceal uncertainty and fear: the silent rock hints at a need for public validation and display of imperial power.[31]

The Lokapaleshvara temple at Pattadakal, known today as the Galaganatha. Observe the curvilinear spire with spines composed of horseshoe-shaped motifs; these are characteristic of the Latina style of north Indian temple architecture.

There might have been less fighting and raiding going on by the early eighth century, but there were other challenges the court had to face. The Chalukya political network had grown both wider and deeper over the last four generations. Take, for example, the Harischandra family of the Konkan, with their power concentrated near Puri (modern Elephanta near Mumbai, not Puri in Odisha), once conquered by Pulakeshin II. Svamichandra, the founder of the line, was established as the hereditary *samanta* – vassal king[32] –

of that region by Vikramaditya I. Two generations down the line, his grandson Bhogashakti was still ruling it under Vikramaditya's grandson Vijayaditya,[33] the current emperor. But the term 'under' is somewhat misleading: vassals of this rank had the right to appoint their own candidates to rule over districts and groups of villages,[34] which meant that in practice they enjoyed considerable autonomy. Bhogashakti was essentially a king in his own right, and is known to have set up a temple to a god named after himself and ordered local merchants to administer it on his behalf, making a land grant of his own to do so.[35] This situation of de facto independence grew over the generations, despite ties through marriage and tribute to the imperial family.

However, these *samantas* were just one rank among a vast hierarchy of local rulers and minor and major lords, with direct or indirect ties to the Chalukya court. This included village chieftains, lords of districts, governors of provinces. And alongside them, of course, were the nouveau riche, the merchants and bankers and monks and courtesans who might not have ruled over land themselves, but nevertheless wielded enormous clout in political affairs. Keeping them all in line required constant alertness and activity from the Chalukya emperor and his court. Titles, honours, marriages, appointments, gifts and submissions had to be negotiated and arranged. Agreements needed to be upheld, challenges dealt with, opportunities exploited. And the court, paralleling the rest of the imperial formation, was also made up of talented and ambitious individuals with hereditary ties to the Chalukya clan. The Punyavallabha family, for example, served Vikramaditya I and his descendants as *maha-sandhi-vigrahakas*,[36] Great Controllers of Peace and War (similar to foreign ministers). They went wherever the Chalukya emperor went in his moving court/military encampment, personally composing the land grants and official documents he issued.[37] And just as the Harischandras of the Konkan sat near the top of the hierarchy of semi-autonomous local rulers, the

Punyavallabhas were the most prominent in the hierarchy of court
offices that many powerful families of the Malaprabha heartland of
the Chalukyas vied for.

Supremely influential among these lobbies were the women of
the *antahpurams*, whom we have previously seen outdone by the
courtesan-queen Vijaya-Mahadevi. As opportunities for advancement,
profit, glory, rivalry and vengeance proliferated, so too did activity in
the Inner Cities of all these powerful men. As has been mentioned,
hierarchies in the *antahpuram* paralleled those of the court. All these
positions flowed from politicking: the question of who would occupy
the position of chief queen was a decision based on talent, public
perception and private negotiations, not on who happened to marry
the king first.[38] The wives and daughters of the rajas, maharajas,
samantas, *mahasandhivigrahakas*, chief priests, senior generals and
so on also occupied ranks to which they had to adhere. These elite
women were expected to attend the 'life-cycle rites of the imperial
family', and served as attendants of the seniormost queens.[39] Within
the *antahpuram*, the women's 'fertile periods' were supposed to be
meticulously tracked by female attendants reporting to the king's
officials, as were their sexual interactions with him.[40] As much power
and influence as a queen could wield, it should be remembered that
(in theory) she was little more than the king's appendage. Only the
most important, connected and qualified women would be allowed
to gain influence by becoming the mothers of the next generation of
potential kings and queens. Royal succession, like so much else in
medieval India, was a complex affair.[41]

Of course, not all women who entered the *antahpuram* did so with
even this degree of autonomy. References to queens and princesses
kidnapped in war and forced to live in their abductor's *antahpuram* are
commonplace in historical texts, and they are unlikely to have been well
treated either by the king or the senior queens. Violent sex – whether
consensual or not – was also not uncommon, being described in the

Kamasutra, a manual on love and relationships meant for a courtly and urbane audience, and probably known to the elites of the Malaprabha valley.[42] Indeed, the *Kamasutra* goes so far as to say that 'Ferocity and roughness are in a man's nature, it is said; for woman it is lack of power, suffering and giving up, and a sense of weakness …'[43] Soon after, it provides examples of kings accidentally killing their wives or dancing girls during sexual intercourse by beating them for pleasure. Though it condemns that extreme as 'hurtful, barbaric, and unworthy of respect',[44] the fact that the practice was brought up in the first place – given it was meant for such an elite audience – is telling.

Moving beyond aristocratic women, the *antahpuram* was also home to a crowd of attendants to provide the former with everything from cosmetic services to musical accompaniment, from dance performances to confidential advice. There were also of course cooks, cleaners, launderers, guards and administrators to run the Inner City and keep potentially seductive or influential male partners well away from the king's women.

A medieval Indian king's visits to his *antahpuram* must have been fraught with political tension. The king was expected to visit the Inner City on a regular basis, where the women would be lined up to meet him. During this interaction, he would confirm or change their hierarchies through a ritualized process of gift giving. Queens would gift him 'garlands, perfumes and unguents', and he would return them 'as forms of grace'.[45] Carefully done up, his body washed and perfumed and adorned with jewellery, he was then supposed to talk and joke with the assembled women 'in keeping with their status and the time they have been in the harem'.[46] He would then repeat the process with 'remarried women' (which is to say, queens abducted in war), as well as the courtesans and dancing girls who resided in the *antahpuram*.[47]

As such, the declaration of Prince Vikramaditya Chalukya as Yuvaraja, *circa* 720 CE – coming decades after his marriage to the Kalachuri princesses – suggests that he was just one of many half-

Sachin Ravikumar / Wikimedia Commons

An amorous aristocratic couple on the walls of a temple in Pattadakal, an important centre of their power in the Malaprabha river valley. The men and women of Vijayaditya's court and Inner City may have been similarly attired.

brothers, sons of the Vallabha Vijayaditya by an array of queens, who were all lobbying for succession. He and his two sister-wives must have had to navigate their own personal dynamics, as well as their relations with the other aforementioned power centres of the Malaprabha valley, to ensure that he was declared the heir.

Once this was done, both princesses, now wives of a middle-aged Yuvaraja under an ageing Vallabha, found their positions immeasurably strengthened. They now had precedence over the wives of other

Chalukya princes, as well as most other women of the court with the exception of their mothers-in-law, the Vallabha's wives. Up to this point, the royal women of the Deccan (with the exception of Vijaya-Mahadevi) had played a relatively muted role in the patronage of religious and architectural projects, often undertaking them with the financial or political support of their male relatives.[48] No longer.

When Trailokya-Mahadevi, the younger of Vikramaditya's two sister-wives, gave birth to his son and heir apparent in the early 720s, she embarked on a project of astonishing scale. She ordered the construction of a Shiva temple at Pattadakal, so ambitious in scale that it sucked Chalukya-employed artisans away from their other building projects in the Malaprabha valley for no less than fourteen years.[49] Pattadakal was the coronation site of Chalukya monarchs, one of the central hubs of their power in the Malaprabha valley, and was also emerging as a major religious centre thanks to the Vallabha Vijayaditya's previous temple projects. At a time when elites were increasingly using temples to establish their position in the valley's pecking order, for a princess to sponsor such a major project, evidently with the Vallabha's support, indicates an extraordinary degree of self-assurance; evidently by this point this foreign princess did not lack for connections and influence of her own in the valley.

Trailokya-Mahadevi, unfortunately, did not live to see the completion of her temple. When her son was still in his teens, she died suddenly of unknown causes, and all the resources and workers gathered for her temple were transferred to her father-in-law's projects, though the old man was apparently touched by her vision and drive.[50] But now her elder sister, Loka-Mahadevi, rose to the apex of the Chalukya *antahpuram*, taking her younger sister's son and her husband under her wing. It is interesting to wonder what the relationships between these people were like: did Loka-Mahadevi spoil the young prince as the son she never had, a memory of a beloved sister, or emotionally torture the child for his status as a rival to her power? We will never know.

Loka-Mahadevi was perhaps one of the most powerful of all medieval Indian queens.[51] Soon after her husband Vikramaditya's appointment as crown prince, despite being lesser in rank than her sister Trailokya-Mahadevi, the mother of the heir, there were already hints of her independence and influence. According to her land grants, she administered two regions in her own right, successfully built a large temple that has not survived to today, and assigned the revenue of many villages to it.[52] If so much evidence of her deeds survives, it stands to reason that her career must have involved even more activity than we are able to see today. Even her sister had never had such influence. For a royal lady to do all this, and do it publicly, was exceptional; the only other one to have done so[53] was Queen Vijaya-Mahadevi. Unlike that former courtesan who had risen to power in a moment of chaos, Loka-Mahadevi flaunted her authority in full view of the Chalukya imperial network, apparently with the full backing of the *antahpuram*, her husband the crown prince, and her father-in-law the Vallabha himself.

By distributing land in her own right instead of asking for the emperor to do so 'at her request' as most other royal ladies did,[54] Loka-Mahadevi was making a bold statement about her importance to the Chalukyas. She seemed almost to imply that if her father-in-law and husband were Vishnu, the ideal king, then she was the female equivalent: the female energy from which Vishnu's power sprung – in a sense the fertile, generative power behind the Chalukya dynasty.[55] *She* was Fortune, Loka-Mahadevi, the Great Goddess of Earth, and Vikramaditya was her favourite.

There can be little question that Loka-Mahadevi's importance was recognized by her contemporaries. Later Chalukya inscriptions would declare that her husband Vikramaditya obtained 'great energy' (*mahotsaha*) from his union with her[56] – a reflection of the idealized relationships of gods and their *shakti*, their female counterparts, but also a striking centring of a queen in otherwise king-centric *prashastis*.

As Loka-Mahadevi took the Chalukya *antahpuram* and her viceregal territories in hand over the decades, her husband, Crown Prince Vikramaditya, proved himself a talented and well-liked administrator and diplomat, displaying little military inclination. He and his father travelled far and wide to maintain the Chalukya imperial network in a reasonably healthy state, constantly negotiating and solidifying ties with local elites. They could be surprisingly pragmatic about this, granting considerable local autonomy in return for an acceptance of their sovereignty and adherence to their overall geopolitical goals.

One particularly famous inscription from Vikramaditya's early career features a 'constitution' he established in a town called Porigere (modern Lakshmeshwar, Karnataka), in agreement with its foremost citizens and representatives of various social groups.[57] According to this deal, royal officers would be responsible for enforcing the Vallabha's proclamations and the terms of land grants in Porigere. However, the income from taxes on various types of households and guilds, as well as fines for theft and other delinquencies, were to be paid not to royal officers, but to the merchant guild. The collection was to be made in the month of Karttika,[58] the start of the campaigning season – a hint that this revenue right was granted to the merchants in return for assistance with maintaining the Chalukya armies. Clearly, the Five Hundred and other such guilds were already more influential in some areas than the imperial court, and the latter understood how to turn these new politico-economic equations to their advantage.

Vikramaditya's father, the Vallabha Vijayaditya, would reign for nearly forty years – quite exceptional for the times, though for the last decade or so of this period it was Vikramaditya and Loka-Mahadevi who ran the affairs of the court, especially after Vikramaditya's installation as crown prince *c.* 720. Through all these years, the Chalukyas had remained relatively at peace, focusing on political competition, temple construction and the like. But as the Vallabha's health continued to deteriorate, Vikramaditya and Loka-Mahadevi seem to have realized they needed a more grandiose display of their power. Perhaps other ambitious claimants were raising their heads, or perhaps the couple wished to establish they were as capable in the arts of war as they were in the arts of peace. After all, every generation of Chalukya kings before them had been extraordinarily militarily successful, maintaining and extending their authority through war. Vikramaditya, living under their shadow, had to publicly establish himself as worthy of ruling in the eyes of the immense pan-Deccan network that watched the court attentively for any sign of faltering or weakness.

And not just Deccanis, either. In 708, a distant superpower, the Umayyad Caliphate, headquartered in Syria, had begun a campaign of conquest and raiding in India that would continue into the 730s and leave much of western and central India reeling.[59] There must have been much fear and uncertainty in the air.

The easiest way for the royal couple to consolidate their position was probably to summon the allies and vassals they had made over their career and unleash them on a common enemy. But, apparently, Vikramaditya did not feel secure enough about his political position or military ability to tackle the terrible threat that was emerging to his north. Instead, he searched around for a softer target. And *c.* 731, just such a target was available to him to his south.[60]

Over the past three decades, the Pallavas had managed to substantially recover from the devastation of the Chalukya king Vikramaditya I's campaigns of the 670s. The new Pallava king, Narasimha-Varman II, was an artistically inclined type, like his great-grandfather Mahendra, the author of the *Farce of the Drunkard's Games*. Part of this may have been due to the influence of his court poet and *acharya* (teacher), Dandin (Stick Wielder).

The Pallavas of Kanchipuram

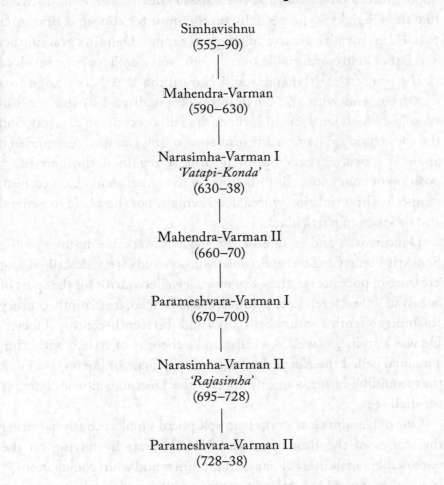

Simhavishnu
(555–90)

Mahendra-Varman
(590–630)

Narasimha-Varman I
'Vatapi-Konda'
(630–38)

Mahendra-Varman II
(660–70)

Parameshvara-Varman I
(670–700)

Narasimha-Varman II
'Rajasimha'
(695–728)

Parameshvara-Varman II
(728–38)

Dandin is an excellent example of the cosmopolitan and multi-generational character of medieval Indian courts, and his life offers us a glimpse of the surprisingly human stories of some of these elites. His great-grandfather had left western Maharashtra to seek easier opportunities down south at the Pallava court.[61] The Pallavas were, like the Chalukyas, perpetually on the hunt for educated Brahmins to build up social, human and religious capital. Dandin's grandfather and father held comfortable courtly jobs, and may have been involved in the projects of Mahendra and Narasimha I. All that came to a disastrous end with the Chalukya Vikramaditya I's expedition of revenge, which left Kanchi sacked, the Pallava court in disarray, and the countryside in flames. The orphaned young Dandin had wandered about for twelve years[62] until he finally regained the hereditary position of court poet. But his time on the streets had changed him, tempering his erudition with a deep cynicism of the world in general and of kings in particular.

Dandin was and is one of the most remarkable figures of the Sanskrit literary canon, a virtuoso whose words were described as a 'treasure of pure nectar, their expanse a jewelled mirror for the sport of Sarasvati',[63] and references to him are 'widespread, from ninth-century Kashmir to tenth-century Sri Lanka and thirteenth-century Tibet'.[64] He was a stylist, as well as a critic and a theorist of style,[65] authoring a manual called the *Kavyadarsha* (Looking-Glass of Poetry) – a book that would be of great significance to the Deccan centuries later, as we shall see.

One of Dandin's lost works is an epic poem simultaneously narrating the stories of the Ramayana and Mahabharata by relying on the remarkable capabilities of Sanskrit grammar and word conjugations.[66] In another, one of the greatest surviving works of Sanskrit prose, he narrates the stories of ten adventurous princes seeking to restore a lost kingdom. This was perhaps designed to impart to his young ward, the Pallava king, lessons on kingship, the morality of dharma, and perhaps also the things he had seen as a wandering orphan.[67] It reveals a great deal about the ethical world and political calculations of the elites of early medieval India.

The heroes of the work, the *Dasakumaracharitam* (Tale of the Ten Princes) freely deploy seduction, riot-mongering, thievery and murder; they impersonate sages, bankrupt rivals and overthrow kings. But, arguably, all the kings they overthrow are unrighteous, do not follow their dharma, and are most often *unwary*. The villains of the *Dasakumaracharitam* are caught up in personal vendettas, have made themselves unpopular with their subjects, or are slaves to their passions, and all these flaws allow the heroic princes the opportunity to overthrow them, usually after a careful calculation of whether their actions will help uphold dharma or not. One prince, for example, holds himself back from sleeping with a queen, another man's wife, for fear of hurting dharma. He then calculates that 'the compilers of the scriptures permit this if both *artha* (material success) and *kama* (sexual pleasure) are also attained at the same time[68]... That should neutralise any sin, and may also reward me with some fraction of *dharma*.'[69] He then spends the night in illicit pleasure, leaving the queen covered in love bites and scratches, savouring her moans and the faint line of sweat on her brow as they make love.[70]

The princes' calculations, and the strategies they devise to achieve their goals, are warnings to an unrighteous and unwary king. They also highlight the overriding importance of dharma as a moral code that Indian kings were expected to follow, or appear to follow. While playing with these complex themes in the *Charitam*, Dandin displays his literary gifts: one prince, his lips bruised by love bites, narrates his entire tale without employing sounds that require the usage of one's lips: *pa, pha, ba, bha, ma*).

The new Pallava monarch would follow these lessons carefully. He recognized there was little that could be done to undermine Chalukya dominance, and there were no further attempts at revenge and wars in the Deccan. Instead, the Pallavas looked to trade, across the seas, to a world utterly transformed.

In West Asia, the Prophet Muhammad had died in 632 CE. In the aftermath, the tribes of the Arabian peninsula, now united under the banner of Islam, had embarked on a programme of conquest hitherto unrivalled in human history. 'Alexander was upstaged, Caesar overshadowed.'[71] The remarkably mobile and capable Arab armies, though they only numbered in the thousands, managed to crush the Romans and Persians, the superpowers of West Asia, who were exhausted and demoralized after decades of war. They quickly secured Iraq, Syria, Egypt and some of the southern Mediterranean coastline. They were driven by a combination of religious conviction and tribal affinity, as well as the more usual medieval thirst for plunder and booty.[72]

By 644, the Arabs were settling into garrison cities to administer this vast empire.[73] In 656, the year after Vikramaditya I ended the Chalukya civil war and declared himself Fortune's Favourite, the Arabs fought their first civil war. This eventually culminated in the foundation of the Syria-based Umayyad Caliphate by 661. Soon after, the entire southern Mediterranean coast fell to Muslim armies; Spain was conquered and used as a base to raid France; Muslim armies began to wrest control of the wealthy oases of the 'Silk Road' trade routes from the Turkic nomads of Central Asia. Even the mighty Chinese were forced to send expeditions against the Arabs.

In 708, the armies of the Umayyad Caliphate were unleashed on the Indian subcontinent. An Arab governor of the Caliphate conquered Sind on India's western periphery. Major trading cities were completely sacked, and the governor sent back to the caliph a treasury of 60 million dirhams – equal to billions of dollars today.[74] The Umayyad capital city of Damascus rapidly grew into one of the greatest urban centres of the world as traders, adventurers and scholars flocked to it from across the Mediterranean.

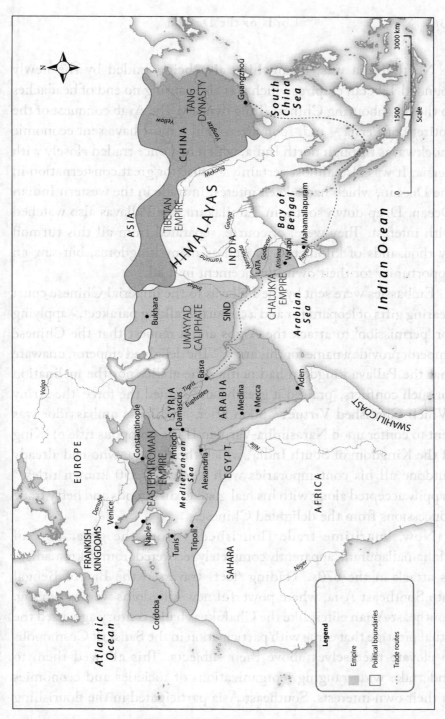

Afro-Eurasia, early eighth century CE.

North India was, meanwhile, also being raided by the newly founded Tibetan empire, which was also causing no end of headaches to the neighbouring Chinese Tang dynasty. The Arab conquest of the entirety of Persia – and, soon after, Sind – must have sent economic shockwaves through north India, which had once traded closely with Persia. It was also almost certainly a cause for great consternation in the Deccan, which had a keen interest in trade in the western Indian Ocean. Deep down south, in Tamilakam, the Pallavas also watched with interest. They were, of course, separated from all this turmoil by thousands of kilometres as well as many kingdoms, but saw an opportunity for their own advancement in it all.

Embassies were sent by the Pallavas to the imperial Chinese court bearing gifts of leopard fur and a colourful talking parakeet,[75] applying for 'permission' to attack the Arabs and a request that the Chinese emperor provide a name for this army.[76] The delighted emperor, unaware that the Pallava kingdom had neither the ability nor the inclination for such conflicts, 'praised it greatly' and named the force 'the Army Which Cherished Virtue'.[77] Soon after, a Chinese ambassador was sent to confer upon Narasimha-Varman II the pompous title of 'King of the Kingdom of South India', which the Pallava, who had already outdone all his contemporaries with a total of 250 known titles,[78] happily accepted along with his real goal: luxury goods and hefty trade concessions from the delighted Chinese.

Now, 'maritime trade flourished'[79] from the great port of Mahamallapuram, apparently completely recovered from Vikramaditya I's attack in the 670s. Trading fleets traversed the Bay of Bengal into Southeast Asia, where powerful new kingdoms were emerging. Southeast Asian elites, like the Chalukyas had a century ago, used the ritual prestige that came with participation in the Sanskrit Cosmopolis to elevate themselves above their subjects. This allowed them to undertake wide-ranging reorganizations of societies and economies in their own interests. Southeast Asia participated in the flourishing

The Shore temple complex at Mahamallapuram. While many Pallava kings would make additions to it, two of the tallest spires are attributed to Narasimha-Varman II, and were built when maritime trade was booming at the royal port. The pyramidical temple spires of the Pallavas are believed to have influenced later temple architecture in Indonesia, a region that medieval Tamilakam frequently traded with.

Sanskrit Cosmopolis, deriving prestige and power from re-adapting its forms and norms to local contexts just as south Indians did,[80] while retaining their indigenous traditions to a significant extent.

In the 720s, while north India burned and the Chinese lost sleep over the marauding Tibetans and Arabs, south Indian and Southeast Asian courts prospered and grew wealthy. The Chalukyas and Pallavas had not completely stopped their competition, except now it unfolded in the field of temple building as opposed to the battlefield. The famous 'Shore temple' at Mahamallapuram was constructed at this time. A grand new temple was also dedicated to Shiva in Kanchi, where the chief Pallava queen's donations were commemorated on walls.[81] All these developments may have been keenly observed by her contemporary, Loka-Mahadevi.[82]

When the Pallava king Narasimha-Varman II died, the Chalukya crown prince and princess, Vikramaditya and Loka-Mahadevi, seized their opportunity before his successor Parameshvara-Varman II could consolidate his power. The elderly couple had, by 731, essentially controlled the Chalukya kingdom for over a decade, with the Vallabha Vijayaditya almost certainly ailing[83] (he would die in 733). Attacking the Pallavas and seizing their wealth would have served to reinforce the couple's domestic position by establishing Prince Vikramaditya's military credentials after a long period of peace,[84] and also help finance more temple building, thus signalling to other vassals the religious and martial primacy of the Chalukyas. It was, apparently, the perfect strategy.

And so, over forty years of relative peace came to a close. Vikramaditya and his commanders brought the boar banner to Tamilakam, leading a combined army with the Pallavas' other nemeses, the Gangas,[85] as well as contingents of troops from the other lords of the Chalukya imperial formation.[86] The young Pallava king was defeated, humiliated and forced to pay a massive ransom to the much older Chalukya crown prince to keep him from marching on Kanchi.[87] Crown Prince Vikramaditya then returned to the Malaprabha valley in triumph. We can imagine him striding into the palace at the head of his elite troops, bowing to his frail old father and laying the symbols of the Pallava royalty – banners, crowns, jewels and musical instruments – at his feet.

The humiliated and infuriated Pallava king then attacked the Gangas, hoping to catch them unawares and recoup his losses. This move was a disaster: he was killed on the battlefield, throwing the Pallava kingdom into crisis as factions at court jostled over which royal child should be appointed the next ruler.[88]

From Prince Vikramaditya's perspective, things were going marvellously. Dharma was a very important part of the medieval Indian worldview, as alluded to in the ravishing tales of the Pallava court-poet Dandin. Now Vikramaditya declared that he had defended his family's honour and upheld the royal dharma by defeating their ancestral enemy. Further improving his position was the fact that his young Pallava rival, who could have been a thorn in the Chalukyas' side for decades, had disposed of himself through a rash attack. Vikramaditya's expedition to Kanchi was thus a resounding success, establishing his credentials for the throne beyond any dispute.

And so, when his father finally died in 733 CE, he came to the throne as Fortune's Favourite, Earth's Beloved, Vikramaditya II – apparently the most powerful Chalukya monarch yet. But external events were moving faster than he could have ever expected. The world was changing, and Vikramaditya's priorities would soon be called into question.

In the early eighth century, as we have seen, the Umayyad Caliph decided to expand into the vast, wealthy lands of India, potentially securing rich new provinces to fund the increasingly desperate internal and external wars he was entangled in. Over the next few years, Umayyad commanders exploited the political chaos of northern India to the fullest, freely allying with any power that would enable them to enrich themselves. In the 720s, the ambitious Shiva-worshipping kings of Kashmir helped[89] these Tajikas,[90] as the Indians called them, burn and sack the Kangra valley.[91] Indian seafarers and pirates also helped them attack the wealthy cities of Gujarat and Rajasthan, sacking Vallamandala (modern-day Barmer) and Marumala (modern-day Jaisalmer). Kaccha (modern-day Kacch), 'al-Mandal' near modern-day Ahmedabad, Saurashtra and Bharuch were conquered outright,[92] and even the outskirts of the ancient fortified city of Ujjain in Malwa were raided for loot and captives.

As the Tajikas went from success to success, many more equally ambitious and unscrupulous Indians saw an opportunity to profit from the loot and slaughter. Thousands of innocents were enslaved and shipped back to Iraq and Syria.[93] In a few years, the Umayyads are estimated to have secured booty worth as much as 250 *million* dirhams – many, many billions of dollars today.[94]

But almost immediately after the initial devastation, the Caliph's new Indian 'subjects', who now understood how the Tajikas fought, struck back.[95] Gujarat, Rajasthan and even the Umayyad's main foothold in the subcontinent, Sind, rose up in revolt. So bloody and costly was the uprising that Umayyad troops outright refused to fight any more in the vast and hostile subcontinent, and 'insisted on leaving the province, refusing to ever go back'.[96] And yet, somehow, convinced that victory was only a matter of time and throwing men at the problem, the Caliphate persisted.[97]

In 731, when Vikramaditya II was attempting to establish his credentials by attacking Kanchi, Umayyad reinforcements reached Sind. Despite a series of setbacks at the hands of ambitious new Indian princelings, they managed to claw back parts of Gujarat, and then decided to attack rich new territories that had hitherto never seen Tajikas before. As they began moving deeper south along the coast of Gujarat, they began to approach the domains of the Chalukyas, or, to be specific, the Chalukyas of Lata, who had been settled there generations ago by Vikramaditya I.

These Chalukyas of Lata had likely been observing Tajika tactics and strategy for the previous decade. They had carefully learned from the defeats of their northern neighbours. While Crown Prince Vikramaditya was busy bullying the Pallavas, the Chalukyas of Lata had been left basically unassisted[98] to deal with this terrible threat.

The Tajikas were coming for them, 'reportedly with the intention of subduing all the southern kingdoms of India'.[99]

And the kingdoms were ready and waiting.

The Lata Chalukya force was commanded by one Pulakeshi-Raja (perhaps named after his grandfather Pulakeshin II). This man was a distant grand-uncle[100] of Vikramaditya II. In 737,[101] Tajika forces entered his territory, intending to sack his capital city, Navasarika (modern-day Navsari in Gujarat), a trading port on the west coast. Pulakeshi knew roughly which route the Tajikas would take, whereas they may have been in the dark about his strategy.

What exactly this strategy was is open to debate. The only primary source from this encounter is a commemorative land grant that Pulakeshi-Raja made soon after. It seems to have been a long and hard-fought battle. Pulakeshi-Raja praises the Tajikas as those who 'had not previously been vanquished even by numerous eminent chiefs among hosts of kings';[102] says that 'they were great warriors and had their sharp swords reddened by the blood flowing from the torn loins and trunks of hostile elephants';[103] and describes a great cloud of dust rising towards the skies as the Arab horses galloped. But after hours of brutal slaughter, the legendary Deccani infantry finally bested their enemies, their armour 'reddened by the streams of blood gushing from intestines spilling out of bellies impaled by spear-heads'.[104]

The Chalukyas – or, to be precise, a Chalukya 'vassal' who was also a Chalukya – had defeated one of the mightiest military forces of the day. The Caliphate had been dealt a blow in India from which it would never recover.[105] From the ashes of once-sacked cities in Gujarat and Rajasthan now rose new dynasties and warlords, determined to drive the marauding Tajikas out once and for all.[106] Henceforth the Arabs[107] would leave the subcontinent in peace. Its treasures were simply not worth the trouble.

Pulakeshi-Raja's astonishing victory over the Tajikas was a critical moment in South Asian, if not global, history. It was one among a series of serious setbacks suffered by the Umayyad Caliphate across the world in the 730s, including defeats at the hands of the Turkic tribes in Persia/Central Asia and the Franks in France in 732. Combined with a series of domestic revolts and a pyrrhic war in the Caucasus, the dynasty would soon collapse[108] and be replaced by a radically different Muslim empire, the Abbasid Caliphate.

However, Pulakeshi-Raja's victory, while it saved the Deccan from devastation, must have rocked Vikramaditya II's position to its foundations. Now that the Tajika threat, which had terrified much of South Asia for the last decade, had been unexpectedly dealt with, the emperor could hardly claim glory for this victory. It certainly seems that Pulakeshi acted on his own initiative, though some scholars have claimed, based on fragmentary evidence, that Vikramaditya II had ordered other vassals to go to his aid.[109] In a matter of days, all the military prestige Vikramaditya II had obtained through his raid on the Pallavas before his coronation had been completely eclipsed. It seemed that a vassal of his could better perform the dharma of protecting his dominions and subjects than the emperor himself!

In an attempt to conciliate the man and keep him within the Chalukya fold, Vikramaditya II had to grant Pulakeshi four very significant titles. These were Dakshinapatha-sadhara (Pillar of the Deccan), Challuki-kula-alamkara (Ornament of the Chalukya Family, a not-so-subtle reminder of their family connection), Anivartaka-anivartayitri (Repeller of the Unrepellable), and, tellingly, Prithivi-Vallabha – the Chalukya imperial title itself.[110]

Pulakeshi, however, had had a taste of glory now. Once again, we see the elements of medieval Indian power coming together. He had inscriptions issued glorifying his own branch of the family tree, post facto granting himself, his elder brother and father imperial titles, and announced that the Goddess of Royal Fortune had chosen him as 'her lord'.[111] Next, just as the Vatapi Chalukyas had brought Brahmins from prestigious, foreign north India to legitimize their rule in Karnataka, Pulakeshi-Raja now imported Brahmins from prestigious, foreign Karnataka to validate his rule in Gujarat.[112] And like the earlier Chalukya kings, he soon set out to expand his kingdom, chasing out the retreating Arabs and attempting to fill the power vacuum they left in Gujarat. Perhaps an attempt on the Chalukya throne in Vatapi itself was in the works.

The Chalukya emperor could not leave this challenge unanswered, though he could do nothing to directly attack his grand-uncle who, it should be noted, still referred to him with the utmost (if perhaps sarcastic) respect in public ('the illustrious Vallabha who is fond of heroism').[113] Instead, Vikramaditya II adopted a three-pronged strategy to shore up the influence of the Vatapi Chalukyas. First, he nurtured another ambitious vassal in the northern Deccan to nibble away at Pulakeshi's heels.[114] The best candidate for this was Pulakeshi's neighbour and grand-nephew from another branch of the family, who may have previously joined in or supported his campaigns against the Arabs. This young man was the leader of a clan called the Rashtrakutas, whose core territories were in the interior of Maharashtra around modern Elichpur,[115] near the Burhanpur gap in the Vindhya hills. He ruled an area of great strategic importance, commanding one of the main routes of the great Dakshinapatha, the Southern Way connecting the trade of north and south India. And his rather unique name, Danti-Durga, 'Elephant Fort', was an almost prophetic allusion to the future that lay in store for him.

In the early 740s, Danti-Durga, unlike his grand-uncle Pulakeshi, made his loyalty and subservience to the Vallabha clear as day, claiming the rank of *maha-samanta-adhipati*, 'High Lord Among Tributaries'.[116] As his military and political career slowly advanced under Vikramaditya II's mentorship and overlordship, his loyalty would be rewarded with the titles of Khadgavaloka (Sword sight) and, surprisingly, Sri-Prithivi-

Vallabha. The award of this supremely significant title to two of the Chalukyas' northernmost vassals, so distant from Vikramaditya II's base in Vatapi, hints at just how desperate the court was to keep the region under its control.

Second, with Lata already pulling out of the Chalukya orbit, Vikramaditya II led a second attack on the Pallavas, to at least shore up his position with his southern vassals.[117] It is possible that Danti-Durga participated in this campaign,[118] perhaps meeting Vikramaditya's heir and promising the old Vallabha that he would be the Chalukyas' most reliable vassal in their northern territories.

It was the perfect time for an attack. The factions at the Pallava court had selected a child from a collateral branch as the next king, and civil war had broken out almost immediately.[119] Soon after the wars resolved in favour of the child king, now a teenager, Vikramaditya decided to invade and establish his dominance, offering us a glimpse of the symbolic texture of medieval Indian wars and the strange 'chivalry' that kings sometimes showed their foes.

After swatting aside the Pallava forces, Vikramaditya II seized the mighty musical instruments which were used to command their troops and drive them into martial frenzies: the drum called 'Roar of the Sea', and the massive trumpet named 'Harsh Sounding'. Also captured were many 'renowned' war elephants and 'a heap of rubies'.[120] He then advanced ominously to Kanchi, where the populace was, no doubt, shivering at the thought of *another* Vikramaditya Chalukya sacking it, as if the first had not been bad enough. Vikramaditya II, however, had something else to prove.

What could be more glorious than sacking? *Not* sacking. Once in Kanchi, the Chalukya emperor confounded all expectations by donating 'heaps of gold' to the great temple of Narasimha-Varman II, the Pallava king who had sent embassies to the Chinese. Having 'inspected' the riches belonging to the god, he returned them.[121] A half-Sanskrit and half-Old Kannada inscription[122] was made on the walls of this Pallava royal shrine, composed by Vikramaditya's Great Minister for Peace and War, Anivarita Punyavallabha. In it, the Chalukya emperor demanded that none destroy this testament to his charity,[123] a commandment that seems to have been obeyed by the stunned populace of this city, given that it survives to this day.

What Vikramaditya was attempting to show his vassals with this generosity was that he had so much wealth to throw around that he did not *need* the petty wealth of campaigns of conquest; furthermore, he had indulged in the campaign not out of any need for money, but rather to restore the 'splendour [of] the previous kings born of his race'.[124] He left his ancestral enemy alive, their royal shrine untouched, because keeping them around as a testimony to his power, benevolence and adherence to dharma was far more useful. He set out to portray himself as the 'righteous' conqueror, loyal to the legacy of his fathers, who restored to his foes after taking from them the most priceless treasure of any medieval Indian king: glory. For now, at least, this decisive display of Chalukya power and prestige was enough to stave off any immediate moves by their vassals.

Queen Loka-Mahadevi may also have been present at this momentous occasion; it was not uncommon for queens, even elderly ones, to accompany the king on his campaigns. If so, she would have seen in this temple an inscription likening one of the Pallava queens to Parvati, commemorating the queen's construction of a tiny sub-shrine in the complex. This was a pitiful achievement compared to those of the Chalukya queen, for Loka-Mahadevi was responsible for a crucial pillar that upheld the trembling edifice of Vikramaditya II's power: a grand temple in the Malaprabha river valley commissioned by her a decade before and which remains, to this day, the most powerful testament to the Chalukya dynasty and to the brilliance of its queens.

As the Malaprabha meanders through its valley, gently flowing towards the Bay of Bengal, it temporarily flows directly to the north, as if pointing to the sacred Ganga, to the Himalayas[125] where the great god Shiva lived. At this sacred site is the town of Pattadakal, the 'Stone of Anointing', the coronation site of the Chalukya monarchs, where we have previously seen the temples of the Chalukya emperor Vijayaditya and his daughter-in-law Trailokya-Mahadevi.

At this most holy place, in the early 730s,[126] Queen Loka-Mahadevi summoned[127] a senior architect by the name of Gundan, master (*acharya*) of a guild of architects called Sarva-Siddhi (Universal Success). At the time, the Sarva-Siddhis seem to have been at the centre of a major scandal which was the talk of the entire Malaprabha valley.[128] Some very influential people were calling for the entire guild to be excommunicated from their caste, potentially rendering them unemployable[129] overnight.

Precisely what the Sarva-Siddhis had done to cause such a scandal is not clear. Legal texts from the period hint at some possibilities, such as embezzlement.[130] Either way, Gundan was probably in a state of high tension as the queen explained to him that the Sarva-Siddhis were in a great deal of trouble, and the only way to save their business was through her intervention.[131] That Loka-Mahadevi was able to promise this was a sign of the extraordinary influence she wielded in her own right at court. Perhaps this is how Gundan came to be commissioned to build the grandest and largest[132] of all Chalukya temples: a temple named not for a king or a place, but for a *queen*.[133] The Lokeshvara temple – for Queen Loka-Mahadevi.

This great project was commissioned soon after Vikramaditya II was declared Fortune's Favourite in 733, and construction would continue for the better part of a decade,[134] ending soon after Pulakeshi-Raja's victory over the Tajikas and the Vallabha's attacks on Kanchi. Built to the southeast of the temple of the queen's dead sister Trailokya-Mahadevi, the Lokeshvara temple employed so many craftsmen that progress on most other large royal temples came to a halt: yet another indication of its importance to the Chalukyas and especially to the queen.[135] On the walls of her new temple, we can still see tantalizing hints of her power and influence. She announced she was confirming the privileges that her deceased father-in-law, the Vallabha Vijayaditya, had bestowed on a guild of local singers[136] and assigned to the temple the revenues of a district of fifty villages.[137] Most importantly, she asserted that Gundan, by building it, had averted the excommunication of the Sarva-Siddhi guild,[138] conferring upon him the 'fillet of honour' called *mume–perjerepu* and the title of Tribhuvanacharya, 'Master of the Three Worlds', and 'the (most eminent) *Sutradhari* [chief architect] of the southern country'.[139]

As we can see, this medieval Indian queen realigned economic and social networks to make her Lokeshvara temple in Pattadakal, now called the Virupaksha temple and a UNESCO World Heritage Site. She created a new engine of religious and social activity, as any medieval Indian king would have. She handed out titles that transformed the social prominence of the Sarva-Siddhis, raising them up to the highest ranks of courtly society.

Why did she do all this? On an inscription on the eastern gateway, issued after the temple's completion, she calls it the 'temple of Lokeshvara of Lokamahadevi, (the queen) of Vikramaditya, who three times conquered Kanchi'.[140] (We have seen two of these expeditions so far, with the third to follow in the next chapter.) This suggests that it was meant to inflate her husband's martial credentials, but the temple was actually commissioned before the second and third expeditions had even taken place, at a time when Loka-Mahadevi and Vikramaditya had just solidified their dominant political position through a successful campaign to Kanchi followed by their coronation. And though Loka-Mahadevi was ostensibly building her temple to support Chalukya power and signal the authority of the Vallabha and his successful performance of his royal dharma, it was an authority in which her own rule, power and performance of dharma were also intertwined. This structure is a temple to Lokeshvara, Loka's Lord – thus to both Vikramaditya and Shiva.[141] But the Lokeshvara is also an unprecedented association of a queen's identity with a temple she made primarily for herself. In contrast, her younger sister's construction of a grand temple – a project that came to an abrupt end with her death – may have been intended to commemorate the birth of the heir and to support her position as a royal mother; Loka-Mahadevi's was unquestionably about her position as Vikramaditya's co-ruler.

Visitors to the Lokeshvara temple paddled their boats along the Malaprabha to alight at ghats of mud which lined the waterfront at Pattadakal, and made their way through bathing devotees and wandering ascetics[142] as they headed to this grand edifice. Stepping through the ornate eastern gateway, they would have immediately come across an elevated mandapa of warm sandstone which shrined an image of Shiva's bull, Nandi, carved out of cool black stone. This mandapa was decorated with niches featuring sculptures of beautiful women, representations of the Mother Goddess[143] and perhaps modelled after powerful members of the queen's own retinue. On its pillars are carved sexually intertwined couples, auspicious symbols of creation and generation.

Cathleen Ann Cummings

A female figure that might be the Chalukya queen Loka-Mahadevi, as suggested by the elephant-surmounted staff she holds, a symbol of royalty.

Today, the carvings on the walls of the Lokeshvara/Virupaksha temple at Pattadakal reveal a great deal about the politics of the queen who commissioned it. Loka-Mahadevi herself can be seen depicted on a pillar; though elderly when the temple was made, she is depicted as a beautiful young woman standing on a throne upheld by three lions,[144] symbols of the warrior-goddess Durga. Her arms are decorated with bands of gold, her hair piled up and fastened with a large jewel. In her hand she holds a standard crowned by an elephant – a symbol of the royalty that she figuratively and literally upheld. She looks down at viewers with a demure expression, even as the fact that this entire building is *hers* tells a different story. Elsewhere on the mandapa, the queen is again alluded to by a large, noble lion under which a little boar takes shelter – a statement that she is Durga, the lion-riding aspect of the Divine Mother that shelters the Chalukya family with her bravery and ferocity.[145] Close to this lion and boar is a slender young woman, her arm draped around a tree branch (a symbol of fertility), with a small boy standing at her feet as she stares off to the northwest. This, perhaps, is her dead sister Trailokya-Mahadevi, mother of the heir, who stands in her sister's temple looking at the temple that she did not live to see completed.[146] One is tempted to see a flash of personal rivalry in this: Loka-Mahadevi never ordered her sister's temple completed through all her years as queen, and yet chose to have her portrayed as a minor sculpture on her own temple and had her positioned in this way. Whatever the truth of this matter, the mandapa of the Lokeshvara, with its repeated imagery of the goddess and the generative powers of the feminine, is a clear symbol of Queen Loka-Mahadevi's position as the mother of the Chalukyas. 'By her erection of the Lokesvara temple the Queen upholds her duties to both god and husband and thus upholds *dharma*.'[147]

The Lokeshvara temple is also is a powerful testament to Vikramaditya II. A single look at this enormous building makes it clear how far the Deccan in general, and the Chalukyas in particular, had come.

The Chalukya king Mangalesha had once donated a single village's revenue to his family deity, Shiva Makuteshvara, in gratitude for his military success against the Kalachuris. Now the Kalachuri wife of his distant descendant, Vikramaditya II, could donate the revenues of fifty villages and mobilize the resources of hundreds of settlements to build a temple in her own name. The Chalukya king Pulakeshin II's temples had been simple, austere structures with their architectural decoration barely visible. Every part of the Lokeshvara temple, in contrast, is beautifully formed and adorned with mini-temples. The dome topping the superstructure seems to cascade down along the cardinal directions, the rhythm expanding at every tier with larger

Dinesh Kannambadi / Wikimedia Commons

The Lokeshvara temple at Pattadakal, known today as the Virupaksha. Observe how the walls, roofs and spires are decorated with beautifully rendered architectural elements, in contrast to earlier temples such as the Upper Shivalaya. The dome-shaped *kuta* on top of the spire is replicated on the corners of the lower tiers. At the central portions of the lower tiers, the *kuta* is replicated by barrel-shaped *shala* miniature shrines, imparting a sense of dynamism.

and larger *shala* (barrel-shaped) and *kuta* (dome-shaped) miniature shrines. This much larger building also has a more complex floor plan: no longer a simple square, but a square with additional squares projecting out of its axes of symmetry. This evokes a sense that the rhythm of the superstructure is carried all the way down to the base, and creates recesses and niches that impart dynamism to the otherwise still walls – a uniquely Deccan architectural innovation.

On this increased surface area of the temple are placed carefully selected sculptures with clear political meanings that would have been obvious to Vikramaditya II's vassals. Shiva the Ganga Bearer, for example, stands there as a reminder of Shiva in Narasimha I Pallava's Great Penance relief that had been defaced by Vikramaditya I; this sculpture also commemorates the conquests of Vikramaditya II's father Vijayaditya, who brought to the south the Ganga and Yamuna banners. Mythological stories abound on the Lokeshvara's walls, images of wrestling warriors symbolizing the long Chalukya–Pallava struggle as well as the divine wrestling match between Arjuna and Shiva. Rama, the ideal hero-king, is depicted, hinting at the supposedly ideal Vikramaditya II. Also featured is his rival the demon-king Ravana, a metaphorical representation of Narasimha Pallava, shaking the great mountain Kailasha on which Shiva lived, only to have his arms crushed by a single tap of the god's foot. This sculpture seems to say that Narasimha Pallava was little more than a demon-king. And now Vikramaditya II, like Shiva, had humiliated and embarrassed the Pallavas with his own mercy.

The Lokeshvara temple has many messages sequestered in its walls by the queen and the *sthapati*. But what appears to dominate is the Chalukya victory over the Pallavas, a message that the royal couple thought best established them as upholders of dharma, and thus worthy to rule and continue to rule.

Perhaps, as many historians have seen it, the Lokeshvara temple is indeed the pinnacle of Chalukya power. Or, perhaps, it is politics

The walls of the Lokeshvara temple, showing how they are decorated with architectural modules and miniature shrines. Note how sections of the wall appear to project out of each other at the base. The sculptures suggest that either the patron or the sculptors of the temple were well aware of Pallava models, especially the Great Penance at Mahamallapuram.

and religion turned into high art, a story, a drama, a statement of power that ignored a present that was far more complex, unfavourable and uncertain than the story it tells. Whatever its true meaning, the resources that had been poured into this enormous publicity stunt would soon be desperately needed elsewhere. For in the north, the young man whom Vikramaditya II had encouraged in his early career was about to transform the Deccan. Danti-Durga Rashtrakuta had big plans.

Part II

Apogee: The World of the Rashtrakutas

5

The Elephant Fort

Monsoon, 737 CE

Let us leave the sandstone cliffs of the Malaprabha river valley and fly north, to meet the dynasty that would bring doom upon the Chalukyas.

What might we see below us, as we traverse these untamed medieval Indian landscapes? It would mostly be the craggy, unrelenting natural beauty of the Deccan. Monsoon clouds break over the land having shed their waters over the Western Ghats. Below us are whorls of red and black soil interspersed with dry vegetation, the remnants of primeval volcanic activity; rain-fed rivers cutting through landscapes of boulders; jungles teeming with wildlife and flocks of thousands of colourful birds. Here and there, we might see tiny villages. Sometimes, along rivers, we might even see small towns, usually along trade routes or at a river ford or confluence. For all the changes we have witnessed over the last two centuries, northern Karnataka was far less urbanized than it would be in its heyday as the seat of the great empires of Vijayanagara and the Deccan Sultanates in the early modern period.

But as we fly over Maharashtra, we see a somewhat different landscape. As we enter the great valley of the Godavari river – one of the subcontinent's largest, third in size to the valleys of the Ganga and

Indus – we might see villages more frequently. We might see cities of considerable antiquity, such as Pratishthana (modern-day Paithan) and Nasikya (modern-day Nashik), where the Chalukya king Pulakeshin II had resided to consolidate his power in the region a century ago. We come across people who speak Maharashtri Prakrit, an Indo-Aryan language very different from the Dravidian Old Kannada spoken by the Chalukyas. We see ancient Buddhist cave temples and trade routes that traverse the Western Ghats, leading to bustling port towns. We see the growing pilgrimage centre of Ilapura (present-day Ellora), not too far from the Dakshinapatha trade route between northern and southern India. Swooping down into misty, rolling hills covered in forests, we would also see many Adivasi peoples, whose history, culture and languages barely survive today. But at the time, they were major power brokers. Ellora had originally been one of their sacred sites. Royals who had settled in this general region, such the Lata Chalukyas, made marriage alliances with them. And they controlled important natural resources, such as luxury woods and elephants.

Moving northwest from Ellora, we would see, in the distance, the Narmada river, where Pulakeshin II defeated Harsha. On its northern bank is Mahishmati, once the seat of power of the Kalachuris, the birth family of the Chalukya queen Loka-Mahadevi. Our view of this town is obscured by the ancient Vindhya hills, but there is a gap between them, through which traders, monks, artists, priests and armies have moved for many centuries – the Burhanpur gap. Off to the southeast of the gap near the Tapti river, close to the trade route and with an eye to the dense forests of central India, is Achalapura (modern-day Elichpur). Here, according to some scholars, the family known as the Rashtrakutas (literally 'state headman'),[1] so distant from Chalukya power at Vatapi, dreamed of empire.

The origins of the Rashtrakutas, as with the Chalukyas, are obscure. Some historians have attempted to prove, based on flimsy evidence, that they were Marathas or at least Marathis. Some even claim that they were Rajputs – though neither of these groups or categories would exist for centuries after. These anachronistic claims are driven by a need to project modern political identities onto a much more complex past: many forgotten ethnicities and groups have risen to and fallen from power in the vast history of the subcontinent, and the Rashtrakutas present a particularly unique case of this. It is most likely that they were Kannada-speaking military aristocrats settled at a strategic point in modern-day Maharasthra by the Chalukyas or some other powerful group, perhaps to keep an eye on trade routes and various tribal peoples. Their 'original' caste and ethnicity is impossible to retrieve; given their journey to imperial status, and the complex intermarriages and new self-presentations this involved – processes we have seen with the Chalukyas – it is not even relevant to their future story.

Here at the northernmost frontier of the Chalukya political network, the Rashtrakutas and the Chalukyas of Lata trod a thin line between obeying the emperor at Vatapi and defiantly pursuing their own relentless ambitions of conquest. By the time of the Chalukya Vikramaditya II's accession, the two families had already clashed once. Bhavanaga, the niece of the Lata Chalukya king Pulakeshi-Raja, defeater of the Umayyads, was married to a Rashtrakuta king. But this does not seem to have been a voluntary marriage according to some: later Rashtrakuta sources claim[2] they kidnapped her on the very day of her wedding to some other nobleman. This might just be propaganda to show them as being more 'virile' and martial than the Lata Chalukyas. And it seems the Lata Chalukyas cared little for what became of their daughter. Either way, this lady represented a major step up, maritally speaking, for the Rashtrakutas, then petty provincial warlords. Bhavanaga's father was a Chalukya, thus granting her descent from Pulakeshin II, Defeater of Harsha. Her mother may have been the daughter of an important Adivasi tribal chief.[3]

Whatever the circumstances of her marriage, Bhavanaga, in public at least, was treated with the utmost respect by her Rashtrakuta in-laws,

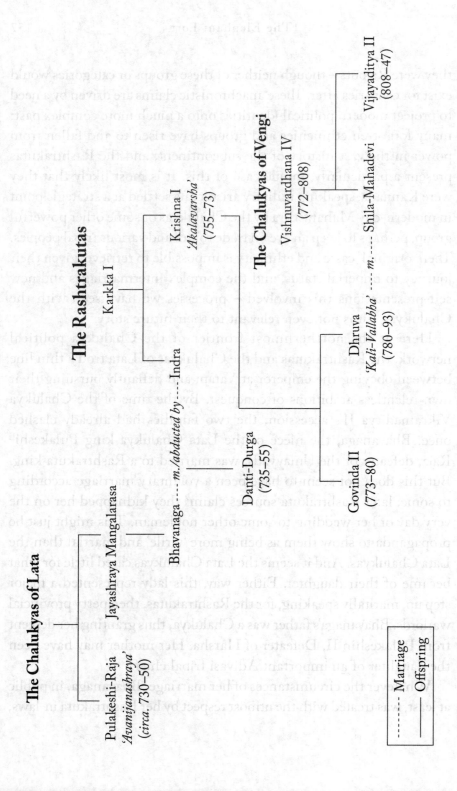

The Chalukyas of Lata

Pulakeshi-Raja
Avanijanashraya
(circa. 730–50)

Jayashraya Mangalarasa

The Rashtrakutas

Karkka I

Krishna I
'Akalavarsha'
(755–73)

Jayashraya Mangalarasa

Bhavanaga ---- m./abducted by ---- Indra

Danti-Durga
(735–55)

Dhruva
'Kali-Vallabha'
(780–93)

Govinda II
(773–80)

The Chalukyas of Vengi

Vishnuvardhana IV
(772–808)

Dhruva
'Kali-Vallabha' ---- m. ---- Shila-Mahadevi
(780–93)

Vijayaditya II
(808–47)

---- Marriage
—— Offspring

for she had (involuntarily) ennobled their line through a direct tie to the imperial clan.[4] And she seems to have reclaimed her agency over the decades as a Rashtrakuta queen – by adopting, as the Kalachuri princess Loka-Mahadevi had, the ambitions of her marital family. Unlike Loka-Mahadevi, though, Bhavanaga seems to have brought up her son, for whatever reason, to take revenge on her Lata Chalukya brothers and then her Vatapi Chalukya relations. This young man, Danti-Durga Rashtrakuta, who was probably raised on tales of his own descent from Pulakeshin II, and of the vacillation and distraction of Vikramaditya II, had in his mother Bhavanaga a powerful ally and adviser.[5] Danti-Durga was a brilliant and canny politician, receiving the title of Prithivi-Vallabha while, at least outwardly, a loyal vassal of Vikramaditya II; he was also conceited and decisive, and was a master of art and propaganda. He led one of the most astonishing lives of eighth-century India, as short as it was transformative, and he would leave the Deccan profoundly changed.

This Rashtrakuta king and his mother watched as Vikramaditya II and Loka-Mahadevi obsessed over the Pallavas and the Lokeshvara temple while the Tajikas overran Sind and Kathiawar and raided Malwa, spreading chaos and confusion. They watched as Pulakeshi-Raja, puffed up with his hard-fought victory over the Tajikas, alienated his overlords, leaving his rear exposed to them. Carefully they planned their move.

In the first part of this book we've observed first-hand how a medieval Indian kingdom was created where none had existed before, and how Sanskrit court culture was adopted by former agriculturists to aid their transformation into sophisticated aristocrats. The Rashtrakutas, starting with their eccentric young king Danti-Durga, will allow us to see in detail the inner workings of medieval Indian kingdoms and aristocrats: their savage military power, their astounding global ambitions, and their sometimes surprising humanity. To do this, we will have to peer beyond the flowery language of *prashastis* and the elaborate symbolism of art, and imagine the living, breathing people beyond the staid, upstanding, 'dharmic' image they try to portray.

When the young Danti-Durga came to the throne in the early eighth century, he and his mother Bhavanaga appear to have first set up a solid military base with which to contest Chalukya supremacy. They seem to have done this by securing the grandest symbol of Indian kingship, the tank of the premodern world, Danti-Durga's namesake: the elephant, *danti*.

By the time of Danti-Durga's accession to the Rashtrakuta throne, the Indian tradition of elephant warfare (*gaja-shastra*) was at least two thousand years old, and Indian mahouts were the envy of the world.[6] Indeed, the use of these animals for war was almost certainly an Indian invention.[7] Given the position of the Rashtrakuta kingdom – at the northern edge of the Deccan plateau, close to the dense forests of central India – Danti-Durga was perfectly positioned to capture these vital military resources.[8] One of the earliest targets of Rashtrakuta expansion seems to have been southern Chhattisgarh (then called Kosala), famed for its elephants.[9] Its rulers, probably mostly Adivasi chiefs or minor kings, were defeated and forced to pay tribute in elephants. A portion of them may have been proffered to Danti-Durga's relative and overlord, the old Chalukya emperor Vikramaditya II, to reassure him of Danti-Durga's good intentions. It is tempting to imagine a queue of the great beasts trudging the hundreds of kilometres to Vatapi, their squeals and trumpets interspersed with the yells of mahouts, the clinking of chains.

A captured elephant – a sensitive, intelligent and tortured creature – is a sorry sight. But a fully trained male war elephant in heat – musth, a state of heightened aggression and sexual energy – must have been magnificent and terrifying to gaze upon. As with those of many powerful medieval kings, Danti-Durga's elephant corps likely consisted of dozens of the animals. Cinnamon-scented fluid leaking from their temporal glands, eyes glowing,, barely restrained by the sharp goad (*ankusha*)[10] that their mahouts dug into their flesh to guide and control their aggression, flicking their man-killing trunks – all this military power gathered in one spot must have been a hair-raising sight. Massive and muscular, painted with designs and decked with garlands, long, gleaming tusks fitted with spikes, a clanging necklace of bells around the neck,[11] an elephant on the battlefield called for a very brave man (or a fool) to stand up to it.

Medieval India, of course, lacked for neither fools nor brave men to fight Danti-Durga's beloved[12] elephant corps. One such individual was his relative, Pulakeshi-Raja of the Lata Chalukyas.

Almost immediately after his victory over the Tajikas in 737, Pulakeshi-Raja was already positioning himself for a takeover of Gujarat, as his propaganda recycled elements from the *prashastis* of older ruling dynasties. He adopted for himself and his forebears the imperial title of Parama-Bhattaraka – without fully realizing how his actions would be perceived in Vatapi. Soon after, Danti-Durga, his ambitious relation, appears to have served in the Chalukya emperor Vikramaditya II's second expedition to Kanchi. The emperor seems to have encouraged the young man's ambitions of expansion[13] as a counterbalance to the increasingly independent Pulakeshi-Raja. Given what we know of Deccani women in *antahpurams*, it is easy to imagine that the Chalukya queen Loka-Mahadevi and the resentful Rashtrakuta queen mother Bhavanaga played a role in these decisions.

But as much as Danti-Durga may have loved his elephants, the real source of this Rashtrakuta's power was masterful politics and propaganda, which enabled the long-term marshalling of economic resources. The northern Deccan, especially in the regions corresponding to modern western Maharasthra, had been urbanized and irrigated for many centuries, and its trade and agricultural networks were vast and ancient – much more so than the Malaprabha river valley. This was why earlier generations of Chalukya kings had devoted considerable attention to keeping their northern frontier under their control with conquest and marriage. Old Pulakeshin II had spent so much time at the city of Nashik that a contemporary Chinese pilgrim believed it to be his capital. Vikramaditya II's father, Vijayaditya, had visited the pilgrimage site of Ilapura/Ellora during one of his northern campaigns, and handed out land there.[14] But now, it seems, the Vatapi emperor no longer had sufficient resources or attention to dedicate to the northern Deccan, relying on his vassals to do the hard work while he focused on easier targets in the south. This allowed Danti-Durga Rashtrakuta to expand his influence nearly 400 kilometres beyond his family's ancestral holdings to one of the most ancient and prestigious religious sites in the entire Deccan. In 742 CE, Danti-Durga came to the *tirtha* of Ellora. Here, we shall see how pluralistic the religious practices of medieval India really were, and observe the brilliance of its artists, propagandists, kings and monks in Ellora – a wondrous and tragically ignored centre of religious, artistic and political flowering.

⁓

Millions of years ago, the Deccan was shaped out of lava flows that engulfed the Indian subcontinent, then an enormous island, as it moved towards its collision with Asia. At Ellora, cliffs of black basalt formed out of the lava. These cliffs would eventually become an important site in the medieval period, and many generations would leave traces of the religious diversity, innovations and struggles of their world in the shrines, temples and sculptures carved here. They also illustrate the continuity of religious practices before and after the coming of kings, Brahmins, and organized temple-based and monastic cults. Though royals, through their inscriptions, portray themselves as the prime movers of all history, the truth of the matter, as we have seen, is rather more complicated.

High up above these basalt cliffs, in hills and forests, the river Ela/Aparnika flows south through sacred groves and pools, cascading into a spectacular waterfall[15] at Ellora, and thence flowing down to the river Shiva and the Godavari.[16] Aparna, 'Leafless', was the goddess of the ancient forest-dwelling peoples[17] who had called this place home for hundreds of years before the coming of Shaivas and other organized religions. Bhavanaga, Danti-Durga's mother, was possibly a descendant of these peoples.

The worship of the river and the goddess had been central to the religious practice of these Adivasis. Indeed, the worship of a river goddess continues there to this day, though Aparna's original worshippers have long since been incorporated into India's teeming, diverse masses.[18] The dominance of tribal forms of worship at Ellora, however, did not last forever. As a holy site that drew worshippers from the neighbourhood as well as itinerant merchants and preachers, it was only a matter of time before kings and chiefs, Buddhists and Brahmins, became interested in Ellora. Indeed, the earliest definite traces of Buddhist activity there can be discerned by the fourth century CE.

As Puranic, temple-based Hinduism began to spread across the subcontinent in the fifth century CE, a new religion arrived at Ellora. According to legend, a chieftain 'marked with the emblems of Shiva'[19] came to the area to find worshippers of Vishnu and the Great Goddess, Jains, assorted ascetics and gurus, and sects called Sauras and Maladharas there already. Evidently, irrespective of its tribal origins, Ellora held a magical allure for all the major sects of the medieval period, and they coexisted without too much political interference. This fifth-century Shaiva chieftain, however, is supposed to have begun the process of claiming the land for Shiva by settling Brahmins in ten villages there.[20] It would be a couple of centuries before Shaivas would dominate the site, however: Buddhists and Jains wielded considerable influence at Ellora. Cave temples carved into the basalt cliffs, often commissioned by communities of non-royal patrons, show that all these cults were served by the same architects and sculptors. They freely exchanged iconographic elements and perhaps even ritual practices,[21] contributing to 'Ellora's fame as a powerful and extraordinary place of worship'.[22]

Patrons, both royal and non-royal, paid for thriving monasteries to be cut into the primordial rock, resounding with the drone-like chants of saffron- and white-clad monks. Epigraphic evidence from the sixth century CE suggests that the early Kalachuris of Mahishmati – Loka-Mahadevi's ancestors – were involved in excavating some of the structures there. At roughly the same time, the Vatapi Chalukyas had taken over the ancient spring at Mahakuta in the Malaprabha valley and remade it in the image of their new family deity, Shiva Makuteshvara, the Crowned Lord. But as Ellora shows, royals are not always needed for the process of religious transition: medieval merchants, pilgrims and preachers were capable of profoundly transforming landscapes by themselves.

As generation after generation of *sthapatis* and patrons came and went, cave temples teeming with sculpture were carved into the primordial Earth, shallow and stiff and small in the first generations, slowly growing to titanic proportions. These elaborate compositions supported some of the most beautiful sculptures the subcontinent had yet seen. By the eighth century, Ellora's sculptors[23] had perfected a sculptural style that depicted stately deities brimming with calm energy. Ellora had many other features that set it apart from other *tirthas*, increasing its appeal for any ambitious king. It is one of the few sites in early medieval India where the Shiva linga – believed to be a symbol of primordial masculine energy – is attested to being actively worshipped by women.[24] According to a story that emerged around this time, Shiva had brought back to life the murdered son of a Brahmin woman who worshipped him at the sacred waterfall,

Anirudh Kanisetti

A Saptamatrika panel from Ellora Cave 24; note the naturalistic poses, elegant hairdos, vertical posture, and calm yet attentive mien of the goddesses.

and female worshippers continued to come to Ellora in the hope of receiving similar blessings.[25]

Through the gradual accretion of such legends, and with the growing influence of Shaivism across the subcontinent, the *tirtha* at Ellora came to be associated primarily with Shiva.[26] The ten tiny villages of the fifth century had grown into a great pilgrimage hub. Hordes of preachers and pilgrims, and the crowds of hawkers and merchants needed to feed them, were drawn there, as well as powerful kingdoms seeking to advertise their wealth and devotion.

It is little wonder, then, that when Danti-Durga set out to solidify Rashtrakuta power, he chose Ellora, associated with so many gods and peoples, as the site to do so. His land grant of the year 742 was given to Brahmins from Navasarika, the capital of the Lata Chalukyas,

The waterfall in Ellora in October 2019. Danti-Durga Rashtrakuta bathed in this lake over 1,200 years ago.

after bathing in the waters of the *tirtha*[27] – this is a waterfall that can still be seen in Ellora today during the monsoon. Just as his Vatapi Chalukya ancestors had imported Brahmins from prestigious northern India, and his Lata Chalukya grand-uncle Pulakeshi-Raja had brought them from prestigious Karnataka, so Danti-Durga imported Brahmins from the Lata Chalukya capital[28] to legitimize himself and establish himself as a royal patron.

This new kingdom of Danti-Durga's – his activities and influence now stretching from Elichpur to Ellora – spanned an area of hundreds of square kilometres, a respectable kingdom by any standard, already equivalent to those of the early Chalukya kings. But the young Rashtrakuta had goals much larger than those of the impatient Pulakeshi-Raja of the Lata Chalukyas. For what Danti-Durga was implying with his performance of the dharma of kings at this ancient site, granting land and flaunting his titles – including Prithivi-Vallabha, granted him by Vikramaditya II – was that his descent from a Lata Chalukya mother entitled him to a claim on the Vatapi Chalukya throne itself. He was declaring himself as martial, righteous, generous, a supporter of Brahmins and of religion before the eyes of the entire Deccan.

Vikramaditya II, meanwhile, was convinced he was doing the same thing – by repeatedly attacking the hapless young Pallava king and funding temples in his home territories. There can be little explanation for his complacency regarding Danti-Durga's activities and ambitions other than that he nurtured a bit of a blind spot towards the young man he saw as an ally against the Lata Chalukyas. Perhaps he was thrilled to hear the Rashtrakuta king had one-upped the headstrong Pulakeshi-Raja by inviting Brahmins from Navasarika to receive land at Ellora.

The year after Danti-Durga made his grant, 743 CE, construction of the Lokeshvara temple reached its final stages. Vikramaditya II sent a third and final expedition to attack Kanchi,[29] this time under the command of his son, Yuvaraja Kirti-Varman, attempting to establish the crown prince's credentials just as he and Loka-Mahadevi had established their own a little more than a decade earlier by attacking the Pallavas. It does not seem this expedition was anywhere near as kind to Kanchi as the one Vikramaditya himself had led a few years earlier. Danti-Durga, 'loyal' vassal that he was, was almost certainly also present in this campaign (as he may have been in Vikramaditya II's second campaign against the Pallavas), and helped himself to a fair share of the booty (he would claim, in his later years, that he had conquered Kanchi all by himself).[30] The old Vallabha Vikramaditya II, now having triumphed three times against this ancestral enemy, and having lived a most exemplary life by the standards of medieval Indian royalty, died soon after, in 745.[31] His son Kirti-Varman II was crowned soon after.

❦

The death of Vikramaditya II was exactly what Danti-Durga had been waiting for. His years as a Chalukya vassal had given him a keen understanding of how their political network worked, and acquainted him with most of the major players in the region. He also understood Vikramaditya II's enormous political miscalculations: not directly attacking the Umayyads; refusing to make his presence felt in the northern Deccan; and repeatedly attacking the already defeated Pallavas to shore up his reputation. While the ambitious Rashtrakuta king had decided not to test his luck against a well-established Vallabha with a solid support base in the southern Deccan, there was no reason not to do so with the successor. By 745, Danti-Durga had been on the throne for more than a decade. As his activities in Ellora show, he was far more confident in his power than the newly crowned Chalukya emperor Kirti-Varman II. He immediately moved to set himself up as a serious competitor to the Vatapi throne in the eyes of the rest of the imperial network.

The most spectacular way to do so was through an ostentatious display of military prowess,[32] a public declaration of his right and ability to reorder the world and uphold the dharma of kings. And so Danti-Durga's elephants headed across the Vindhyas to the ancient city of Ujjain. Ujjain had successfully withstood the raids of the Umayyads little more than a decade earlier. But by the late 740s, the region was torn by strife between two branches of the ruling clan,[33] the Pratiharas.

What the Tajikas had been unable to achieve, Danti-Durga now accomplished. His war elephants served him well in this campaign, battering down fortifications, charging down the streets, clearing the way for his infantry to secure Ujjain. As his *prashastis* tell us, 'the turreted fortresses of his enemies fell down, together with their hearts'.[34]

Now, with the eyes of half the subcontinent on him, in a city immortalized in poetry, plays and legend – a 'hallowed piece of heaven'[35] as the celebrated poet Kalidasa once called it – Danti-Durga performed the great sacrifice known as the Hiranyagarbha,[36] the 'Golden Womb'. This would establish him as an individual capable of restoring cosmic order[37] through his connection to the gods and upholding of dharma. He was doing exactly what his distant ancestor, Pulakeshin I, founder of the Chalukyas, had done almost two hundred years before with his performance of the Ashvamedha.[38] He was declaring himself a truly independent, world-ordering sovereign.

Like all the most important sacrifices, the Hiranyagarbha was a spectacle, meant to awe visitors with its performance and impress upon them the interconnected cosmic and political changes that were being enacted. Around the sacrificial pavilion, doorways of fine wood must have been set up, one in each cardinal direction, where the aristocrats of Ujjain defeated by Danti-Durga[39] were forced to stand as ceremonial gatekeepers. Ritual manuals demanded that gold coins and gems be handed out to 'the poor, the helpless, the good, the worthy, and the Brahmanas',[40] amounting to as much as 90–100 kilograms. We can imagine crowds thronging and cheering the young king as the wealth was flaunted and distributed.

The sacrificial pavilion itself probably had fire pits in each of the cardinal directions; it was most likely decorated with brightly coloured cloth banners in red, yellow, green and blue,[41] in addition to bells and the Rashtrakuta imperial emblem, which was an eagle. Brahmins dressed in white silk, wearing gold ornaments, droned on while Danti-Durga waited at the centre of the pavilion in a great golden jar emblazoned with a sun, representing the Cosmic Egg from which all Creation had sprung. The Egg used in the sacrifice that day was fashioned from 'gold in great quantity, dazzling in splendour … strung with pearls and studded with rubies'.[42] At long last, as the chanting grew to a crescendo, there was a great fanfare of trumpets and drums, and the triumphant young king emerged to the roars of crowds of onlookers. Danti-Durga would henceforth be regarded as having obtained a 'celestial body' befitting an emperor, after his rebirth from the 'Earthly body' that his mother had given him.[43] A number of ceremonies, such as the *jatakarman*, were then 'celebrated as if he was a newly born child',[44] with Danti-Durga's wife playing the ceremonial role of a mother.

The entire Hiranyagarbha ceremony was carefully planned to convince the performer and his witnesses of his rebirth and the new-found power and authority that came with it. The exhilarated Rashtrakuta distributed 'gifts of sandals, shoes, umbrellas, seats, utensils, villages, countries'[45] to his loyal vassals, to the hosts of defeated aristocrats major and minor, and the Brahmins who had gathered at Ujjain to bless him and seek his patronage, as well as the crowds who gathered to watch and cheer this spectacular royal ritual. The message was clear: the rulers of the Deccan now had not one but two potential Vallabhas to whom they could offer their loyalties. And Danti-Durga was very clearly wealthier, more powerful and more generous than the new Chalukya emperor on the throne of Vatapi.

The Rashtrakuta and his Chalukya mother Bhavanaga wasted no time in capitalizing on their position, as vassals began to flock to his eagle banner, the Garuda-*dhvaja* of Vishnu. Whatever was left of his grand-uncle Pulakeshi-Raja's rule in Lata was now overrun by Danti-Durga's rampaging forces,[46] and he boasted that 'mankind gazed intently upon the … rending asunder of the high banks of the great river Mahi and of the Reva, [the core of the Lata Chalukya kingdom] accomplished by his victorious elephants'.[47] Navasarika, once Bhavanaga's home, was seized, and a Rashtrakuta princeling installed as governor. And yet the new Chalukya emperor, Kirti-Varman II, did not respond. Meanwhile, correctly interpreting Danti-Durga's triumphant Hiranyagarbha as a moment of humiliation and dispersal for the moribund Chalukya imperial network, one of the Tamil kings led an attack on the most loyal of the Chalukyas' southern partners, the Gangas. The Chalukya emperor headed south to confront him – and was disastrously defeated in the battle of Venbai in 748.[48] His performance of royal duties now in question, he seems to have realized the only way left to stabilize his position was by defeating Danti-Durga.

By 749,[49] he was heading north, attempting to give land to loyalists: but the further he went, the less support he found. Danti-Durga was now handing out grants to his loyalists in villages and towns all across the enormous basin of the Godavari.[50] He even claimed that his mother Bhavanaga Chalukya had made land grants in 400,000 villages[51] – certainly an exaggeration, but an indication that local power brokers, Brahmins and village communities were much enthused by Rashtrakuta promises of a more just and attentive rule. The Godavari river basin, under Rashtrakuta domination, offered a much better base to a would-be Deccan empire than the Chalukya-controlled Malaprabha river valley. Growing in confidence, Danti-Durga expanded his footprint on the western coast by seizing parts of the Konkan from the Vatapi Chalukyas in 751.[52] An inscription commissioned by merchants in this region shows that they acknowledged Danti-Durga's overlordship but were not yet confident enough to call him their ultimate sovereign,[53] waiting until the struggle was resolved one way or another.

By 754, that resolution seemed imminent. The Rashtrakuta imperial network, through feverish political activity, embraced most of modern Maharashtra. Danti-Durga boasted that he had 'straightaway conquered Vallabha with a spike of wild rice that served him as a mace',[54] an indicator of how crucial control over agrarian resources was. Significantly, this claim was written in Nagari script – a distant ancestor of the modern Devanagari script used mostly in northern India at the time, a contrast to the Old Kannada script generally used by the Vatapi Chalukyas. This is the earliest known instance of this script being used south of the Narmada, and its use may have been meant to align Danti-Durga with the prestige of the Sanskrit Cosmopolis, imbuing him with what the scholar Whitney Cox calls 'imperial charisma'.[55] This reminds us, once again, of how symbols of prestige played a significant role in medieval Indian power struggles.

Danti-Durga may also have scored a few decisive victories against the Chalukyas on the battlefield, though the inscriptional evidence is hazy. As the balance of power shifted, the Rashtrakuta king set out on more propaganda campaigns to garner support. And so we return once again to Ellora for a final crowning display of Danti-Durga's imperial might. The Rashtrakuta king decided to build a more splendid edifice than had ever existed at the site, taking over a Buddhist monastery that had only just begun to be cut into the cliffs.[56]

Danti-Durga now set out, in the footsteps of the Pallava king Narasimha I, to put the Chalukyas to shame through art and architecture. He ordered the excavation of a cave temple that to this day is one of the largest in the subcontinent. Here, the artists of Ellora would give free rein to their talent with the unprecedented resources of a Deccan imperial formation – rather than those of small communities of worshippers – at their disposal. Their iconographic, compositional and sculptural talents were unleashed by this ambitious young ruler with little patience for doing things the old way.

This new temple of Danti-Durga's, which posterity would call the Dashavatara cave at Ellora, has forty-four elegant pillars[57] on its first floor. The *sthapatis* understood that there was only one major light source in the cave temple: the sun, filtering in from the façade. As you enter the temple and look deeper into the cave, your perspective shifts and refracts along a seemingly infinite expanse of pillars. As the sculptor and photographer Carmel Berkson puts it:

> like Indra's gem which reflects light from a million cut planes ... No single view can reveal the composite totality. The shifting scenes seem to be limitless. With each step ... the reality of the cave begins to change, as the participant is plummeted into different relationships with the elements in the cave, the columns, the space and the relief panels.[58]

The first aisle of pillars at the Dashavatara cave at Ellora, with the Narasimha – Hiranyakashipu panel at the end. The arrangement of pillars is almost certainly a deliberate design choice, intended to adjust the spatial and visual experience of the cave.

Your eyes are drawn to what lies straight ahead of you in the first pillared corridor. Sunlight bathes the front row of pillars with their auspicious overflowing pots, floral patterns, serpents and dwarves. As though drawn through elegant gateways, you get closer and closer to the work of a true master sculptor, of a calibre that puts the artistry of the Chalukyas' Lokeshvara temple to shame. In a panel taller than the average man, a deep cavity has been cut into the rock, around the sculpture, making it almost pop out into the open space where one stands. It is a sculpture of Narasimha, Vishnu the Man-Lion, locked in a titanic struggle with the demon Hiranyakashipu (the brother of Hiranyaksha, the demon who stole the Earth and was killed by Varaha). The stillness, the calm energy, you see in older caves at Ellora is absent here.[59] Instead, the sculptors of the Dashavatara cave have created beings *in motion*, the energy and thrust of their movement boldly positioned along diagonal axes.[60] The strictly delineated ideal proportions of orthodox *shastras* are dispensed with, imbuing a raw, primal character to the sculptures' heads, hands and feet. Though one leg of each of its protagonists has long since fallen away, at one point their feet were planted powerfully on the floor, directing their strength and energy towards the clash at the centre. The multi-armed god radiates power, the effect amplified by his many outstretched arms; his demonic rival holds a shield and a thick straight sword, leaning slightly backwards for a powerful slash. Evidently the two have been captured the very second before the god disembowels the demon. The god and the demon are likely meant to be analogies for Danti-Durga and his Chalukya rival. And this is just one among the many priceless sculptures at the Dashavatara cave. (Despite its name, it is dedicated not to Vishnu but to Shiva.)

As you approach the linga, an ancient silence descends upon you, close to the heart of the mountain.[61] In the dim light, Shiva slaughters demons, Vishnu strides over the three worlds, and a powerful Varaha bears the Earth upwards. How could anyone doubt that the person

Anirudh Kanisetti

The Narasimha–Hiranyakashipu panel at the Dashavatara cave; compare this to the Saptamatrika panel in Cave 14. Note the exaggerated proportions of the limbs and heads and the dynamism of the poses.

who created such masterpieces was any less worthy to rule over the Earth than Vishnu himself? Danti-Durga claimed for himself the full complement of Chalukya imperial titles: Sri-Prithivi-Vallabha (Fortune's Favourite, Earth's Beloved), Maharajadhiraja (Great King of Kings), Parameshvara (Supreme Lord), Parama-Bhattaraka (Foremost Revered One), Khadgavaloka (Sword Sight), Sri Danti-Durga-Raja-Deva. And perhaps he deserved them.

Danti-Durga was preparing for a final diplomatic or military offensive by 756, aiming to capture the support of the most long-standing and loyal Chalukya partners, such as the Sendrakas and the Gangas – who, being bound to them by marriage, were prepared to defend their coalition with bloody warfare. A great inscription was issued on the walls of the Dashavatara, a full-fledged Rashtrakuta imperial *prashasti*. But when the thirtieth verse was being carved, mere months before the army was due to set out,[62] disaster struck. What exactly happened, we do not know. We are only told that word of the heroic Danti-Durga had reached the heavens, and he was bombarded with the 'pressing requests of the heavenly damsels',[63] to which he understandably acquiesced.

One of the most remarkable individuals of the eighth century – administrator, publicist, diplomat, aesthete – was dead.[64] His beloved elephant corps may have lined up solemnly as his corpse, so young that it had left no heir,[65] was carried to the grand funeral pyre. The overlordship of the Deccan was not yet settled.

❧

The Chalukya Vallabha Kirti-Varman II, his morale restored by this apparent sign of divine favour, tried to bounce back. In fact, the man had never really lost hope despite Danti-Durga's activities over the 750s. While Danti-Durga had claimed control over Maharashtra by 754, Kirti-Varman had indulged in counter-propaganda, erecting a great pillar to remind his remaining vassals in the south of his credentials. The pillar was prominently positioned outside the Lokeshvara temple so that visitors would be sure to see it and, hopefully, be reminded of the prestige and achievements of his clan.

The dedicatory inscription began with an ode to the union of Shiva (Hara) and his wife Uma (Gauri), 'in which the face and breasts of the goddess are passionately kissed [caressed] by the left arm of the god',[66] drawing a parallel between Shiva and Uma and his own parents. He declared that the Lokeshvara temple was built by Loka-Mahadevi, 'who, like the divine goddess Uma, was the very mother of mankind', and that she had been the wife of Vikramaditya II, Fortune's Favourite, Earth's Beloved, 'the bruiser of the town of Kanchi'. He also restarted construction on his mother Trailokya-Mahadevi's temple, which had been in abeyance for many years after her death. Finally, the pillar attests that the emperor gave land to a learned Brahmin brought at great expense from the north bank of the Ganga,[67] and gave him responsibility over the temple built by Kirti-Varman's grandfather Vijayaditya: the Vijayeshvara, Lord of Victory. He was evidently attempting to reassure his vassals with a display of his reach, devotion and influence. It was only appropriate that some effort be put into pleasing the Lord of Victory, the lord of Vijayaditya, the Vallabha who had raided north India. Interestingly, this inscription of Kirti-Varman's – like those of his rival Danti-Durga – was in the Nagari script, suggesting that he, too, was now vying for legitimacy in the eyes of cosmopolitan elites.[68]

The year after the Rashtrakuta king's death, Kirti-Varman II finally gathered his forces and moved north, perhaps hoping to replicate his grandfather's achievements.[69]

But the Rashtrakuta family was not as fragmented as the Chalukyas might have hoped. One of their foremost military commanders – Danti-Durga's paternal uncle Krishna – seized the throne for himself. Krishna may already have fought the Chalukya emperor as a general in the early 750s, while Danti-Durga occupied the throne. Now, in 757, the long-awaited Chalukya–Rashtrakuta confrontation had arrived: and the Chalukyas found that Krishna's might could not be matched. The Rashtrakuta network was simply too vast, and its economic and military resources beyond anything the Chalukyas could hope to muster at this point. The Great Boar, according to later Rashtrakuta propaganda, 'turned into a she-deer',[70] and the last emperor of the

Vatapi Chalukyas and all his sons were killed.[71] No trace remains of how, when and where that battle was fought, but it was undoubtedly a military disaster for the Chalukyas from which there was no recovery. Krishna, we are told, 'forcibly wrested away … on the battle-field' the Goddess of Royal Fortune of the Vatapi Chalukyas,[72] 'wearing the garland of the fluttering banner in rows',[73] composed of the boar banner and all the dozens of other standards that the Chalukyas had seized from their defeated rivals over centuries. The goddess, supposedly overcome by Krishna's martial virility to the point where she was 'listless', acceded to his affections.[74] One wonders what Bhavanaga, the former Chalukya princess and mother of the dead Danti-Durga Rashtrakuta, thought of all this. At long last, she had finally had her revenge on her family.

The final defeat of the Vatapi Chalukyas sent political shockwaves through Karnataka. All of a sudden, this dynasty, which had practically become an institution over the past two hundred years, was gone – and there was almost no hope of it returning. Local rulers and strongmen – ranging from the priests of important shrines to wealthy merchants to vassal kings – had to reconsider their position and decide whether to support a Chalukya claimant or submit to this new superpower of the Deccan.

The Rashtrakutas moved quickly. Krishna Rashtrakuta, the new Vallabha, took on the majestic titles of Subhatunga (Foremost in Fortune), Akalavarsha (Rainer of Unexpected Favours),[75] and, most tellingly, Sri-Pralaya-Maha-Varaha[76] – Great Boar of the Apocalypse. For in the deluge that ended one age in an apocalyptic flood, Varaha the Great Boar had rescued the Earth from the waters, allowing for new life and the beginning of a new age. In Rashtrakuta propaganda, as Danti-Durga's successful conquests, sacrifices and temple building proved, the Chalukyas' conduct had not been righteous or strong enough. We are expected to believe that old Krishna Rashtrakuta, 'of fierce disposition towards the fierce, a mighty repository of generosity towards the poor, most dear to women',[77] was merely saving the Earth from the Chalukyas by taking it into his own hands and regenerating it with his rule. It was a strange parallel to the Chalukyas' own vicious overthrow of the Kadambas.

While there is little information of the tribulations that followed for the Chalukya family and the Malaprabha valley, we know a good deal about the horrors that the Rashtrakutas inflicted on other Deccan powers, specifically the Gangas. The Ganga rulers had been personal friends and relations by marriage of the Chalukya monarchs for generations. They were too involved with the old structure of the network, especially given their own primacy within it, to consent to a sudden shift in the political centre of gravity to the northern Deccan – which would reduce their strategic importance and thus their status in the long run. Nor did they have any reason to think they would be better off submitting to a new emperor when they themselves were such an ancient, prestigious and successful clan.

And so, war came once again to southern Karnataka, leaving its footprints in the form of families torn apart, blood spilled, homes burned and silent memorials to the dead. The Ganga ruler was a wiry and experienced old man, and, despite his defeat by the Tamils a few years earlier and the death of the Chalukya emperor, his nephew by marriage,[78] he decided to fight it out to the last breath. He assumed the title of Sri-Prithivi-Vallabha[79] and ordered the vassal kings Mutta, Nagata, Jadiya, Kitta, Pulikkada and Siyagella to marshal their forces and rally to fight the invaders.[80] They, and many of the greatest heroes of the Ganga polity – distinguished in raids against the Pallavas, celebrated warriors all – fought and died in desperate battles against the Rashtrakutas in Pinchanur, Kagemogeyur, Ogaballi and Baygeur.[81] After each one, the devastated Gangas set up hero stones to commemorate valiant dead warriors and give their deaths some sort of meaning in the chaos. Sons, brothers, uncles, commanders, subordinates – all were equal before the bloody tusks of the Rashtrakuta elephants, those gleaming swords which cut through the Ganga armies like the flames of a forest fire.

On these hero stones, the valiant dead were celebrated for their loyalty to their overlords and adherence to the dharma.[82] Decorated with flowers and cloth,[83] worshipped with blood, rice and ritual self-mutilation,[84] these memorials became rallying points for the heartbroken men who had outlived their comrades. To the sound of throbbing drums and chants, these warriors fell into trances, as they were supposedly possessed by the vengeful dead,[85] and went again and again to battle the Rashtrakutas.

But all their desperate resistance was to no avail. The hero stones of Gangavadi, the Ganga kingdom, sprang up like meadows of flowers blooming in the blood-soaked ground as Krishna Rashtrakuta systematically devastated that country, unleashing his vassals and armies to loot, sack and kill any who dared resist his authority as Vallabha, the sole superpower of the Deccan. Sacrificed to the clash were men at every level – ranging from nameless soldiers, who served only as background imagery in their commander's hero stone, to one of the Ganga king's own sons.[86] A warrior called Kittayya, who has recently become a minor celebrity after his hero stone was rediscovered, was killed by Rashtrakuta forces where the modern city of Bengaluru[87] would eventually emerge.

In 768, eleven years after the death of the last Chalukya Vallabha, the new Rashtrakuta Vallabha finally occupied the Ganga capital, Manyapura (Manne in the modern-day district of Bengaluru Rural). Krishna ordered the donation of land to Brahmins there[88] to establish his right to distribute Ganga territory as he saw fit, signalling his status as the overlord of their lands. All other imperial claims except his own now lay in bloody tatters. Like all those who had claimed the paramount sovereignty of the Deccan before him, he had proved his 'right' to seize and hold the region with violence. He had earned with blood and fire the titles of Sri-Prithivi-Vallabha Maharajadhiraja,

The Kittayya hero stone at Hebbal, Bengaluru. It depicts the warrior Kittayya (left) as he is being killed by javelins thrown by a horse-riding Rashtrakuta warrior on the right. Commissioned by a local family, the sculptural and aesthetic style of the stone is quite different from that preferred by the wealthy patrons and experienced *sthapatis* of a site like Ellora.

Fortune's Favourite, Earth's Beloved, Great King of Kings.

And so the Chalukyas of Vatapi, those sackers of Kanchi, those devotees of Shiva, those builders of mighty temples, blood-soaked, vengeful, tenacious, passed at last into history. They would raise their heads no more. All that are left of them are stories, legends, the silent testimony of the monuments they erected, the bustling of towns and markets they helped create.

But the Deccan had been transformed. The process that the Chalukyas had begun two centuries ago, gradually merging the ancient networks of the northern Deccan with those of the south through war, diplomacy and patronage, was reaching a culmination. If we look deeper, beyond the turbulent lives of all these vicious and glamorous royals – Pulakeshin I and II, Vikramaditya I and II, Loka-Mahadevi, Bhavanaga, Pulakeshi-Raja, Danti-Durga, Krishna Rashtrakuta – we can see a profound change in the ambitions and worldview of the peoples of the Deccan. A vast imperial formation now stretched from the Narmada to the borders of the Tamil country – a tapestry weaving together rich market towns, multicultural ports, thriving cities, dense forests, expanding irrigation networks, growing temples and intensifying political, social and cultural complexity – under the firm grasp of ruthless and powerful Kannada-speaking emperors.

It was now time for the Deccan to terrify and astonish the subcontinent and the world.

6

To Kailasha

Winter, 769 CE

With Gangavadi in flames, Vatapi cowed, and Chalukya blood flowing in the Malaprabha river, Krishna Rashtrakuta returned in triumph to Ellora, increasingly a centre of Rashtrakuta power.[1]

We cannot know what may have occupied his mind, as the great army of the Rashtrakutas and their vassals returned to their homes to enjoy their new wealth and prominence. But we do know of one idea he had. Krishna Rashtrakuta, Fortune's Favourite, needed to prove his newly imperial dynasty's authority and dominance in all directions, in all ways. He thus decided to commission at Ellora a temple of such stupendous scale and craftsmanship that it would humble all that had come before. This temple dedicated to Krishna Rashtrakuta's lord, Shiva Krishneshvara, needed to be twice as massive as the Lokeshvara at Pattadakal, eclipsing the crowning glory of the Vatapi Chalukyas. Its iconography would showcase the latest Shaiva innovations and ideas, thus making it a great engine for the development of Shaivism, now the Deccan's royal religion par excellence.

The Krishneshvara would be a radical departure from its predecessors. It would not be assembled painstakingly from carved

183

and jointed panels. Rather, it would be *excavated* straight down a colossal basalt hill at Ellora. A gigantic mass of rock was to be isolated and carved to make the Krishneshvara – a building that was really a sculpture, a cave temple of hitherto unimagined proportions and complexity. In comparison, the cave temples of the early Vatapi Chalukyas would be damp, unimaginative grottos, and Narasimha Pallava's temple monoliths at Mahamallapuram mere pebbles. But we will return to the Krishneshvara temple soon. For the moment, suffice it to say that by leaving the architectural, iconographic and religious 'arms races' of the Chalukyas and Pallavas in the dust, it was intended to proclaim to the subcontinent that the Rashtrakutas were the wealthiest, most martial, most devoted to Shiva of all south Indian royal clans; the most deserving to rule the peoples of the Deccan and to claim the supreme authority and ornate regalia of sovereign emperors.

But the Rashtrakutas were not the only Indian superpowers interested in making claims to unprecedented supremacy at this time. In Rajasthan, Malwa and Gujarat, a clan calling themselves the Pratiharas, Keepers of the Gateways, managed to consolidate power. They previously had been forced by Danti-Durga Rashtrakuta to serve as his 'doorkeepers' in the great Hiranyagarbha sacrifice that he performed in Ujjain. ('Doorkeeper' was a cruelly appropriate pun on their title.) But now, by slowly expanding their power towards the fertile Gangetic plains, the Pratiharas were becoming one of the most successful polities that north India had seen since Harsha's death nearly two hundred years earlier; they, like the Rashtrakutas, claimed the title of Maharajadhiraja.

Indeed, Harsha's ghost still loomed large over the turbulent north. His capital, Kannauj, like Delhi a thousand years later, had become the ultimate prize, the crown jewel that any would-be emperor of northern India had to control. Commanding a geopolitical crossroads between the fertile lands of Punjab and the Gangetic plains, armies and adventurers from Kashmir to Malwa had flocked to Kannauj in the centuries since Harsha's death. Even the Tajikas had made an abortive attempt to seize the city before being routed by one such adventurer.[2] But by the eighth century, most rulers of Kannauj tended to control little more than the vast city itself. They must have watched with trepidation the growth of powers like the Pratiharas and others, such as the Karkotas of Kashmir, and far to the east in Bengal, the Palas. Unlike the Rashtrakuta and Pratihara clans, who came from fairly well-established military aristocracies, the Palas were almost certainly commoners. Near-contemporary sources describe them as either belonging to the 'menial' castes, or as being administrators and scribes. Their birth was no barrier to the growth of their power, however, as the Palas successfully consolidated the fertile and populous eastern Ganga valley, declared themselves emperors and began to look beyond. From across these vast, lush, and urbanised territories, they began to wrestle with the Pratiharas for influence and control. Kannauj was crucial to both polities: controlling it would help secure the Pratiharas' northwest frontier and offer a useful staging ground for campaigns into the Gangetic plains; to the Palas, it would secure their control over the vast river system while offering a route into Central Asian markets.

By the late eighth century, these once-regional kingdoms were, like the Deccan, emerging as subcontinental superpowers. Their rulers were no longer interested in merely being acknowledged by the petty rajas and maharajas of their immediate neighbourhood. Now, their superiority needed to be recognized by the defeat and conquest of their equals and rivals, the *maharajadhirajas*. This, they imagined, would grant them primacy over *all* the dynastic polities that constituted their world. In the late eighth century, as geopolitical tension crackled in the air, these dominant polities of eastern and western India circled

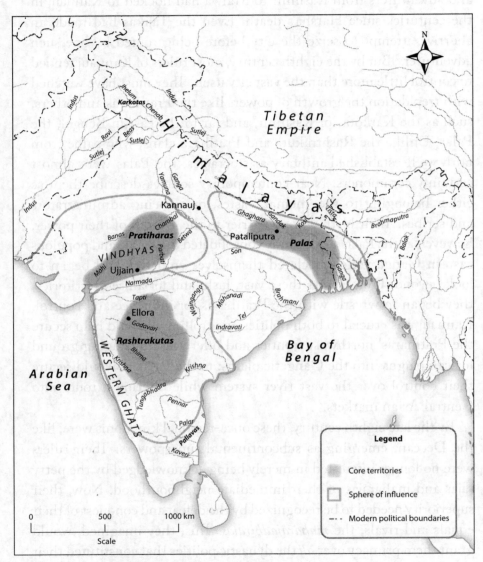

The imperial formations of South Asia, late eighth century CE.

Harsha's old capital and dreamed of undisputed supremacy. And, meanwhile, south of the Narmada, the lord of the Deccan watched them both carefully and made his plans.

~

Every few centuries or so, at least in the premodern period, a constellation of factors comes together and an explosion of art follows. We've seen this before with the artistic competition of the Chalukyas and Pallavas, and met the talented masters Mandhatar of Mahamallapuram and Gundan of Pattadakal. It is a tragedy that when one of southern India's most extraordinary such confluences came together, we do not know the name of the person or persons who designed the greatest marvel of the time: the Krishneshvara temple at Ellora, known today as the Kailashanatha temple or Cave 16.

Let us briefly dwell on this enigmatic building, which to this day inspires awe and wonder in sightseers, emotions we certainly share with its long-forgotten eighth-century visitors. Why did this Nameless *Sthapati*, as we shall call him, shape the Krishneshvara this way?

This man was most likely a veteran of Ellora's sculpture and architecture industry, and may even have worked with Danti-Durga on his innovative Dashavatara cave temple.[3] Ellora before the Rashtrakutas was a small, if bustling, sacred centre; after the Rashtrakutas commissioned the Krishneshvara and began to frequent the site, the glamour and wealth of this medieval imperial court must have reshaped the contours of the town. What must it have been like for the Nameless *Sthapati* to meet his new colleagues, the guilds of northern Karnataka and the Tamil country, that came to Ellora attracted by Rashtrakuta blood money? What were the streets of Ellora like when full of Rashtrakuta warriors, rowdy and drunk, or crowded with impoverished labourers in huts of mud and thatch? Large-scale excavations are desperately needed across the Ellora UNESCO World Heritage Site for more information.

Whatever his experiences with Krishna and the Rashtrakutas, the Nameless *Sthapati* struck upon a genius design to meet the Vallabha's vision. Had he simply doubled the size of the Lokeshvara at Pattadakal and carved it into a hill, the bottom part of the temple would have been damp and in perpetual darkness, ruining the spatial experience of circumambulation and rendering it ineffective. The Nameless *Sthapati* solved this by excavating in the rock hill a truly gigantic cavity, leaving there a temple of humongous proportions. It would stand on a much higher plinth than ever used in either northern or southern temples,[4] an entire storey by itself, boosting the main structure into the open space of the excavated cliff and exposing both the ground floor and the first floor to sunlight. The first floor would carry the main shrine, hall, secondary shrines and the primary spire – a tiered Dravidian superstructure, the farthest north this design had ever appeared. The

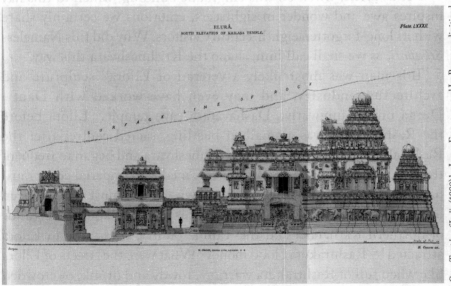

Cave Temples of India (1880) by James Fergusson and Jas Burgess, digitized by the University of Heidelberg

An elevation of the Kailashanatha or Krishneshvara temple at Ellora, as seen from the south. The entire structure seen here is a single colossal monolith, an architectural sculpture. The human silhouettes have been added for scale.

elevated bottom storey, plinth included, would be decorated with imposing sculptures almost twice the height of a man, creating a dramatic aesthetic juxtaposing the raw cliff side, towering monolith and bright sky. The scale of the excavation needed to execute this plan was unprecedented in the subcontinent: 2 million cubic feet of rock had to be removed,[5] leaving behind a temple that would be one of the largest constructions of the eighth-century world, and certainly the largest free-standing structure in the Indian subcontinent at the time.

An undertaking such as the Krishneshvara could only have been imagined by an individual who had imbibed the knowledge of generations of cave temple makers, with logistical, sculptural and iconographic solutions for diverse patrons and religions. It could only have been paid for by the resources of a vast imperial formation with something to prove. And it could only have been made with the help of teams of talented priests, monks and sculptors, coming from rich artistic and religious traditions across southern India. All of these, which we have observed evolve over the last few chapters, had congregated in Ellora by the late eighth century.

But a temple is not merely the work of architect, patron, sculptor and labourer. As a gigantic curation of religious art, it also requires the services of the priest. A temple like the Krishneshvara offers hundreds if not thousands of surfaces for decoration, and there must have been teams of *sthapatis* and priests who worked together to curate and assign elements to each surface. These were layered in striking ways: the roof of the temple, for example, features four roaring lions facing the ordinal directions (northeast, southeast, southwest, northwest), their powerfully muscled paws gripping a large lotus. This was probably meant to reflect the Rashtrakutas' military supremacy over the rest of their world, and may have had other meanings that have since been lost. The priests who worked with the *sthapatis* were most likely members of the school or monastery that was on the ascendant at the

Rashtrakuta court at the time, and were plugged into the latest ritual, scriptural and mythological developments of Deccan Shaivism. The Krishneshvara's sculptures thus also offer us a snapshot of Hinduism in evolution in the eighth century, a topic we will return to.

Finally, how did the Nameless *Sthapati* actually carve out this architectural sculpture? Contemporary architects tend to think he deliberately chose a part of the Ellora hills with a relatively gentle incline and turned it into a ramp. At or near its top, a football field-sized rectangle was carved *into* the rock so that it paralleled the ground, creating a 'floor' for sculptors to work on, hundreds of feet above ground level. This plane, including the top of the ramp, was then meticulously carved downwards towards the ground foot by foot, leaving, at every level, a large block of the correct size and shape in the middle for sculptors to carve. The slope was retained till the very end, to dispose of the debris of the carving.[6] One can imagine that extreme care needed to be taken with measurement, alignment, demarcation and carving to ensure that the design of the temple

Archaeological Survey of Western India, Vol. V: Report on the Elura Cave Temples (1883) by

A transverse section of the Kailashanatha or Krishneshvara temple. Observe the multi-storeyed design and the large plinth, designed to lift the entire structure into the light. Carving out multiple storeys both downward and laterally into the rock, at such a scale, must have presented enormous logistical challenges. The human silhouettes have been added for scale.

remained intact throughout the process. This hints at a powerful grasp of mathematical, architectural and engineering principles.

The actual execution of the project was a logistical and managerial challenge unprecedented in the subcontinent, if one does not count military campaigns. The Krishneshvara's main designers and executors were almost certainly a multi-ethnic, multilingual, highly experienced and self-confident group of individuals. They had to figuratively dive downwards into the black rock, and trust that they could collectively deal with the challenges that were sure to arise[7] in the years to come as they fashioned this 150-foot-tall monolith. And so sometime in the late 760s, this group of people set out to make a wonder of the world.

The excavation of the temple must have been an impressive sight. As the rough surfaces of the temple emerged, level by level, foot by foot, ever larger teams of master sculptors were brought in to work on more surfaces simultaneously. Meanwhile, toiling labourers removed chunks of rock around them in layers, rolling them down the gentle incline of the hill. No scaffolding was needed for the sculptors or the debris removal[8] as the temple gradually took shape, every level being finished before the next was excavated. We can imagine that arguments and fights broke out as tempestuous master sculptors declared that they would do things their way and no other. Or, perhaps, new friendships and loves blossomed as they delighted in the creativity of their peers, and Ellora resounded with the sound of laughter and feasts and weddings between clans who would never otherwise have met.

By the time the Krishneshvara's sculptors finally reached the bottom floor, the project had gathered together the greatest sculptors of the subcontinent and kept them rich and well fed and busy for around twelve years, allowing them to learn from and compete with each other. Together, they unleashed a flourishing of artistic ability[9] that is among the most extraordinary legacies of the medieval Deccan.

We will return to see this, alongside the Rashtrakuta kings who commissioned it, towards the end of this chapter.

∽

Ellora's architects were not the only Deccanis busy with grand and world-shaping deeds in the late eighth century. In 769, soon after brutally forcing the Gangas to submit, Krishna Rashtrakuta made sure that the Chalukyas of Vengi, the only royal Chalukyas left standing, could not make their own bid for sovereignty in the Deccan. His sons were ordered to lead an army into the fertile coastal lands of Andhra.[10] This pair, Govinda and Dhruva Rashtrakuta, Danti-Durga's cousins, had probably been partners in the project of overthrowing the Vatapi Chalukyas from its very inception. But though the Rashtrakutas' sovereignty was very much a family enterprise, like most medieval polities tended to be, they were not directly in the line of succession in Danti-Durga's lifetime. At best, they might have expected a life as generals or provincial governors under Danti-Durga and his heirs. The young Rashtrakuta king's sudden death, and his uncle Krishna's successful bid for the throne, had led to an abrupt change of fortune.

By 769, the brothers almost certainly had quite a reputation in south Indian circles thanks to the sudden shock of their defeat of the Vatapi Chalukyas. The younger, Dhruva, was a ruthless warlord, who preferred to be called Kali-Vallabha, Strife's Beloved.[11] The Vengi Chalukyas, despite their vaunted ancestral name, very astutely decided not to test him and instead threw themselves on the mercies of Dhruva's gentler elder brother, Govinda.[12] Soon after,[13] Dhruva, who already had two sons[14] by an earlier wife, was married to the Vengi Chalukya princess Shila-Mahadevi. She was almost two decades his junior, being in her late teens.

The Vallabha Krishna Rashtrakuta would not live to see the completion of his magnificent temple.[15] His death in 773, followed by the accession of Govinda II, gave these newlyweds an opportunity to seize power. Dhruva was appointed governor of Nashik and Khandesh,[16] two critical territories. However, it seems he began to put out word that Govinda had given himself to a life of pleasure and debauchery, and was getting too friendly with the vassals of the Rashtrakutas, instead of devoting himself to his royal dharma and strengthening the kingdom through war.[17] It does seem that the Gangas were already preparing a challenge to Rashtrakuta power, or that the political situation was otherwise sensitive enough that many grandees saw Dhruva as offering better solutions than his elder brother. After some deft politicking, Dhruva attempted to issue his own independent land grants, without referring to the authority of Govinda.[18] This challenge provoked an immediate response from Govinda, who stripped his younger brother of his titles. Now claiming to be the aggrieved party, Dhruva rebelled and led a coup d'état against the Vallabha. Govinda II, like so many who had held the throne of the Deccan before him, vanished into darkness.

In 780, Dhruva Rashtrakuta and his wife Shila-Mahadevi were ritually crowned.[19] Shila-Mahadevi, the young Chalukya princess from Vengi whose Vatapi relations had been overthrown by the Rashtrakutas, seems nevertheless to have convinced Dhruva to allow her a degree of prominence similar to that of Loka-Mahadevi, her distant Kalachuri predecessor as the Deccan's most powerful queen. Soon after his coronation, she was probably also invested with a magnificent coronet called the *patta-bandha*, thus attaining the enviable status of *patta-mahadevi*, the highest possible status for any Indian queen still associated with a king[20] (queens who ruled in their own right – of which we have examples from medieval Odisha and Kashmir – preferred to simply use the male title of maharaja or *maharajadhiraja*). A *patta-bandha*, possibly adapted from earlier Persian styles,[21] was a 'fillet or band-like piece of silken cloth or gold which was fixed around the head and displayed … on the forehead'.[22] This investiture was part of a consecration ritual of its own, which conferred on the queen 'either the gift of land, sovereignty or other powers'.[23] By awarding Shila such a status, Dhruva was essentially proclaiming her as his equal partner in the cosmic powers he had attained through various coronation rituals.[24]

The new Rashtrakuta emperor now set out to perform a *digvijaya*, the Conquest of the Directions or Quarters, the greatest possible achievement for any warlike dharma-upholding crowned monarch. It was the act by which he could reconstitute the circle of kings around him, the *raja-mandala*, the network of medieval India's many violent and competing polities, into 'an imperial formation, a single polity'.[25] His armies would subjugate the Four Quarters, and loot and conquer and reorder them as his position as Fortune's Favourite demanded. Over the next decade, Dhruva would begin the process of expanding the Deccan's influence to proportions it would not reach again until the rise of the Marathas, a thousand years later. In order to do this, however, Rashtrakuta power needed to be secured once again against any challengers. It is difficult to reconstruct this process in detail, but it seems that by 786/87, Rashtrakuta forces had completed raids into southern Karnataka and Tamilakam, brutalizing what remained of the unfortunate Pallavas. One Rashtrakuta poet had a picturesque way of putting it: the Pallava king surrendered as he saw he was trapped between the two oceans that were the Rashtrakuta army and the Bay of Bengal.[26]

On 27 September 786, the day after a total solar eclipse, the empress Shila-Mahadevi, having bathed and purified herself, ordered her personal officers to execute a land grant to some Brahmins. She, like Dhruva, seems to have travelled around with her own personal court, her ladies-in-waiting – the wives or daughters of vassal kings – as well as administrators, tax collectors, messengers, scribes and panegyrists.[27] On this brisk September day, she ordered the engraving of a powerful *prashasti*, allowing us a glimpse of this eighth-century queen's relationship with her husband and the marvellous possibilities of the Sanskrit language which aristocrats like herself used. The empress announced:

> As (Dhruva) subjected forts which were the essence of the three worlds, augmented his fame by stopping the flow of the Ganga, and made his own the prosperity of the [Pallava] ruler exalted by the bull-banner, he alone in this world displayed the quality of *Parameshvara* [Paramount Lordship] clearly and powerfully.[28]

Though the Sanskrit double meanings have been lost in translation, the subtle parallel between Dhruva and the god Shiva is apparent. The 'flow of the Ganga', the river entwined in Shiva's locks, is an allusion to how Dhruva had entrapped and stopped the Ganga family. The defeat of the Pallavas, who used the bull banner, added to his glory.[29] Only *her* world-conquering husband was worthy of being a true king, worthy of paramountcy, said the young empress. It would seem that Shila was not exaggerating. By 788, the Rashtrakuta royal pair finally crushed the Gangas and imprisoned the young Ganga king.[30] Dhruva's eldest surviving son was appointed the ruler of Gangavadi. His father-in-law ruled in Vengi, securing his eastern flank. The roaring waves of the Arabian Sea secured his west. The Indian subcontinent south of the Narmada river was now pacified: the Gangas, Cholas, Cheras, Pandyas and Vengi Chalukyas had all submitted, as had hosts of minor kings and chiefs. Dhruva had come very close indeed to a successful Conquest of the Directions, one of the duties of the 'ideal' ruler. But this was hardly enough for this ambitious and power-hungry warlord, perpetually on the hunt for opportunities to expand and aggrandise himself.

In the late 780s,[31] when Dhruva Rashtrakuta's position in the Deccan was finally secure, a tiny event set off a chain reaction leading to an explosive confrontation between medieval India's superpowers. The kingdom of Kashmir – a pugilistic and culturally sophisticated Himalayan power – raided Kannauj, imprisoning its king. As the Kashmiris attempted to ransom him, the Pratihara emperor Vatsaraja advanced to the city and set up his own candidate on the throne; he thus announced that the Pratiharas were claiming the sovereignty of north India, and that they saw the fertile Gangetic plains as their rightful sphere of influence.

The Palas immediately retaliated by choosing their own candidate to the throne of Kannauj. The Pala emperor, Dharmapala, moved west to install him at the head of an army of his own, but Vatsaraja Pratihara was ready and waiting. The Palas were defeated – though not conclusively – and driven away. The two white imperial umbrellas which were symbols of Pala sovereignty were gleefully seized by Vatsaraja, whose claim to north Indian supremacy now seemed indisputable.

Meanwhile, Dhruva Rashtrakuta had been carefully observing these events unfolding hundreds of kilometres away, and saw an opening. The overconfident Vatsaraja had left his southern flank, Malwa, completely exposed – a critical strategic error. We do not know the precise details of what followed. Did Dhruva initially set out only to conquer Malwa, or was he always planning on securing a symbolic submission from the two arrogant north Indian monarchs? How much did he know of what had happened between Vatsaraja and Dharmapala, and how did he plan his logistics and route of advance to confront them? Did his army consist of Rashtrakuta forces alone, or did vassal kings – such as his father-in-law, the Chalukya king of Vengi – join in?

All we know for certain is that the Rashtrakuta Vallabha did indeed march to war. Rituals were performed beforehand, astrologers consulted, plans made, and a great army of infantry, elephantry and cavalry was gathered and ordered to march. Along with the troops followed thousands of labourers, cooks, physicians, dancers, musicians, courtesans, poets, panegyrists, priests and preachers,[32] the army stretching out for many kilometres, shaking the Earth, advancing like an immense, noisy, colourful serpent. Harsha, Lord of the North, had so fatefully crossed the Narmada into the Deccan almost exactly one hundred and eighty years earlier. Now Dhruva, Lord of the South, crossed the same Narmada from the Deccan into north India. How the tables had turned: the time had come for the Deccan, which once trembled at north India's might, to terrify that ancient seat of empires.

It would not have been long before the Pratihara emperor Vatsaraja, concerned about the loss of his core territories, rushed to confront Dhruva. The precise location and date of their collision are unclear, but it is likely to have occurred somewhere in northern Malwa, perhaps near Vidisha or Jhansi, before Dhruva could erupt into the Gangetic plains. It was probably one of the most spectacular set-piece battles of the medieval period: a head-on collision between two almost equally brash and untested Indian imperial powers, two equally power-hungry warlords.

What might this climactic battlefield have looked like? We might see two immense armies arrayed to face each other as huge drums are beaten, trumpets and conch shells blown in a 'tumultuous uproar'.[33] Perhaps the might of southern India was gathered there that day: men from the many kingdoms and provinces of Maharashtra, Karnataka, the Konkan, Andhra and Tamilakam. The vast majority were certainly on foot, while some were mounted on elephants from dense jungles, others on horses from Arabia or Persia across the ocean. Mercenaries and troops of elite aristocratic families, in clean, organized lines, may have rubbed shoulders with crowds of levied farmers, pastoralists and artisans. All must have been gathered there that day with banners and standards and round shields painted with animals and flowers, long hair tied into topknots and side knots, loins girded with bright cotton cloth.

A description of what may be the ferocious infantry maintained by the Rashtrakuta imperial household survives today: their wavy black hair was fastened with vibrant cloth bands tied around their foreheads, their bare chests draped in 'triple necklaces made of many-coloured beads',[34] and their forearms, up to the elbows, covered in thick iron bracelets. Their legs were covered in loincloth tucked around their knees, a band around the waist held a dagger, and their hands clasped their weapon of choice – anything from a mace to a sword. Rashtrakuta murals from the eighth and ninth centuries also depict light cavalry: sword-wielding riders wearing Persian caps and armour made of overlapping scales, riding expensive imported steeds festooned with ribbons.[35] Such warriors were organized in complex, overlapping hierarchies – language, region, overlord, caste and many others – culminating in Dhruva himself, a stocky, muscular old man with a hairy chest[36] seated on a mighty elephant. The aristocrats and generals surrounding Dhruva must have watched their opponents silently amidst a host of banners, including the imperial *pali-dhvaja*, the Banner in Rows, featuring the Rashtrakuta Garuda and other glittering emblems. Eventually, the *pataha* and *dhakka*[37] drums broke into a roar like the ocean in a raging storm, while embroidered and painted flags and banners snapped and waved.

Studies of medieval warfare suggest that the two vast armies then advanced slowly, watching each other for the slightest gap or vulnerability. When they came within range of each other, flocks of barbed arrows were launched, and then javelins and stones, continuing for a few hours to attempt to wear down the enemy and score a few easy kills. The first screams of pain and the first cries for help were heard, the first spatters of blood appeared. The infantry then advanced steadily to clash, building up momentum like a huge wave, attacking each other in compact rectangular or square[38] formations, pushing and shoving at each other, stabbing and chopping at any exposed individuals or body parts.[39] This lasted for about 20 minutes,[40] after which both sides withdrew for a brief rest, screaming insults at the other, flinging missiles, and dragging back their dead and wounded – as well as any well-adorned enemy corpses that could be looted. They then charged again when sufficiently prepared. This cycle played out over many hours: battles were long-drawn-out affairs.

Here and there, we might see small elite squadrons of war elephants or cavalry charging at each other, opening up into 'alleys' so that their riders could duel. In other areas, bloodthirsty elephants may have smashed into and trampled down crowds of men, routing them and leaving them to be cut down by Rashtrakuta light cavalry. Among these daring and deadly warriors may have been Dhruva and Shila-Mahadevi's son, the heir apparent Govinda, who would later rise to the Rashtrakuta throne as Govinda III and repeat his father's military exploits.

The screams of maddened elephants, of horses whose bellies had been punctured by sharp spears, and of dying men missing limbs or drowning in pools of their own blood, filled the skies. Every now and then, the drumbeats might change tempo, a horn would be heard through the madness, and one unit would withdraw, only to be replaced by another. The average foot soldier knew little more than chaos, dust, blood, pain, terror and the thrill of a kill, of survival, of booty. Tactics and strategy were reserved for the men sending them to their deaths sitting on elephants well behind the front line.

As the battle wore on, the neat formations seen at dawn probably turned into a bloody, confused mess. Huge clouds of dust suffocated the increasingly exhausted warriors and animals as Dhruva and Vatsaraja sent them to their deaths in their contest for supremacy. But more than either emperor, the outcome of any battle was determined by the force of crowd psychology. Which side could convince people on the other that they would be slaughtered if they didn't run away? On that day, the answer to that was the Rashtrakuta side: the collapse of the Pratihara forces appears to have been sudden, not a planned retreat in any way (even if it started as such).[41]

The ferocious Deccan army pressed the advantage as panic spread through the north Indian army, and a fatal rout set in. For Dhruva to have a free hand in Malwa or a secure road onward to Kannauj, he could leave absolutely no Pratihara forces intact, and there seems to have been a brutal slaughter. Vatsaraja was chased away, leaving behind him the dust of the battlefield, the dust of his ambitions, and the two precious imperial umbrellas he had so gleefully seized from the Pala emperor.[42] The Pratihara fled deep into the deserts of Rajasthan,[43] where he was safe but also too distant to be anything more than a nuisance to the victorious Deccanis until his shattered forces were able to rest, recover and regroup. Dhruva, however, had no time to lose. Perhaps it only now dawned on him that such a decisive victory offered him a way to claim dominance over the entire subcontinent.

When the Rashtrakuta army, victors over the Deccan, victors over the south, victors over the west, finally burst on to the Gangetic plains – where the subcontinent's mightiest empires had risen and fallen for a thousand years already – they found one last challenger waiting. The Pala emperor Dharmapala may not have expected Dhruva to defeat Vatsaraja so decisively, and seems to have planned to seize Kannauj while the two were at each other's throats. He may even have entertained ambitions of reclaiming his lost umbrellas, which Dhruva had now brought with him after seizing them from Vatsaraja; perhaps he thought the southern Indian army would be too tired to mount any sort of effective resistance. He was in for a rude shock: not only did Dhruva successfully drive him off, but he also relieved the Pala of the two *new* umbrellas he had brought to the battlefield![44]

The capture of all these umbrellas might seem trivial to us, but it was hugely significant in the symbol- and status-obsessed worlds of medieval Indian courts. An imperial parasol, gleaming white, jewel-encrusted, was as representative of a ruler's sovereignty as his crown. Dhruva's victories and capture of the imperial regalia of the Pratiharas and the Palas signified that he was now their overlord – which technically made him paramount sovereign of all India. In the space of barely a year, this second son, this king's cousin, Fortune's Favourite, Strife's Beloved, had emerged as the most powerful ruler in the entire Indian subcontinent. In doing so, a Deccan ruler had now become one of the medieval world's most powerful individuals.

The Metropolitan Museum of Art, New York

A seated Tara, a Buddhist saviour goddess, from the Pala period. Bengal and Bihar remained strongholds of Buddhism till the late twelfth–early thirteenth centuries. Unlike in southern India, Buddhism in the region retained its relevance for the state through incorporating tantric ritual ideas. The Pala rulers were major patrons of tantric Buddhism.

And so the Rashtrakuta Vallabha, his Conquest of the Directions complete, his dominance over the subcontinent symbolically and violently established, returned to the Deccan to celebrate his triumph. With him went the treasuries of the Pratihara and Pala emperors and many new additions to the Rashtrakuta *pali-dhvaja*. To the high central flagstaff mounted with the image of 'Garuda, the eagle, Vishnu's emblem'[45] were tied in each cardinal direction, at heights corresponding to their rank, rows of banners of the kings of the subjugated directions of the Rashtrakuta world. The Pandya fish, the Pallava bull, the Chola tiger, the Chalukya boar and the Chera bow of the south now shared space with the Pratihara Lakshmana (brother of the god-king Rama), and the Pala Tara (a Buddhist goddess),[46] representing the extraordinary prowess and military dominance of Fortune's Favourite. But now all these were shifted to the side in favour of two resplendent new additions. Henceforth the Rashtrakuta *pali-dhvaja* would also carry a banner symbolizing the Ganga and the Yamuna rivers, a reminder, a boast, of overlordship over the whole of north India.

❧

In the year 792 the Rashtrakuta imperial family may have held a festival at the Krishneshvara.

The monumental temple, by now finished, was oriented almost perfectly to the west.[47] Anyone standing in front of it in the darkness of the early morning saw the sun rise from behind the magnificent black cliffs like the temple's halo, ascending to a great din of clanging bells and throbbing drums. Soon, crowds may have started to appear, thronging into the dozens of cave temples at Ellora, staring at the murals, silently praying, giving gifts to their gods, asking for blessings. As the sun climbed higher, Ellora's cliffs must have grown noisier and noisier. In rowdy dirt arenas, animals fought and wrestlers wrangled as bets were made and audiences cheered; there could have been plays, dances and musical performances as well.[48] Princes and ministers wearing *patta* fillets and coronets came with their retinues, preceded by the *pancha-maha-shabdas* – the Five Great Instruments, the horn, conch, drum, victory bell and something called a 'tammata' (whose meaning is unclear).[49] These were granted exclusively to the highest ranks of the Rashtrakuta imperial network, and were loudly sounded to warn the crowds to stay out of the way of these lords of the great houses.[50] If they were important enough, they would have had a small coloured parasol of their own, and perhaps one or two attendants with a *chauri*, the fly whisk made of a yak's tail.[51] Sometime during the day, the emperor Dhruva himself may have put in an appearance, in the company of vassal kings, ministers, chamberlains and attendants. His splendour eclipsed all his subordinates, marking him out as many times wealthier and more prominent. Dhruva might have looked in many ways like the classical Indian king we imagine; in other ways, he certainly was not.

Above his head was held aloft a huge parasol of white silk, adorned with gold and precious gems; on his head was a tall, heavy gold crown, perhaps encrusted with rubies and carved with fantastic creatures; his chest was covered with thick necklaces of pearls, gold, jewels, and fragrant garlands of rare flowers; his mouth was probably red with exotic betel.[52] Behind him was a crowd of gorgeous female attendants in the finest of clothes, fanning him with *chauris*, fluttering around his shoulders like birds.[53] Shila-Mahadevi may have been present, attended by the wives of Dhruva's vassals,[54] and her sons, the heirs,[55] attended by the sons of Dhruva's vassals. The Nameless *Sthapati*, his head covered with a turban and fillets of honour, was in all likelihood also part of this parade. All these people were probably resplendent in festive finery, with elaborate garlands and coiffures and make-up.

The crowds must have cheered, clapped and gawked at the procession, drinking in the sight of the tall, well-fed men and women, the handful of elite, sophisticated, ruthless families that ruled them now and would do so for generations after. They must have almost seemed to have descended from a heavenly world, perfumed water sprinkled before them, fans waving, music playing and women dancing before their splendid parade in the sweltering heat. Though the masses were unlikely to have been allowed into the priceless Krishneshvara, worth hundreds of millions of dollars in today's currency, Dhruva's retinue were welcomed obsequiously into its hallowed portal. They would immediately have been struck by the remarkable *experience*, the tangible presence of divinity, that the Nameless *Sthapati*'s design unfolded before their eyes.[56]

Let us join them as they step through the shadowed gateway of the monolithic temple. They see a sunlit panel welcoming them in, a relief of that same Royal Fortune whom Krishna Rashtrakuta had supposedly seized on the battlefield: the goddess Sri or Lakshmi, the emblem of Indian kingship, accompanied by royal elephants showering her with water – signifying the ablution that accompanied the royal consecration. She is seated on a field of lotus leaves, which the sculptor

The royal goddess Sri or Lakshmi, attended by elephants and two colossal deities guarding the entrance to the Krishneshvara.

cunningly carved to give the illusion of perspective and depth to the relief: the pads at the bottom are larger than the ones higher up, thus drawing the viewer's eyes towards the goddess. From darkness to light, the goddess seems to say. From the mundane world to the divine world.[57] Dhruva would then have taken a left into the sun-drenched courtyard. There stands an immense statue of an elephant, carved by Tamil sculptor guilds into a figure of unmatched 'grace, volume, and swiftness of movement'[58] to delineate the space[59] and act as a nod to the creator of the Rashtrakuta family's fortunes: Danti-Durga, the Elephant Fort. On Dhruva's left were stark cliff faces decorated with caves for worship, vanishing into the darkness of the living rock, decorated with torches and garlands. Above and around him were thousands of tonnes of sacred stone, suspended as if defying the laws of

WL / Wikimedia Commons

Shiva the Slayer of the Elephant Demon, on the ground floor of the Krishneshvara. Twice the size of a man, the titanic deity seems to whirl around his torso, flinging the skin of the slain elephant demon around him like a mantle. One hand nevertheless gently caresses the cheek of his consort, the goddess Parvati, on the right. Only a master sculptor could have made a sculpture so large convey such dynamism and energy.

gravity, and above that the sapphire-blue sky. And we can imagine that
Dhruva couldn't tear his eyes off what was emerging on his right: the
spectacular temple proper, rising like the peak of the sacred mountain

The plinth of the Krishneshvara. The monolith's scale is difficult to capture in a single
photograph, but the plinth alone clearly dwarfs visitors (visible on the right).

The entire Krishneshvara monolith.

Kailasha, painted white and decorated with vibrant colours. Here was the snowy abode of Shiva and his raucous retinue, recreated in all its glory, as though the Rashtrakutas had brought the heavens themselves to the Deccan,[60] along with the Ganga and Yamuna banners.

Here the retinue could have stopped to admire a relief of Durga slaying the buffalo-demon Mahisha, a representation of the indomitable, terrifying energies of the Divine Female[61] with her weapons arrayed around her like a halo of blades. There they may have shuddered at the titanic carving of Shiva in his horrific form as the Slayer of the Elephant Demon. Everywhere they saw potent combinations of political and religious iconography, entirely new forms which are present only here at the Krishneshvara. For example, the plinth is made up of dozens upon dozens of powerful elephants and lions in combat, evidently made by sculptors who had seen the beasts in action. They leap out of the monolith at the worshipper, bearing the weight of the imposing artificial mountain above, lifting it into the air and light. They could also be interpreted as an indicator of the importance of the royal war elephant to the Rashtrakutas,[62] and another nod to Danti-Durga.

In the cliff sides on the ground floor were galleries cut under the line of the rock, which artificially increased the space of the courtyard and created a pillared colonnade through which light filtered into tall, framed sculptures. Here, the royal retinue may have admired a sculpture depicting Ravana sacrificing his ten heads to Shiva for unbounded power. Its quality may not have been comparable with some of the others in the temple, but it was probably interesting to any initiated Shaivas in the group because what it depicted was actually fairly new at the time.[63]

In literary works completed centuries earlier, such as the Ramayana and *Raghuvamsa*, Ravana is depicted as sacrificing his heads to Brahma, the Creator, in return for magical powers.[64] Yet in literature composed a few centuries after the Krishneshvara was excavated, such as the *Shiva Purana* of eleventh–twelfth-century Varanasi, they narrated a tale of Ravana sacrificing his heads to obtain powers from Shiva instead, making him out to be an ideal Shaiva devotee – just as the panel in the Krishneshvara does.[65] What this suggests is that we are seeing Shaiva theology and myth in motion, captured on the rock of the Krishneshvara. Similarly, scholars have noted that the Krishneshvara's depictions of the lives of the hero-gods Rama[66] and Krishna[67] are not what we see in the classical texts, but seem instead to reflect contemporary south Indian narratives of the myths, which Dhruva Rashtrakuta and his retinue were probably most familiar with. The Krishneshvara temple is thus not only a political or artistic achievement: it is an invaluable historical artefact which could tell us a great deal about the evolution of Shaivism and Indian religions in the Deccan. It challenges our stereotype of unchanging Indian rituals and myths with a history where priests, kings and communities instead actively participated in making and remaking them.

Moving away from this gallery, perhaps Dhruva's retinue next climbed up the stairs into the main hall, seeing its murals illuminated by flickering oil lamps, as gold leaf and semi-precious stones glittered in the dark. And there in the heart of the temple, in a cell blazing with light, was the splendid manifestation of Shiva Krishneshvara himself, a linga decked with 'rubies, gold, and all other precious things'.[68] The victorious Dhruva must have heaped it with jewels and prostrated himself to the chanting of priests and clanging of bells, decorating with the bloody spoils of war this representation of the awesome power of human creativity and determination.

At sunset an observer on the other side of Ilapura's cliffs could have watched the sun's red glow vanish behind the cliffs to the west, only to be replaced by the faint glow of the temple's lamps, as if the sun 'had descended of its own accord'.[69] Day and night, it blazed like the subcontinent's crown jewel, 'billowing smoke and incense … courtyards sprinkled with pure scented water'[70] – a heady, intoxicating,

Shiva Krishneshvara. This humble linga would once have been decorated with the most splendid spoils of war that the Rashtrakuta imperial formation could obtain.

overwhelming religious experience. According to later inscriptions, gods flying above it stopped to stare in astonishment and concluded that a creation of such beauty could not have been the artifice of mere human hands but was a self-generated manifestation of Shiva himself.[71]

What remains now of Krishna and Dhruva Rashtrakuta except the dry testimonies of *prashasti* propaganda, that leave no trace of their humanity and complexity? What remains of their conquests, of their boasts, of their politics and their betrayals? Where is the immortality and glory they were supposed to have earned by killing thousands?

But what the Nameless *Sthapati* created – that will stand till the end of time.

7

King of Poets

Summer, 814 CE

It is barely thirty years since Dhruva Rashtrakuta's splendid military triumph in the Gangetic plains and the completion of the Krishneshvara temple. But the Rashtrakuta imperial network is already at risk of collapsing.

The lords of the sixteen[1] huge principalities and dozens of smaller states which together made up the Rashtrakuta polity had gathered in a temporary town[2] built to accommodate them on the outskirts of the still new Rashtrakuta capital Manyakheta,[3] modern Malkhed,[4] near Gulbarga. Some of these mighty aristocrats came from other Rashtrakuta lines. Many more came from established local dynasties with their own unruly vassals, ambitions and claims. These included the Gangas and the Vengi Chalukyas. All of them knew very well what magnificent treasures Manyakheta contained, and they knew these treasures were, all of a sudden, within their grasp. After all, they were there to witness a fourteen-year-old, a mere boy, being crowned their lord and master.

His name was Sarva Rashtrakuta, and he had once seemed a child of destiny. He had been born in the town of Sri-Bhavana, nestled within the ancient Vindhya hills, during the monsoon season of the year 800. His parents were Dhruva's son, the dashing young[5] Vallabha Govinda III Jagattunga, 'Pinnacle of the World', and his queen Asagavva. The prince was born in the immediate aftermath of a series of brilliant Rashtrakuta campaigns, almost as if he were a reward from the gods for the dynasty's upholding of the royal dharma. His father Govinda III had crushed a coalition of twelve south Indian kings including those of Vengi and the Ganga country, executed a lightning expedition to north India, and forced the lords of central India to pay him tribute; he may even have forayed into Odisha. Though some of these regions had already been subdued by Dhruva, medieval Indian emperors could only be sure of the loyalties of the core territories their families ruled directly. They were less certain of territories ruled by dynasties tied closely to their own through bonds of family or military alliance, as we have seen with the Vatapi Chalukyas and their fractious relations in Lata. Regions ruled over by dynasties with their own storied legacies – especially those brought into the fold recently, as Vengi had been into the Rashtrakuta political formation – often stopped paying tribute upon the accession of a new ruler, or whenever an established overlord's grip was seen to be faltering.

Early in Govinda III's reign, his military successes had established that he was an overlord best not crossed. Indeed, it seems that the minor rulers of the subcontinent had been reduced to a state of abject terror at Govinda III's display of Rashtrakuta military might. One of them, Govinda's mother's relation, the Chalukya king of Vengi, had scrambled to show his devotion by helping build sections of the wall for Govinda's grand new city of Manyakheta, which the delighted imperial court claimed 'touched the summit of the sky'.[6] Another, the king of Sri Lanka, sent Govinda two idols of the Buddha, 'his own personal lord and the highest lord of the Sinhala polity'.[7] These were set up, according to the Rashtrakutas, 'like pillars of fame' in a Shiva temple in Manyakheta, yet another endorsement (no matter if only symbolic) of the Deccan's dominance[8] over the entire subcontinent.

After such a violently triumphant start, it might have seemed that Govinda III was on the verge of a long and successful reign – and yet in 814, barely middle-aged, the Vallabha was dead. Prince Sarva Rashtrakuta was now left to control a vast and multi-centric empire, surrounded by the relentlessly ambitious lords of the Deccan. While Govinda had been able to find the resources and inclination to repeatedly crush them into subordination or overawe them with propaganda and public ritual, it certainly seemed that Sarva would not be able to do so.

One can only imagine what the boy went through at his coronation, feeling the heat of the sacrificial fire as the chanting of verses was almost drowned out by the roars of the Manyakheta crowds. As his rivals and relations and vassal kings watched with hungry eyes, the waters of the royal ablution were poured over his head, transforming him. No more would he be the boy Sarva: from this day to his death, he was Fortune's Favourite, Earth's Beloved, Paramount Lord, the Great King of Kings: Amoghavarsha-Raja-Deva, the Unfailing Rainer of Gifts.[9] A long period of deadly peril lay on the horizon for the young Vallabha.

Nobody in the coronation pavilion that day – probably not even the newly minted Amoghavarsha himself – could have expected that he would rule with charm, refinement and violence for sixty-four years, preserving the Deccan as one of the subcontinent's dominant powers for most of the 800s, and profoundly impacting the cultural history of southern India. He would leave a legacy that would be sung of by Arab and Kannadiga alike for centuries. In observing his career, we'll embark on an odyssey from the intensely personal to the global, and see how the Deccan under the Rashtrakutas participated in the emergence of the global system of trade and interaction that still exists.

Deccan kingship had come a long way from its early days under the Chalukyas, who had initiated the institution's gradual integration into the Sanskrit Cosmopolis. By the ninth century, we can infer from inscriptions that rulers like Amoghavarsha were exposed to the gamut of knowledge and attitudes circulated across this vast geocultural formation. The young Vallabha learned of the Three Goals of human life: following and upholding dharma, the acquisition and protection of wealth (*artha*), and the pursuit and enjoyment of pleasure (*kama*).[10] Parts of encyclopaedic *shastras*, explaining the correct means to achieve these goals,[11] were probably drilled into his head until he could recall them from memory. These could include everything from 'logic, law, royal policy, composition and metrics … stories and poetry, *itihasa* (epics) and the *Puranas*', to 'musical instruments, dancing, painting, leaf-cutting, gambling, knowledge of omens and astronomy, architecture, carpentry, gem-testing' and so on.[12] He seems to have learned how to use force and wealth to win others to his side,[13] and been taught how to regain and steward his kingdom and his family's glory. But most importantly, he learned – or was taught – how to manage the people of his court.

As a young prince, before his accession, Amoghavarsha probably imbibed the complex gestural and verbal protocols he would need to navigate courtly hierarchies: to rise from his seat; to touch the feet of his elders; to fold his hands above his head, in front of his face, or in front of his chest according to the rank of the addressee; to bend at the head or waist or touch various parts of his body to the ground as a prostration.[14] He needed to cultivate a low, pleasant voice[15] and get used to formal modes of address even for those closest to him: higher-ups could not be referred to by their names unless permission was explicitly granted; the term *deva* (Your Highness) used for vassal kings and queens, *arya* or *bhadra* (noble one/sir) for learned Brahmins and accomplished artists and so on.[16] The boy would not have interacted with his father, the Vallabha Govinda III, very much, appearing before him mostly on very formal occasions, during which he had to adhere to a strict verbal and gestural protocol.

After his coronation in 814, as suggested by normative texts as well as royal inscriptions from across the Sanskrit Cosmopolis, Amoghavarsha had to learn how to carefully control his every facial movement. In medieval Indian courts, even the eyes, like the rest of the body, were considered to be capable of making gestures.[17] A single miscalculated smile might be interpreted by the palace crowd as a bestowal of royal favour and lead them all to recalculate their opinion of the king and the lucky recipient.[18] A furrowed eyebrow or a harsh word might be taken as a sign of a terrible falling out.[19] A sidelong glance might be interpreted as one of great intimacy.[20] It must have been a stressful life for a child to lead.

The Rashtrakutas had come to power by overthrowing their Chalukya overlords when they were distracted and vulnerable. In 814, in the aftermath of Govinda III's death and Amoghavarsha's accession, things had come full circle, as their vassals plotted against them in this moment of vulnerability.[21] The political crisis came to a head in 815/16, when Amoghavarsha had been on the throne for little more than a year. The Chalukyas of Vengi – cowed down by Govinda III and Dhruva Rashtrakuta, and tied by blood to the Rashtrakutas through the empress Shila-Mahadevi – sought their revenge. Her brother, the king of Vengi[22] and Amoghavarsha's grand-uncle, allied himself with the Gangas[23] and led an army through the Eastern Ghats and Telangana, appearing straight in the heart of Vidarbha (eastern Maharashtra).[24]

It was a bold move. Without a leader of Dhruva's or Govinda III's charisma and military ability, the Rashtrakuta armies and vassals seem to have been unable or unwilling to resist determined opponents. A scholarly adolescent, Amoghavarsha must not have cut a very inspirational figure to the battle-hardened veterans who had served under his brilliant and brutal father and grandfather. The armies of the Vengi Chalukyas hacked and burned their way deep into the Rashtrakuta heartland with little serious resistance. Simultaneously, in the south, the Gangas raised their elephant banners and defeated the armies the boy-emperor sent to punish them.[25] Parts of the Deccan sank into anarchy,[26] casting, we are told, 'the glory of the Rashtrakuta house into the Chalukya ocean'.[27]

The imperial court was forced to flee, seeking the assistance of the dead emperor Govinda III's general and nephew, Karkka Rashtrakuta: a man bearing the awe-inspiring title of Patala-Malla, Hell Wrestler.[28] As a member of a cadet lineage of a Deccan imperial house, like the Lata Chalukya king Pulakeshi-Raja before him, Karrka ruled in Lata in southern Gujarat with the rank of maharaja, ensuring that the Rashtrakuta imperial centre retained its crucial connections to Indian Ocean trade.

We do not know how the loss of his throne changed Amoghavarsha, what he must have seen, and what it must have taught him about the world and his place in it. It is difficult not to sympathize with the boy's situation. Meeting Karkka Rashtrakuta, the Hell Wrestler, and convincing him to throw his lot in with the imperial court – perhaps through tools we know other medieval kings used, such as expensive and prestigious gifts, praises of his martial valour, and calls to familial loyalty and personal virtue – must have been one of the early successes of the young Vallabha's political and diplomatic career. It would not be the last.

By May 821,[29] the Hell Wrestler had worked out an arrangement with the Vengi Chalukyas by offering his sister to the Chalukya crown prince in marriage.[30] The Gangas seem to have settled for an uneasy truce with the Rashtrakutas as well, though both dynasties continued to fear and distrust the other. Amoghavarsha, by now probably a rather world-weary and determined twenty-one-year-old, could at last return to take the throne of Manyakheta. The first deadly challenge to his rule had, for now, been dealt with. As he paraded into the city, the

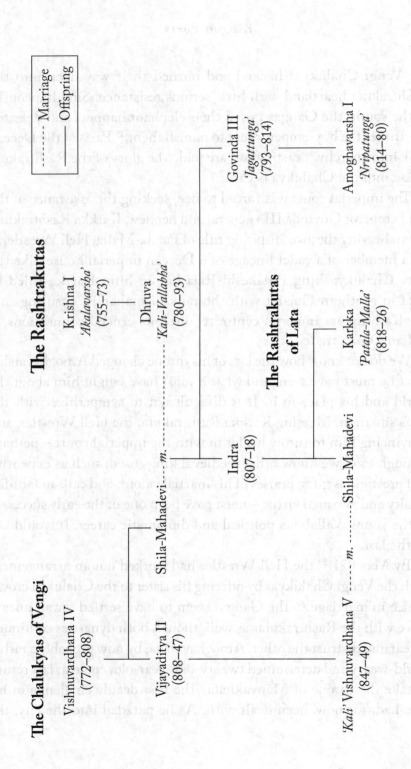

The Rashtrakutas

Krishna I
'*Akalavarsha*'
(755–73)

Dhruva
'*Kali-Vallabha*'
(780–93)

Govinda III
'*Jagattunga*'
(793–814)

Amoghavarsha I
'*Nripatunga*'
(814–80)

- - - Marriage
——— Offspring

**The Rashtrakutas
of Lata**

Karkka
'*Patala-Malla*'
(818–26)

Indra
(807–18)

The Chalukyas of Vengi

Vishnuvardhana IV
(772–808)

Shila-Mahadevi - - - *m.*

Vijayaditya II
(808–47)

Shila-Mahadevi

Indra - - - *m.* - - - Shila-Mahadevi

'*Kali*' Vishnuvardhana V
(847–49)

imperial Garuda banner was raised on a towering flagstaff to the blasts of trumpets, signifying that the Vallabha had finally returned, that the King of Kings had once again assumed his rightful place at the axis of the four quarters,[31] that order was at last restored to the world.

♋

Amoghavarsha had left Manyakheta as a boy, now he returned as a man. Self-control, astuteness in diplomacy and an unusually introspective turn of character would characterize his public image. 'What does one fear?' he would write, decades later. 'Death. Who is in even worse plight than the blind man? The passionate man. What is hell? Dependence upon another.[32] What is truth? The welfare of the beings.'[33] This attitude informs many of his later inscriptions, and he would one day famously sacrifice his little finger to the goddess Mahalakshmi,[34] ostensibly to save his subjects from a famine or outbreak of disease, an almost unheard-of act for any contemporary ruler.

It is doubtful that most kings in the early ninth century were anywhere near this contemplative.[35] Many of them were raised as though they were gods on Earth (with all the suffocating rituals and duties that entailed). Rulers, as we know from historical records across millennia, could often be spoiled, selfish, arrogant and intolerant of those below them, insulated from the consequences of their actions by layers upon layers of security and protocol.

But just as life today is not completely defined by presidents and prime ministers, medieval life was not entirely defined by kings. Amoghavarsha might have been a great force in the Rashtrakuta palace, but outside those pleasant, perfumed environs, his capital, Manyakheta, was a diverse, crowded melting pot where the Vallabha's activities were generally peripheral to the humdrum daily lives of the people of the Deccan.[36] We know very little about what the city

actually looked like, thanks to centuries of war, neglect and the lack
of archaeological study of its probable site. But if the worldview of
Rashtrakuta courtly literature is any indication, its residents came from
all over the Deccan and beyond, from Bengal, the Gangetic plains,
Rajashtan, Malwa, Chhattisgarh, Gujarat, Maharashtra, Andhra, the
Konkan, Karnataka and so on – a true microcosm of the Deccan's
far-flung politico-economic networks. Sanskrit literature on cities
describes occupations ranging from 'ministers of the king, judges of
the court of justice, and *ācāryas* or professors, to scribes, physicians,
merchants, grammarians, guards, bards, courtesans, *viṭas* [libertines],
dhūrtas [knaves], *pīthamardas* [companions], *vīnā* players, dance
masters, drummers, master painters, and *sabhikas* (club keepers), down
to male and female servants ... carpenters, gardeners, elephant riders,
cart drivers... cowherds, horse keepers, masseurs',[37] and butchers,
cobblers, carpenters, doctors, monks, bureaucrats, generals, *sthapatis*
and more.

This diversity in occupation was matched by religious plurality
and proliferation. All the major Shaiva sects probably ensured they
were represented in the Deccan's most important city, from the
Pashupatas to the Kapalins to the Kalamukhas. So too did the Jains,
whose expansive network of monasteries ensured they were still one of
western and southern India's dominant religious forces, the fulmination
of Tamil bhakti poets notwithstanding. Today, though Jainism has
almost vanished in the south, retaining a foothold only in the balmy
shores of coastal Karnataka, it continues to be a major force in Gujarat
and Rajasthan.

But one would have been laughed out of Manyakheta in the ninth
century if one had claimed that south Indian Jainism would some day
vanish. In the centuries since the Chalukya king Vikramaditya I's
initiation into Shaivism in the seventh century, Jains in the Deccan
had proven every bit as innovative and responsive to new religious and
political trends as the Shaivas. The idea of the *jina*, the ascetic who

Shriram Rajagopalan / Wikimedia Commons

Matanga, Jain god of prosperity, from Ellora Cave 12. Medieval Deccan Jains worshipped many deities in addition to the *tirthankaras*, the great sages and teachers who conquered their senses.

conquered the senses, was creatively presented as analogous to the warrior who conquered his enemies,[38] thus making this once-peaceful religion (which theoretically could not even stand for an insect to be harmed) most appealing to some warlike south Indian aristocrats. Indeed, ninth-century Jains offer a striking insight into the continuing development of religions in the subcontinent.

South Indian Jain sects, such as the Yapaniyas, allowed women to be ordained as nuns, and made active attempts to entice householders into the fold.[39] The Yapaniyas also adopted practices that are commonly identified with Hinduism today, including the idea of

caste,[40] permanent monasteries dependent on agriculture, the worship
of goddesses such as Jvalamalini, Bearer of a Fire Garland, and the
propitiation of astrological deities on behalf of laypeople.[41] Many Jain
schools even ran full-fledged temple establishments complete with
ritual bathing of the deity, festivals, processions and musical soirees.[42]
Like contemporary Shaiva monastic orders,[43] they were also wealthy
enough to build temples in their own right, or at least influential
enough to request it as a form of royal grace. These were functionally
almost indistinguishable from Shaiva temples, acting as religious,
social and political centres just as the Lokeshvara and Krishneshvara
temples had, hiring the same *sthapati* guilds and drawing patrons
from similar classes. (Jain temples, however, tended to be somewhat
more austere with their sculptural decorations than Shaiva shrines.)
All these innovations, which were shrewd responses to extant
socio-economic trends, powered Jainism to a nearly 800-year-long
reign,[44] alongside Shaivism, over south India's religious landscape.
The striking similarity between the two religions (in practice, if not
in theology) also challenges us to think of developments in Indian
religions as long-term overall trends that evidently cut across sectarian
boundaries. From this perspective, Indian religion in general is
perhaps best understood as a response to, and driver of, evolving
social, economic and political patterns.

The Gangas, those implacable rivals of the Rashtrakutas, were great
patrons of Jains. Now, in the aftermath of a devastating war, sitting
precariously on his throne, Amoghavarsha saw an opportunity. Just
as the old Chalukya Vallabha Vikramaditya I had cultivated closer
ties with the Shaivas in a moment of crisis, the Rashtrakuta Vallabha
Amoghavarsha encouraged Jain literature and patronized that religion's
powerful network of monasteries and temples.[45] Indeed, he and his
successors would construct a number of Jain shrines and cave temples
at Badami and Pattadakal: the Malaprabha river valley seems to have
continued to be an invaluable economic centre to the lords of the

Deccan even after the fall of the Chalukyas of Vatapi, now a fading memory.

This is not to say definitively that Amoghavarsha *was* a Jain: these boundaries are difficult to establish in medieval India. Religiosity at the time was fluid,[46] and monarchs liked to spread their devotions and patronage as widely as possible to appeal to the broadest possible cross-section of society. For example, Amoghavarsha would refer to himself in his own inscriptions as Vira-Narayana, the Valiant Vishnu, and as mentioned, sacrificed his little finger to the goddess Mahalakshmi.[47] The Jains were only one of the many squabbling and ambitious social groups of Manyakheta amongst whom the Rashtrakuta Vallabha spread his largesse.

Another favoured group – and perhaps far more significant both to Amoghavarsha and to us – were poets. The young Vallabha was a master of aesthetic theory and poetry, especially in the world of Sanskrit literature, and had rather strong opinions about what comprised good poetry and what did not.[48] The Deccan had come a long way from the days when the Chalukya Vallabhas had slowly, tentatively, begun to popularize the use of Sanskrit for its prestige and political utility. Now centuries later, Manyakheta, the Deccan's new imperial centre, thrived with poets as the great lordly houses competed with the Rashtrakuta Vallabha to attract poetic talent. Poets were well respected and highly specialized professionals with considerable presence in aristocratic daily lives. For example, the contemporary Deccan text *Yashastilaka*, a Jain epic, describes royal officials selecting an elephant and a horse for a king. An elephant named Udayagiri, sent by the king of Kalinga (southern Odisha)[49] as part of his annual tribute, was presented to him with

> an elaborate report on the characteristics of the chosen animal, full
> of technical details. Meanwhile, a bard named Karikalabha recited
> a number of verses in praise of elephants. Similarly, a notable white

horse of Kamboja [most likely Central Asia in this context] was selected by a committee of experts ... after which a bard named Vajivinodamakaranda recited some verses in praise of horses.[50]

Like all the Vallabhas who had come before him, Amoghavarsha also toured the dozens of cities and towns of which he was the hereditary lord, as well as the temples and monasteries and cities of his many vassals. During these travels, he appears to have noticed the gulf between the urbane, intellectual, Sanskrit-speaking world and the overwhelmingly Kannada-speaking world of orally transmitted legends and stories – the world inhabited by the lower ranks of his vassals, who were much more in awe of him than those in the court of Manyakheta.

Perhaps, as he heard Jain myths and fantastical legends of Rashtrakuta and Chalukya kings, local heroes and deities, and regional takes on stories from Sanskrit epics and *Puranas*, as he judged and rewarded bright young Kannada poets in Pattadakal and Koppana and Porigere and Okkunda,[51] the outlines of a magnum opus began to take shape. But it would take considerable resources, time and talent to bring it to life. For now, the Vallabha had other things on his mind.

Constantly pressed for resources and goods to reward his loyalists and to maintain his pre-eminent status within the Deccan, and lacking the military capabilities of his father and grandfather, Amoghavarsha was in desperate need of wealth and luxury goods. By the ninth century, an unprecedented constellation of global and local factors were beginning to come together. Far to his west and east, two vast political formations – the Abbasid Caliphate in West Asia, and the later Tang dynasty of China – were growing increasingly interested in the profits of global trade. As the young Deccan emperor toured the dusty plateau and its noisy cities, interactions in the Indian Ocean were growing to unprecedented levels. This would offer the young

Vallabha a means to maintain the splendour of the Rashtrakuta court without having to rely primarily on ceaseless war and tribute, as his predecessors had.

∾

Let us pause and look at the enormous world of which Amoghavarsha Rashtrakuta and other medieval Indian kings were an integral part.

As anyone who has traversed modern India by road will attest to, the subcontinent is almost incomprehensibly vast. And yet it is dwarfed by the size of the Indian Ocean and the continents that surround it. By the ninth century, the subcontinent, as a result of its geographical location in the centre of the Indian Ocean, the sophistication of its craftsmanship, and its bounteous natural resources, had emerged as the central link in the exchange chain between Europe, Africa and much of Asia. The scale and depth of this interconnectivity is exemplified by stunning archaeological discoveries dating to the sixth–eleventh centuries on the Swedish island of Helgo, not far from Stockholm. These include a sixth-century bronze Buddha from Kashmir and a bronze ladle from North Africa, as well as 'Arabic coins, Frankish glass and metal-work from across western Europe'.[52]

By the ninth century, great tides of people were in motion across the Afro-Eurasian landmass, interacting with new goods, languages and ethnicities. Moving from west to east across this landmass, we would see Scandinavians beginning to move into the British Isles as well as down the Volga river into Ukraine. We would fly over Frankish kingdoms – the ancestors of the later kingdoms of France – preserving Latin knowledge in monasteries and manufacturing glass and metalwork, sending embassies to the courts of Iraq, and receiving elephants in return: the first time the animals had set foot in France since the Roman Empire centuries ago. We might pause in awe to behold the glittering palaces, libraries and ports of Constantinople on

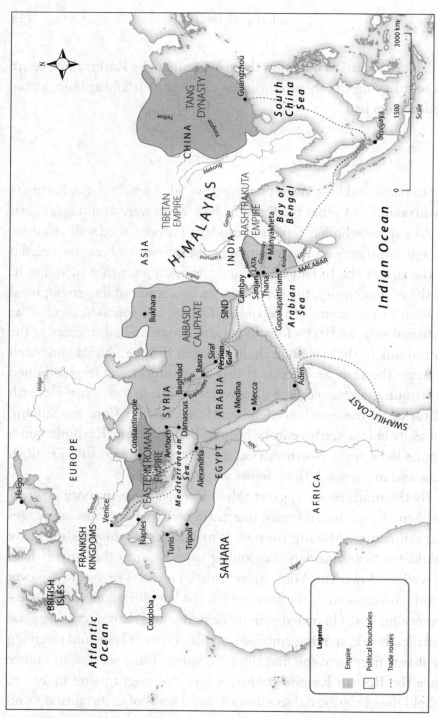

Afro-Eurasia, ninth century CE.

the Bosporous, the direct medieval descendant of Rome, overflowing with perfumes, silks, spices and gold. We would traverse the vast Abbasid Caliphate, which had overthrown the Umayyads, connected the markets of Egypt, Iraq and Persia, and established the metropolis of Baghdad as the world's premier centre of trade, education and scientific research. Moving south into Africa, we would see vanishing into the distance the wealthy city-states of the Swahili coast, a region that has historically been deeply connected to India, exporting gold, 'ambergris, ivory, leopard skins and tortoise shell'.[53] Leaping across the ocean, we would traverse the dusty plateaus of Iran with their underground canals and rich cities, pass the thriving oasis towns of Central Asia, and reach China, where the superpower that was the Tang dynasty matched the 'gravitational pull' exerted on the global economy by the remnants of Rome, the Islamic world and the Indian subcontinent.[54] (For context, the early Tang emperors had been rough contemporaries of Harsha, Pulakeshin and the Prophet Muhammad.) By the ninth century, the Chinese too had developed an interest in international trade.[55] Across Europe, East Africa, West Asia and East Asia, the ninth century thus saw unprecedented attention to the profit and prestige to be gained through global interactions.

But this continent-spanning network of interactions depended on ninth-century South Asia's thriving ports, merchant organizations, avaricious aristocrats and toiling agrarian masses. In a war-torn time, where military success and control over land had made fortunes for many dynasties, merchant organizations such as the Five Hundred Lords of Aihole (whose emergence we witnessed in Chapter 4) helped connect producers and markets, and moved goods across vast geographical extents. Such organizations could mobilize large amounts of capital; insulate members against the risk of banditry, piracy or natural disaster; and hire mercenaries to protect their depots and caravans. They could also, as we will see, secure consignments of rare goods or strategic resources for warlords, and use their political networks to connect international traders and Indian markets. Meanwhile, for rulers such as Amoghavarsha, control over important ports was critical because it allowed a degree of taxation, and because international trade allowed them to obtain luxury goods that were crucial to maintaining their status and prestige over competing lords. However, the exact degree to which Indian royals and their agents succeeded in taxing or directly profiting from international trade is a matter of considerable debate.

To get a better sense of the subcontinent's importance in ninth-century global trade, we will further explore systems of production and exchange within the subcontinent. We will then try to catch some glimpses of Amoghavarsha's own activities through the testimony of Arab merchants and travellers, as well as evidence from archaeology and inscriptions in the great Rashtrakuta port of Sanjan.

Over the last few chapters, we have seen medieval Indian kings making land grants to local elites to create regional power bases. But these actions were also tied to the development and encouragement of commerce. By granting land and giving grandees the right to pay less tax in return for irrigation and rainwater harvesting works, kings sought to deepen and widen networks of agrarian production, supporting further economic specialization. The surplus agricultural produce that new landowning elites (temples, monasteries, Brahmin landlords and local warlords) collected were moved to local exchange centres which began to emerge as commercial hubs: we have seen this process earlier with the emergence of the Five Hundred Lords of Aihole in the Malaprabha river valley. Such exchange centres supplied the growing cities and towns of the Deccan with food and crafts, and also established routes for the exchange of other goods, both imported luxury items and local manufactures, especially cloth. However, the commercial economy was not yet mature enough to support large-scale artisanal specialization. Many local artisans used their craft as a way to supplement agricultural and raiding activity, with true specialists being confined to cities, which had both the economic surplus and constant consumption required to sustain them.[56]

The evolution of a complex and stratified economic structure is always a complicated process – and often tragic. The transformation of the dry lands of the Deccan into networks of irrigated, commercially productive hubs was often enforced at sword-point, and inscriptions speak of defiant villages slaughtered, of women raped, even of children attacked.[57] However, for those with the social and fiscal capital to manoeuvre themselves, all this was a great opportunity for profit.

None were better positioned to do so in the ninth century than the Five Hundred Lords of Aihole. A century earlier, as the Vatapi Chalukya Vallabha Vikramaditya II raided the Pallavas and his queen Loka-Mahadevi erected her temple, the Five Hundred had rapidly expanded their influence across the Deccan. By the late 800s, when the Rashtrakutas had seized paramountcy in the Deccan, the Five Hundred had managed to establish a franchise of sorts in Pudukkottai, in the Palar river valley of the Tamil country.[58] This location was crucial for trade between the two regions.[59] This sudden leap in their influence – from dominating a hub connecting manufacturers and traders in the northern Deccan to establishing a presence in another hub, straddling trade routes into the Tamil country – may have been connected to Rashtrakuta aggression in the region under Dhruva and Govinda III, and helped establish them as one of southern India's most powerful merchant associations.

Meanwhile, on the subcontinent's west coast, Zoroastrian and Christian merchants from Persia visited every year and settled down. Some moved inland, some intermarried with locals, and some formed their own diverse guilds, such as the Anjuvannam, a name possibly derived from the Persian *anjuman*, 'association'.[60] Alongside them, in Malabar, were the Manigramam, an indigenous merchant group which worked closely[61] with pepper-cultivating indigenous Christians[62] organized under the aegis of native churches. These two organizations seemed to have worked together, monopolizing the purchase of pepper and its sale to buyers across the western Indian Ocean. The Manigramam ensured that local chiefs turned a benign eye to the trade[63] and probably focused on buying and sorting pepper, while the Anjuvannam used its far-flung international networks to find buyers and secure capital for shipments. During the eighth–twelfth centuries, similar merchant networks stretched all the way from India to Iran, Iraq, Central Asia, the Mediterranean world, North Africa and even Spain.[64]

Inscriptions of both the Anjuvannam and Manigramam are often found in association with the much vaster organization that was the Five Hundred. It therefore seems that the expansion of the Five Hundred by the ninth century helped connect newly productive agrarian hinterlands controlled by Deccan warlords – as well as ravenous urban markets such as Manyakheta – to international trading networks through these coastal merchant organizations. In response to blossoming forces of supply and demand within India, Arab ships increasingly began to make journeys through the year instead of primarily during the monsoon season, as earlier. These ships usually moved in a circuit from Siraf on the Persian Gulf to ports in Gujarat and the northern Konkan, making fortunes for their owners in the process. All this was also aided by the actions of Indian rulers great and small with a presence on the west coast, eager for a slice of the extremely lucrative trade[65] through tariffs and the purchase and sale of luxury goods and horses. In the Konkan, for example, a dynasty called the Shilaharas managed to conquer and unite the three great emporia of Gopakapattinam (now Old Goa), Balipattana and Chandrapura (which Arabs called Sindabur) into a single 'regional economic unit' that would emerge as one of the major trading centres of the west coast,[66] acting as an international and regional hub for coastal trade.[67] This was accomplished in the same decade that Amoghavarsha returned to the throne of Manyakheta, c. 830.

Other ports that emerged as thriving trading hubs for Arabs include 'Kanbaya (Cambay), Sandan (Sanjan) [both in Gujarat], Tana (Thana), Subara (Sopara), Saimur (Chaul) [all in coastal Maharashtra], and Manibar or Mulaybar (Malabar)'.[68] All of these, with the exception of Malabar and probably Cambay, were within the Rashtrakuta sphere of influence in the ninth century. Arab traders were aware that their local partners owed ultimate allegiance to a distant, splendid monarch far off in the interior. Over the next two hundred years, stories of the 'Balhara king', the Vallabha-Raja, would attain almost legendary proportions, and Arab merchants in the ninth century would insist 'there is in fact no [Indian] king who has greater affection for the Arabs than the Balhara'.[69] This almost certainly refers to Amoghavarsha, suggesting that the Vallabha was well aware of the profits to be made from trade and sought to systematically encourage it.

West Asians – Muslim Persians and Arabs, as well as Zoroastrians, Jews and Christians of diverse ethnicities – were soon settling down in these major ports, establishing permanent bases for trade. The modern ideals of chauvinistic religious and linguistic nationalism scarcely existed in the medieval Indian Ocean world, despite the violent conquests of the Umayyad Caliphate a few generations before this time. It appears that occasional elite-directed violence was not allowed to get in the way of much more frequent people-to-people interactions. The Rashtrakutas, for example, were pleased to allow these wealthy immigrants the right to build mosques: Amoghavarsha and his successors even appointed Muslim officers to administer personal law[70] to traders. In Chaul, Maharashtra, there is evidence of a group called the Bayasira – born to West Asian fathers and Indian mothers.[71]

These immigrants also integrated themselves with gusto into the cosmopolitan culture of the times. One fascinating example is a Persian Muslim known to us as Madhumati, son of Sahiyarahara (a Sanskritized form of Muhammad, son of Shahryar). In the tenth century, Madhumati was appointed the Rashtrakuta governor of the entire region of Sanjan, including much of the northern Konkan, a region crucial to the Rashtrakutas' global connections. As with any contemporary Indian king, Madhumati's *prashasti* declares that he had 'conquered the chiefs of all the harbours', indicating his appointment as governor was due to his naval expertise as a seaman. He claims to have spent on public charity, establishing two free ferries and a feeding house which served 'rice, curries and ghee' free of cost.[72] Madhumati worked closely with a diverse city assembly which included both Indian and West Asian merchants,[73] and was served by a loyal Indian minister – whose friend, a well-connected Brahmin aristocrat, set up a 'monastery or temple' in the city with Madhumati's approval.[74] West Asians would also serve as witnesses and important community members when land grants were made to shrines by their Indian colleagues. Indeed, Madhumati himself made a land grant to a Durga temple in the region.[75]

It should be noted that such activities were sometimes met with orthodox disapproval, and varied significantly by ethnicity and region. Documentary evidence suggests that Arab merchants at times had to obtain special legal dispensations to trade with ostensible 'infidels',[76] whereas some Indian merchants sometimes insisted on separate quarters for eating for reasons of caste purity. With all of this, they nevertheless seemed to have maintained warm business and interpersonal relationships. All this suggests that the Rashtrakutas were highly involved in the multi-ethnic, multilingual, cosmopolitan and 'globalizing' world of the ninth century.

But why did the Rashtrakutas, an inland Deccan empire, put so much effort into encouraging trade on the subcontinent's coasts? The benefits to them were strategic, political and economic.

Acquiring horses was a priority for Deccan kings from the earliest times: recall Chitrakantha, the famous steed of the Chalukya ruler Vikramaditya I. Coins of Govinda III, Amoghavarsha's father,

A gold *dinara* of Govinda III, using an imitation of the Arabic script (probably Kufic) on the obverse as a decorative element. These coins may have been made specifically for trade on the west coast, and are an indication of how important links to West Asia were for the Rashtrakutas.

A Rashtrakuta gold coin dated to the ninth century, inspired by Abbasid models. The punch marks suggest that it was carried with similar coins in a drawstring, or worn as a necklace.

constitute another example: gold *dinaras* have been found of him as a turban-clad shirtless warrior sitting on an Arab stallion, one arm holding a sword with a wicked, decapitating hook on top, the other raised. These and other Rashtrakuta coins are marked with decorative patterns inspired by the Arabic script, which Indian courts appear to have found a beautiful curiosity; they also feature the auspicious symbols of the Garuda eagle, lotus, and conch shell. They declare Govinda to be Apratihata, 'Invincible'.[77]

On these small pieces of portable propaganda, Govinda III seems to be depicting himself as a military man adapting to the latest global

trends of his time: a stark contrast to the stereotype of medieval Indian
monarchs as disinterested in new technologies and the benefits of
international trade. It is also a most striking parallel to the similarly
innovative emperors of fifteenth- and sixteenth-century Vijayanagara:
Deccan rulers who relied on Portuguese and Arab traders to secure
cavalry for their armies.

As the Deccan grew more connected to global trade during the reign
of Govinda III's son, Amoghavarsha, the scale of its exchange with
the world in general, and the Islamic world in particular, expanded
further. These exchanges were complex and multidimensional, taking
advantage of developments from across continents. Medieval Indians
exported sugar produced by cutting-edge Indian technology,[78] which
would eventually be adopted by the Chinese;[79] salt produced from
seaside pans, based on Chinese technology learned by the Arabs from
interactions in Central Asia;[80] mangoes and citrus fruits grown in vast
estates,[81] and jewels and semi-precious stones set in 'bowls, knife-
handles, paper-weights, beads and bangles',[82] among many other items.
Also on the list of Indian exports were extremely fine cotton cloth
'which could pass through a small ring'[83] and indigo (correspondence

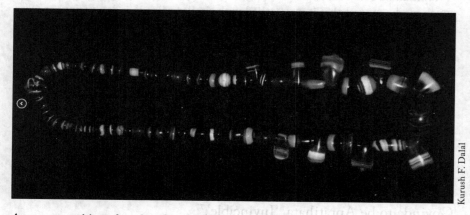

Kurush F. Dalal

An agate necklace found at Sanjan, Gujarat, the premier port of the Rashtrakutas.
Probably of Indian origin, this and similar items were exported all over West Asia
and perhaps beyond.

from the period even gives some West Asian indigo merchants the name *nili*, blue, a term derived from Sanskrit[84]). Sanjan in Gujarat, where the Persian Madhumati ruled on behalf of the Rashtrakutas, was a major centre for the indigo trade,[85] hinting at intense commercial cultivation around the region.

Excavations conducted by the Indian Council for Historical Research at Sanjan in the early 2000s found the remains of a 'prosperous and flourishing city',[86] including glass beads, bangles and semi-precious stones. Most importantly, large quantities of West Asian glass[87] and Chinese ceramics[88] were discovered, signs of Sanjan's globe-spanning import and export networks. In another indication of the complex and intertwined nature of history, Sanjan appears to have been the site where Zoroastrian refugees from Persia, fleeing Umayyad persecution, made their landfall in India in the eighth century. Little more than a

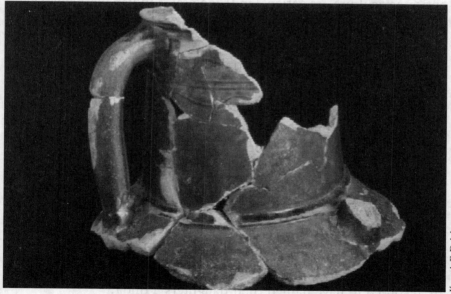

Kurush F. Dalal

Turquoise glazed pottery, perhaps from Iran, discovered at Sanjan. The port was also an important entry point for ceramics and other materials from the western Indian Ocean to reach markets in the inland Deccan.

century later, descendants of these refugees were conducting a brisk international trade under oversight of Madhumati, the Muslim Persian governor appointed by Amoghavarsha's successors, who were Kannada-speaking kings who patronized Hinduism and Jainism.

Indians also exported perfumes, cloves, nutmeg, pepper, mace and cardamom, alongside the odd peacock, rhinoceros or even elephant[89] for particularly rich menageries in Baghdad. Arabs are recorded to have been aware of 'thousands of such [Indian] commodities',[90] which poured into the expensive kitchens and fashionable salons of Baghdad. In the high-stakes world of Abbasid politics, Indian poisons, swords and jewellery were well regarded.[91] So too was Indian knowledge: the Abbasids brought together scholars and texts from the East and the West to develop their understanding of 'philosophy, spiritualism, cosmology, geography, geology, history, botany, mineralogy, physics, mathematics, astronomy, astrology, medicine, pharmacology, anatomy, optics, agriculture, irrigation, [and] zoology'.[92] Indian mathematicians, physicians and philosophers lived in Baghdad, and some were employed in the courts of the Abbasid caliphs Al-Mansur and Harun Al-Rashid, contemporaries of the early Rashtrakutas.[93] Indian scholars are attested to have worked alongside Abbasid scholars in the great library known as the 'House of Wisdom', and Indian numerals, arithmetic, geometry and natural philosophy had a profound impact on the development of the sciences in the Islamic world.[94] Though the evidence is extremely fragmentary, there are some suggestions in Rashtrakuta texts that Abbasid innovations – especially in the realm of 'fine technology', producing sophisticated mechanical devices such as water clocks, fountains and automata – were reaching the Deccan even as Indian knowledge moved West.[95] At a more intimate level, there is evidence that some Arab merchants were so enamoured with India that they are recorded to have named their daughters 'Hinda'.[96]

Caches of letters from the period reveal not just good professional relationships between Indians and their Indian Ocean business partners, but strikingly human tales of friendship, greed, adventure, loss and the sorrow of parting.[97] A story from medieval Kerala describes merchants from Karnataka, Malwa, Gujarat, Andhra, Odisha, Greece (or Anatolia), China and Arabia (or Central Asia) sitting on black carpets, counting money and chatting.

A senior merchant among them tried to impress his juniors in a bragging tone:

If I sell a *jonakuttira* (Arab horse) in the Cōḷa [Tamil] country, I will immediately get two thousand *anayaccu* [coins] … in cash. For my elephant I will get eight thousand … If I go to Kollam (Quilon) and Kollapuram (Kolhapur) I can sell quickly all the good *karpuram* (camphor) …[98]

Evidently, as the historian Ranabir Chakravarti points out, the merchant is attempting to impress his audience with the fact that he is trading in high-value commodities, the only buyers of which could have been landowning military elites and religious institutions. This is no common merchant, it seems. He then continues his boast, in a telling revelation of the closeness of mercantile and political interests in early medieval India: 'I have to get a hundred thousand *accu* [coins] by way of interest on the loan I gave to Vallabha.'[99]

Meanwhile, as the ports of the west coast buzzed with activity, some particularly enterprising Arabs, seeking to write travelogues and on the hunt for commercial opportunity, entered the Deccan, reaching the Rashtrakuta heartland itself. Their writings portray India as a strange land of great splendour and prosperity. Such depictions were intended to instil wonder among their readers – a major concern in Arabic poetics – rather than being factual representations of travels. Nevertheless, it is fair to say that India's 'wonders' were an important component of Arabic travel literature, and a crucial part of their imagination of the world.

One Arab writer was particularly taken by the ascetics who wandered the jungles and peaks of the Western Ghats. Some of them went about naked with a ring on their penises 'to prevent all sexual relationships with women', while others wore leopard skins.[100] With their matted hair, wild eyes and pungent odour, they must have made quite an impression. One of them stood facing the sun somewhere in the Konkan, where this Arab traveller first saw him. He was apparently still there sixteen years later, when the Arab visited again and was stupefied by the man's discipline and by the fact that his eyes had apparently not been burned into empty husks over all those years.[101]

The Rashtrakuta capital, Manyakheta, was also fertile ground for Arab travellers' imaginations. Manyakheta, now a hub of subcontinent-spanning political and economic networks, may have rivalled Baghdad itself (though large-scale archaeology is needed to say for certain). Through the ninth century, as the Rashtrakuta imperial network and the merchants it patronized flourished, the city seems to have been remade through the profits of war and trade; indeed, inscriptions often claim that Amoghavarsha 'made' the city. In the absence of major military adventures during his reign, this may be read as a hint of the wealth that global trade brought the Rashtrakutas. Decked with temples, markets and mansions, surrounded by rivers on three sides,[102] Manyakheta had a great moat[103] and rampart fluttering with the *pali-dhvaja* of the imperial dynasty and banners of its most powerful lords, its gods and its guilds. One Arab visitor, clearly awed by what he saw and seeking to impress a cosmopolitan audience in Iraq, wrote (rather hyperbolically):

'In that city there are for the ordinary people one million elephants which carry the merchandise ... In this temple there are about twenty thousand idols made of a variety of precious metals ... and various carved stones mounted with shaped and artistically worked precious jewels ... In that house is an idol whose height is twelve cubits and is placed on a throne of gold in the centre of a golden cupola, the whole of which is set with jewels like white pearl, ruby, sapphire, blue and emerald stone.[104]

Amoghavarsha Rashtrakuta, Vallabha of the Deccan, had, it seems, made a wise choice in relying on trade rather than the tribute and ceaseless warfare used by his predecessors to fund their politico-military machines. As his coffers swelled, the sophisticated young emperor finally had the resources for a different kind of magnum opus than we have seen up to this point.

After the setbacks he had faced early in his reign due to his inability to personally command and motivate his armies, Amoghavarsha had developed a flair for diplomacy and politics, an eye for talent, and a knack for promoting and inculcating loyalty. A master of literature and aesthetics, he now brought together an unprecedented concentration of poets and teachers to decorate his court at Manyakheta. He could have merely set them to the banal task of composing *prashastis* and dramas, but Amoghavarsha did something else, of exceptional vision, that would echo down to the very languages that Indians speak today.

❧

Amoghavarsha's court poet Srivijaya, working on guidelines laid down by the Vallabha,[105] was given the task of composing a great manual of courtly Kannada grammar – the first the language had ever seen. This *Kavi-raja-margam* (The Way of the King of Poets) was the first text in the world to 'self-consciously' theorize the relationship between a vernacular language and the cosmopolitan Sanskrit, the domain of urban and courtly elites.[106] This work reflects the extraordinary sophistication that the science of linguistics and poetics had reached in the subcontinent by this time; there is nothing comparable to it across the Afro-Eurasian world.

Amoghavarsha's intention in propounding The Way of the King of Poets was to create a register of Kannada with aesthetic and poetic qualities comparable to the elite literature of the Sanskrit Cosmopolis.[107] For this, the structure of older works on Sanskrit poetics – especially the *Kavyadarsha* of the old Pallava court poet Dandin[108] – was systematically reworked to establish the grammatical, metrical and aesthetic rules this courtly Kannada would require.

Dandin's text had marked out the limits of the Sanskrit-speaking universe, discussing the extent of the Indian subcontinent and the varieties of regional Sanskrit styles within it; now Amoghavarsha and Srivijaya did the same for the world of Kannada, declaring it to be the land between the Godavari and Kaveri rivers[109] and classifying a 'northern' and 'southern' variety of Kannada poetic styles.[110] 'Sanskrit and Prakrit are well-established languages, with their characteristic features and examples,'[111] said the Rashtrakuta Vallabha and his poet.

'It is difficult to create poetry in Kannada ...[112] With the native language having so many variations, even Vasuki [the thousand-headed king of serpents, the paragon of scholarship] would become frustrated, unable to identify and fix the faults in the usage of Kannada dialects.'[113]

These 'faults' included unpalatable and harsh sounds, incorrect meanings and difficulty in comprehension[114] – all of which were regarded with horror in Dandin's *Kavyadarsha*. (It is debatable whether local Kannada poets, storytellers and singers, who had been plying their craft well before Amoghavarsha set out on this project, thought so harshly of their language, but their opinions have not survived.)

In their newly developed courtly Kannada, the Vallabha and his poet now set out their own definition of Kannada literature, the qualities to be sought in its two varieties (poetry and prose), and the assorted blemishes they thought made Kannada poetry less than perfect. They also provided nearly two hundred examples[115] – taken from older Sanskrit manuals but reworked into their new vision of Kannada literature – of the proper rules of composition and mixing of Sanskrit, Prakrit and Kannada sounds and grammatical rules. These were developed from deep scholarly engagement with well-established Sanskrit and Prakrit grammars, linguistics, aesthetics and rhetoric, as well as a detailed survey of extant Kannada poetry, prose and metres.[116] The purpose Amoghavarsha had in mind was clear: now, at last, Kannada could match the aesthetic and expressive capabilities of Sanskrit. At last, it could be a language of power and prestige and appear in the *prashastis* of kings; at last, it could be a language of beauty and be admitted into and celebrated in courts. It could compete with that ancient language of prestige on its own terms.

This new 'courtly' Kannada struck enormously fertile ground. Amoghavarsha's hundreds of vassals and rivals, and their thousands of poets and panegyrists, now unleashed a new wave of literary production in their own language, a wave of literature that was more intelligible than Sanskrit was to their peers and subjects, more open to the participation of new social groups, and thus far more politically instrumental. The transformation was immediate and dramatic: 'the proportion of records in Sanskrit shrank from about 80 percent in the period 741–819 (the approximate level of the Bādāmi [Vatapi] Cāḷukyas) to 15 percent in the period 819–974', and to a negligible 5 per cent by 996.[117] Henceforth in the Deccan, Sanskrit, the once-dominant language of Indian literary, philosophical and scientific works, would increasingly be used with Kannada compounds, and in many cases be replaced by it altogether – except in some very significant cases, as we will see later in this book.

This was a landmark in the history of world literature, a moment of transformation. In addition to the emperor Amoghavarsha Rashtrakuta, the illustrious litterateurs involved in this project included Parama-Srivijaya (Paramount Victory of Fortune), Kavishvara (Lord of Poets),

A Jain painting from the Ellora caves dated to the ninth or tenth century, probably depicting a Deccan royal (on the right, looking at a supplicant) with his retainers. Amoghavarsha and his court poets may have looked similar to this group, except in more elaborate costumes.

Panditachandra (Moon Among Pandits), and Lokapala (Guardian of the World).[118] These titles were all honours granted to them by the emperor as rewards for their work. For all future Kannada poets – down to this very day, when there are more speakers of Kannada than the entire population of some countries – this moment would stand out as 'a rupture in time, a moment of discontinuity, when something new began'.[119] It was the moment when predominantly Kannada-speaking polities began to shift their gaze from the Sanskrit Cosmopolis and its connections to subcontinent-wide cosmopolitan literary cultures, to audiences closer to home, more directly relevant to their political networks.[120]

But Kannada had existed before Amoghavarsha, and it had certainly been used by those toiling at the bottom of the political and religious hierarchy to tell their stories and sing their songs for centuries before, irrespective of the sophisticated aesthetics of the Sanskrit Cosmopolis. From this perspective, Amoghavarsha's establishment of 'courtly' Kannada could also be interpreted as an appropriation of an already thriving vernacular culture to suit the aesthetic of power to which he and his vassals were accustomed. What might the average Deccani have thought of this 'aestheticization' and elite transformation of a language they had spoken for centuries?

∽

All these intellectual activities did not make Amoghavarsha a pacifist by any stretch of the imagination. His sheer will to power could put any Mughal emperor to shame. His relation, Dhruva of Lata, the son of Karkka Patala-Malla (the man who had helped Amoghavarsha retain his crown when he was a boy-king) followed in the tradition of Deccan cadet branches based in the wealthy coastal region, and rebelled against the Vallabha in the 840s. Amoghavarsha's armies would end up killing the young man, spawning a family vendetta lasting almost twenty years.[121] Meanwhile, Ganga *prashastis* inform us, their kings were also occupied with 'illuminating the sky of their own kingdoms, which had been overcast by the darkness of the night of the Rashtrakuta'.[122]

By the mid-850s, Amoghavarsha attempted to crush the Gangas once and for all. He was now at the peak of his power, with awestruck Arab visitors acclaiming him as one of the Four Great Kings of the World, his only other rivals being the Byzantine Emperor, the Emperor of China and the Abbasid Caliph himself.[123] His general Bankeya, the commander of the fearsome Rashtrakuta elite hereditary guard corps, was ordered to 'extirpate that lofty forest of fig-trees – Gangavadi, difficult to be cut down'.[124]

Bankeya's story is interesting: his meteoric ascent from the son of a village chieftain[125] was accompanied by increasingly elaborate titles and governorships, from Bankesha (Lord Bankeya) to Bankeyaraja (King Bankeya). It appears that as a member of the Kannada-speaking peasant elite, Bankeya was able to take advantage of Amoghavarsha's new courtly Kannada culture. Through a display of the courtly ideals of valour and military brilliance, he had risen far beyond his station and catapulted himself into the innermost circles of aristocrats. The man would even establish a city named after himself, Bankapura,[126] which would become an important centre of Deccan Jainism; it will feature again in this book.

The campaign was derailed, however, when one of Amoghavarsha's sons rose in rebellion, joining up with his relatives in Lata and attempting to overthrow the elderly Vallabha. But the loyalty Amoghavarsha was able to inspire among his subordinates saved the day. Returning to Manyakheta post-haste, Bankeya promised he would either end the rebellion in three months and make the emperor 'drink milk'[127] to calm his mind, or he would immolate himself. He then unceremoniously killed the disloyal prince and scattered the Vallabha's enemies, though precisely how this was done is unknown. After the crisis had passed, the delighted Amoghavarsha issued an edict which 'till the world's end proclaims him [Bankeya] a hero', eulogized the general's loyalty, fame and fury, granted him additional lands and titles, and confirmed and expanded Bankeya's donations to a Jain monastery.[128]

However, more invasions and rebellions would follow as Amoghavarsha continued to age. The Pratiharas of western India, now on the ascendant, conquered Malwa and parts of Gujarat; meanwhile, a new king of Vengi began to raid Maharashtra,[129] though the Rashtrakutas claimed a great victory against him, having 'offered the Chalukyas [of Vengi] like a sacrifice to Yama', the god of death, at the battle of Vingavalli.[130] Nearing seventy, Amoghavarsha finally sought a diplomatic resolution to the Ganga problem: two of Amoghavarsha's daughters were married to Ganga princes, and the

Ganga king, who had successfully brought the subcontinent's greatest power to terms, was only too happy to establish a military alliance with the Rashtrakutas[131] after generations of bloodshed. This would last until the collapse of both houses in the late tenth century. From the Rashtrakuta perspective, this was at least if not more significant than the north Indian adventures which captivate the modern imagination. Gangavadi's terrain was extremely hilly, with an average elevation comparable to the Vindhya mountains; it thus offered them a secure southern frontier and staging ground for campaigns in the Tamil country. We will witness this later in the book.

Ageing rapidly, Amoghavarsha finally appointed one of his younger sons as crown prince. This man would eventually rise to the throne as Krishna II[132] and face (with somewhat less success) the challenges of the vast, unwieldy empire. His life had been one of high drama and low betrayal, of creative brilliance and hard administrative work, of decades of peace ended by a decade of war. Nevertheless, by the late 870s, Amoghavarsha had dominated the Deccan for over sixty years, a feat no other monarch before him had managed, one that none after him – not even the emperors of Vijayanagara and Delhi – would be able to repeat. His encouragement of trade and development of courtly Kannada would long outlive him.

Fortune, it is said, favours the brave, the audacious, but she also favours the tenacious. Well could Amoghavarsha claim to be Vallabha-Narendra, the Beloved Lord of Men, the Beloved Indra of Mortals, and Nripatunga, Pinnacle of Kings, and have his poets declare that 'the seals of all kings he has broken with his Garuda seal'.[133]

What might the people of Manyakheta have thought about this man when they saw him during seasonal festivals and public rituals? Generations had come of age under his reign, knowing no Vallabha other than him. His wrinkled face was perhaps arranged into the calm, benevolent expression he had learned so many decades ago, dispensing nods and glances and smiles graciously.

The Vallabha Amoghavarsha, Sarva Rashtrakuta, once a boy who
lost his father, once terrified of the intrigues of older men, had outlasted
them all. To his contemporaries in the subcontinent and the world,
he was *the* Vallabha, perhaps the most iconic of all Deccan emperors
– though his importance as a South Asian historical figure has faded
since. Amoghavarsha had held the Deccan together at all costs. Would
those who followed be able to do the same?

Part III

Twilight: The Kalyana Chalukyas and the Chola Empire

8

King of Kings

Spring, 959 CE

We return to the medieval Deccan nearly a century after the career of Amoghavarsha I.

Through this intervening period, South Asia saw an intensification of the trends we have witnessed so far. Courtly Kannada literature, especially by south Indian Jain writers, continued to be produced in ever-larger quantities. The Rashtrakuta imperial family involved themselves deeply in the politics of central India through intermarriage with the Kalachuri family of Tripuri, based in modern Madhya Pradesh and Chhattisgarh. The Gangas of southern Karnataka also gradually became the Rashtrakutas' closest allies as a result of generations of intermarriage, a trend Amoghavarsha I had inaugurated.

The Rashtrakutas also gradually regained an overwhelming influence over the politics of Vengi: many Vallabhas would sack the region, often encouraging bloody dynastic conflict among the Chalukyas of Vengi to ensure their unquestioned dominance. However, the aristocratic houses of the Deccan grew more powerful, often involving themselves in these political struggles, joining factions opposed to their Rashtrakuta overlords, and on occasion successfully intervening in succession crises within the imperial family.

To their north, the influence of the Pratiharas initially rose rapidly under a series of energetic rulers. Kannauj, Harsha's erstwhile capital commanding the eastern Gangetic plains, became one of the major centres of their power. However, by the early tenth century, the Rashtrakuta emperor Indra III once again led a Deccan army north and sacked the city and its environs, dealing a mortal blow to Pratihara power. Their ensuing decline led to the establishment of smaller regional kingdoms in western India, some of which, such as the Paramaras of Malwa, were loosely integrated into the Rashtrakuta imperial network through ties of tribute. Further east, the Palas of Bengal also lost their predominance over the eastern Gangetic plains, with their ostensible vassals having far more influence and power in the region.

To the south of the Rashtrakuta imperial formation, in Tamilakam, the Tamil country, Pallava power had significantly eroded. Once the region's predominant dynasty, it was now under threat from innovative new polities: the Cheras, trading with the western Indian Ocean from their base of Mahodayapuram (modern Kodungallur) in what is now Kerala; the Pandyas of Madurai; and an ambitious dynasty based in the Kaveri river valley, calling themselves the Cholas.

By the late tenth century, all the great imperial houses of the early medieval period were in terminal decline, waiting only for an ambitious vassal to overthrow them at last and create new regional imperial states of their own. The Rashtrakutas appeared to be the sole exception to the rule. The powerful Vallabha Krishna III, succeeding a string of weak and incompetent rulers, had managed to convince the aristocratic houses of the Deccan to join him in a series of campaigns north and south, propelling the Rashtrakuta imperial formation to its territorial apogee. As it would turn out, the empire was nowhere near as strong as it appeared: Krishna III's vassals, the aristocratic houses of the

Deccan, were merely biding their time and waiting for an opportunity to seek their own fortunes on the battlefield.

As we witness the final collapse of this imperial dynasty, we will see how the actions of the Rashtrakuta Vallabhas inadvertently created the political conditions needed for these new regional kingdoms to rise in south and central India. And as it fades in confusion and chaos, we will see how, in a world very different from that in which the earliest Chalukyas had established their power in the Deccan, a new dynasty calling themselves the Chalukyas would be established as an innovative, resilient, new Deccan superpower.

In March 959, Amoghavarsha's descendant, the Rashtrakuta emperor Krishna III, Gandamartandaditya (Sun among Sun-like Warriors), built a victory-pillar[1] and two temples to gods named after himself – Krishneshvara and Gandamartandadityeshvara – on the southernmost tip of the subcontinent.[2] Rampaging over the Tamil lands, his armies had brutally slain the crown prince of the up-and-coming Cholas, a local Tamil dynasty, at the battle of Takkolam in 949. In the ensuing decade, Krishna III outdid all previous Vallabhas: whereas they had been content with subduing and extracting tribute from the Tamil kings, Krishna divided the Tamil lands among his vassals and followers, perhaps with the intention of creating a new power base loyal to him and preventing any new imperial power from rising in the region. This conquest was commemorated through inscriptions in Kannada,[3] not Sanskrit, previously the premier language of power in the south.

A few years later, the Rashtrakuta emperor led an expedition into Malwa alongside his relation,[4] the Ganga king Marasimha II. As a reward, Marasimha – descended from a family once implacably opposed to the Rashtrakutas – had proudly accepted from Krishna the title of Gurjaradhiraja, Supreme King of the Gurjaras, claimed the honour of personally organizing and protecting the emperor's camp, and awarded two of his generals the title of Ujjenibhujanga, Conqueror of Ujjain. This attack of Krishna's would be responsible for the spread of Kannada inscriptions to the furthest north they would ever reach, near Jabalpur in modern-day Madhya Pradesh. Evidently, a century after Amoghavarsha Rashtrakuta, the inscriptions of south Indian kings now sought to speak to their vassals in their very own language of prestige, no longer bothered with the distant, hallowed world of the Sanskrit Cosmopolis.[5]

Krishna III's title, Gandamartandaditya, Sun among Sun-Like Warriors, was a compound of Kannada and Sanskrit, only allowed by the grammarians – following the lead established by his ancestor Amoghavarsha I – in royal titles such as this.[6] By his death in 967, it seemed that no other king had ever been the overlord of the subcontinent's entire southern peninsula as completely as Krishna III Rashtrakuta.[7] And yet, in 972, five years after his death,[8] the great Rashtrakuta capital of Manyakheta, which had awed south Indian kings and Arab travellers for nearly two centuries and sent out armies to ravage much of the subcontinent, was sacked for the first time.

On the banks of the Narmada, at the ford called Kalighatta[9] near modern Thalghat[10] – three and a half centuries after the Chalukya Vallabha Pulakeshin II had humbled Harsha, lord of the north, on the same shores – a new Harsha faced the armies of the Deccan. He was called Siyaka 'Harsha' Paramara, king of Malwa in Madhya Pradesh, of a dynasty of military aristocrats once subservient to the Pratiharas of northern India. The warlords of the Deccan had sacked his capital at Ujjain barely a decade earlier[11] and forced him to prostrate before Krishna III. Now that Krishna was dead, succeeded by his elderly and incompetent brother, Siyaka's time had come.

At Kalighatta, the Rashtrakuta armies tried to hold off Siyaka's bands of boat-riding troops, killing one of his generals in hails of

Stephen Paa / Hole Narasipura / Wikimedia Commons

The Atakur hero stone, one of the most unique surviving Deccan hero stones. Rather than commemorate the death of a warrior, it praises a hound named Kali, 'the ostentatious barker'. Kali (on the left) belonged to the Ganga king Butuga II, who fought alongside the Rashtrakuta emperor Krishna III against the Cholas at the battle of Takkolam in 949 CE. He was then gifted to Butuga's knight Manalera as a reward for the latter's valour in that battle. Soon after, when Manalera was hunting in his fief, Kali and a boar fought to the death, leading to this stone being set up. Today it constitutes a reminder of the tapestry of emotions that accompanied the political and military turbulence of the early medieval world.

javelins and flaming projectiles.[12] But the Paramara king, coming up with reinforcements, outmanoeuvred the Deccanis and inflicted a devastating defeat on them.[13] This defeat would slowly snowball into one of the most unprecedented military disasters in the subcontinent's entire history.

A man bearing the title of 'Harsha' had finally crossed the Narmada and entered the Deccan.

The subcontinent must have reeled in shock as news of the disaster began to spread. As we have seen, the tenth century had been one of war and tumult in northern India as the Palas and Pratiharas declined and new regional kingdoms emerged. Now chaos was coming to the Deccan as well.

Perhaps the Malwans rushed through the gates like a river through a broken embankment, pouring down the royal avenue.[14] They stormed past whitewashed mansions with balconies and terraces from where aristocrats had watched parades.[15] They saw the splendid elephant racecourses of the city, where the Rashtrakuta emperors, preceded by troupes of dancers, came to enjoy the cinnamon scent of the tuskers' musth, the cheers of their subjects.[16] Perhaps they paused before sacking the dozens of temples that decorated Manyakheta. What would they have thought of the beautiful tiered southern architecture unfamiliar to their eyes?

Everywhere, like other armies across the medieval world, and as implied by Indian inscriptions, they probably ran about in gangs in the neighbourhoods, slaughtering, raping, plundering. They may have pried out the gold panels, made piles of loot out of family heirlooms, and assaulted their captives, gloating over their power. 'Do not the hand devoid of wristlets, the breast devoid of necklace, the eyes deprived of collyrium [kohl], the ear without the ear-ornament, the waist bare of girdle and the tender-leaf-like feet wanting the anklet, of the wives of his enemies … bespeak the heroism, the overpowering capacity, and the prosperity of the king …?' asks a medieval Deccan poet, offering us an insight into the attitudes of the warlike aristocrats of the period.[17]

It must have been surreal for King Siyaka Paramara to enter the imperial palace, outside whose gates crowds of vassal lords had once gathered to the beat of the Rashtrakuta drum. He strode past its intricate series of courtyards, accompanied by a platoon of guards and senior generals, including his son Vakpati Paramara, Lord of Speech, a poet and capable military leader. In those courtyards, Siyaka had once waited in humiliation with other subjugated kings as the Vallabha's officers displayed captured horses and elephants before them,[18] waiting for the palace chamberlains to strike the floor with their golden staves and admit them to the next courtyard and the next. This continued until they finally reached the imperial court where they had to gaze upon their Rashtrakuta overlord with compulsory adoration,[19] and should they be called to do so, touch their crowned heads to his feet.[20]

Siyaka inspected the offices and sub-offices of the Manyakheta palace, and had their records, carved on copper plates, seized.[21] What might he have seen as he explored and ransacked the palace? Rashtrakuta literature speaks of exquisite murals and carvings and lush gardens: flowers, waterworks, artificial hillocks, and trees carefully manicured and arranged.[22] There were pleasure pavilions and bathhouses with exquisite fountains and tanks, water-powered automata ingeniously crafted into the shapes of lotuses, animals and women: hydraulic marvels[23] inspired by developments in Baghdad and Constantinople. Perhaps the Malwan king sat on Amoghavarsha Rashtrakuta's lion throne, gloating in his new-found power and the woe of his vanquished enemies.

Within weeks, Ganga troops, led by Krishna III's loyal general Marasimha II, had chased Siyaka out of the Deccan.[24] But it was too late. Fortune had finally abandoned the Rashtrakutas, though there would still be Rashtrakutas claiming the title of Sri-Prithivi-Vallabha for years after.[25] However, with neither an army nor the great capital and its wealthy surrounding territories to support them and enforce their authority over the Deccan's kingdoms, nobody paid them any attention.

The sudden evaporation of the Rashtrakuta dynasty might appear surprising given that it seemed to have reached its apogee under Krishna III less than a decade ago – but it also reveals how military and political successes are an inadequate lens through which to study historical change. A nuanced understanding of the power relations between the Rashtrakuta court and its vassals, situated within the changing political economy of the tenth century, awaits the discovery of more primary sources and archaeological evidence from the period. Until then, the collapse of the Rashtrakuta Vallabhas will remain a dramatic tale of hubris, imperial overreach and the fragility of even the mightiest dynasties in the face of the tides of history.

In the aftermath of the sack of Manyakheta and the collapse of the Rashtrakuta imperial house, a man called Taila emerges onto the historical scene. As for who exactly he was and where he came from, we have only fragmentary evidence and the unreliable testimony of his descendants. He was a high-ranking officer in Krishna III's army and did very well for himself through the emperor's reign, rising to the rank of raja, and assigned the status of guard over a hefty thousand-village district in the vicinity of Manyakheta.[26] He was also connected to a minor Rashtrakuta line through his wife,[27] a marital alliance that may well have been arranged by the Vallabha to honour this loyal subordinate of moderate means and prestige.

Taila would later claim to be descended from one of the many Chalukya families that still survived in the Deccan, some of them minor branches of the Vatapi line, others that seem to have used the name mostly because of its prestige and allure. Whether or not his ancestors were actually one of those long-forgotten kings, it is difficult to say, but as one of the Rashtrakuta emperor's military officers, Taila was likely well connected in the Manyakheta court, understood how the cut-throat world of high politics worked, and personally knew many of the warlords who would now emerge to stake their claim to be Fortune's Favourite.

Soon after Siyaka's departure from Manyakheta, Taila seems to have managed to seize the city, thus guaranteeing his own eminence in the new political order that would inevitably emerge.[28] As war whittled away other claimants and his confidence grew, a large faction gradually began to gather around him, claiming that Taila was a Chalukya. However, all concrete memories of that ancient line – their fantastic *prashasti* claims of being nourished by the breasts of the Seven Mothers[29] and their Sanskrit verses on each king's reign and descent – seem to have faded by this time. Only the Chalukya name, the boar banner and the iconic 'Victorious is Vishnu made manifest as the Boar!' invocation still remained in popular memory, 'like dimly remembered formulas of a lost heroic language'.[30] In medieval south India, though, remembered histories were a powerful and potent political force, and it was something that Taila's new 'Chalukyas' would exploit with great success.

Though his descendants' inscriptions (and some modern historians) have construed Taila's rise as inevitable, this was by no means guaranteed in the late tenth century. He was far from the largest fish in this pond – or even the most powerful contender of ostensibly Chalukya descent. That distinction belonged to Rajaditya Chalukya, apparently an actual descendant of that ancient family, who was married to one Ganga and one Rashtrakuta princess,[31] and the foremost leader of the forces arrayed against a Rashtrakuta restoration. Opposing him was the Ganga king Marasimha II, leader of the pro-Rashtrakuta faction represented by a grandson of Krishna III.

Meanwhile, Siyaka's son and heir Vakpati Paramara, sacker of Manyakheta, master of Malwa, claimed the titles of Maharajadhiraja, Sri-Prithivi-Vallabha and Amoghavarsha,[32] comparing his own poetic talents to those of the celebrated Deccan monarch of the ninth century. He would cross the Narmada multiple times to raid the Deccan,[33] attempting to carve out an empire that spanned the great river. Rounding out the list of contenders to the overlordship of the

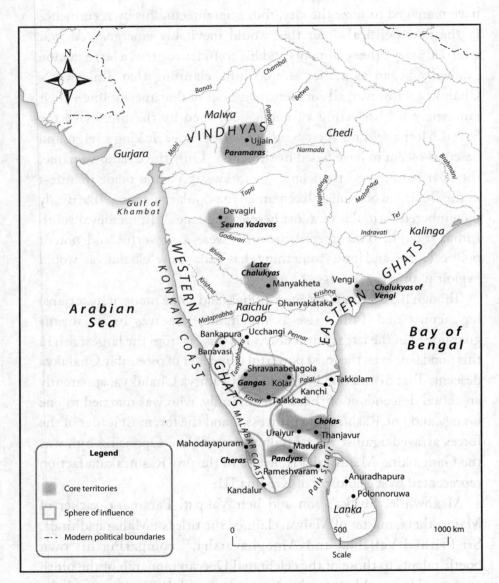

Southern India, late tenth century CE.

Deccan was yet another Rashtrakuta princeling, propped up by two powerful hereditary ministers.[34] And in every part of the Deccan, there were now practically independent regional kingdoms that were hardly enthusiastic about returning to an imperial network with distant Manyakheta at the centre.

Precisely how Taila went about consolidating his position is unclear. As with most events of the time, all that survives are flashes of complex warfare and politicking that lasted till the very end of the tenth century. Taila appears to have drawn to himself similarly upstart, ambitious men of aristocratic backgrounds, often provincial governors or landed magnates[35] who were richly rewarded with titles and wealth in return for their personal loyalty to him and the efforts they undertook on his behalf. The upper echelons of Taila's faction were highly militarily competent: one of them bore the title of Giri-Durga-Malla, Wrestler of Hill Forts.[36] They worked together to cajole or otherwise convince remnants of the Rashtrakuta imperial formation to accede to a reworked 'Chalukya' imperial formation. As one might imagine, the creation of this new polity was a bloody process, and this is attested to in many of Taila's inscriptions. The picture that they suggest is that Taila's faction astutely chose its moment to strike, waiting until after the biggest contenders had eliminated themselves.

This moment came in 974. At the beginning of that year, the Ganga king Marasimha II seemed to be at the peak of his power. His territories had vastly expanded due to lands granted to him by Krishna III in gratitude[37] for his participation in imperial campaigns in the north and south, and even securing the submission of some Tamil kings. Had Marasimha prevailed, he might have reinstalled a puppet Rashtrakuta emperor at Manyakheta – but it was not to be. He and the most powerful Chalukya claimant, Rajaditya,[38] fought a gruelling, exhausting campaign around the great citadel of Ucchangi (near modern-day Davanagere, Karnataka). The horrors inflicted by both sides seem to have eliminated Rajaditya from contention and convinced this great Ganga king to give up his ambitions. An ordained Jain, Marasimha gave up his crown and spent a year moving across his territories before ritually starving himself to death at the feet of his preceptor Ajitasena in a three-day fast in Bankapura[39] near modern-day Hubli-Dharwad. This was the very same city founded by Amoghavarsha Rashtrakuta's general Bankeya. 'Aho! Chola king, quiet down by gently rubbing thy palpitating heart! O Pandya, give up weeping! O Pallava, run not away in fear; O retreat not from thy territory, but remain …! The Ganga chieftain … has gone in triumph to the abode of the gods!'[40] wailed a poet. Soon after, Taila and his army arrived on the borders of Gangavadi proper,[41] and subdued it.

Vinaya Raj / Wikimedia Commons

A colossal monolithic statue of Gomateshvara Bahubali, a popular figure in Deccan Jainism. This statue was commissioned at the pilgrimage site of Shravanabelagola by Chamundaraya, a feudatory of the Gangas, in 981, seven years after the death of Marasimha II. The scale of the image, given that it was paid for by a feudatory ruler, suggests that the power of the Gangas was already on the wane. Shravanabelagola today is home to the epitaph of Marasimha.

By 980, Taila was the acknowledged Chalukya overlord of much of northern and southern Karnataka, and his armies had quelled the families that controlled the Western Ghats.[42] Shortly thereafter, his generals attacked Goa and forced its rulers to surrender. With most of the southern and western Deccan now subservient to the Chalukya Varaha, Taila finally turned to deal with the last powerful remaining claimant to the lordship of the Deccan, a man whose sacking of Manyakheta had caused the anarchy pervading the plateau: Vakpati Paramara, the north Indian who dared to claim the title of Prithivi-Vallabha.

Realizing that Taila had emerged as the dominant force south of the Narmada, Vakpati, sometime around 994–996, decided to gamble it all in an open confrontation.[43] Raids were no longer enough to maintain his claims to Deccan overlordship. Taila had to be defeated, and Manyakheta, which Vakpati's father Siyaka had sacked in 972, had to be permanently occupied. This would lead to a showdown so memorable that it would pass into oral legend and eventually be included in a Sanskrit storybook by the Jain monk Merutungacharya in fourteenth-century Gujarat. According to this work,[44] when Vakpati decided to mount a full-scale invasion of the Deccan, his minister[45] warned him that disaster was waiting for him across the Godavari. The king ignored the advice and set out, and the distraught minister immolated himself.[46] Should this be even a dim memory of real events, it seems that Vakpati was betting he would be able to beat Taila decisively deep in the Deccan. But his dead minister was right: this was a suicidal mistake.

As the Malwan armies marched across the Narmada, the Vindhyas and the Godavari, into the heart of the Deccan, a trap was sprung. The Seuna Yadavas of northern Deccan, who had accepted a position as Taila's vassal kings, swung in and cut off Vakpati's supply lines and channels of communication to his core territories in Malwa.[47] The Malwan king was left at Taila's mercy. Vakpati's army was annihilated and the Paramara king captured.

And so one of the biggest military blunders in medieval Indian history came to a close. The supremacy of Taila's 'Chalukyas', and their claim to the title of Sri-Prithivi-Vallabha Maharajadhiraja, was indisputable: the Gangas, Rashtrakutas, Paramaras and other Chalukyas had all been crushed, and the Silaharas, Seuna Yadavas, minor Rashtrakuta lines and dozens, if not hundreds, of other political groups and clans had all yielded.

Krishna I Rashtrakuta, nearly two centuries earlier, had described his defeat of the Vatapi Chalukyas as his having 'forcibly wrested away' on the 'battlefield that was the auspicious hall of marriage' the Goddess of the Royal Fortune.[48] The Seuna Yadavas, vassals of Taila's new Chalukyas, now described how they gave Fortune 'a sound thrashing'[49] for associating with Vakpati and 'forced her to take to the life of an obedient house-wife'[50] in Taila's palace. (These, incidentally, were the same Seuna Yadavas who would be defeated by Alauddin Khilji centuries later and have their capital, Devagiri/Daulatabad, taken over by the Tughlaq Sultans of Delhi.)

Vakpati came to an unpleasant end. After his capture, legend tells us that he was stripped, put in a cage, paraded through the streets of Manyakheta, and forced to go from household to household begging for food.[51] If this is true, he must have been bound and chained and carefully watched by guards through this humiliation. It is unlikely that anyone was so forgiving as to feed the son of Siyaka Paramara, the man who had sacked their city.

And so, after a miserable and humiliating few days, the unrecognizable Malwan monarch, his once-glorious moustache torn and yanked, his fair skin probably splattered with mud and excrement and blistering in the harsh Deccan sun, was dragged to a public execution site on the city outskirts. Here he was brutally impaled on a stake[52] to the roar of cheering crowds before being beheaded. His rotting head, covered with 'thick sour milk',[53] was put on display for visitors to the new court of Manyakheta, leaving them in no doubt as to the power and intentions of the 'Chalukyas' who had returned to claim the mantle of Fortune's Favourite.

∽

These had been momentous decades for the Deccan, but also for the world. Even as regional kingdoms had emerged across northern India over the tenth century, the Abbasid Caliphate headquartered in Baghdad had faded, and governors of various parts of the far-flung Abbasid empire turned their provinces into power bases of their own.[54] In 969, Egypt became the seat of a new Caliphate:[55] the Fatimids, supposedly descended from the daughter of the Prophet Muhammad, Fatima, and her husband, the Imam Ali.

The Fatimids soon founded a new capital city that would rival Manyakheta and Baghdad in splendour. This was al-Qahira,[56] Cairo – which has certainly fared better than these two rival cities in its thousand-year history. The Fatimid Caliph took up court there in 973,[57] the year after the Paramaras' sack of Manyakheta. The Fatimids nurtured Egypt's fertile agrarian tracts and encouraged international trade. Cairo's markets boomed. The ancient trade routes of the Red Sea, where fleets of hundreds of Roman ships had once gathered in the early centuries CE to be blown to India by the gale-force winds of the southwest monsoon,[58] once again roared back to life.

However, it was in many ways China that emerged as the 'world axis' of the time, and its interaction with the rest of Afro-Eurasia would accelerate the formation of a 'thickening world system'.[59] A new dynasty, the Song, rose to power around 960, inaugurating a period of artistic, intellectual and technological achievements – including, for example, large-scale iron manufacturing verging on an 'industrial revolution',[60] and the invention of gunpowder.[61] In addition, 'new varieties of crops were introduced into China from Southeast Asia, improved irrigation machines and techniques spread rapidly, and the

Chinese population started migrating towards the fertile southern region of the country'.[62] China's population would grow 'almost fourfold' from 32 million to 121 million during 961–1109, urbanizing all the while.[63]

To feed these ravenous new cities and provide them with the good things of life – 'frankincense, sandalwood, black pepper and cloves'[64] – and luxury goods such as rose water, coral, glass, printed textiles and carved ivories – private enterprise was encouraged,[65] with spectacular results. Merchants from across the world flocked to the coasts of China in the tenth century.[66] Goods from far-flung regions arrived here in unprecedented quantities.

The share of international commerce in China's state revenue exploded to nearly twenty times[67] what it had been under earlier dynasties. In 987, the Song court sent out four missions 'invested with imperial authority ... to foreign countries ... to come more frequently to the Chinese ports on the promise of special facilities and import licences'.[68] These missions travelled west by sea, first visiting the archipelagos of Southeast Asia, dominated by the Srivijaya confederacy: a loose-knit alliance of trading cities that stretched from Sumatra through the Malay Peninsula, led by Srivijaya (modern-day Palembang in Indonesia), which gave the confederacy its name. The confederacy's many allied fleets dominated the Straits of Malacca, the gateway to the Indian Ocean.

After crossing the straits, the next stop for the Song ambassadors was southern India. The arrival of these missions in the region, coinciding with the rise of the Fatimids and the Chalukyas, would inadvertently assist the emergence of a polity that profoundly impacted the history of the Indian Ocean.

❧

In Tamilakam, the Rashtrakuta Vallabha Krishna III's killing of the Chola crown prince in 949 had consequences which rapidly took on a life of their own. Krishna III had, as mentioned, redistributed lands in the Tamil country to his Deccan vassals, significantly eroding the power of minor local dynasties and the Pallavas alike. After the death of the Vallabha in 967, his vassals retreated from the Tamil country to compete in the Deccan political arena; and the remaining Tamil dynasties rapidly expanded into the political vacuum. The Cholas, now led by the energetic younger brothers of the dead crown prince, rapidly regained much of their lost territories in the Kaveri river valley, and expanded into the erstwhile Pallava heartland. To their east, the Chera dynasty of Mahodayapuram (modern-day Kodungallur) controlled the thriving ports of the region corresponding to Kerala today, while to their south, the Pandya dynasty of Madurai dominated the southeast tip of the subcontinent. All these medieval dynasties identified with ancient patrons of Tamil Sangam poetry from the late centuries BCE/early centuries CE, thus connecting themselves to a long-vanished 'classical' age.[69] (As with Taila's 'Chalukyas', there is almost no way to verify these unlikely claims.)

Any would-be Tamil superpower also had to grapple with the autonomy of hundreds of smaller polities, village assemblies, local magnates and Brahmin settlements[70] that had emerged over the centuries. Tamilakam's multicentric political system may well have continued for centuries, just as the Deccan could well have shifted to a pattern of subregional kingdoms after the Rashtrakuta collapse. But in both cases, ruthless competition led to the emergence of leaders of extraordinary political and military ability.

In July 985, when the Cholas had finally gained the upper hand over the Pandyas and emerged as the primary power in the northern and eastern parts of the Tamil country, a prince by the name of Arulmozhivarman acceded to the throne, adopting the regnal title of Rajaraja, King of Kings. The screaming of trumpets, the clanging of bells and chanting of priests at the ceremony may have all seemed to portend a subcontinent – and a world – that would be changed forever.

Rajaraja Chola understood that domination of lucrative trade routes was a sure way to distinguish himself and his court from the other fragmented polities of the Tamil country. But he soon learned that rival polities to his east were suddenly receiving more and more traders from across the seas. This was because traders from prosperous Fatimid Egypt were now reaching the Malabar coast, under the control of the Chera dynasty. Within a few years of his accession, the young[71] Chola king moved to seize the riches of the region by attacking the great port of Kandalur,[72] ruled by a Chera vassal. This happened around the same time as the arrival of the first embassies from Song China to the Indian Ocean region, and its timing cannot have been a coincidence. What was possibly south India's largest collection of ships at the time was gathered at Kandalur port. The fleet probably numbered at least a few hundred, and would primarily have been composed of vessels owned by merchant corporations. Rajaraja appears to have caught it at its most vulnerable – in harbour, perhaps preparing to set out for that year's trading season – and ordered it burned.

It must have been a spectacular and horrifying sight. Medieval Indian texts describe ships painted white, red, yellow and blue; with prows shaped like lions, buffaloes, snakes, elephants, tigers, birds and people; and with sails of white, red, yellow and black.[73] As the burning cloth snapped in the sea breeze, scattering sparks and smoke, the unbearable heat spread from one ship to another. Masts must have collapsed, teakwood cracked and slipped under the roiling waves, probably to the cheers of thousands of Chola soldiers as they ransacked the populace and held back weeping merchants at spear-point. Rajaraja had seized a colossal loot and violently established himself and the Cholas as one of the rising powers of the southern tip of the subcontinent. Trade would only be allowed to flow if merchants reached an accommodation with the Cholas, it seemed.

It was a sign of things to come. Over the next decade, Rajaraja Chola would display an extraordinary grasp of political and military strategy, tactics and operations. If an opportunity presented itself, Rajaraja Chola could be relied upon to exploit it – and to use it to send a message. By the 990s, inscriptions suggest he had overrun much of the erstwhile Pandya territories and appointed his own governors there.

Soon after, a merchant informed him of a mutiny of mercenaries from Karnataka and Kerala, who served as the private army of the Sri Lankan king. Lanka at the time was quite deeply integrated into south Indian movements of goods, labour and capital. Rajaraja immediately moved to take advantage of the chaos in the island. A Chola army penetrated deep inland and completely sacked the nearly thousand-year-old Sinhala capital, Anuradhapura. The chief queen[74] was captured and sent to Rajaraja, as were the royal jewels, crown and sword.[75] Northern Lanka was then savagely looted: stupas were broken apart and golden images, reliquaries and offerings within stolen.[76] A temple to Shiva was set up after the capture of the city of Polonnaruwa.[77] The ransacking of the great Buddhist viharas – some of which were home to hundreds of monks and supported by the produce of villages and bonded labour,[78] just like temples in India – was so comprehensive that later Sinhala chroniclers would describe the Chola troops as 'blood-sucking *yakkhas* [capricious nature-deities]'.[79] Lanka, like the Pandya country, would now also become home to a permanent Chola presence as Rajaraja built a number of Shiva temples and established a garrison at Polonnaruwa.

After the conquest of Lanka, the Cholas dominated not only the southern tip of India, but also the Palk Strait, the gateway between the eastern and western Indian Ocean. Control of this crucial geopolitical crossroads allowed Rajaraja Chola, and merchant guilds connected to him, to extract profits from the movement of goods between East, West and South Asia.

The death of the Ganga king Marasimha II in 974 provided Rajaraja another opportunity to expand. He now made an attempt to seize control of the trade routes between the southern Deccan and Tamilakam. His generals first conquered the many hill forts that dotted Kongu, the drylands where the rocky plateau transitioned into the lush green fields of Tamilakam. In 991, Rajaraja himself was in Gangavadi.[80] Encountering no opposition, he headed further north, only to find Taila Chalukya, by now the Deccan's dominant ruler, heading towards him at speed at the head of an army. In this first major clash between Chalukya and Chola, the Chola was thrashed, apparently losing one hundred and fifty war elephants[81] to the older and more experienced Chalukya. This was a serious setback, especially given the close ties between a warlord's prestige and the size of his elephant corps. But Rajaraja was given a reprieve: before Taila could decisively deal with the brash young Tamil king, he was forced to turn north to repel Vakpati Paramara, thus leaving Gangavadi in Rajaraja's hands. Nevertheless the defeat humiliated Rajaraja: he supposedly vowed he would never hunt again until he had sacked Manyakheta.[82]

Taila Chalukya died in 997, having regained some of the Deccan empire's lost territory and founded a new imperial dynasty. He was succeeded by his son Satyashraya – a title apparently meant to connect him to his illustrious purported ancestor, Pulakeshin II, who had used Satyashraya, Refuge of Truth, as one of his titles. By this point, the Cholas had successfully overrun most of Gangavadi,[83] which had so heroically resisted generations of Deccan Vallabhas; they had also wiped out the Pallavas, dominated the Cheras and Pandyas, and conquered much of Sri Lanka. The hill chiefs and kings of the southern Deccan were gradually being integrated into the burgeoning Chola state; indeed, one can still find Chola temples to Shiva in modern-day Bengaluru. Never before had the Deccan faced such a dangerous foe. And the Cholas were only just getting started.

Temporarily stymied by Chalukya power to his northwest, Rajaraja Chola cast about for easier targets. In Vengi – crucial for Chola dominance of east coast trade – he found one, taking advantage of the mess the Rashtrakutas had left behind. By persistently interfering in the politics of Vengi for nearly two hundred years, the Rashtrakutas had created a situation of perpetual dynastic strife within the Chalukya dynasty of Vengi – the only truly royal descendants of the old Chalukyas of Vatapi. In the aftermath of a civil war, two Vengi Chalukya princes fled south to the Chola court,[84] and Rajaraja was only too pleased to intervene on their behalf. He invaded Vengi and installed the elder prince as king. The younger remained in the Chola court and was married to Rajaraja's daughter.[85] Their children's story, as we'll see, would be tied to the ultimate doom of Rajaraja's male line.

By 1000 CE, Chola military and political successes had responded to and influenced crucial long-term trends in global history. The achievements of Rajaraja Chola, this singularly ambitious and capable man, would have ramifications for centuries. Thanks in part to his career, powerful, stable and commercially inclined polities now controlled each of the nodes and access routes to the thriving trade networks of the Indian Ocean: the Red Sea by the Fatimids; the Palk Strait by the Cholas; the Malacca Strait by Srivijaya; and China by the Song dynasty. International trade boomed and Chola coffers swelled.

The wealth this dynasty had gained from their military success and the control of trade is readily apparent in the gigantic Rajarajeshvaram (Rajaraja's Lord) temple, today known as the Brihadishvara or 'Big' temple in Thanjavur, which Rajaraja endowed in 1003.[86] This building was so huge that it contained about *forty times* as much stone as the average Chola temple,[87] and its construction is a testament to the scale of the resources Rajaraja was able to mobilize. Over the next decade, until his death, the Rajarajeshvaram would be showered with the wealth of Chola conquests north, south and west. It was, as the Krishneshvara at Ellora was for the Rashtrakutas, a potent statement

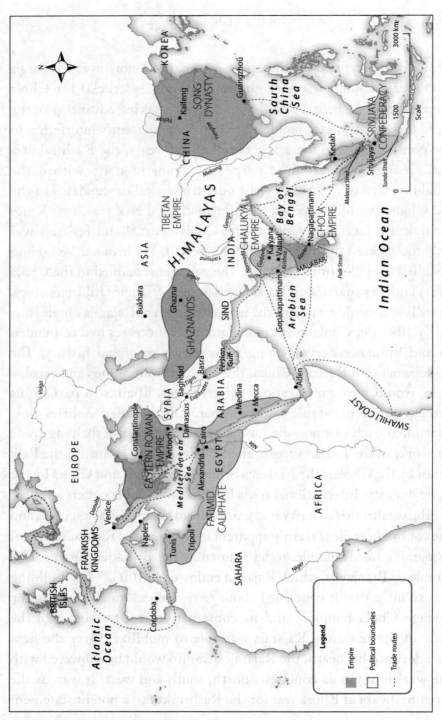

Afro-Eurasia, early tenth century CE.

Marcllendr / Wikimedia Commons

The *vimana* of the Rajarajeshvaram or Brihadishvara temple at Thanjavur, Tamil Nadu, exhibiting its enormous scale. The ambition and resources required to make this building are singularly impressive.

of the abilities and vision of this dynasty. The gifts that the king, his elder sister, his vassals, his army regiments and the temple women dedicated to the god added up to thousands of kilograms of gold and silver, alongside hundreds of valuable gemstones[88] and dozens of trumpets, parasols and other royal and military paraphernalia.[89] These had been seized from the newly arisen Chalukyas in the Deccan, the Buddhist monasteries and stupas of Sri Lanka, the ports of Kerala, and the sacked hill forts and towns of recalcitrant south Indian chiefs and kings. Luxurious and exotic gifts to Rajaraja's Lord – incense, camphor, musk – were sourced from merchants increasingly connected to globe-spanning trade networks. The temple itself was built by importing thousands of tonnes of granite from higher up the Kaveri river valley at great expense,[90] and maintained with produce from villages across Chola dominions, even as far away as Sri Lanka.[91] All these were deliberately arranged to reflect the immense reach of Chola royal power.

The Rajarajeshvaram's colossal pyramidal *vimana* (temple spire) rose to a height of 190 feet in fourteen storeys, dwarfing even the Krishneshvara, its only competitor in southern India at the time for sheer scale. It was topped by an 80-tonne granite *shikhara* (a dome atop the temple spire) – probably raised by teams of dozens of elephants and, according to oral legend, a stupendous earthen ramp 4 kilometres long. The Rajarajeshvaram towers over a vast open courtyard a quarter kilometre long and an eighth of a kilometre wide, behind imposing gateways flanked by colossal *dvarapalas* (door guardians). A human is just barely as tall as its plinth. At the time of its construction, it was one of the largest free-standing structures anywhere in the world.

Some inscriptions refer to this extraordinary edifice as Dakshinameru,[92] the World Mountain of the South, a counterpart to Shiva's residence, Mount Kailasha, the northern World Mountain. 'It is a measure of the ambition embodied in this imperial act that Rajaraja could portray himself as having offered Siva a new home in the south, equal to Siva's Himalayan abode,' writes Shaivism scholar Richard H. Davis.[93] The Cholas had outdone the wondrous monolithic residence the Rashtrakutas had once made for the god in the Deccan, and brought Shiva to watch as they conquered all in his name.

While Rajaraja's fortune rose, the Vallabhas of the Deccan had not been idle. It was all well and good to claim they were Chalukyas and seize the throne of Manyakheta by force. But something more concrete had to be done if anyone were to take their claim of descent from those half-forgotten Pulakeshins and Vikramadityas seriously, when the shadow of the Rashtrakuta Amoghavarshas and Krishnas still stretched even into the heart of Malwa – and when actual Chalukyas, descended from Pulakeshin I, performer of the Ashvamedha sacrifice, still ruled in Vengi. And so, they turned, as previous Vallabhas had, to masterful literary propaganda. This will allow us a glimpse of one of the most vibrant periods of the development of courtly Kannada, and see how these new Chalukyas legitimized their power in their chaotic world.

The first tentative steps towards the reinvention of Taila's new Chalukyas were made by the brilliant poet Ranna, who had risen from the courts of petty chieftains to those of Rashtrakuta vassals and finally received the title of Kavi-Chakravarti, Emperor among Poets, from the Vallabha Taila himself.[94]

In the 980s, soon after Taila's forces had subdued former Rashtrakuta vassals in the Konkan, Ranna was set the task of turning this bloody campaign, fought on red hillsides and lush coastal jungles, into a work of glory and legend. To do so, he adapted a story from that grandest of all Indian epics, the Mahabharata: specifically the deadly duel between the cousins Bhima, strongest of the heroic Pandava brothers, and Duryodhana, eldest of the wicked Kaurava brothers. The pair develop a memorable rivalry in both the Mahabharata and in Ranna's retelling. After Duryodhana and his brothers attempt to strip the Pandavas' wife Draupadi in full view of the court, Bhima promises to one day wash her hair with Duryodhana's blood. He eventually does so after shattering Duryodhana's thighs with his mace towards the very end of the devastating familial conflict.

Ranna's magnum opus, the *Gadayuddham* (Duel of the Maces), also called the *Sahasa-Bhima-Vijayam* (The Victory of the Bold Bhima), mixed verse and prose, as well as Kannada and Sanskrit, as standardized by Amoghavarsha Rashtrakuta a century ago.[95] It was designed to be read out in the *gamaka* tradition still extant in Karnataka today, with musical accompaniment and pauses to allow audiences to fully experience the complicated array of emotions[96] of the protagonists. The *Gadayuddham* is filled with martial imagery, including, for example, a depiction of a war elephant strike corps in action: 'His cardinal elephant stomps to the fore against the famous Gurjaras on their elephant army. The princes' elephants follow the leading elephant ... so the thread follows the needle, and princes follow [the then crown prince] Satyashraya's elephants.'[97] This was, no doubt, meant to flatter Taila's successor Satyashraya 'Irivabedanga' (A Wonder among Those Who Pierce in Battle), an Old Kannada title.

All these, combined with the depiction of Duryodhana as an unusually compelling antihero, made the work an immediate hit; indeed, it is considered one of the classics of the Kannada courtly tradition to this day. It was a perfectly timed meditation on the human costs of the brutal wars that had been fought to restore order to the Deccan after the anarchy and horror of the previous decades. It was a reminder that the Earth would renew itself just as it had after the devastation of the Mahabharata war, especially under the stewardship of virile, sophisticated and martial Chalukya kings.

In the *Gadayuddham*, Ranna also initiated a process of directly connecting these new Chalukyas to the old. He had dug into extant oral legends to uncover Pulakeshin I's glorious horse sacrifice all those centuries ago and then inserted in his composition a reference to it.[98] By the time Taila's grandsons[99] came to the throne in the early 1000s, this process of creating links to the old Vatapi Chalukyas was further systematized and expanded.[100]

Scholars were dispatched to Aihole, 200 kilometres away from Manyakheta, to examine a great *prashasti* composed for Pulakeshin II.[101] Soon after, we see its opening verses replicated in the land grants of these new Chalukyas, using chaste Sanskrit, not courtly Kannada as was then in fashion.[102] All those marvellous formulations, which had not been heard in the Deccan for two hundred years, reappeared:[103] from the image of Varaha, the Ocean, shaking as he raised Earth on his right tusk, to the Chalukya's nourishment at the breasts of the Seven Mothers, to their 'uninterrupted' dominance over other kings granted by Skanda, to their acquisition of the ever-victorious boar banner at the hands of Vishnu himself.[104] This was not some mindless replication but a self-aware one, designed to tell a new story of new Chalukyas suited to drastically different political circumstances.

In this version, Pulakeshin II never rebelled against his uncle Mangalesha. Instead, Mangalesha merely acted as the boy's dutiful regent and handed over the throne to him as soon as he was mature, for as the *prashasti*'s rewriter puts it, 'what member of the Chalukya dynasty would ever stray from the path of the *dharma*?'[105] This must have dovetailed beautifully with new grants to Brahmins and temples across the Chalukya imperial formation, as elites celebrated the new Chalukya Vallabha's restoration of the supposed dharma of his ancestors, a dharma that we have seen always existed more in the elite political imagination than in actual fact for most of their subjects.

Definitive family connections to the Vallabhas from Vatapi were also dreamed up and included in the *prashasti*, 'setting right once and for all the historical relationship'[106] between the two families. According to these new Chalukyas, Taila was actually the heir of an obscure son of Vikramaditya II. This individual's descendants, according to the new genealogy, had continued to rule some unspecified territories while the treacherous Rashtrakutas reigned over the Deccan – just as Pulakeshin II's sons had survived the anarchy of the Pallava invasion.[107]

All this self-conscious moral and historical positioning was enormously useful in legitimizing this new dynasty. The new Chalukya history, with the inferred prestige it conferred on the Vallabha, was likely circulated and carefully analysed by *maha-sandhi-vigrahakas* (Great Controllers of Peace and War, chancellors-cum-foreign ministers) and kings within and outside their vassal network to assess the martial, territorial and ritual claims it was attempting to make.[108] A connection to the Deccan's seventh-century superpower certainly helped consolidate the 'Chalukya' family's claims to primacy within this turbulent region in the eleventh century.

This connection also served external geopolitical objectives. In particular, by establishing these new Chalukyas as directly tied to Pulakeshin II, it established a connection to his younger brother Kubja-Vishnuvardhana, and thence to Vengi, which Rajaraja Chola had practically taken over only a few years earlier. This fertile coastal belt, well connected to the trading networks of the eastern Indian Ocean, had also recently emerged as a hub of Kannada poetry.[109] The Chalukya Vallabha was searching for ways to take Rajaraja Chola down a notch after the endowment of the splendid Rajarajeshvaram temple, and the Chola king's success in incorporating the Vengi Chalukyas into his own lineage. And so the lords of the Deccan once again plotted to conquer Vengi, that blood-drenched and fertile land between the Krishna and Godavari deltas.

The Chalukyas attacked Vengi in 1006, looting and burning the ancient Buddhist site of Dhanyakataka/Amaravati[110] before being chased out by Chola forces.

The next year, the Tamil chiefs and viceroys and generals gathered to the beating of drums and the blowing of trumpets, and retaliated with a devastating raid of the Deccan. They were led by Rajaraja's equally violent son, Rajendra Chola (Lord of Kings). This sort of an attack was both political and economic activity.[111] It was intended to do much more than slaughter the enemy: a successful raid was the ultimate symbol of a king's ability to subordinate his rivals and reward his vassals with the wealth of their enemies.

According to the Chalukyas, Rajendra, 'the constant joy of Rajaraja, the ornament of the Chola family',[112] attacked with 'a host of nine hundred thousand' (more realistically a tenth, if that, of that number) and 'was ravaging the whole country, perpetrating murders of women, children, and Brahmans'.[113] Their inscription is also quite emphatic that the invaders 'caught hold of girls and destroyed their caste'.[114] Which is to say, Rajendra's army committed mass rape and plunder. Though the scale of this activity is unclear, this testimony cannot be dismissed as unreliable out of some misguided desire to portray the Cholas as chivalric heroes. The capture of women in raids and war in medieval India is extremely well documented,[115] and we have repeatedly seen how violence against enemy women was associated with martial success and royal virility. On the other hand, ostentatious respect for the highborn wives and daughters of one's subjects was considered a mark of chivalry; it is rare to find a medieval king claiming to respect women as people.

Chalukya propaganda thus sought to portray the Cholas as violating dharma through these atrocities, just as the Chola attacks served to humiliate the Chalukyas, and portrayed them as unable to follow the dharma of protecting and enriching their subjects and loyal followers.

When the expedition returned to Tamilakam, the delighted Rajaraja Chola had golden flowers crafted out of his son's loot, and 'worshipped the feet of the god' in the altar of the Rajarajeshvaram.[116] Attended by all the new warlords of the Tamil country and their wives and children in glittering jewels and Chinese silks, and accompanied by the clanging of cymbals and bells and the pungent odour of wet flowers and Arabian incense, this must have been a sight to behold.

And so began the Chola–Chalukya wars: a series of devastating annual attacks and counter-attacks that would destroy cities and towns across southern India and leave thousands, if not tens of thousands, dead and displaced. The stakes of the conflict rose higher every year as the two imperial dynasties sought to outdo each other, leading to ever-escalating campaigns to secure or seize glory and wealth. This vicious pattern had emerged in full force by the time of Rajaraja's death in 1014: in 1010, the Chalukya Vallabha Jayasimha II would describe

P.S. Sriraman, Archaeological Survey of India

'*Rajaraja Worshipping Nataraja at the Koyil*', a mural from the interior of the Rajarajeshvaram temple. Rajaraja, who was probably much older at the time this mural was made, is depicted as a young, fit man wearing simple clothes on this religious occasion. He sports a beard, a moustache, and long hair arranged in a bun. His queens, standing behind him, wear ostentatious jewellery. In the early eleventh century, Thanjavur witnessed many similar royal religious ceremonies.

himself as 'the Lion to that Elephant, Rajendra-Chola'[117] and award one of his generals the title Tigularamari, Death to the Tamils.[118]

But the Cholas were not the only deadly threat the Deccan now had to contend with. The Malwans, under a new king, Bhoja Paramara, known also as Bhoja of Dhara, were out for revenge for Taila's brutal slaughter of Vakpati. Bhoja was one of the most brilliant kings of the medieval world, eclipsing his contemporaries with his encyclopaedic knowledge – which spanned disciplines from aesthetics to architecture

The Paramaras of Malwa

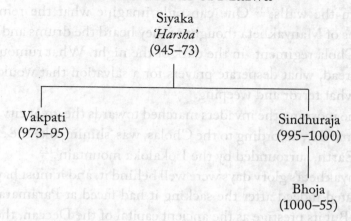

Siyaka
'Harsha'
(945–73)

Vakpati
(973–95)

Sindhuraja
(995–1000)

Bhoja
(1000–55)

– and extraordinary poetic talent. 'In the courtyard of his tongue,' we are told, 'the goddess Sarasvati used to dance in ecstasy.'[119]

His artistic inclinations notwithstanding, Bhoja's armies crossed the Narmada in the mid-1010s, reaching southern Gujarat, and headed south, along the west coast, to the lucrative emporia of the Konkan.[120] The Vallabha Jayasimha II was forced to move to repel them. Rajendra, now the Chola emperor and on the lookout for any opportunity to loot and seize glory, saw a gaping patch in the Deccan's defences, and did not hesitate to take advantage of it.

Around 1016[121] CE, Manyakheta, once the glittering crown jewel of the Deccan's peoples, would be sacked for the last time.

The invading Chola army seems to have encountered almost no serious resistance as it punched past the Krishna river and headed for the city. A huge exodus probably began as news of the invading Tamils spread, panicking denizens clogging the bejewelled gates under which Amoghavarsha Rashtrakuta once paraded. The Chola army camped in orchards of tall sal trees on the Manyakheta outskirts as they prepared to storm the walls.[122] One can only imagine what the remaining denizens of Manyakheta thought as they heard the drums and chants of the Chola regiments in the dark of the night. What rumours may have spread, what desperate prayers for a salvation that would never come, what terror and weeping.

In the morning the invaders marched towards the great city, which on its final day, according to the Cholas, was 'shining like the expanse of the Earth, surrounded by the Lokaloka mountain'.[123]

Manyakheta's glory days were well behind it, and it must have been dilapidated indeed after the sacking it had faced at Paramara hands in 972. But its prestige as the ancient capital of the Deccan, the home of the Vallabhas, was still intact, and it was probably slowly limping to a fresh lease of life as the new imperial centre of the Chalukyas. Destroying it once and for all would send a painful and devastating message. And Rajendra Chola had ordered[124] his generals to do exactly that. Manyakheta's great teakwood gates were pushed open for the last time. The city was once again systematically looted, and Chola sources tell us it was set afire by thousands of torches thrown by Rajendra's army.[125] 'The women running through the smoke in the terraces of the bejewelled mansions looked like lightning flashing through groups of clouds,' a Chola poet would say.[126]

As the flames leapt higher, ash and screams clogged the air. We can scarcely imagine what was destroyed that day: utensils, tiny idols, jewellery, trinkets, manuscripts carefully inscribed and painted by centuries of Deccan Shaivas and Jains, the knowledge of generations of poets, administrators, generals and connoisseurs. Spectacular palaces, carefully built over generations, crumbled. Hovels of mud and thatch, homes to migrating manual labourers, were incinerated. And, as Chola sources tell us, many of Manyakheta's inhabitants must have suffered agonizing deaths through burning or suffocation. 'The gods, abandoning their palaces set alight by the terrible fire burning aloft from that city, suddenly fled away out of fear, suspecting it to be the fire of the apocalypse,' they claim.[127]

Manyakheta – where generations of merchants and kings and poets and courtesans and queens, fisherfolk and sculptors and priests had built communities and families and livelihoods, where Arabs had been bedazzled and emperors had poured scented water and milk over idols of gods and rested their feet on their vassals' crowned heads – was dead. Today, at modern-day Malkhed in Karnataka, the likely site of that city, nothing remains of its glorious past. It has been erased, consigned to oblivion, and there has been little archaeological excavation conducted to precisely locate and study the site.

We do not know how the news of Manyakheta's destruction reached the Chalukya ruler Jayasimha II, Taila's grandson. Thanks to the Paramara king Bhoja, he was already on the back foot in the Konkan. We do not know how he reacted to the disaster when he heard of it. All we know is that the man himself did not give up the struggle, and continued to fight on the Deccan's northern and southern fronts. And unlike after Siyaka's sack of Manyakheta in 972, this time vassals stuck with the Chalukya emperor. This Chalukya court was only three generations old. Its vassals and generals as a group were much more cohesive and invested in the survival of their imperial formation than the huge, unwieldy Rashtrakuta court had been, which was nine rulers and many worlds away from its initial founding members. The Chalukyas even had in their service men (and women[128]) who remembered Taila's precarious rise, and who had fought and defeated Tamils, perhaps even under the command of Krishna III before the Rashtrakuta collapse.

Of course, any thoughts of revenge had to wait. The destruction of Manyakheta, when the Chalukyas were already so vulnerable, must have been a devastating blow to their wealth, prestige and morale. It annihilated a major hub of agrarian, trade and religious networks, which had been crucial to the prestige and power of the Vallabha.

But not all was lost. In reality, the Chalukya capital was wherever the Vallabha's court was, and the court at this time was in a moving military encampment in the Konkan, fighting the forces of the Paramaras and their allies. It seems to have moved quickly to the smoking ruins of the city, leaving the Malwans to prematurely celebrate their conquest of the Konkan in 1020.[129] Meanwhile, an old city on the route from Ellora to Manyakheta – close enough to Manyakheta that the refugees from the scorched city could settle there – was chosen to be a new capital. This city would give these later Chalukyas the name by which they are still remembered, to set them apart from their putative ancestors from Vatapi and their fractious relations in Vengi: Kalyana.

Rajendra Chola cared little for what these 'Kalyana Chalukyas' did or did not do. The loot of Manyakheta was paraded and used in public festivals and in the Chola capital, where Rajendra appeared on a horse surrounded by similarly mounted princes, 'a hero in the midst of the cavalry',[130] as inscriptions put it. His cheering subjects were informed that through this act, his father Rajaraja's vow to destroy that city had been fulfilled.

Rajendra now sent his armies south, where Chola control over the former Pandya territory and in Lanka remained contested and unpopular, and looted the Sinhalas again in a brutal two-year campaign.[131] The Cholas could not afford to lose their dominant position in the Palk Strait, the gap between India and Lanka, the gateway between the eastern and western Indian Ocean. Ships conveying goods between Egypt, Arabia, Persia, Indonesia, Malaysia and China needed to pass through this crossroads, offering enormous business potential to Tamil merchant guilds close to the Cholas, as well as an opportunity to the Cholas to levy transit fees. The Palk Strait offered an unavoidable geopolitical choke point where maritime traffic was concentrated: there was no escaping a polity which controlled both of its shores. In comparison, the geography of the Konkan coast allowed daring captains and merchants to avoid hostile ports, which was why it was so important for the Paramaras and Chalukyas to control it in its entirety. But to medieval Indian rulers, all these risky and expensive military campaigns were well worth it, because there were real fortunes being made in the Indian Ocean trade. Pottery from China has been found all across the coast of Tamil Nadu in recent archaeological excavations, hinting at an explosion in the scale and value of maritime interactions across the eastern Indian Ocean in the eleventh century.[132]

The best evidence we have of the scale of the Indian Ocean trade in the ninth–twelfth centuries comes from a shipwreck from 830 CE, discovered near Belitung, an island off the east coast of Sumatra. The ship was an Arab dhow on a return voyage from China, carrying nearly 60,000 ceramic items, attesting to industrial-level mass production for global markets, specifically for buyers in West Asia.[133] Its cargo also included extremely fine gold and silver items apparently intended as gifts from the imperial Chinese court to the Sailendra dynasty of Java.[134] Other objects recovered from the wreck included a paperweight, 'a re-soldered bracelet sized for a woman's wrist', 'a ceramic whistle shaped like a fat bird, and a small, charming ceramic dog'[135] – all remnants of lives just as human as ours, a diplomat's writing equipment perhaps, a gift for a beloved, souvenirs for a child.

The ceramics found in the wreck had been produced in their tens of thousands in Changsha in south-central China, and then packed and shipped to the embarkation port of Guangzhou. Here there were large communities of international traders: Persians, Arabs, and various groups from South and Southeast Asia.[136] The consignment consisted of bulk orders placed by merchants based in West Asia, as revealed by the decorative motifs used on the ceramics, which were similar to

Jack Lee / Wikimedia Commons

Ninth-century mass-manufactured bowls from Changsha, China, discovered in the Belitung shipwreck. They were made using a rudimentary assembly line, often associated with modern mass manufacturing. The production of such items suggests both technological sophistication and significant global connectivity.

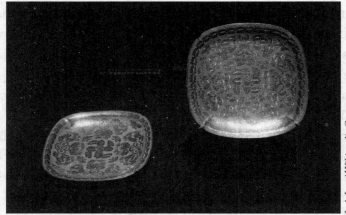

Jack Lee / Wikimedia Commons

Gold dishes from the Belitung shipwreck. These objects required considerable (and very expensive) craftsmanship: they were probably commissioned by a wealthy foreign buyer, or for a diplomatic mission that was travelling on the ship.

examples from Iraq and the Persian Gulf. The ceramics were mass-produced according to consistent templates. As Professor Geraldine Heng elegantly puts it, they and the other objects in the ship 'are summaries of the socioeconomic relations that propelled international commerce; a shorthand for deciphering political and diplomatic initiatives that were taking place in the world; and a dramatization of the artistic exchanges that were crisscrossing the world's creative pathways as early as the ninth century'.[137] This is all the more striking because it is so reminiscent of our modern, globalized world.

If not for the roaring trade of the medieval Indian Ocean world, both India's coastline and the great cities in its interior would have looked profoundly different. Rajaraja Chola, his son Rajendra and their contemporaries worked closely with the growing merchant corporations of southern India to reshape the region's economic and social landscape.

By this point, the Five Hundred Lords of Aihole had evolved into a vast organization called the 'Five Hundred of the Thousand Directions, known in every direction in all the Eighteen Lands'[138] and had brought together almost 'all possible specialist merchant groups, itinerant and sedentary, local and foreign'.[139] Including its commercial partners, suppliers, artisans, guard groups and so on, tens of thousands of individuals were probably associated with it, making it one of the most powerful groups in medieval India, far more so than most petty kings. The Five Hundred's influence expanded in the wake of the politics of military aristocrats – entering the Tamil country alongside Rashtrakuta attacks, and now expanding through Gangavadi, Lanka and Malabar alongside the Cholas.[140]

To defend their diverse and spread-out interests, merchant groups like the 'Five Hundred' hobnobbed not only with emperors, but with other medieval power centres as well: local kings, administrators of minor cities, and temples. The last two often went hand in hand – in the eleventh and twelfth centuries, temple building helped catalyse a great

wave of urbanization along the east coast, often described as India's
'third urbanization', after the urbanization of the Indus and Ganga
river valleys. Merchants, artisans, landowners and city administrators
worked in a symbiotic and mutually beneficial relationship that led to
an explosion in economic specialization and an array of goods produced
in newly prominent southern Indian cities.[141] These ranged from low-
cost, easily available staples such as grains, straw and beans to more
expensive pepper, areca nuts and cinnamon; from imported horses,
camels and pedigree cattle to exotic and sophisticated goods such as
conch shells, silk, musk, garlands, incense, sandal paste, camphor and
iron ingots.[142]

The amount of economic activity that merchants could generate by
linking up local economies to global supply and demand, and the clout
they wielded made working with them a smart move. Merchants could
secure all sorts of concessions from rulers. One group in the Malabar
coast, for example, obtained from a local king the right not to pay
customs duties 'if they feel wronged (by the officials)', to try their own
members for crimes they had committed, and permission to 'carry on
elephants the purification water for their rituals'.[143] Another, led by
a Jewish man by the name of Issuppu Irappan (Joseph Rabban), was
even allowed the free use of boats and vehicles and exempted from
paying duties entirely.[144] The race to make money from global, regional
and local trade would shape the dynamics of societies and states across
southern India for centuries thereafter.

As Rajendra Chola exulted in his conquests in the Deccan and Sri
Lanka, global trade opportunities and the military interests of south
India's new superpower now aligned to give rise to one of the most
extraordinary events of the eleventh-century world.

~

From the 990s onwards, diplomatic missions from across the world to
the Song court had drastically expanded in frequency and opulence

as people from across the Indian Ocean smelled fortunes to be made. Those embassies that made a favourable impression in the Song court would be rewarded with higher diplomatic status and thus preferential access to Chinese markets[145] – something that both kings and merchants, especially the Five Hundred and their partners, were eager for.

The first Chola embassy to the Song court, sent by Rajendra's father Rajaraja, was received on 17 October 1015, arriving roughly a year after his death.[146] The gifts from the Chola to the Song court included 'one robe and one cap adorned with real pearls, 21,000 ounces of real pearls, 60 elephant tusks, 60 catties [half-kilos] of frankincense, jade, glass, and cotton fabrics'.[147] The ambassadors – wealthy members perhaps of the Five Hundred, or powerful port guilds seeking trade concessions for themselves – 'presented *on their own* 6,600 ounces of pearls and 3,300 catties of aromatic drugs'.[148]

The Song were highly impressed by the embassy and the dignified conduct of these supposed barbarians (medieval Chinese considered all people barbarians by default, unless convinced otherwise by overwhelming wealth and sophisticated mannerisms). The emperor ordered his officials to treat them with 'great regard',[149] and they were invited to participate in the emperor's birthday festivities in early 1016. They departed soon after, bearing an 'imperial edict and rich gifts'[150] and perhaps some trade concessions. That was not all they carried with them, for they had learned something very worrisome about the activities of Srivijaya, the maritime confederation that ruled the Straits of Malacca. The historian Tansen Sen argues that until the Chola embassy had arrived in the Song court, merchants from Srivijaya had been informing the Chinese that the Cholas – who were actually south India's undisputed superpower – were mere vassals of Srivijaya.[151] This had secured preferential trade licences for them, as representatives of an ostensibly greater kingdom.

Rajendra Chola was neither going to accept such a humiliation, nor pass up the opportunity to make money. A seaborne raid was immediately sent to punish Kadaha/Kadaram (modern-day Kedah, a state in Malaysia), a major city of the Srivijayan confederation that controlled the entry point to the Malacca Strait. Somehow, the undoubtedly rather seasick Chola expedition appears to have taken those doughty Srivijayan traders and sea lords by surprise, or so Rajendra's poet would claim: 'It is no wonder that the fire of his [Rajendra's] prowess consumed the great race of Taila [the Chalukya – an insulting comparison of his name to oil/*tailu*] ... But it is a wonder that having crossed the ocean [that which is sealed], it burnt Kadaha [Kedah/*kadai*, a cooking vessel].'[152]

The Srivijayans seem to have dismissed this raid as a one-off. In 1018, the king of Kedah sent a large gift of gold for a temple and its undoubtedly well-connected Brahmins in Nagapattinam, the premier Chola port on the Indian Ocean, perhaps in thanks for their assistance in smoothing things over with Rajendra's court. Perhaps he thought that was atonement enough.[153] In any case, the many other wealthy Srivijayan ports that studded the island of Sumatra and the coast of the Malay Peninsula had been totally unaffected by Rajendra's raid. They were, for the time being at least, left to their own devices, as the Chola emperor turned his attention to other projects.

❧

By the mid- to late 1020s, the Chalukya Vallabha Jayasimha II finally managed to uproot most of the Paramara presence in the Konkan.[154] He then set out to weaken Chola control over the Deccan and ensure there was no repeat of the disaster at Manyakheta, pushing his influence incrementally further south towards the Krishna river.[155] His son and crown prince, Someshvara (Lord of the Moon), a shrewd politician, also involved himself in Vengi to try and create a new front to engage the Cholas.

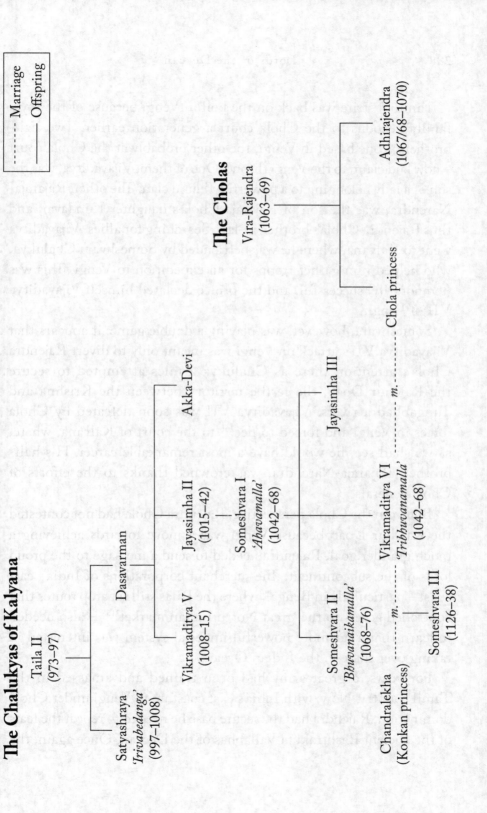

The Chalukyas of Kalyana

Taila II
(973–97)

Satyashraya
'Irivabedanga'
(997–1008)

Dasavarman

Vikramaditya V
(1008–15)

Jayasimha II
(1015–42)

Akka-Devi

Someshvara I
'Ahavamalla'
(1042–68)

Someshvara II
'Bhuvanaikamalla'
(1068–76)

Vikramaditya VI
'Tribhuvanamalla'
(1042–68) .... m. .... Chola princess

Jayasimha III

Chandralekha
(Konkan princess) .... m. ....

Someshvara III
(1126–38)

The Cholas

Vira-Rajendra
(1063–69)

Adhirajendra
(1067/68–1070)

---- Marriage

——— Offspring

Familial strife was back on the boil in Vengi because of the royal family's exodus to the Chola court a generation earlier. Two half-brothers – one based in Vengi, the other probably at the Chola court – now laid claim to the Vengi throne. One of them, Vijayaditya, was the son of a lady belonging to a powerful Telugu clan. The other, Rajaraja-Narendra, was the son of Rajaraja Chola's daughter Kundavai, and thus Rajendra Chola's brother-in-law. Searching for allies, Vijayaditya went to Kalyana, where he was befriended by Someshvara Chalukya, who helped him gather troops for an expedition to Vengi. This was (temporarily) successful, and the prince declared himself Vijayaditya VII of Vengi.

Someshvara, however, was playing a double game: it appears that Vijayaditya VII's attack on Vengi was meant only to divert Rajendra Chola's attention there as Chalukya armies attempted to secure the Raichur Doab, the fertile territory between the Krishna and Tungabhadra rivers. Vijayaditya VII was soon defeated by Chola forces in Vengi and forced to flee[156] to the court of Kalyana, where, as we shall see, he would have a most remarkable career. His half-brother, Rajaraja-Narendra, was crowned thanks to the efforts of Chola generals.[157]

But from the Chola perspective, Rajendra Chola had not contested the Raichur Doab because Vengi was a move towards achieving a much grander goal. Rajendra needed to send a message to the proud lords of the subcontinent. The merchant corporations of India's east coast – particularly in Bengal, where the Palas still sat atop routes that controlled access to the 'great North Indian market'[158] – also needed to learn that a far more powerful imperial system was interested in taking over trade in the Indian Ocean.

For years, a great army had been trained and amassed in the Tamil country. Now, with India's east coast up to Vengi under Chola domination, Rajendra had the secure base he needed to repeat the feats of the ancient Rashtrakuta Vallabhas of the Deccan. Once again, the drums and trumpets of a south Indian army would resound along the banks of the Ganga, and shatter the peace of northern India.

In 1022–23, an expedition was dispatched under a veteran Chola commander, bearing (among others) the titles of Araiyan Rajarajan (Rajaraja's Noble) and Jayasinga-Kula-Kala (God of Death to the Chalukya Clan). Moving along the subcontinent's east coast over a two-year campaign, the expedition seized forts and destroyed and captured towns in the regions corresponding to modern-day Odisha, Chhattisgarh and Bengal. Chola sources claim the cities of Tandabutti, Takkanaladam and Uttiraladam were sacked, and Madura-mandalam, Namanaikkonam, and Panchapalli destroyed (their precise locations are debated to this day). No less than three kings who attempted to fight off the marauders in Bengal – vassals of the Palas[159] – were defeated and their elephants, women and treasure seized.[160] The size of the list of raided cities and regions that appears in Rajendra Chola's propaganda, the geopolitical awareness it presumes in its original readers, and the strategic, tactical and operational abilities needed to execute such long-distance operations are all astounding. As Professor Nilakanta Sastri puts it, even if Chola accounts of it 'gloss over reverses and exaggerate successes', the campaign was an extraordinary 'exhibition of the power of the Chola empire and a demonstration of its strength'[161] to other Indian kings and to Rajendra's own subjects. At its end, waters of the Ganga were transported south, perhaps on elephant-back, in huge containers made from the mud of Bengal. The Rashtrakutas were totally outdone. Loot flowed with the Ganga's waters to Rajendra's new capital city, named after himself: Gangai-Konda-Chola-Puram, the City of the Chola who Conquered the Ganga.

∽

What the Chalukya Vallabha Jayasimha II and his son Someshvara must have thought of all this can scarcely be imagined. Before Rajendra

Chola's north India expedition, there must have been celebration in the Deccan early in the 1020s. Though there was much more to do, the Paramaras, their deadly enemies from Madhya Pradesh, had been removed from the Konkan, and the ports of the west coast were once again beginning to acknowledge the Chalukya Vallabha, Jayasimha II. Vengi had been gained and lost, but that was a small price to pay for conquering the fertile lands between the Krishna and Tungabhadra rivers. Crown Prince Someshvara was celebrated in his father's great moving military camp, showered with flowers by the women of the court, praises composed to his political astuteness in Kannada and Sanskrit, jewels and titles heaped on him by delighted generals and ministers. It may have seemed that, at long last, Fortune had granted a respite to the tenacious Chalukyas. Perhaps campaigns were being planned to reconquer Gangavadi, to contest Vengi, to fully assimilate the Konkan, or raid Malwa.

And then, in 1022–23, the years of the Cholas' north India expeditions, the Chalukya dreams must have begun to unravel as the true might of the Cholas began to dawn on them, and dismaying reports from its network of informants, clients and vassals poured in. In an attempt to sabotage and humiliate their Chola rivals as they carried out their audacious campaign, the Chalukyas even appear to have indirectly aided the kings of Odisha and Chhattisgarh,[162] but in vain. The Chola armies – which also included significant numbers of Deccani fighters and commanders,[163] reminding us that medieval India was far more heterogeneous than modern nationalism would have us believe – overpowered all. There was no coalition of Indian kings, merchants and religious institutions that could challenge the Chola imperial formation. Submission was the only option in the face of such might.

Chalukya court factions squabbled over their course of action, and it was not long before the Vallabha's leadership was being questioned. The men of the court, who spent 'large portions of their youth' in arduous military training, seem to have clamoured for an opportunity to perform in the great theatres of war where they could display their prowess before their peers and superiors.[164] There were probably many young nobles, born in the generation after the collapse of the Rashtrakutas, steeped in the propaganda of the Chalukyas, who now demanded that the Vallabha take the field for glory and fortune.

Jayasimha II, the Chalukya Vallabha who called himself 'The Lion to that Elephant, Rajendra Chola', would come very close to losing his throne in these fraught years. For obvious reasons his records are tight-lipped about the matter, but it appears that he was just barely rescued from a coup attempt by the prompt actions of the senior general Kalidasa;[165] we know little else of the conspiracy. The general claims only to have 'maintained with vigour the burden of government which had become dissolute when those generals and vassals proved false to King Simha'.[166] Yet the worst days for the Deccan still lay well in the future.

Someshvara, the Chalukya crown prince, learned from this shock, just as he learned from the Cholas' successes and atrocities. This young man had already developed a taste for politics: we have seen how he encouraged his Chalukya 'relation' from Vengi, Vijayaditya VII, in his attempt to seize the throne. Over the course of the 1020s, the two developed a close, almost familial relationship, with Vijayaditya serving as Someshvara's right-hand man through many of the hardships that followed. We can imagine the pair riding next to each other on garlanded elephants, exulting in the momentum of the great beasts, or perhaps chasing and shooting down fleeing animals from their imported steeds in royal hunts, surrounded by the baying of pedigree hounds,[167] meant to exhibit Someshvara's martial prowess and suitability to succeed his father as emperor.

The Cholas were an enemy unlike any that the Deccan had faced. The Paramaras could be defeated; the vassal lords of the Deccan guarded against, crushed, cajoled, flattered. But the Cholas didn't play by the rules – not even by the violent and anarchic standards of medieval India. To an educated prince like Someshvara Chalukya, violence (at least in theory if not in practice) was 'ritualised and honourable', to be 'exercised with restraint, to be combined and complemented with the virtues of compassion, kindness and gentility'.[168] To accept the submissions of defeated highborn enemies and restore them to power – as the Chalukya Vallabha Vikramaditya II had done with the Pallavas, as the Rashtrakuta Vallabhas Govinda III and Dhruva had done with the Vengi Chalukyas, Palas and Pratiharas – was to publicly display one's adherence to the correct, orderly rules of this world.

But the Cholas did nothing of the sort. Driven by hard-nosed geopolitical realism, they paid no heed to the rules of the game – and in return they had received victory after victory. Rajaraja and Rajendra Chola conquered outright the territories they deemed important, garrisoned them with Chola armies and Chola viceroys of royal blood, and renamed them after themselves. Lanka, that ancient Buddhist kingdom which had sent its idols as submission to the Deccan emperor Govinda III, was now to be called Mummudi-Chola-Mandalam, The Circle (territorial division) of the Chola Who Wears Three Crowns. The former Pallava heartland in northern Tamilakam, which so many Deccan Vallabhas had sacked but left otherwise untouched, was now to be called Jayan-Gonda-Chola-Mandalam, the Circle of the Victorious Chola.[169] The Kaveri river valley and the coastal area around it were renamed Cholamandalam, the Chola Circle – a name that survives to this day as 'Coromandel'.

The Chola machine was kept going with incessant warfare, looting, temple building and urbanization at an unprecedented scale. The fortunes of the Tamil country burned bright, its cities teemed with people, its palaces were full of captured women from the many kingdoms of the Deccan, Kerala, Lanka, Andhra, Odisha, Bengal and Chhattisgarh, forced to be the servants of Chola queens and princesses, the concubines of the royal guards of the princes.[170] Someshvara could do nothing but survive against such a terrible enemy.

But Rajendra Chola's ambitions were still far from fulfilled. Now, in the eleventh century, Rajendra Chola had the resources and the inclination needed to perform the most spectacular of all medieval Indian military expeditions.

Srivijaya would learn its lesson.

In a daring and extremely risky expedition – not replicated by any South Asian power until the British Raj – Rajendra Chola, having conquered the north, south and west, sent an army east, across the thundering sea, to raid as many Srivijayan cities as it could. It was intended as punishment for their audacious attempt to claim primacy over the Cholas in the rich Song court. Though how the Chola armada was organized and how it executed its objectives are unknown, it appears that by January/February 1026, it returned to the Coromandel coast laden with booty from those cities across the seas.[171] The huge, colourful fleet returning to its home shores must have been a sight to behold.

This Chola campaign was spectacular like no other Indian undertaking in the medieval period. The Krishneshvara at Ellora was outdone, the campaigns of Dhruva Rashtrakuta eclipsed. Even Rajaraja Chola's conquests and enormous temple at Thanjavur could not match his son Rajendra's crossing of the ocean itself to plunder Srivijaya.

In Gangai-Konda-Chola-Puram, Rajendra made a display of the wealth he had seized, making a particular example of Kedah, the city on which he had ordered an attack in 1017–18. In 1024–25, Rajendra's armies had supposedly 'caught' the 'King of Kadaram (the Chola name for Kedah), along with (his) rutting elephants, [which were as impetuous as] the sea in fighting'[172] and '(took) the larger heap of treasures, which he had rightfully accumulated'.[173] The great Vidyadhara gate of Kedah had been torn down and was now put on display in the Chola capital. So, too, were a 'jewel-gate, adorned with great splendour', and another 'gate of large jewels'.[174] These gates, transported back to Thanjavur or Gangai-Konda-Chola-Puram, were likely put on display for Rajendra's subjects as a testament to this extraordinary feat.

Also on display, perhaps, were treasures from Srivijaya (modern-day Palembang[175]) itself, the eponymous capital of the Srivijaya confederacy. This was a commercial hub of such density that an Arab trader reported that in one street alone he had counted *eight hundred* money changers.[176] Palembang could not have been sacked with anywhere near as much aplomb as its ally, Kedah; it was guarded by two straits and estuarine terrain that the Cholas would have found extremely difficult to navigate in the limited time they had. This, of course, did not stop Rajendra from claiming to have captured it anyway, but details of the defeat of the city's king and its supposed sacking are, unsurprisingly, lacking.

In his propaganda, Rajendra also claimed, on the east coast of Sumatra, the capture of 'Pannai' (modern-day Panei), 'Malaiyur' (modern-day Jambi) and 'Ilamuridesam'[177] (modern-day Lamuri). The list of the cities he claimed to have captured is even more extensive along the Malay Peninsula – either because the Chola army had based itself around Kedah, or because there were simply more cities there. Here, his forces supposedly captured 'Yirudingam', 'Pappalam', 'Ilibangam', 'Valaippanduru', 'Takkolam' and 'Tamalingam',[178] all accompanied with descriptions, including brief praise of their defences and martial valour, which apparently did them no good against his armies. To round out this maritime 'Conquest of the Directions', Rajendra also informs us that his forces had supposedly attacked the Nicobar Islands – 'the great Nakkavaram, whose flower-gardens (resembled) the girdle (of the nymph) of the southern sea'.[179]

These were all places the people who saw Rajendra's parades and displays were probably familiar with to some degree. Word of the success of these raids spread like wildfire across trade and pilgrimage routes, and Rajendra's own status as a celebrity king rose to a level none of his contemporaries could hope to challenge. In medieval India, neighbouring kingdoms were seen as foreign land. The further away the enemy kingdom, the more prestige gained by the king who successfully plundered it: thus the Rashtrakuta expeditions to north India and Tamilakam, and the Chola expedition to Bengal. But the sack of Srivijaya, involving an audacious crossing of the seas, put it in a different category altogether. Through this, Rajendra Chola almost completely eclipsed the Chalukya emperor Jayasimha II and his heir apparent, Someshvara, whose military encampment was even then roving around the Deccan,[180] still attempting to piece together their shattered political and economic networks.

Today, we tend to think of what Rajendra Chola did as something all South Asians should be proud of. But in the medieval Deccan, there must have been a sense of doom at this man's meteoric rise, his display of dominance, and the fact that this destroyer of cities and despoiler of lands seemed utterly unassailable.

But Rajendra Chola's success was more superficial than it seemed, despite the awe-inspiring spectacles of paraded loot from distant Bengal and Indonesia. Many Srivijayan cities had been bankrupted by the devastation caused by the Chola army, but the confederacy was very much still in business.[181] Rajendra's raid captured booty, sent a message and played to his domestic audience, but it was by no means a 'conquest' or 'colonization'. Srivijaya didn't even take that long to return to the China trade: by 1028, merchants from there were once again thronging the docks of Guangzhou.[182] Rajendra himself soon lost interest in Srivijaya now that it had been put in its place, though he seems to have arranged some intermarriages with prominent local dynasties. His eyes were on the big picture, the profits of trade which

Babel Stone / Wikimedia Commons

A Sino-Indian goddess from Quanzhou, produced using local stone. The style and iconography suggests that the panel was carved either by Tamil artisans or by locals trained by Tamil artisans, who appear to have been present at the port along with a booming Tamil merchant population. Such a medieval diaspora is strikingly reminiscent of immigrant communities in the modern world.

could fuel his wars in the Indian subcontinent. The Chola emperor sent another embassy to the Song court in 1033, with a letter written in gold leaf, and his ambassador scattered pearls from a silver bowl before the emperor, receiving in return the honorary titles of Grand Master of the Palace with Golden Seal and Purple Ribbon, and Civilizing General.[183]

But the cultural and economic opportunities that the Chola attack on Srivijaya created would lead to deep and persistent changes in world history. Through the 1024–25 campaign to Srivijiaya, the Chola state had, without intending to do so, made an immense leap towards the 'emergence of a world market'[184] by clearing the way for deeper, direct connections between southern India and eastern Asia. A 'new wave of cultural influence'[185] was now borne deep into Sumatra by the expanding Tamil merchant guilds, who were granted trading outposts and ports.[186] Art styles fused, interacted, bloomed.[187] Sculptures, spices, handicrafts and Indian textiles – pleated, painted, patterned with geometry, petals, stars, suns and flowers – were exported from south India to East Asia.[188] Foreign kings and nobles luxuriated in them. From the eleventh century onwards, we see the footprint of Tamil merchants in China rapidly expanding;[189] in the port of Quanzhou, for example, there is evidence of Shaiva temples and Tamil inscriptions left by these traders. Remains of Tamil architectural elements and a sculpture of an Indian goddess depicted by what seem to be Sino-Indian *sthapatis* are visible today in the Quanzhou Maritime Museum. These remind us, once again, that globalization and syncreticism are by no means unique to the modern world. Though competition with the Srivijayans and Chinese would continue in the ensuing centuries, it appears that the biggest winners of the Chola expedition were, at the end of the day, Tamil merchants.

Rajendra Chola might not have agreed with such an assessment. In 1034, when his embassy returned laden with gifts from the Song court of China, it had been barely half a century since his father's coronation in 985. And now the Chola dynasty was without question the richest, most powerful and most famous in the entire subcontinent, without any indication the situation would change any time soon. In his great palace at Gangai-Konda-Chola-Puram, Rajendra lounged on silks imported from China, inhaling exotic incenses from Ethiopia and Arabia burning in bronzes cast by the skilled artisans of Tamilakam, surrounded by gorgeous attendants from Bengal, Odisha, Andhra,

Karnataka and Sri Lanka waving fly whisks made of the tails of Himalayan yaks. All around him were the towering spires of the gleaming temples he had built and the cities he had enriched. His new 'Kailasa-like imperial Shiva temple', the Gangaikondacholeshvaram, rivalled his father's Dakshinameru in size, and its great temple reservoir was purified with the waters of the distant Ganga.[190]

Gangai-Konda-Chola-Puram was full of trophies, the symbols he had seized from all over the world and brought here to signify his power over all. 'From the [Kalyana] Chalukyas a sun-pedestal, several images of Durga, and a Ganesa-image' had been seized and placed in shrines attached to his own massive temples. The city was also decorated with other images: 'from the Eastern [Vengi] Chalukyas, a resting Nandi, Shiva's bull mount; from the Kalingas of Odisha, three large stone images of Bhairava and Bhairavi and an awesome eight-armed Kali image; from the Palas of Bengal, a bronze image of Shiva dancing on Nandi's back',[191] and many others. At the four towering gates of the city, images of Durga – one stolen from the Chalukya emperor – guarded his subjects.[192]

Rajendra had three adult sons who would now have to rule the empire their father had raised to unprecedented heights. It was time for a transition. How many gates and walls would they add, he may have asked himself. How high would their temples ascend?

Certainly he would never have imagined that these three – who would one day bear the titles 'The Victorious Rajendra', 'The Divine Rajendra' and 'The Heroic Rajendra' – would be the last of his direct male descendants to sit on his throne.

9

Lord of the Moon

Summer, 1042 CE

Pattadakal, the ancient coronation site of the Chalukya Vallabhas of the Deccan.[1]

Here, on the shores of the Malaprabha river where generations of Vatapi Chalukyas had built their temples and made their boasts of conquest, a new Vallabha, Someshvara I of the Kalyana Chalukyas, was about to be crowned. The ancient royal consecration of Fortune's Favourite was enacted once again, as it had been for centuries. His family's ancient crown – probably very similar to the crown on the cover of this book[2] – was lowered onto his head. The dharma of kings was to conquer, to protect, to seek fame. Perhaps Someshvara believed it was his duty to carry that burden against the might of the Chola juggernaut.

It would take all of the new Vallabha's political, diplomatic and strategic guile to do so. The Chola imperium was now led by the ruthless Rajadhiraja Chola: Rajendra Chola's eldest son and co-ruler, the deadliest enemy the Deccan had yet seen. Those present at Someshvara's coronation in 1042 must have expected that horrific destruction lay on the horizon. They knew that the subcontinent's great superpowers, the Chalukyas and Cholas, were preparing for a new round of brutal competition across the vast geopolitical chessboard of south India. Aristocrats and merchants, poets and priests from the Konkan to Vengi, from Dhara to Kanchipuram, waited with bated breath for the emperors to make their move.

✧

Rajadhiraja Chola had burst onto the geopolitical chessboard of southern India in the 1030s. Less than a decade after his father Rajendra's expeditions to the Ganga and Srivijaya, the old aristocracy of Tamilakam proved that they were far from overawed. Other royal south Indian dynasties whom the Cholas had supplanted, such as the Cheras and Pandyas,[3] rose in revolt. Warriors flocked to their ancient banners: the Chera bow and the Pandya fish.

Rajadhiraja Chola now set out to punish the kings who had dared to challenge the Conqueror of the Ganga. One royal rebel, we are told, possessed a handsome head '(adorned with) large jewels, inseparable from the golden crown'.[4] Rajadhiraja had the rebel's head cut off, crown and all. Another heroic upstart, whose thick legs were normally adorned with gold ankle rings, was captured in battle. Rajadhiraja had the ankle rings replaced by fetters, after which he was 'pleased to get him trampled'[5] to death by his elephant, Attivarana. Another aristocrat fled desperately from the battlefield into exile. In Kerala, a somewhat braver group of minor kings were summarily 'sent ... to the country of heaven'.[6] Finally, replicating his grandfather Rajaraja Chola's feats, a fleet of ships at Kandalur was burned to ashes, after Rajadhiraja had forced the ruler of the city to flee and hide in the thick jungles of the Western Ghats.[7]

While the Chola armies were thus occupied in the 1030s, the Chalukyas, under Someshvara's father Jayasimha II, had crossed the Tungabhadra. They subdued the kings of the south-eastern Deccan[8] and even expanded into southern Chhattisgarh. The citadel of Chakrakuta (modern-day Chitrakoot in Bastar district), previously seized by the Cholas during Rajendra's 1022–1023 Ganga expedition, was captured[9] to act as a base for Chalukya diplomatic and military efforts along the east coast. The Kalyana Chalukyas planned to use the lords of Chhattisgarh and Odisha to hem in Chola expansion in that direction. This was accompanied by another Chalukya attempt to seize Vengi and install their close ally Vijayaditya VII of the Vengi Chalukyas as king. This attempt was ultimately repelled by Chola forces, but by the late 1030s, it was clear to all the rulers of the subcontinent that the apparently invincible Chola tiger had been bloodied.

It is possible to discern some broad patterns in Someshvara's geopolitical manoeuvres against the Cholas after he came to the throne in 1042. He seems to have understood that the Kaveri river valley alone would not be able to provide the agrarian revenue and military manpower to sustain the Cholas against the many challenges they faced. This was why the Cholas had attempted, time and again, to seize the Raichur doab, between the Tungabhadra and Krishna rivers. This 'Idutarainadu', as the Cholas termed it, was so important to them that Rajendra Chola often mentioned it first among his lists of conquests in his *prashastis*.[10] Despite early Chola successes in the region, Someshvara's father Jayasimha II had managed to retain Chalukya influence in Raichur, or Edudorevishaya (as the Chalukyas called it). Vengi, between the Krishna and Godavari rivers, offered another such fertile base for Chola power, and unlike Raichur, it was firmly under the Chola sphere of influence. Meanwhile, the lucrative Konkan coast had only recently been regained by the Chalukyas from the Paramaras. As Vallabha, Someshvara would thus need to better integrate the Raichur doab and the Konkan into his domains. Furthermore, he had to ensure that the Cholas could no longer draw sustenance from Vengi.

And so, when Rajendra Chola died in 1044, Someshvara Chalukya

immediately moved to take advantage. Vijayaditya VII was once again
sent to Vengi with a Deccan army to overthrow his half-Chola half-
brother Rajaraja-Narendra. In this third and most serious attempt,
so far, to claim his birthright, Vijayaditya had the assistance of a new
generation of Deccan generals, who had earned their titles in decades
of campaigns against the Cholas. The Chalukyas also appear to have
increased the size and capability of their armies in the nearly twenty
years since Rajendra Chola's Bengal and Srivijaya campaigns. The
beleaguered Narendra desperately requested Chola assistance, and an
'equally matched'[11] army commanded by three of Rajendra Chola's
top generals set out to defend him.

But the toll of the Cholas' endless raids and wars was becoming
apparent. The flower of the Chola army, the units and officers that had
successfully raided across the seas, were ageing. They had also taken
severe losses over thirty years of campaigning. Though constantly
swelled by recruits from hill forts and rice fields, the effectiveness of
the Chola military machine seems to have declined somewhat. All
three commanders of this relief army were killed by the Chalukyas in
a pitched battle at Kalidindi in the modern-day Krishna district. The
Cholas were forced to temporarily retreat south beyond the Krishna
river, leaving the unfortunate Narendra to build temples to Shiva over
their generals' ashes.[12]

Rajadhiraja Chola, who had by now been crowned emperor, took the
field. A challenge so early in his reign, in such a geopolitically crucial
region, could not go unpunished. With him, he probably brought
substantial reinforcements and new officers from his campaigns against
the rebellious Pandya and Chera kings. Successfully rallying the Chola
forces, he managed to blunt the Chalukya advance at Amaravati in
1045. 'Vikki [perhaps a disparaging reference to a general with the
title of Vikramaditya] and Vijayadityan [Vijayaditya VII of Vengi] ...
retreated like cowards!'[13] declared Rajadhiraja's eulogist.

The Chalukyas retreated, following the Godavari back west towards

Kalyana. At this point, two different versions of what happened emerge. The Chalukyas claimed to have successfully fought off the Cholas at Kollipakam (modern-day Kollipaka in Telangana): Someshvara Chalukya awarded one of his vassals the title 'Protector of Kollipaka' that year.[14] Rajadhiraja Chola, on the other hand, claimed in his inscriptions to have burned Kollipakam.[15]

Though the Chalukyas had been unable to install their candidate in Vengi, news of the Cholas' struggles in this war spread rapidly through the subcontinent. One after another, subjugated powers spluttered back to life. Lanka rose in rebellion, with adventurers from across the subcontinent seeking their fortunes in the chaos.[16] The Chola emperor withdrew from his conflict with Someshvara and moved to quell the uprisings to his south.

The Vallabha Someshvara, however, did not attempt to seize Vengi again at this point of time. He had other scores to settle.

❧

Over the past century, we have seen how Malwa – once little more than the Deccan's forward base for north Indian campaigns – had taken a deadly revenge on its former overlords. First, Siyaka 'Harsha' Paramara had sacked Manyakheta in 972. Next, Vakpati Paramara, the poet-king, had attempted to claim the titles of Amoghavarsha and Sri-Prithivi-Vallabha, Fortune's Favourite, before being brutally killed by Taila, the Chalukya ruler of the Deccan, c. 994. Bhoja Paramara, arguably the most acerbic and brilliant of the Paramara family, had then wrested the Konkan from Taila's grandson Jayasimha II, c. 1020, and Chalukya authority in the region remained weak despite later attempts to reclaim it. Now, Taila's great-grandson Someshvara would settle the score once and for all.

Rajendra Chola, after decades of war, had become the Indian subcontinent's great military celebrity king. But Bhoja Paramara had embraced a more complex route to royal superstardom. Bhoja was the greatest of royal Sanskrit litterateurs, acknowledged and celebrated by critics and connoisseurs across South Asia. He was among the greatest medieval patrons of Sanskrit literature, eclipsing Amoghavarsha Rashtrakuta in a world still obsessed with that ancient language's marvellous sounds. (Indeed, as far as Bhoja was concerned, vernacular languages, including that of his own subjects, were too unrefined to even be considered worthy of literature.[17])

Though it is generally believed Sanskrit had its golden age during the Gupta period in northern India in the fourth to fifth centuries, it was really now, in the eleventh century, that Sanskrit literature began to reach its apogee. Courts across South Asia presided over waves of *prashastis* and poetry and dramatic productions: this literary golden age of Sanskrit produced hundreds if not thousands of texts across the vast subcontinent. From Kashmir to Kannauj, from Varanasi to Vengi, from Gauda to Gujarat, from Kalyana to the Kaveri river valley, salons and courts resounded with Sanskrit literature – much of which is now lost. And none exemplified this zenith of Sanskrit literature better than Bhoja.

With interests spanning a range of subjects from grammar to yoga to astronomy to architecture,[18] this Paramara king was a remarkable polymath, seeking to compose, versify, patronize and write his way into eternal fame. Encyclopaedic *shastras*, bringing together centuries of theoretical and practical knowledge transmitted in Sanskrit, were composed under his direct supervision. Poets from all directions converged upon his capital, Dhara, where one of the Indian subcontinent's greatest libraries of texts was being amassed. The Paramara court resounded with urbane conversation, poetry, drama and erudite debate on everything from aesthetics to metaphysics. Bhoja himself oversaw it all. So qualified was he, so appreciated for his generous patronage and marvellous insights, that his salons soon became part of the subcontinent's tapestry of legends. Twelfth-century Kashmiri poets would bemoan never being able to meet him and receive his gifts; the sixteenth-century Deccan emperor Krishna Raya of Vijayanagara would declare himself Abhinava-Bhoja, the 'New Bhoja'.[19]

Bhoja was also a builder of vision. On the Betwa river, he constructed a dam of extraordinary proportions. On the shores of its reservoir, he began the construction of a temple – the Bhojeshvara – intended to be nearly one and a half times the size of the Rajarajeshvaram temple at Thanjavur, with a 10-foot-tall Shiva linga at its heart, still visible today. Referring to this colossal project, architect Adam Hardy writes: 'Mirrored in its lake it would have doubled up like an expanding *śivaliṅga*. Would Bhoja have declared anything less?'[20]

This Bhojeshvara was, unfortunately, to remain the greatest temple never built, as the Deccan Vallabha Someshvara finally wreaked his vengeance on the flamboyant, brilliant old Paramara king.

In 1046–47, four senior generals of the Kalyana Chalukyas – Nagadeva, Gundamaya, Jomarasa and Madhuva[21] – crossed the Narmada. The first would declare himself a 'Garuda to the serpent Bhoja', the second, 'a royal swan strolling on both banks of the Narmada, an evil comet to the Malavas', the third, 'the flame of doom to Bhoja'.[22] Crossing the Narmada, the citadel of Mandu was captured and burned by the Deccani armies, and then Dhara itself besieged. Bhoja, pulled from his poetry and his building projects, surrendered[23] in a futile attempt to salvage the situation, but to no avail. The Chalukya Vallabha was not interested in maintaining a vassal in such a dangerous territory. Unlike his Rashtrakuta predecessors, Someshvara had no ambitions for expeditions to northern India. Malwa was important only insofar as it had to be reduced to the status of a secure northern flank, which meant Paramara power had to be smashed once and for all.

And so Dhara, with its spires and pinnacles and poetry halls and temples, was captured. Chalukya generals tore apart Bhoja's palace,

Yann / Wikimedia Commons

The remains of the Bhojeshvara temple at Bhojpur, Madhya Pradesh. The domed pavilions in the foreground are later additions. In the background is what would have been the sanctum sanctorum, suggesting the enormous size of the building should it have been completed.

Apoorva Lakshmi Ragi

The linga in the Bhojeshvara temple at Bhojpur, emphasizing the scale at which Bhoja imagined his temple.

named after one of his grammatical treatises,[24] *Sarasvati-kantha-abharana* (The Necklace of the Goddess of Knowledge), and seized its jewels and treasures. (To his credit, Someshvara seems to have ordered that Bhoja's library be left intact; it was carted away by a Gujarati warlord soon after.[25])The city was then comprehensively sacked and set on fire. So too was the ancient city of Ujjain, where Danti-Durga Rashtrakuta had once performed his Sacrifice of the Golden Egg.

The kohl of the weeping widows of Malwa, dragged back along with the victorious Deccan armies, supposedly turned the waters of the Narmada as black as those of the Yamuna.[26] So memorable was this event for Deccan armies that one of the Chalukyas' vassal dynasties – the famous temple builders called the Hoysalas, who would later rule their own kingdom in southern Karnataka – would integrate tales of their participation in this campaign into their *prashastis* as evidence of their martial prowess. Indeed, they would even replicate the architectural forms of Malwa in their great twelfth-century imperial temple at Belur, 200 kilometres away from modern-day Bengaluru.

As his generals returned in triumph, Malwa at last reduced to a state from which it would never again rise to challenge the Deccan, Someshvara himself attacked the Konkan, captured the last of its recalcitrant lords, and 'wrung his neck'.[27] Marriage alliances were arranged between Someshvara's family and local dynasties.[28] His aunt, the fearsome warrior-queen Akkadevi, 'whose lotus-like feet are touched by the diadems of opponent kings',[29] was positioned to guard the passes of the Western Ghats as the Vallabha withdrew in triumph. His armies laden with loot, Someshvara headed to Kalyana, preparing for a glorious celebration.

Unfortunately, Someshvara Chalukya was not the only emperor headed to Kalyana that year.

Over the past two years, Rajadhiraja Chola had savagely defeated all challengers to his power. In Lanka alone, the Chola emperor had seized no less than four splendid jewel-studded royal crowns, capturing and mutilating kings, queens and their mothers alike.[30] A fragile peace had fallen upon the brutalized island.

Then, in 1047, Rajadhiraja decided he could do to the Deccan what the Deccan had done to Malwa. He would burn cities and temples, and unleash his armies to rape and sack and slaughter. He would at last integrate the Raichur doab into the Chola dominions, and he would secure it by seizing *tirthas*, setting up victory pillars, and destroying cities. In Kalyana's ashes, Rajadhiraja Chola planned to perform a ritual known as the *virabhisheka*, the Hero's Consecration, with the Chalukya court as hapless witnesses and attendees. He would thus destroy every shred of glory and divine favour that the Chalukya Vallabha could claim. He would make sure that no lord of Kalyana or Manyakheta would dare threaten the Cholas again.

As Rajadhiraja Chola entered the Deccan, he was immediately attacked by a swarm of smaller armies. The minor kings Gandaraditya, Naranan, Ganapati and Madhusudhanan 'of the fragrant garland'[31] were swatted away. Rajadhiraja then headed to the city of Kampili, 'whose gardens diffuse fragrance',[32] near the future site of Hampi/ Vijayanagara on the Tungabhadra river. Here, in what was likely the southern base of the Chalukya emperors, Someshvara's palace was captured, looted of all its precious treasures – imported vases and plush clothing and jewellery, idols and banners and gateways – and burned to the ground. Someshvara quickly dispatched an army to intercept the invaders. The commander was one Viccaya, a Telugu speaker,[33] suggesting that by this time Someshvara had begun to cultivate the chiefs of the Telugu country as well.

The two armies met at Pundur, on the south bank of the Krishna. Here Viccaya was defeated, his parents, officers and elephants captured, and paraded before Rajadhiraja in the Chola camp.[34] The

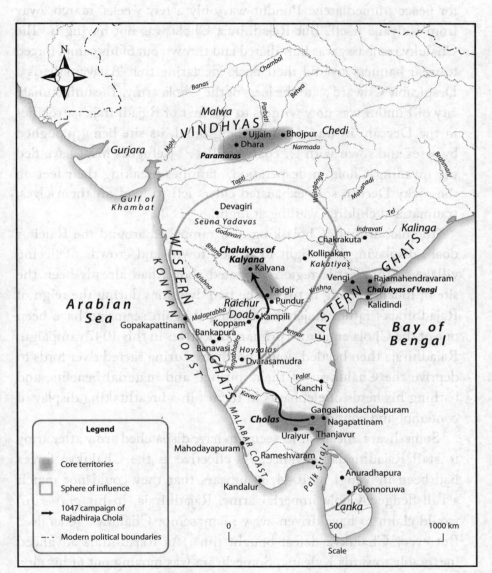

Southern India, mid-eleventh century CE.

Chalukya emperor Someshvara 'Ahavamalla', Great in Battle, sued for peace immediately: Pundur was only a few weeks' march away from Kalyana itself. But Rajadhiraja Chola was not having it. The Chalukya embassy was humiliated and thrown out of his camp, forced to wear banners around their necks declaring that 'Ahavamalla is a Despicable Coward',[35] to the jeers of the Chola army. The unfortunate city of Pundur was now witness to the first of Rajadhiraja's atrocities in the Deccan: it 'was razed to the ground, its site being ploughed by asses and sown with … coarse millet'.[36] Refugees must have fled the invading Chola in desperation, families breaking their feet on the rocky Deccan soil, exhausted elders left to fend for themselves, traumatized children wailing at night.

The bloodthirsty Chola king now rampaged around the Raichur doab, displaying his might to ruined towns and crowds of fleeing villagers. This fertile region, as noted above, had already been the site of much warring between the two dynasties during the reign of Rajadhiraja's father Rajendra. Seizing it again seems to have been one of the Chola emperor's primary objectives in this 1047 campaign. Rajadhiraja then headed slowly north, capturing sacred river fords to deprive the Chalukyas of their spiritual and material benefits, and bathing his herds of elephants in them[37] in a breathtaking display of contempt and confidence.

Someshvara, meanwhile, seems to have dispatched army after army to stall Rajadhiraja's advance. As effective as the Chalukya forces had been in Vengi in 1044, it appears that they could not match a full-fledged Chola imperial army. Rajadhiraja, in his *prashastis*, would claim to have driven away many senior Chalukya generals.[38] But every Chalukya defeat bought time. As Rajadhiraja advanced inexorably towards Kalyana, Someshvara was moving out of his city, transporting his court and treasury to safer territory in the east, where the Cholas could not follow without stretching their lines of supply and communication to breaking point.[39]

Meanwhile, Rajadhiraja crossed the Krishna and planted a victor pillar at Yadgir, emblazoned with the crest of the Cholas, the leaping tiger.[40] Now, his camp decorated with fluttering flags, he received yet more ambassadors from Someshvara. These, too, were humiliated: one of them was forced into a sari and dubbed 'Ahavamalli'. Another's head was shaved badly, leaving cuts and scrapes and five tufts, and was declared 'Ahavamalla'.[41] Then, covered with bruises, their status stripped away, they were thrown out of the Chola camp. The message was clear: no peace; only complete defeat. Rajadhiraja then continued onwards to Kalyana. The capital of the Deccan's foremost dynasty was captured and methodically sacked and burned, like Manyakheta before it.

But Rajadhiraja's arch-enemy Someshvara was nowhere to be found. Though he had wished to humiliate the Chalukya emperor by forcing him to witness his Hero's Consecration, the *virabhisheka*, Rajadhiraja could not 'force his rival to take the role of ceremonial doorkeeper in person',[42] as Danti-Durga Rashtrakuta had once done to the Pratihara kings of Malwa during his Golden Womb sacrifice in the captured city of Ujjain, *c.* 750. Instead, a statue of a door guardian[43] was seized from a Chalukya temple to 'witness' Rajadhiraja's reconsecration, his rebirth as 'Vijaya-Rajendra', the Victorious Rajendra, Lord of Kings, in an elaborately staged spectacle at which loot and captives were paraded.[44] The Deccan, it seemed, lay broken at the Chola emperor's feet.

⌎

The Vallabha still had some contingencies he could call upon in this moment of apparent Chola apotheosis. Moving east, into Telangana, what remained of the Chalukyas' armies were joined by the forces of an ambitious local chiefdom, the Kakatiyas. Telangana at the time was similar to the ancient homeland of the Chalukyas, the Malaprabha river valley: it was a dry, war-torn inland region watered by rain-fed rivers, home to itinerant pastoral groups. The Kakatiyas would one day transform it with an imperial network of vassals and temples and tanks, akin to that of the rest of the Deccan. That day was, however, far in the future.

In the sweltering, dry heat of Telangana in 1048, fanned by attendants and sipping on buttermilk[45] cooled in earthen pots, Someshvara and his generals probably argued over how best to dislodge Rajadhiraja Chola. The Kakatiya ruler and his son were almost certainly present with them.[46] It is tempting to imagine what these planning sessions looked like: it is unknown whether medieval Indian strategists even used maps, but we can guess that military officers and aristocrats of various ethnic, religious and linguistic groups, clad in everything from simple cotton to luxurious silks, presented their ideas to the Vallabha.

Rajadhiraja, now back in the Raichur doab, was gradually spreading his devastation west.[47] It was only a matter of time before the grandees of the region began to swear their loyalty to Rajadhiraja out of sheer desperation. The Chalukya court settled on a risky solution: they would take advantage of Rajadhiraja's preoccupation with the Deccan to raid Tamilakam itself, forcing him to turn back and defend his core territories. It was the only way to ensure that Someshvara's imperial network would not unwind and collapse. Kakatiya reinforcements – probably light infantry used to raiding in the drylands of Telangana – were gathered. A Chalukya general with the title of Pulakeshin was appointed to lead the force alongside the son of the Kakatiya chief. This Pulakeshin was ordered to raid and set fire[48] to what was, for the Chalukyas, the most symbolically important of all the Tamil cities: Kanchi, the ancient capital of their dead rivals the Pallavas, previously seized by two Vikramaditya Chalukyas.

Precisely how this raid was put together and sent on its way is unclear, but it must have been a race against time: should the Cholas get wind of it too soon, Rajadhiraja would certainly move to stop this Chalukya force before it got anywhere near Tamilakam. The Chola emperor could not afford to be humiliated in Kanchi.

For just as the old Pandya and Chera heartlands had proved recalcitrant to Chola authority, so had the Pallava core region around Kanchi. Here, in drier territory quite unlike the fertile valley of the Kaveri, the Cholas had only poorly integrated the patchwork of powerful warrior gentry, agriculturist groups and local 'independent zones' around Brahmin settlements established by the Pallavas centuries ago.[49] Nevertheless, the territory had been renamed soon after Rajaraja Chola conquered it in the late tenth century, and it bore the name of Jayan-Gonda-Chola-Mandalam – one of Rajadhiraja Chola's titles.[50] It was integral to the prestige of the Chola emperor and the polity that his grandfather had designed.

General Pulakeshin and his Kakatiya forces were more successful than his namesake, the long-dead Vatapi Chalukya Vallabha Pulakeshin II, more than four hundred years ago. Kanchi was captured, its gates torn down,[51] its suburbs ransacked and burned, and fires lit to cover the raiders' escape. This sacking – made all the more humiliating because of the fact that it was a 'Pulakeshin' doing it – forced Rajadhiraja Chola to finally withdraw from the Deccan with whatever loot he had seized.

This entire series of events – Rajadhiraja's repeated humiliation of Chalukya ambassadors, the erection of victory pillars, his use of the door guardian at his *virabhisheka* at Kalyana, and Pulakeshin's raid of Kanchi – remind us once again that for medieval Indian kings, military campaigns were as much about stating and reinforcing power through symbols as they were about capturing territory and treasure.

By August 1049, after the horrible deaths of thousands and incalculable destruction, Rajadhiraja Chola had failed to secure his grip over the Raichur doab. It would be years before he managed to gather enough forces to attempt another invasion. Someshvara and his queens made land grants in the southeast Deccan,[52] not too far from Chola territory, a defiant show of normalcy and Chalukya suzerainty. Despite all the destruction and humiliation that Rajadhiraja Chola had rained down upon the Chalukyas, attempting to reduce them to political subjection[53] as he had the rest of the south, Someshvara Ahavamalla had maintained his grip over the Deccan.[54] The Cholas had, for now, been wrestled to a standstill, and Raichur still remained under Chalukya influence, though it had taken a desperate gamble and the loss of Kalyana itself to do so.

Now, Kalyana would be remade. At a strategic site straddling the crossroads of the emerging regional language zones of Kannada, Marathi and Telugu,[55] Someshvara Chalukya would build a new Kalyana, a capital of such magnificence that it would dominate the Deccan imagination till well into the sixteenth century.

Someshvara and his architects chose an area close to the ruins of the old Kalyana that Rajadhiraja Chola had destroyed, or perhaps cleared the rubble and ash to create a new layout.[56] According to architectural texts from medieval southern India, such as the *Manasara Shilpashastram*, a wide area at the city centre, or slightly away from it, would first have been measured and cordoned off for the Vallabha's palace[57] and temples associated with the royal family. This would act as the city's sacred, political and administrative centre. A road would then have been demarcated around it, and from there, arterial roads laid out aligned to the cardinal directions. In theory, these would act as the basic anchor points of an enormous geometric grid, positioned so that its 'energy'[58] radiated from Someshvara's own residence, creating a complex pattern of plots intersected by streets and lanes, with areas demarcated for castes. Brahmins, courtiers and generals were supposed to be closest to the palace; merchants and traders next to arterial roads; and the productive 'lower' castes – tailors, shoemakers, butchers, cowherds, weavers, servants, blacksmiths, oil pressers and so on – were to be segregated into streets and neighbourhoods[59] well away from the main ritual hubs.

This, at least, is how the *shastras* describe it. However, archaeological evidence from a major medieval Deccan city, Dvarasamudra (modern-day Halebidu), built by the Hoysalas, vassals and successors of the Chalukyas, complicates the picture. If Dvarasamudra is any indication, caste and class divisions in the layout of medieval Deccan cities were rather more fluid[60] in practice. Here, the most prominent occupational groups (not just of high caste) were clustered around the city's main arterial road as well as the royal palace and temples.[61] The city was encircled by a wall in turn surrounded by a wide ditch, with enormous gateways where the arterial roads met it at the cardinal directions.[62] Dvarasamudra was not particularly large by modern standards: the walled city was about as big as a modern residential neighbourhood, and home to only a few thousand people. Someshvara's Kalyana was most likely of a much larger scale. We know from literature that Kalyana had suburbs, temple complexes, and lanes populated by goldsmiths, silversmiths, jewellers and merchants of exotic imported goods to serve the tastes of its elites. As inscriptional depictions of other Deccan towns suggest, Kalyana probably blurred the lines between a 'rural' and 'urban' area, with agricultural land, gardens and orchards both within and outside the city walls. The Chalukyas certainly planned it to be a most imposing place; as one Sanskrit text puts it, 'There is not, was not, nor will ever be a city on this Earth like Kalyana.'[63] It may have been one of the densest urban centres in the Deccan at the time. Further archaeological work at its site – modern Basavakalyan – is needed in order to learn more about it.

The Chalukya court had defiantly returned to the very site of its greatest defeat – where, not so long ago, a Chola emperor had smeared himself with its ashes and performed his Hero's Consecration. Generals and ministers hobnobbed with courtesans and merchants in glittering two- to three-storey edifices with luxuriously appointed salons with gilded wooden furniture, residential suites decked with sumptuous Chinese silks and elegant murals.[64] But outside these rarefied circles, drawn by all variety of social, political, spiritual and economic opportunity, the people of the Deccan flocked to Kalyana. Unfortunately, the archaeological record is too fragmentary to build an understanding of the struggles and joys of the lives of this vast majority of the Deccan's peoples.

A fragile peace now fell across the Deccan. Nearly three centuries ago, the Vatapi Chalukya prince Vikramaditya II and his father Vijayaditya had toured the Deccan, establishing the rights and duties through which cities and guilds were bound to the royal family. So too would Someshvara and his family.

However, by this time, the social and political context within which these Deccani royals were operating was quite different. The ambitions and scale of this Deccan imperial polity were vast. There were now dozens more major cities that required the direct attention of the court, and far more powerful local aristocrats needed to be won over through titles, grants, alliances and privileges. Inscriptions mention a number of 'royal cities', probably directly linked with the imperial family: Annigere, Mulugunda, Nadapura, Kohalli, Mandaligere, Belgali, Banavasi, Karividi, Navile, Nandavadige and Peruru.[65] The inscriptions of the long-faded Vatapi Chalukyas, in comparison, rarely mention anything approaching this degree of urban complexity.

In comparison to the Vatapi Chalukyas and Rashtrakutas, many more of the imperial ladies played important roles in the consolidation of Kalyana Chalukya power.[66] This was, perhaps, a tacit acknowledgement of the increasing power of local Deccan aristocracy, the birth families of the Vallabha's wives, in relation to the imperial court. These families, once petty warlords leading raids from the security of mud forts, had gradually transformed into kings, the owners of immense plantations toiled over by bonded agricultural labourers. Their hill forts were now urban and commercial hubs[67] that funded retinues, armies and courts steeped in both Sanskritic and Kannadiga courtly culture. The Hoysalas of southern Karnataka, tribespeople from the Western Ghats who had risen to the status of rulers, are an excellent example: they had achieved considerable wealth and status as feudatories and generals of the Chalukyas, as we have seen earlier. One of Someshvara's queens, Hoysaladevi, came from that family.[68]

Another queen of Someshvara's, Ketaladevi, managed a major Brahmin *agrahara*. A senior queen, Mailaladevi, governed the Banavasi 12,000 in 1053.[69] (The number in medieval Deccan district names establishes their 'rank' in comparison to other territories, and might refer either to the actual number of villages within them or merely be a designation of status.) Banavasi was once the seat of the ancient Kadambas whom the Chalukyas of Vatapi had overthrown centuries ago, and thus the intention behind Mailaladevi's appointment seems to have been to declare the imperial court's personal commitments to these prestigious and long-standing hubs of social and political power. The governorship of the Banavasi 12,000 would later be held by Someshvara's cousin, the son of his aunt Akkadevi by a princeling

Sarah Welch / Wikimedia Commons

A Jain mural at Ellora, depicting women attending upon a deity or teacher. Commissioned in the tenth or eleventh century, the regional aristocracy who were intermarrying with the Kalyana Chalukyas may have looked very similar.

descended from the Kadambas,[70] and by Someshvara's second son, Prince Vikramaditya.[71]

This queen, Akkadevi, is worth briefly dwelling on. She is described as 'a very Bhairavi in battle and in destroying hostile kings',[72] ruling over the districts of the Kisukadu 70, Roragare 60 and Masavadi 140,[73] which suggests that she controlled a total of two hundred and seventy villages. This formidable queen thus seems to have commanded armies in her own right – generally an exclusively male prerogative – and had even been involved in Someshvara's subjugation of the Konkan in 1047. By 1050, she was invested with the authority to send out 'seven royal ministers and other administrative officials' who granted to 'the eight Settis [senior merchants] and eighty households' of the town of Sudi 'a renewal of their corporate constitution which had partly broken down in the stress of the war with the Cholas'.[74] Sudi was an important commercial and urban centre, a transregional trading hub with the authority to mint its own coins to facilitate exchange – and thus crucial to Chalukya power.[75]

Someshvara, meanwhile, seems to have set in motion a serious attempt to connect the Deccan's many power centres directly to the imperial court, expanding the reach of the Chalukya chancellery and an institution called the 'Office of Records'. In the late tenth–early eleventh centuries, when Taila Chalukya had seized the title of Fortune's Favourite in anarchy, and his sons and grandsons struggled to fend off invasions from two fronts, the process through which the court interacted with the Deccan's many local power centres was somewhat ad hoc. High-ranking military officers ruled over them under the direct authority of the Vallabha, with awe-inspiring titles such as Maha-Prachanda-Danda-Nayaka, Great Furious Commanders of the Forces. These grandees conducted the administration of justice, tax collection, land grant composition and so on, through members of their personal retinues.[76]

But by Someshvara's reign, 'a process of regularisation or rationalisation' had set in.[77] An 'imperial chancellery' of sorts was beginning to emerge: some varieties of local administrative functions, especially related to the composition and recording of land grants, were permanently associated with official positions tied directly to the imperial authority.[78] These officials now executed their duties at the *authorization*, rather than the *command*, of whatever aristocrat happened to be shuffled around to oversee a region by the imperial court. This does not seem a professional bureaucracy as we would know it, but rather a new, non-military elite class, often highly mobile Brahmins: pandits from Kashmir, especially, were drawn to lucrative careers in the Deccan. As scribes, poets and administrators without local roots and thus loyal only to the imperial court at Kalyana, they appear to have been integral to Someshvara's attempts to counterbalance the influence of powerful aristocrats.[79] These individuals helped standardize another policy of the Chalukyas of Kalyana: the resurgence of Sanskrit in imperial land grants.

We have seen how, after the composition of Amoghavarsha Rashtrakuta's landmark *Kavirajamarga*, Kannada had very rapidly begun to replace Sanskrit in royal land grants. The Rashtrakuta emperors had even begun to adopt titles of mixed Sanskrit and Kannada. By the time of the Kalyana Chalukya grants, while the vast majority of stone inscriptions – usually commissioned by local grandees declaring fealty to the imperial court – were in Kannada, the land grants of the Chalukya emperors themselves, usually made on copper plates roughly the size of modern A4 sheets, were all in Sanskrit. Apparently, the ambitions and worldviews of the Vallabhas had shifted again: Someshvara's family were seeking to associate themselves once again with the prestige, transregional appeal and eternal allure of the subcontinent's grandest language of power. The imperial chancellery seems to have ensured a remarkably consistent standard Sanskrit script across the reign of the Kalyana Chalukyas: Nagari (rather than, say, Old Kannada letters, which was more frequently used to write Sanskrit words in the region). Nagari was the script used in the inscriptions of the Vatapi Chalukya king Kirti-Varman II and his Rashtrakuta rival Danti-Durga, when they had struggled with each other for imperial dominance of the Deccan in the eighth century.[80] It had an extraordinary currency and usage across the Indian subcontinent's elites in the eleventh century. It seems that Nagari witnessed a resurgence in eleventh-century Deccan, and Sanskrit began to reappear in Chalukya land grants, in order to reflect the imperial and transregional ambitions of Someshvara's court. As the land grants put it, they were meant to be maintained by all dynasties that came after: how else should the Chalukyas command future generations than through Sanskrit in the prestigious Nagari script? We shall return to this Nagari script, related to the modern Devanagari script used for Hindi, in the next chapter.

Let us now move beyond the court and see how far the Deccan has come from when we first saw it: a dry, war-torn land with few cities and dynasties, and an economy primarily based on loot and barter.

Half a millennium after our story began, we would see a society and economy of vast scale. Perhaps the most significant change we would see is the preponderance of currency: coins were now being minted by private workshops (under royal supervision) in ever-larger numbers,[81] not just gold but lower denomination coins of copper as well. These coins were being used with increasing regularity for everything from purchasing goods to paying construction workers.[82] The importance of this transformation cannot be understated. Money is far more fungible than bushels of grain. It can be moved around faster, and used to buy more varied and complex goods and services. The increased availability of coinage helped establish financial networks to extend credit, exchange currencies and pay interest on deposits.[83] The biggest owners of fixed assets – temples and landlords – had also leapt into the game, lured by exorbitant interest rates ranging from 30 to 40 per

Classical Numismatics Gallery

A gold coin issued by a Kalyana Chalukya feudatory, depicting the dynasty's boar crest.

cent per annum. The money supply exploded, and commercial activity with it.[84]

Everything from 'drugs, clothes, spices, perfumes, oil-seeds, jaggery, white sugar, gems of every description and also grain, areca-nuts and betel leaves'[85] was available in prosperous market villages as also in large urban centres. People even outside of cities no longer had to split their time between cultivating and manufacturing as they had done for centuries. They could simply manufacture and sell goods, and use the cash to buy food from great agricultural estates which used bonded labour to undercut each other in the markets. Lords and peasant groups went out of their way to invite merchants and producers to their towns and markets, giving them free land or concessionary tax rates in return for their aid in developing commercial centres.[86] Some towns were even administered by merchant princes with the title of Pattanasvami, Lord of the City, working in close conjunction with minor kings and landlords.[87]

This diverse, polycentric ruling elite, coming from an array of caste backgrounds, occupying ever-shifting positions in relation to each other and to various glittering courts shifting around Someshvara's, all competed for social status and for material possessions, kindling a ravenous appetite for exotic produce from the farthest corners of the world.[88] As we compare all this to the relatively simple, pastoral, and barely urbanized landscapes of northern Karnataka in the seventh and eighth centuries, the picture that emerges is of a land that has been totally transformed through centuries of warfare, agrarian and religious expansion, and growing political complexity. Much of the Indian subcontinent went through similar processes through the early medieval period, *c.* 600–1200, setting the foundation for many of the social, economic, religious and political structures that survive in some form today.

Medieval India had great cities, tournaments, forts, lords and ladies, poets and priests, peasants and craftsmen, monasteries and temples. Its kings and queens wore costumes of great diversity and sophisticated style, its lordly houses wielded insignia granted by emperors, and even followed a code of honour, as we've seen. Yet, today, the word 'medieval' in the global context generally conjures up either an image of a European knight in shining armour, or perhaps a sultan in the Middle East. This image of a medieval Indian past that was as complicated as our present seems to have totally vanished from our imagining of our own history, not to mention that of the world.

❧

Such a profusion of wealthy, status-conscious people, with the means to hire flourishing *sthapati* guilds from the rapidly expanding market cities of the Deccan, naturally led to a profusion of those most iconic of medieval buildings: temples.

The eleventh century was a flourishing age of temple construction, just as it was for Sanskrit literature. The Paramara king Bhoja of Malwa had been able to dream of creating such a colossus as the Bhojeshvara because the means and expertise to create it finally existed. The visions of great pillared halls and temple spires that Bhoja probably saw in his mind as he composed or revised great architectural tomes such as the *Samaranganasutradhara,* could now be brought to life. The scale of the projects that we see in the eleventh century, including Rajendra Chola's Gangaikondacholeshvara and the 'Rani ki Vav' stepwell in Patan, Gujarat (both UNESCO World Heritage Sites today), prove that *sthapatis* could create load-bearing structures of enormous size and weight, and adapt them to a plurality of local conditions and design requirements. Their existence is a testament to the considerable resources and engineering capabilities that states and *sthapatis* had managed to accumulate since the fledgling stone temples of the sixth–seventh centuries.

Sudeep M. / Wikimedia Commons

The Amriteshvara temple at Annigeri, a splendid example of Deccan architecture. Observe the sheer dynamism of its walls, and how the architectural elements at the corners and axes of symmetry are layered upon each other. While it looks very different from the Lokeshvara at Pattadakal, it is a descendant of the same design logic. Observe also how the walls feature little to no sculpture; all decoration is architectural, leading the scholar Gerard Foekema to describe medieval Deccan temples as 'architecture decorated with architecture'.

In the eleventh century, Deccani architects unleashed a vast wave of temple building that has left us with a truly 'glorious body of monuments'[89] in Karnataka. Whereas in the seventh–eighth centuries royals were the most important patrons of temples, the vast majority of eleventh-century temples were built by feudatories and subordinates of the imperial court. Unfortunately, many of these masterpieces are relatively unknown, subsumed in our imagination of south Indian architecture by the thriving pilgrimage sites and imposing temple gateways of Tamil Nadu. They can be seen at Sudi: the Mallikarjuna and Joda Kalasa temples; Annigeri: the Amriteshvara temple; Ittagi: the Mahadeva temple; and Badami, the old home of the Vatapi Chalukyas, right in front of the great reservoir that still exists today, the Yellamma temple.

The floor plans of the Lokeshvara and Krishneshvara temples built by the early Chalukyas and Rashtrakutas had resembled squares projecting from squares, with walls decorated with niches for sculpture. Their roofs rose up in tiers, studded with carvings of miniature buildings. Made of hard rock such as sandstone and basalt, these architectural decorations had a certain thickness and weight to them; Gerard Foekema describes them as 'chubby'. But now, by the eleventh century, Deccan architects had arrived at floor plans of greater complexity: squares projecting out of squares projecting out of squares projecting out of squares projecting out of squares. They even introduced a floor plan inspired by designs current in Malwa and northern India, embedding rotated squares into other squares, creating stellate designs – stars with anywhere from sixteen to thirty-two points. The Dodda Basappa temple at Dambal, perhaps the most remarkable example of a stellate temple in existence, is based on a twenty-four-point star.[90]

With exponentially more surfaces to ornament, *sthapatis* incorporated new materials to meet this design requirement. In the Dharwad region, south of the Krishna river, soapstone and potstone[91]

P. Madhusudhan / Wikimedia Commons

The Dodda Basappa temple at Dambal, an example of the Deccan trend towards complex floor plans and architectural decoration. The star shape is a logical extension of the increasingly complex outward projections that characterize medieval Deccan temples.

were worked into astonishingly florid architectural decorations depicting all sorts of fantastic creatures and foliage.[92] Pillars inside the temple took on polished, rounded shapes almost reminiscent of lathe-turned carvings.[93] The temple spires maintained the tiered logic of Dravidian temples,[94] but with many more projections and repetitions of the main spire along the central axes, following the floor plan composed of squares projecting from squares. The emanating walls of these temples were decorated with carved pillar forms bearing miniature depictions of dozens of different temple styles, reflecting the vast variety of regional architectural idioms that its cosmopolitan *sthapatis* were now familiar with – a far cry from the relatively simple architectural depictions seen in early Deccan temples in Vatapi. The result is temples that seem truly *alive*, almost dancing. The Ittagi Mahadeva temple can be considered an example of this type.

North of the Krishna river, closer to the heart of Chalukya power, the preference seems to have been for harder varieties of stone.[95] The architectural style also reflects north Indian influences, with tall plinths taking up most of the bottom half of the wall, and tall, curvilinear brick towers on the superstructure.[96] Pillars in the halls generally look as though assembled from stacked square or octagonal forms decorated with abstract geometric shapes.[97] Instead of pillar forms decorated with miniature temples, the walls are adorned with sculptures of dancing women contrasted against elegant flat surfaces – the sophisticated 'Metropolitan' style of Kalyana and its environs.[98] The Dattatreya temple at Chattarki, in the modern Vijayapura district, exemplifies this style. The importance of these two new Deccan architectural lineages will become apparent when we discuss the successors of the Chalukyas in the next chapter.

Deccan *sthapatis* in the eleventh century competed to create the most innovative floor plans, the most imposing temples, the most elaborate sculptural ornamentations. The greatest shrines could be declared, just like the greatest poets, 'emperors among temples',[99] admired by rivals and inspire imitations.

༄

The thriving economic and cultural structures of the eleventh-century Deccan could not have existed without a stable and resilient polity of vast scale to enable them. The temples, coinage and land grants that have survived to this period establish that such a polity did indeed exist, and that unlike Sri Lanka or the kingdoms of India's east coast, it was able to successfully withstand the might of the Cholas on multiple occasions. And the credit for this should go to the grit, determination and political abilities of the court of Someshvara, Fortune's Favourite, the Vallabha. Though his career is eclipsed in popular memory by those of his contemporaries, especially Rajaraja Chola and his sons, he deserves to be recognized for manifesting and anchoring an ambitious and powerful imperial polity in the Deccan, and for successfully holding his own against the forces arrayed against him. Someshvara Kalyana Chalukya is one of the subcontinent's unsung political masterminds. His history, like that of the Deccan, is unfortunately eclipsed by the stories of kings who fit better into nationalist and militaristic representations of our past.

Someshvara's consolidation of the Chalukya imperial network came not a minute too soon. In 1054, Rajadhiraja Chola, having recovered from the exertions of his 1048 campaign, once again invaded the Deccan.[100] For six years, he had trumpeted his successes and flaunted the door guardian he seized from the ashes of Kalyana, inscribed prominently with the label 'The door-keeper brought by Sri-Vijaya-Rajendra-Deva after burning Kalyanapuram',[101] a stand-in for the supposedly subjugated Vallabha,[102] still visible today at a museum in Gangai-Konda-Chola-Puram. Now, the Deccan was ready to show the Cholas just how wrong their king's claim of victory was.

Rajadhiraja 'Vijaya-Rajendra' Chola, Victorious Lord of Kings, does not seem to have anticipated what was in store for him. While he was busy boasting of his victories, the 'proud and furious'[103] Someshvara had steadily strengthened his own positions, dispatching an army led by a number of veteran commanders to Koppam[104] on the north bank of the Tungabhadra. Koppam protected a crucial ford that Rajadhiraja would have to cross in order to invade the Deccan again.

Rajadhiraja began his campaign with the same moves he always adopted. Moving from the southern Deccan towards the Raichur doab, he 'began to ravage the country by defiling its rivers and demolishing its towns and villages'.[105] It would appear that his strategy was, once again, to parade his forces around the region, loot it and perhaps capture the rebuilt Kalyana, in which Someshvara had invested so much treasure. However, with a Chalukya force at Koppam now prepared to challenge Chola attempts to move beyond the Tungabhadra, he would have to deal with it first.

The commanders of the Chola and Chalukya armies would probably have arrayed their troops with the river protecting one side of their formations, and advanced towards each other.

There were probably vast regiments of infantry bearing spears, swords, maces and everything in between. According to a late tenth-century source, Tamil soldiers wore short-cropped hair and thick beards, with gold rings swinging from their ears;[106] it is possible that many continued to be costumed as such in the mid-eleventh century. Their bodies were painted with turmeric, their shields covered in blood-red lead.[107] Evidence from travellers' accounts and Chola inscriptions suggest that on this day, Rajadhiraja Chola, standing on a splendid howdah on the back of an enormous elephant alongside his bodyguards, advanced near the front.[108] He was surrounded by a dense formation of heavily armed elephantry painted with frightful designs; the lordly beasts, like Rajadhiraja and his officers, bore titles awarded to commemorate their valour and prowess on the battlefield.[109]

Arrayed against them were the senior generals of the Deccan, also on elephants. Present on that day, supposedly, was one of Someshvara's younger brothers, as well as General Pulakeshin, the burner of Kanchi.[110] They carried bamboo bows, coated with red arsenic, vermilion and lac, decorated with jewels and tied to their hands with leather cords.[111] These men were trained to shoot at high speed, supposedly having an arrow ready to launch as soon as one had been dispatched towards its target.[112]

After a period of skirmishing, when both sides traded projectiles, the order to attack was given. Rank after rank of infantry clashed with an enormous roar. As desperate foot soldiers yelled at each other, moving back and forth across the battlefield, attempting to break their enemy's cohesion and stay alive in the chaos, the elephant-riding men of rank sought each other out[113] to display their combat abilities and bravery. 'The battlefield was to the warrior what the court or salon was to the poet.'[114] The poor foot soldiers were there to kill and be killed. But, as we saw in the previous chapter, the aristocrats were there to *perform*, to display their prowess to their followers and the Vallabha. Studying medieval hero stones and inscriptions, and comparing with warfare in other parts of the world, we can deduce that these warlords were drawn to the front lines by the banners of enemy commanders, their approach accompanied by the cheering of their troops, with poets announcing their lineages and achievements, and the blowing of conches and trumpets. Some might even fling themselves into knots of heavy fighting, inspiring their troops to fight ever harder; many Deccan hero stones seem to commemorate precisely these kinds of deaths, as do depictions in literature. For example:

> A good fighter ... holding with his left hand his restless head which, half-cut by an arrow, remained on his neck, made everyone praise (him) ... Some one, holding his mouth into which the enemy-elephant thrust its small tusk ... appeared as if sportively drinking the juice of the nectar of fame with a lotus-stalk.[115]

On this day in 1054, Rajadhiraja Chola's leaping red tiger banner was sought out by just such a team of braves, riding crack elephants, probably with a light infantry escort, led by the generals Mararasa and Bachiraja;[116] the latter descended from the general Kalidasa who had rescued the Chalukya emperor Jayasimha II, Someshvara's father, from a coup attempt in the 1020s. For whatever reason, the Chola emperor himself seems to have ended up in the thick of combat – perhaps he was lured into a weak point in the Chalukya line and attacked it without enough support, perhaps he was overconfident about his abilities and led a cohort of elephants directly into the thick of the fighting. Either way, in the chaos of the battle, Mararasa found him, vulnerable, and attacked.

Rajadhiraja's elephant probably came under a hail of Chalukya arrows,[117] dispatched from Mararasa's squadron on foot and from their elephant-back howdahs. The Chola's bodyguards must have desperately attempted to cover him with heavy shields of cow and horse leather.[118] Sharp elephant lances, the heads twenty-one fingers across, with a curved hook and sharp backward-facing triangular blades below,[119] would have been stabbed by Chalukya riders into any exposed patches of the Rajadhiraja's elephant's skin that they could find – its eyes, trunk, genitals, belly and mouth, shredding its flesh as the weapons were yanked out, forcing the screaming animal to collapse.

An emperor of Rajadhiraja's rank may well have been given the chance to surrender, but that was not the Chola's style. One is tempted to imagine the Chalukya generals calling down to him in Sanskrit, only to be met with a barrage of curses in Tamil. And so the 'Victorious Rajendra' was brutally put to death on the battlefield, dying as he had lived, his head – perhaps still anointed with the perfumed oil of his morning ablution – grabbed by a bloodstained hand and hacked off.

The death of Rajadhiraja was a crushing blow to the Chola army's morale, but his younger brother Rajendra-deva was able to bring up the reserves and drive away the Chalukya elephant squadrons before they could take advantage.[120] It was, even according to usually chest-thumping Chola accounts, a desperate and closely fought affair, though of course they still claimed victory. Though many senior Chalukya officers were killed at Koppam – including General Pulakeshin,[121] burner of Kanchi – and the Cholas were left in possession of the battlefield, their 'victory' was entirely hollow. Rajadhiraja Chola, the Victorious Rajendra, had gone 'up into the sky, welcomed by the women of the world of Indra',[122] and was eulogized as Anaimerrunjina

Devar, the King Who Died on the Back of an Elephant.[123] His younger brother crowned himself Rajendra II on the blood-soaked ground the next day,[124] and quickly retreated to forestall any succession struggles or rebellions at home. No matter how much the Cholas attempted to portray themselves as victors of the battle of Koppam, it was evident to the entire subcontinent that they had been struck a devastating blow. Lanka once again smouldered into rebellion,[125] drawing away Chola forces. The Deccan was saved.

Celebrations must have broken out across Someshvara's cities, thanks given to Shiva to the sound of bells, drums and conch shells. 'The wicked Chola, that deadly sinner, failing in his [royal] duty, abandoning the ancient *dharma* of his family, invaded … he burned down a multitude of temples … his guilt bore an immediate harvest in his hand and he gave his live head to Trailokyamalla [Someshvara],'[126] declared the triumphant Chalukyas. The Chola emperor's death was a resounding reminder, trumpeted by the court to all who would hear it, that Someshvara was, indeed, Fortune's beloved.

The general Mararasa was awarded the unique title of Rajadhiraja-Chola-Gonda, the Destroyer of Rajadhiraja Chola, and declared Queen Mailaladevi's Champion,[127] while Bachiraja's family boasted of how he had delivered the 'freshly decapitated head' of the 'savage enemy' to Someshvara.[128] This grisly trophy must have been the target of no small amount of merriment in Kalyana, the object of parades and humiliation, payback for the burning, rape, murder and looting it had once inflicted when attached to a body. After all the struggles of the previous decades, it must have appeared that Someshvara had, at last, saved the Deccan and established it as the premier power of the south, as it had once been.

10

Fortune's Favourites

Winter, 1054 CE

After the death of the emperor Rajadhiraja in 1054, as the Cholas turned inwards, the Kalyana Chalukyas turned outwards. It seemed that Someshvara's career had reached a splendid apogee: Raichur was firmly held by the Chalukyas, the Konkan had submitted, Malwa had been crushed, and Vengi too would soon be captured.

Rajaraja-Narendra, the Chalukya king of Vengi, finally realized that there could be no more resistance to the influence of the Vallabha of the Deccan. His entire career had been spent chasing his half-brother Vijayaditya VII, Someshvara's dear ally, out of Vengi as their 'political and martial fortunes seesawed, intensified by their alliances with their powerful, self-interested neighbours to the west and south'.[1] As the growing weight of the Kalyana court tipped south India's centre of gravity once more to the west, it seemed that Vijayaditya's moment had come. But Narendra was not ousted and replaced. Instead, the Vallabha Someshvara made a deal with him and allowed him to keep his throne as the vassal king of Vengi. The Vallabha's eldest son, also named Someshvara, was appointed the 'Lord of the City of Vengi',[2]

332

suggesting that the Deccan emperor intended Vengi to be ruled directly from Kalyana after Narendra's death.

Vijayaditya VII must have been aggrieved. He was compensated with splendid governorships and titles elsewhere in the Deccan.[3] But to a man with his 'incisive political mind,'[4] this deal with his half-brother Narendra must have been a humiliating betrayal by Someshvara. Vijayaditya kept his peace for now, but he seems to have found a powerful ally, also sidelined, also ignored: Someshvara's second son, Prince Vikramaditya of the Kalyana Chalukyas, who had fought in his father's armies alongside Vijayaditya for years. And so he began to plot with this man, as masterful a politician as the old Vallabha himself.

Narendra, meanwhile, subsided into a sorrowful retirement under Someshvara's shadow, far away from his Chola relations. Narendra was the son of a Vengi Chalukya prince and the Chola princess Kundavai, daughter of Rajaraja I; he was married to Ammangai, daughter of Rajendra I and his first cousin. Their son, named Rajiga[5] for his Chola grandfather Rajendra, was now far away in Tamilakam. This young man seems to have spent much of his early life enamoured by the opportunities his maternal uncles, the Cholas, could provide him – rather than what his father could offer. We will hear from Rajiga again soon.

Apparently seeking a project to keep himself occupied, and perhaps inspired by old Amoghavarsha Rashtrakuta's success at creating a new courtly Kannada, Narendra now commissioned one Nannayya, a Brahmin from Tamilakam,[6] to compose the first great poem in a new, courtly Telugu – a classicized register of the language spoken in Vengi and its environs. Narendra had a simple request for Nannayya, which also reveals to us how seriously kings took the claims of divine descent that their ancestors included in their *prashastis*, and the complex motivations which led them to patronize poets:

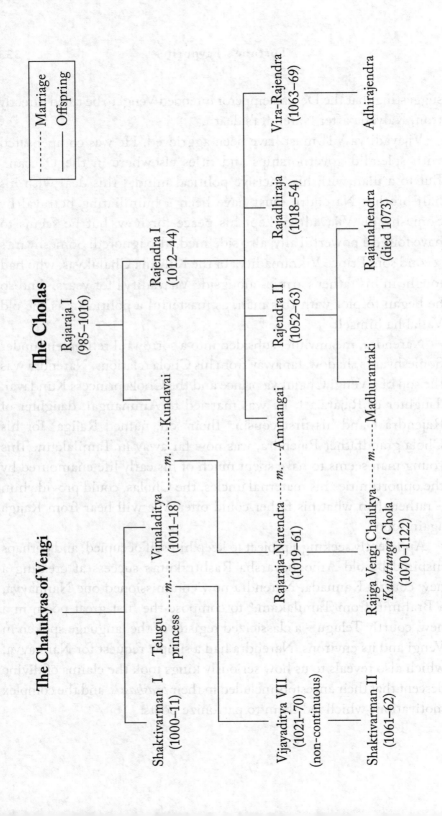

The Chalukyas of Vengi   **The Cholas**

Rajaraja I
(985–1016)

Shaktivarman I   Vimaladitya   Rajendra I
(1000–11)   m.   (1011–18)   (1012–44)

Telugu   Kundavai
princess

                    m.

Vijayaditya VII   Rajaraja-Narendra   m.   Ammangai   Rajendra II   Rajadhiraja   Vira-Rajendra
(1021–70)   (1019–61)   (1052–63)   (1018–54)   (1063–69)
(non-continuous)

                    m.

Shaktivarman II   Rajiga Vengi Chalukya   m.   Madhurantaki   Rajamahendra   Adhirajendra
(1061–62)   'Kulottunga' Chola   (died 1073)
                    (1070–1122)

- - - - - Marriage
———— Offspring

My lineage begins with the moon, and then proceeds through Puru, Bharata, Kuru, and King Pandu. The stories of Pandu's famous sons [the Pandavas], virtuous and beyond blame, are ever close to my heart ... My mind inclines day and night to those stories. With all your learning, please compose in Telugu a book that makes clear ... the proven meaning bound to the *Mahabharata* text.[7]

The Mahabharata, one of the longest poems ever composed, was now slowly reborn in Telugu, in what Professors V.N. Rao and David Shulman call a 'lyrical, laconic and precise' form 'combining long Sanskrit compounds and Dravidian-based Telugu words and adapting a variety of Sanskrit and regional meters'.[8] It was a distant parallel to the birth of courtly Kannada poetry under the rigorous Sanskrit-inspired grammars of Amoghavarsha's court. Nannayya would never finish this great undertaking: that was a task left to the generations of master poets who came after him. But courtly Telugu, which would one day grow in splendour to the point where it practically eclipsed the literature of the Kannada and Tamil regions that had so cruelly attacked and exploited the fertile coast, had been born. It was the founding moment of a glorious literary tradition. Courtly Telugu would reach its apogee in sixteenth-century Vijayanagara, the mighty empire of the southern Deccan, and continue to flourish in the Qutb Shahi court of Golconda and the Nayaka states of Tamil Nadu in the seventeenth and eighteenth centuries.[9]

Returning to the eleventh century: as poetry flourished in courts across the subcontinent, in 1055, the greatest of its royal patrons – Bhoja Paramara – died under a cloud of shame and sorrow. The brilliant old king had never recovered from Someshvara's 1046 sack of Dhara. His beloved capital was sacked again soon after by the rising power of the Chaulukyas of neighbouring Gujarat (not to be confused with the Chalukyas of Kalyana), and then the Kalachuris of central India. A later story tells us that Bhoja, attacked by these two kings, 'lost his pride, as a snake, overcome with a charm, loses its poison'.[10] The Paramaras fell into anarchy and dynastic squabbling: one candidate sought the help of his family's enemies, the Kalachuris and the Kalyana Chalukyas.[11] The Vallabha Someshvara seems to have realized this could potentially help settle his northern frontier. His second son, Prince Vikramaditya (who, as noted earlier, was already searching for allies of his own) was sent to ensure that the ambitious Paramara prince succeeded to Bhoja's vacant throne.[12]

Bhoja had been the most extraordinary of the medieval Paramara line of poet-kings. Despite the brilliance and tragedy of his life and almost total absence from narratives of world history, Bhoja finally did become immortal in Indian storytelling and literature: he would be remembered for centuries after as the 'ultimate arbiter of grammatical correctness, rhetorical propriety, and literary good taste',[13] rewarding courtiers and litterateurs for witty or unique turns of phrase.

By 1061, Prince Vikramaditya had returned from Dhara to the south, where the Cholas were once again seeking to wrest back the Raichur doab. Rajadhiraja's brutal death on the battlefield was hardly conducive to future peace, and the Cholas sought revenge for this humiliation. The Tamil kingdom was also facing some political churn. Rajendra II's succession to the throne in a moment of deadly crisis had not been disputed by his elder brother Rajadhiraja's sons. However, he now appointed *his* son Rajamahendra as crown prince, sidelining the claims of his ambitious younger brother – the youngest of Rajendra I's three sons, Vira-Rajendra. To help secure the heir's future, Rajiga Vengi Chalukya, the son of their sister Ammangai and Rajaraja-Narendra of Vengi, was married to Rajendra II's daughter Madhurantaki (Rajiga's first cousin). The emperor also seems to have promised that Rajiga would be seated on his father's throne, and that Vengi would be freed of the influence of the Kalyana Chalukyas.

But Prince Vikramaditya of the Kalyana Chalukyas moved on the Cholas before they had a chance to attack – apparently while they

were still gathering their forces in the former Ganga territories in the
southern Deccan. Vikramaditya's attempt was not successful. Indeed,
the new Chola crown prince, Rajamahendra, dramatically claimed
to have forced the Chalukyas back with a single war elephant at an
inconclusive battle in 1061 at Kudala-Sangama,[14] where the Tunga
and Bhadra rivers merge to become the Tungabhadra.

But before the war could unfold any further, all plots and plans
and preparations were thrown out of the window by a new crisis.
The fuse was lit in Vengi, where, in 1061, Rajaraja-Narendra, part
Chola, part Chalukya, died. The first on the scene was his half-brother
and deadliest rival, Vijayaditya VII, who entered Vengi, at last, in
triumph. The goal that had driven him for nearly half a century was
at last achieved. It seems that by this point Someshvara Chalukya
had modified his plans for the kingdom and agreed to Vijayaditya's
reclamation of his ancestral throne. However, Vijayaditya would not
forget his old ally's earlier betrayal so easily, as we shall see.

Vijayaditya VII, his life's ambition apparently fulfilled, now
crowned his son as the new king of Vengi. But the Chola royal family
had already realized what was happening and were moving to turn
the situation to their advantage. Rajiga Vengi Chalukya, son of the
dead Narendra, nephew and son-in-law of Chola emperors, had just
as strong a claim to Vengi as his paternal uncle Vijayaditya VII. An
army was dispatched under the command of Vira-Rajendra Chola,
younger brother of the emperor Rajendra II.

In 1062, the Chalukya and Chola armies, with all their pent-up
enmity and hatred, clashed in battle. Vijayaditya's son, the new king
of Vengi, was killed, though his side apparently managed to drag his
body away before the Cholas could seize it. Another senior Chalukya
commander who was killed was not so lucky: as with Rajadhiraja, his
body was beheaded. The commander's daughter, 'who resembled a
peacock in beauty', was captured, and the elderly Chola prince Vira-
Rajendra cruelly ordered her nose to be cut off.[15] It was a chilling

reminder of how women's bodies were the most frequent targets of aristocrats who wished to humiliate and underline their dominance over their enemies.[16]

Vijayaditya was devastated.[17] According to his inscriptions, it was not until 'hereditary well-wishers'[18] managed to get through to him that he agreed to seat himself on the sorrowful throne of Vengi. The twisted humour with which Fortune had seen it fit to grant his dearest wish, only to tear it away and return it to him, seems particularly cruel.

A year later, in 1063, the Chola emperor Rajendra II died. Rather than continue to conduct the war in Vengi, his younger brother Vira-Rajendra returned to Gangai-Konda-Chola-Puram, hell-bent on seizing the throne. Rajendra II's son, the crown prince Rajamahendra, disappeared in somewhat murky circumstances. It is not entirely clear whether or not he predeceased his father. Vira-Rajendra had abandoned Vengi to Vijayaditya VII. The claims of his nephew Rajiga were not to be enforced. Rajiga had lost his patrimony.[19] This young man's allies and his branch of the Chola–Chalukya family now began to cast about for opportunities of their own.

The new Chola emperor Vira-Rajendra, meanwhile, had much bigger challenges facing him. A half-century of incessant war, the loss of crucial spheres of influence to the Kalyana Chalukyas, and the growing power and autonomy of Tamil lords, merchants, cities and chiefs needed to be urgently addressed. The military successes that had fuelled the careers of the last four Chola emperors were increasingly untenable in the face of constant rebellions, dwindling military resources and agricultural surplus, and the ascendant power of the Chalukyas.

Sitting on his throne in Gangai-Konda-Chola-Puram, twenty years after his father Rajendra Chola's death, Vira-Rajendra had neither the resources nor the power with which his predecessors had pursued their ambitions. Continuous rebellions in Lanka and requests for intervention in the politics of the Srivijaya federation[20] – which Prince

Rajiga was dispatched to attend to with a small force, *c.* 1068 – were straining his resources enormously. More importantly, he was already advanced in age, and was determined to ensure that his beloved son Adhirajendra would be able to succeed him and maintain Chola power. He would need to do something radical, and he was not the only south Indian ruler who faced this imperative. Vijayaditya VII of Vengi, despite the tragic loss of his son, was once again back to his political manoeuvring, alongside his partner-in-arms, Prince Vikramaditya of the Kalyana Chalukyas.

By 1067, the Kalyana Chalukya Vallabha Someshvara was seized by a mysterious disease, a 'malignant fever' according to a Chalukya poet.[21] Priests and physicians were anxiously attempting to cure him. His heir, Crown Prince Someshvara, was increasingly taking charge of affairs in Kalyana, while his most capable son, Prince Vikramaditya was elsewhere, busy with his own machinations. Under these circumstances, a Chola raid led to the capture of some Chalukya officers, whose heads were nailed to the walls of Gangai-Konda-Chola-Puram.[22] A ritual humiliation was also performed, whereby a Chalukya diplomat was garlanded with a banner declaring that Someshvara was a coward[23] (which appears to have been an occupational hazard for any Chalukya ambassador to the Cholas). Around this poorly attested incident, the Chola court poets fabricated a feverish fantasy claiming that the humiliated Someshvara had demanded a rematch of the battle of Kudala-Sangama, providing a date and place for the contest; apparently Vira-Rajendra adhered to it, but Someshvara, that 'liar', did not show up and instead 'ran away until his legs became sore, and hid himself in the western ocean', leaving the Chola emperor to conquer and burn the entire Deccan![24]

Nothing of the sort had happened. This was all for show, for the amusement of the crowds of his subjects, demanding war and loot and entertainment. Vira-Rajendra had subtler plans in motion.

Around 1067, as his old ally Someshvara I of the Kalyana

Chalukyas lay dying, Vijayaditya VII of Vengi, unseated and humiliated by two generations of Chola emperors, who had lost his own son to Vira-Rajendra's armies, humbly submitted to the Chola emperor. He received in return a position as an honoured vassal.[25] The Chola emperor now declared that his dead brother Rajendra II's vow regarding Vengi had been fulfilled.[26] It was yet another blow for the young Rajiga Vengi Chalukya,[27] who must have been infuriated. However, apparently learning from his *paternal* uncle Vijayaditya VII that patience might eventually bring him what he sought, he contented himself for now with the position of a minor lord in Chhattisgarh, protecting Chola control over Vengi. Here he butted heads with Prince Vikramaditya[28] of the Kalyana Chalukyas, the beginning of a lifelong enmity. In return for his apparently calm resignation to his fate, Rajiga Vengi Chalukya, this 'seemingly loyal and indebted near-relation', was also 'compensated by being allowed to exercise a certain authority ... in the area linking his two dynastic heartlands', the ancient Pallava domains around Kanchi,[29] between Vengi and the Chola core territories. However, as the scholar Whitney Cox puts it, Vira-Rajendra had fatally underestimated this young man's own ambitions and abilities.[30]

As much as he might have been frustrated with his new-found struggles with Rajiga Vengi Chalukya, Prince Vikramaditya of the Kalyana Chalukyas was probably not too discomfited by Vijayaditya VII's betrayal. He may, in fact, have been responsible for it in the first place. By facilitating Chola control over Vengi, he hoped to gain Vira-Rajendra's support for his own bid for the Chalukya throne. By bringing together the Kalyana Chalukyas and the Cholas, Vikramaditya could finally end the perpetually escalating conflict that was consuming both families.[31]

At this point, it is worth discussing what sort of man this Prince Vikramaditya of the Kalyana Chalukyas really was. Of course, as with so many things in medieval India, all we have are snapshots of the man's furiously active life. Uniquely, we also have access to a *mahakavya* called the *Vikramankadevacharitam*, an epic poem written in Sanskrit by Bilhana, a Kashmiri poet who joined the court of Kalyana, rewriting Vikramaditya's personal history and depicting him as an ideal king, another Rama. In truth, Vikramaditya, for all his undoubted capabilities, was far removed from that god-king of legend.

This prince was born in the generation after the destruction of Manyakheta by the Cholas[32] – which made him and his siblings

Wikimedia Commons

Vikramaditya Chalukya as depicted in Hutchinson's *Story of the Nations*, published in 1915. He sits on a throne, attended by women. The depiction is not completely based on medieval Deccan art and is somewhat inaccurate.

among the first generation of truly 'Kalyana' Chalukyas, some of the
first members of the dynasty to see that city as their home. Growing
up in the palace at Kalyana, he had been surrounded by the women of
the Inner City. He received instruction from senior Brahmins while
his father and grandfather – Someshvara and Jayasimha II – were
constantly away battling the many deadly rivals of the Chalukyas.
Vikramaditya's court poet claimed that he showed signs of bravery and
military potential very early on: 'He loved to chase the royal swans
and to tease the lion-whelps in their cages.'[33] (Whether true or not,
this interesting nugget hints to us that perhaps the Chalukya palace
at Kalyana maintained a zoo or menagerie.)

Vikramaditya learned the skills of sexual pleasure and connoisseurship
of art, poetry, architecture and adornment; he learned to fight with
dagger, sword, shield and spear, exhibiting his abilities before the
court in an arena attached to the palace.[34] He went about in expensive
patterned silks, his hair oiled, shoulders and chest marked with
moon-shaped symbols of sandal paste, neck adorned with expensive
jewellery.[35] He personally knew the Chalukyas' great generals and
vassal kings, who visited the city on ceremonial occasions to pay
obeisance to his father and grandfather, and exchanged gifts and
refined conversation with them in the salons of Kalyana. It did not
take long for a faction to form around him, supporting his claim to
the throne.

Vikramaditya's father Someshvara, who had become Fortune's
Favourite in 1042, could do little about this sort of politicking. His
sons had been lectured in filial piety from legends and *shastra* texts,
but that artifice was no guarantee of loyalty to their father. Someshvara
nevertheless allowed Vikramaditya a position of prominence: he needed
his son's talents desperately to meet the challenges the Deccan was
facing from all directions. The prince was married to Chandralekha,
the daughter of an important Konkan family, probably soon after
Someshvara's campaign there in 1046–47. As has been mentioned

earlier, soon after, Vikramaditya was commanding armies against the Cholas, and served as his father's representative in Malwa in 1055. By this point, Vikramaditya's elder brother Someshvara already appears to have been the preferred candidate for succession, despite his relative lack of achievements. Having played an important role in the installation of the ruler of Malwa, Vikramaditya returned to the south by 1061, where he fought the Cholas at Kudala-Sangama, before the death of Rajaraja-Narendra in Vengi upended the political equations of south India. He then moved to Chhattisgarh, where, alongside the forces of the ambitious and ever-eager Hoysala chiefs of southern Karnataka, he battled Rajiga Vengi Chalukya for control over the strategic fort of Chakrakuta. All these activities indicate that Vikramaditya had diplomatic and military abilities of a very high order. He was, therefore, understandably averse to letting his elder brother succeed their father to the throne of Kalyana.

By 1067, as Someshvara Kalyana Chalukya, Great King of Kings, Fortune's Favourite, lay on his deathbed, Vikramaditya was in the province of Banavasi – the ancient capital of the Kadamba dynasty, where his supposed ancestor Pulakeshin II had first made his name by sacking their capital. Here, he and his younger brother Jayasimha plotted treason against their father and elder brother. The Kadamba lords of Goa as well as the Alupas, a lordly dynasty of southern Karnataka, swore their loyalty to Vikramaditya. They seem to have arranged for a direct meeting between him and the Chola emperor[36] Vira-Rajendra. Supposedly, Vikramaditya shared a seat with this deadly enemy of his family, exchanging vows of friendship. Vira-Rajendra appears to have promised to help Vikramaditya seize the throne of Kalyana, in return for Vengi remaining under Chola control.

Soon after, like his long-forgotten namesake, the Vatapi Chalukya emperor Vikramaditya II, this ambitious new Vikramaditya also entered Kanchi. But instead of the Pallava royal shrine, it was a palace that he visited, and instead of being preceded by an invading army, he was preceded by the beating drums of a wedding party. Vikramaditya Kalyana Chalukya married the daughter of Vira-Rajendra Chola,[37] thus declaring that he would support Vira-Rajendra's heir Adhirajendra in return for the Chola emperor's help in seizing Kalyana.

Someshvara, in a delirious fever, may not have known that any of this was happening. Or perhaps he saw the ominous machinations taking place as clear as day. We will never know. But in 1068, as it became increasingly clear that he would not recover from his illness, the emperor Someshvara informed the court that his career was at an end.

The 29th of March 1068 was an important and terrible day in the history of the Deccan.[38] That morning, the cool waters of the Tungabhadra swirled around Someshvara Kalyana Chalukya's feet, as his court stood around him solemnly.[39] He had already said his last words, his farewells.[40]

Someshvara stepped forward. Eddies swirled around his calves, his knees, his chest, his neck and finally the Vallabha submerged himself. A Chalukya poet writes a few decades later: '...and so it was then that, to the crashing accompaniment/of the river's surging wave/he went to the city of moon-crested Shiva.'[41]

Thus ended the life of the Someshvara Kalyana Chalukya, Fortune's Favourite, Earth's Beloved, Great King of Kings.

On 11 April 1068, less than two weeks after their father's suicide, Vikramaditya's elder brother rose to the throne of Kalyana as Fortune's Favourite, Someshvara II 'Bhuvanaikamalla', Sole Wrestler of the Earth – a significant title, hinting at the fact that this unfortunate prince understood his younger brothers' intrigues very well. He was, nevertheless, forced to grant them formal recognition as the 'governors' of various provinces in southern Karnataka. He surrounded himself with loyal generals, hoping to strengthen his grip on power and eventually humble his treacherous siblings.

Meanwhile, events were working out in Vikramaditya's favour. His Chola father-in-law, Vira-Rajendra, mounted a limited invasion of the Deccan, subduing a cursory attempt at defence by Someshvara II. Vikramaditya then declared himself the sovereign ruler of Gangavadi, southern Karnataka, along the Chola border,[42] and adopted imperial titles. As Vikramaditya and Vira-Rajendra now gathered their forces, it would seem that a Chola ruler was on the verge of a full-scale intervention in a Chalukya succession crisis.[43]

And then, in 1070, Vira-Rajendra suddenly fell ill and died. Vikramaditya was stymied. Had the old Chola emperor lived a little longer and guaranteed his accession to the imperial throne of the Deccan, Vikramaditya had planned to ensure the succession to the Chola throne of his brother-in-law, Vira-Rajendra's son Adhirajendra. But now, he had other matters to attend to: there was little he could do but wait and attempt to overthrow his brother Someshvara II by himself. He could only hope that his brother-in-law was capable of establishing himself as the next Chola emperor in his own right. Someshvara II, meanwhile, was encouraged by the news of Vira-Rajendra's death. That same year, 1070, he gathered his armies together and mounted an expedition to Malwa, where his brother Vikramaditya had so carefully appointed a loyal successor to Bhoja in 1055–56, and dethroned him.

Meanwhile, the political situation in the Tamil country had become far more complicated after Vira-Rajendra's death. His son, Adhirajendra Chola, had no martial accomplishments to his name – especially in comparison to a new claimant to the Chola throne, who had emerged almost out of the blue. This was none other than Vikramaditya Kalyana Chalukya's rival, Rajiga Vengi Chalukya, ruler of the territories around Kanchi, now calling himself Rajendra Chola. In his inscriptions and public documents, this Rajiga-Rajendra's court masterfully recounted his successes in Chhattisgarh, where he had supposedly distinguished himself against Vikramaditya Chalukya with behaviour becoming of a king.[44] In a manner unprecedented for any Chola before him, his inscriptions drew on the mythology of the *Puranas* to emphasize his descent from both the Chola and Chalukya families, the mythical dynasties of the Sun and the Moon supposedly united in his blood.[45] The Chalukya boar, which generations of Tamils had excoriated, was now presented as the gentle restorer of Earth, analogous to this new 'Rajendra' himself.[46]

His rival, Vikramaditya's young brother-in-law Adhirajendra, had 'his father's courtiers and the resources of the Kāveri delta nominally at his command'.[47] Perhaps, given time, he could have emphasized his legitimacy as a patrilineal descendant of the great conqueror Rajendra I Chola and eventually unseated this Rajiga-Rajendra, his Chalukya–Chola cousin. But it was not to be: in late 1071, the young king followed his father to the grave, possibly dying of gangrene.[48]

The courtiers of Rajiga-Rajendra now triumphantly fanned out across the Pallava heartland, which the Cholas had, up to this point, failed to truly integrate into their court society, confirming the privileges of magnates and agrarian assemblies. As Whitney Cox puts it, a new, decentralized network was being born in the Tamil country, a new realpolitik was at play, there was a new series of political equations.[49] By 1074, Rajiga-Rajendra, who could, in the male line, draw his ancestry hundreds of years back to Pulakeshin I, the chieftain-turned-king who performed the horse sacrifice in a distant time and place, rose to the glittering throne of the City of the Chola Who Conquered the Ganga. He adopted the title of Kulottunga Chola, Pinnacle of His Race. Henceforth he will be referred to as Rajiga-Kulottunga in this book.

With his brother Someshvara II now far more secure on his throne to his north and his rival Rajiga-Kulottunga established to his south, Vikramaditya Kalyana Chalukya was under enormous pressure.

Luckily for him, his successful military career seems to have convinced most of the Deccan that he was a sounder choice as emperor than his brother was, and his superb self-confidence,[50] at least in public, had already led to a virtual partition of the Chalukya political network.[51] Someshvara II stuck close to Kalyana, where his father's generals still remained loyal to him, and toured the Deccan making his own land grants and attempting to rally the support of new power centres.[52] But he was running out of time. South of the Tungabhadra, Vikramaditya had adopted the imperial title of Tribhuvanamalla, Wrestler of the Three Worlds.[53] Vassal kings from the Konkan to the Narmada had taken sides in a civil war which Vikramaditya was sure to win: the only question was when it would begin.

In 1075, Rajiga-Kulottunga Chola finally asserted his claims to Vengi with the entire resources of the Chola imperial network at his disposal. He was not content with leaving his paternal uncle Vijayaditya VII in control, given their personal history. The Kalyana Chalukyas were too divided to contest this move, which would finally grant the Cholas undisputed control over this fertile territory. Vijayaditya, his machinations and betrayals over so many decades having come to naught, fled Vengi and joined Vikramaditya Chalukya in Gangavadi.[54] The next year, Someshvara II attempted to ally with Rajiga-Kulottunga, who sent an expedition to fight his old rival Vikramaditya, who managed to fend it off. Claiming (apparently with no trace of irony) that his elder brother had betrayed the Chalukya family by allying with their ancestral rival,[55] he then advanced to Kalyana, his forces swelling larger and larger with the armies of his adherents.

After some desultory resistance, the elder brother that Vikramaditya had perhaps hated for being his father's favourite despite all his hard work over the years, was captured. Like so many others who had attempted to seize the glittering, bloody throne of the Deccan for themselves over the centuries – Mangalesha Chalukya, the courtesan queen Vijaya-Mahadevi, the Rashtrakuta kings Danti-Durga and

Govinda II, the Paramara ruler Vakpati – Someshvara Chalukya's eldest son vanishes from history.

The father's favourite was dead.[56] Long live Fortune's Favourite, Vikramaditya VI.

❧

Vikramaditya VI would reign for fifty years, casting himself as a millennial sovereign, the greatest of all Deccan emperors. Coming to the throne in roughly the year 999 of the Shaka era (1076 CE), one of the most widespread year-counting systems in the Indian subcontinent, he would inaugurate a new era, the Vikrama, used in Chalukya inscriptions through his rule and after.[57] He would reign over the vast, warlike and increasingly prosperous region with the same furious energy he had displayed as a prince, diplomat and general under his father: his inscriptions are found in Kalyana, Banavasi, Ponuguppe, Etagiri, Pottalakere, Appayanadakuppa, Ballakunde, Manyakere, Kollipake, Jananathapuram and Bijapur[58] – a wide swathe of territory extending through the heart of the Deccan, from present-day north Karnataka to the southwest. His feudatories are known from Nagpur in the north to Gangavadi in south Karnataka and Draksharama in coastal Andhra,[59] though the degree of allegiance to the Chalukya emperor varied across this vast landmass. Following in his father Someshvara I's footsteps, he ensured the production of large amounts of Sanskrit documents and texts through his reign, contributing significantly to Kalyana's status, prestige and legend. 'Subsequent generations, in particular those of the sixteenth century, would recall his long and prosperous reign with admiration and view the Chalukya house generally as having embodied the epitome of imperial glory and moral righteousness.'[60]

Under Vikramaditya VI, the glamorous court of Kalyana attracted a number of talented poets and religious leaders – including, as

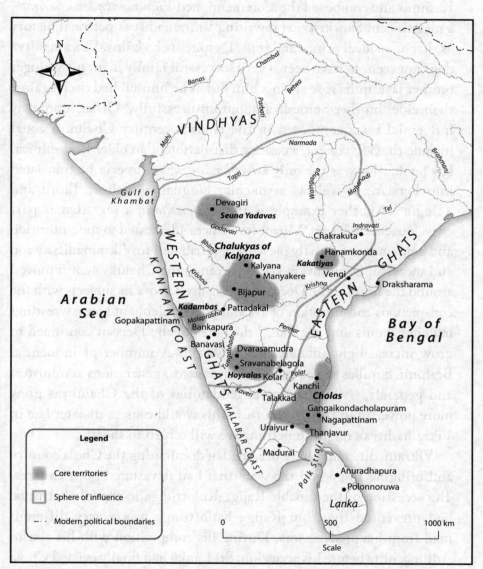

Southern India, late eleventh century CE.

mentioned before, Bilhana, a Brahmin who emigrated from distant
Kashmir and composed the aforementioned *Vikramankadevacharitam*,
a magnificent Sanskrit text rewriting Vikramaditya's personal history
as that of an ideal prince and son. (Despite such claims, Vikramaditya
does not seem to have been a very successful family man: his younger
brother Jayasimha rose against him just as he himself had risen against
their elder brother Someshvara, but unsucessfully.) Other supremely
influential texts composed in the twelfth-century Chalukya court
include the *Mitakshara*, a concise distillation of an older Brahminical
law book. This was the only *Dharmashastra* text to ever be translated
into Persian, as well as vernacular languages such as Tamil and
Telugu.[61] Another example is the *Manasollasa*, a text that is part
encyclopaedia and part 'Mirror for Princes' (dedicated to the cultivation
and enjoyment of courtly pleasures), attributed to Vikramaditya's son
and successor Someshvara III. But even as the Chalukya court moved
around the heart of the Deccan, setting itself above its subjects with the
conspicuous consumption of art and poetry, elephant races, wrestling
matches, hunts and the like,[62] the elites of the Deccan continued to
grow increasingly affluent and powerful. A number of influential
Brahmin families served the Chalukyas across generations as ministers
and generals,[63] while the royal feudatories of the Chalukyas grew
more powerful in their territories. This would cause a disaster late in
Vikramaditya's reign, something we will return to shortly.

Vikramaditya may have dreamed of dominating the Chola country
and bringing to an end the wars that had devastated both empires.
The accession of the capable Rajiga-Kulottunga to the Chola throne
had prevented that, but Rajiga-Kulottunga was a very different
man from his predecessors. During his competition with his cousin
Adhirajendra before his accession, Sri Lanka had finally evicted Chola
power, *c.* 1070–73,[64] and he made no serious attempt to reconquer it.
Instead, Rajiga-Kulottunga's former base, the old Pallava heartland,
was more deeply integrated into the Chola state. Vengi became a

Chola viceroyalty, a proving ground for his sons, and here he would go by the title of Vishnuvardhana[65] – that ancient name once borne by Pulakeshin II's hunchback brother Kubja-Vishnu-Vardhana, the first Chalukya king of Vengi. North of Vengi, near the lands of modern-day Odisha, Rajiga bound himself to local dynasties through marriage and shows of military might.[66] But the terrible Deccan and oceanic expeditions of previous Cholas were not repeated during his reign. Through considerable political pragmatism, personal charm and deep engagement with varied local power centres, Rajiga-Kulottunga successfully (and perhaps more realistically) recast the Chola empire as a 'purely Tamil power', as Professor K.A. Nilakanta Sastri puts it.[67]

Rajiga-Kulottunga and his great rival Vikramaditya VI might not have fought as relentlessly as their predecessors, but their personal enmity was never truly forgotten. As the Chola aged, the Chalukya emperor successfully conquered swathes of northern Vengi; he may have done more if not for the fact that an uprising by a coalition of his vassals – led by the increasingly powerful Hoysalas of southern Karnataka, in alliance with the Kadambas of Goa – shook his throne to its foundations.[68] These dynasties had, ironically, served Vikramaditya closely in his early career and in his rise to the throne. Indeed, Gangavadi, the core territory of the Hoysalas, was Vikramaditya's temporary base before he overthrew his brother Someshvara II. All this lays bare the ruthlessness of power-obsessed medieval aristocrats.

Though this uprising was savagely defeated and Gopakapattinam, the Kadamba capital, sacked, the Hoysalas remained unbroken. Their king, Hoysala Vishnuvardhana, would successfully drive the Cholas out of the former Ganga kingdom in southern Karnataka and seize the ancient Ganga capital of Talakkad for himself by 1118.[69] Indeed, Professor Nilakanta Sastri suggests that the Hoysalas raided parts of Tamilakam, broke open temples and seized images within.[70] Meanwhile, Vishnuvardhana embarked on an ambitious programme of temple building, agricultural expansion and political consolidation, repeating the pattern of medieval Indian kingship that we have seen the emperors of the Deccan deploy before in northern Karnataka. After Vikramaditya VI's death in 1126, Hoysala Vishnuvardhana would adopt imperial titles. He and his successors, as well as other former vassals of the Kalyana Chalukyas such as the Seuna Yadavas and Kakatiyas, would reduce both the Chalukyas and the Cholas to insignificance.

With Kalyana unable to enforce any sort of control over them, the Hoysalas set out to create an empire of their own, conquering parts of the upper Kaveri valley from the Cholas. Capitalizing on this, the Pandya dynasty, centred around Madurai, rose up and sacked Rajendra Chola's great capital of Gangai-Konda-Chola-Puram,[71] bringing Chola power to an end by the thirteenth century.[72]

⤳

This might seem like a repetition of the same endless pattern of dynastic rise and fall that we have seen so often through the course of five hundred years. But when we look at the symbolic texture and political geography of these events, we catch a glimpse of something grander. In the beginning of this book we saw how the Chalukyas of Vatapi had been cultivators or pastoralists. Out of nothing, out of a political vacuum, they built an empire in northern Karnataka. We take terms like 'king', 'empire', 'aristocrat', 'governor', 'vassal', 'monastery', 'temple', 'patronage' and so on for granted today. But the Chalukyas had applied these concepts to geographical and political spheres that had never seen these things. They had created the first Deccan empire, based in north Karnataka, by adapting to this region the Sanskritic imperial rituals and systems that had originated elsewhere, but now became the framework of a uniquely Deccan polity.

We saw this imperial system grow to a vast scale in the centuries that followed. It fused with the ancient agrarian centres of the Godavari

river basin in Maharashtra, and the flourishing trade ports of the
west coast, and reached an apogee under the Rashtrakutas. Courtly
Kannada then added further depth and reach to the Deccan imperial
system, as the Rashtrakutas began to use it as a courtly language of
power adopted by the warlike aristocrats of the Deccan. After the
Rashtrakuta collapse, we saw the Chalukyas of Kalyana lead the region
to a remarkable period of cultural confidence and military dominance,
using both Kannada and Sanskrit in a variety of inscriptions. The
Kalyana Chalukyas formulated new hierarchies of power as their
rulers moved across a vast geopolitical chessboard to fight off another
equally ambitious, powerful and transregional imperial Indian polity:
the Chola empire. All through this, the Deccan's connections to the
trading world of the Indian Ocean continued to expand and thrive.

And now we see the logical continuation of these patterns. Within
the broader context of the Indian subcontinent, the Chalukyas had
created a framework of imperial power that expanded in both breadth
and depth over centuries through the Deccan. They had created the
architecture of a Deccan empire, the vocabulary of political and
religious power, the backbone of agrarian control, the networks of
commercial production and interaction. And now, *within the context
of the Deccan*, the feudatories, rivals and sub-imperial dynasties of
the Chalukyas would re-adapt these frameworks of imperial power
to their own territories. What the Chalukyas had done in northern
Karnataka, their vassals would do in Telangana, southern Karnataka
and Maharashtra. These regions had ascended to royal status and begun
to participate in pan-Indian networks of knowledge and exchange as
feudatories of the Vallabhas; now, as their ruling dynasties challenged
the Vallabhas, they would become new imperial centres in the Deccan's
micro regions.

Urbanization, military expansion, temple building, artistic
and literary innovation in regional languages: the Chalukyas and
Rashtrakutas had established an exemplar of successful southern

Indian kingship and a repertoire of cultural and material paraphernalia to build and negotiate ties with a dizzying array of potential power centres. This template would be imitated by many of the dynasties we have seen in previous chapters to successfully consolidate their regions under new imperial formations. The Seuna Yadavas, who had assisted the Vallabha Taila in defeating the Paramara king Vakpati in 994, gradually transitioned from Kannada-speaking warlords to powerful patrons of Marathi and Sanskrit, ruling over much of Maharashtra by the thirteenth century, centred around the citadel of Devagiri. The Hoysalas, whom we have seen serve the Vallabha Someshvara I in campaigns in Malwa and fight alongside Prince Vikramaditya in Chakrakuta in Chhattisgarh, established a mighty kingdom in southern Karnataka, stretching at times deep into the Kaveri river valley. The Kakatiyas, who had fought alongside the forces of Someshvara I at Kanchi in 1047–48, created a powerful state in Telangana, using many of the concepts and methods of the Chalukya kings while establishing their independence in the late twelfth century. The Kakatiyas would also successfully expand into Vengi, devastated over the centuries by the depredations of Kannada- and Tamil-speaking polities, and thus create the first empire to rule all of the Telugu-speaking lands together. This initiated a vast movement of Telugu peasant-warriors from the fertile coast into the dry upland Deccan and through much of southern India in the centuries to come.

These three dynasties – the Kakatiyas, Seuna Yadavas and Hoysalas – would fight many savage wars with each other over the supreme overlordship of the Deccan. They would also compete architecturally, as previous Deccan dynasties had: the Kakatiya Ramappa temple at Palampet (one of India's newest UNESCO World Heritage Sites), the Hoysala Vijayanarayana/Chennakeshava temple at Belur, and the Seuna Yadava Gondeshvara temple at Sinnar were descended from the stellate and staggered-square architectural forms established by patrons and *sthapatis* in the eleventh-century Chalukya imperium.[73]

As these new regional dynamics emerged, Kalyana, the imperial centre which once dominated the Kannada, Marathi and Telugu lands, began to fade. The once-glittering Chalukya Vallabhas of Kalyana were overthrown by a Kalachuri dynast called Bijjala in the twelfth century, bringing to a rather unceremonious end the name that had awed the Deccan on and off for half a millennium.[74]

But beyond this political turmoil, the Chalukyas had already set in motion religious and political trends of extreme importance. The

Clockwise: The Kakatiya Ramappa temple at Palampet, the Hoysala Vijayanarayana/Chennakeshava temple at Belur, and the Seuna Yadava Gondeshvara temple at Sinnar. While each of these are totally distinct styles, their descent from Kalyana Chalukya architecture is evident in the projecting walls. While the Chennakeshava has lost its roof, it originally had one similar to the Gondeshvara; such curvilinear spires were used in the northern reaches of Chalukya territories as well as in Malwa.

Sarah Welch / Wikimedia Commons

Akshatha Inamdar / Wikimedia Commons

Sharvari SM / Wikimedia Commons

constant expansion of elite temples, the increasing concentration
of power and wealth among the upper-caste aristocracy, and the
relatively low status of women and of the bevy of other castes and
professions led to the emergence of a new bhakti movement in the late
twelfth century: the Virashaivism. These Heroic Shaivas, as the name
suggests, bravely defied the hierarchy of political and religious power
upon which the imperial structure of the Deccan depended. Singing
of the accessibility of Shiva to all in a vast hall in Kalyana called the
Anubhava Mandapa, they rejected caste and gender discrimination,
the authority of the Vedas, and even the idea that temples could lead
to an experience of Shiva. Their poetry also reveals a deep discontent
against the wealthy landed aristocrats who were so important to the
Chalukya court.

The Virashaivas' activities were actively encouraged by the
religious leader Basavanna, a Kalachuri minister,[75] and popularized by
hundreds of remarkable male and female poets, from assorted social
backgrounds, singing in Kannada. This group of people includes the
relatively well-known Akka Mahadevi, who according to legend was
married to a minor king; Allama Prabhu, who may have been a temple
musician; Basavanna, who was a Brahmin; cobblers such as Madara
Channayya, cowherds such as Siddharama, a sex worker by the name
of Sankavve, and a thread maker, Remmavve, among many others.[76]
Their activities, over just a few decades, shook the balance of power at
Kalyana to its foundations. According to the *Basava Purana*, composed
about a century after these events, this led to a violent response from
the lords of Kalyana that seems to have escalated into widespread
destruction, the assassination of Bijjala Kalachuri, the annihilation of
much of the great city of Kalyana, and the scattering of the Virashaivas
across the Deccan.[77] *Kettittu kalyana* – 'Kalyana is wrecked' – would
become a common phrase in Kannada literature and folk narratives
in the centuries after.[78] There is a strange romance in devotees of
Shiva – who, in the eighth century, had been crucial to renewing the

power of the Vatapi Chalukyas – bringing to an end the last remnant of Kalyana Chalukya power in the twelfth century. Today, a town at the site of Kalyana is known as Basavakalyan, after Basavanna, considered one of the most important saints of the Virashaiva and closely related Lingayat traditions. Kannada literature and poetry would be profoundly shaped by the poetry of the Virashaivas. Indeed, Professor H.S. Shivaprakash argues that in terms of literature, the Virashaiva movement and its successors were more influential than the courtly Kannada epics composed by powerful Deccan dynasties up to this point.[79]

Even grander changes were afoot in the rest of the world. The rest of the subcontinent had seen similar trends as the Deccan, with new polities forming in Madhya Pradesh, the northwest and the Gangetic plains, such as the Chandellas (known for their construction of the temples of Khajuraho) and the Chahamanas (more famously remembered as the Chauhans). From the tenth century onwards, these polities had to contend with waves of Central Asian nomads who began to expand into South Asia as well as West and East Asia. By the late twelfth century, one of these waves – led by Turkic warriors – had overrun a number of north Indian dynasties and founded the Sultanate of Delhi, just decades after the collapse of Kalyana in the Deccan. Partly in order to fund wars against other Central Asian peoples such as the Mongols, the armies of Delhi would lead the collective military might of much of northern India to raid the Deccan in the late thirteenth century. By the early fourteenth century, the Hoysalas, Seuna Yadavas and Kakatiyas had been uprooted by Delhi's armies, and the Sultanate established garrison towns across the Deccan.

Attempts to integrate the Deccan into a north India–centric imperial network failed spectacularly, however. From the remnants of the

Chalukya successor states, radically new south Indian polities, deeply integrated into the broader 'Persianate' world, emerged. North of the Krishna river, a powerful new kingdom, the Bahmani Sultanate based in Gulbarga in the fifteenth century, had given way to five Deccan Sultanates of varying size and power by the sixteenth century. South of the Tungabhadra, the mighty empire of Vijayanagara dominated southern Karnataka and the Tamil country that had defied so many Deccan emperors.

Vijayanagara and the Deccan Sultanates, especially the Sultanate of Bijapur (centred in a former Chalukya royal city), were among the most populous and vibrant polities of the sixteenth-century world. Both states substantially expanded the Deccan's integration into global networks of trade, a process the Vallabhas encouraged, as we have seen. But they would seek to attract not just goods but also people from the wider world, especially Persians and Turks, and even the Portuguese. The innovative nature of these polities is indicated in a letter written by Alfonso de Albuquerque, Portuguese viceroy of Goa – based, incidentally, in the city that was once Gopakapattinam, the capital of the Kadambas of Goa – to King Manuel I of Portugal. According to Albuquerque, Bijapuri gunsmiths from Goa were as skilled as those of Germany.[80] Vijayanagara, meanwhile, dedicated enormous resources to obtaining horses from across the Indian Ocean,[81] resurrecting the ancient geopolitical strategies of the Rashtrakuta kings.

Both Vijayanagara and Bijapur also competed to claim the imperial mantle of the Chalukyas of Kalyana. Elements from Chalukya temples south of the Krishna – with their lush soapstone decorations and 'lathe-turned' circular pillars – would be reused in temples and marketplaces in Vijayanagara. Indeed, these can be seen today in the sixteenth-century Bhuvaneshvari shrine in Hampi's Virupaksha temple,[82] and in one of the pillared hallways in the vast Vijayanagara period bazaar outside.[83] A Kalyana Chalukya tank was also relocated stone by stone to the royal compound of the city,[84] where it is still visible

A Kalyana Chalukya tank in the royal compound of Hampi, Karnataka.

The boar sigil of Vijayanagara, positioned in the colossal gateway of the Achutaraya or Tiruvengalanatha temple at Hampi. Vijayanagara's emblem, a boar with a dagger, sun and moon, is a direct descendant of the Chalukya boar crest we saw in Chapter 1.

today. The powerful sixteenth-century Vijayanagara ruler Rama Raya used the Chalukya boar banner and he would explicitly call himself Chalukya-Chakravarti and 'Lord of the Excellent City of Kalyana':[85] a major goal of his foreign policy seems to have been to capture the city of Kalyana from the rival Deccan Sultanates to add additional symbolic support to his status.

Bijapur, meanwhile, seamlessly integrated the grand halls, pillars and elegant architectural ornamentation of Chalukya temples north of the Krishna into their mosques, forts and palaces. Quite contrary to modern stereotypes of Muslim intolerance towards 'Hindus', the curiosity and respect that many rulers of Bijapur (such as Ali Adil Shah I in the late sixteenth century, and his successor Ibrahim Adil Shah II) had towards Deccani religions and cultural norms is well attested. Indeed, in the mid-sixteenth century, it was Bijapur that was expelling Persian speakers and encouraging the use of Kannada and Marathi, while Vijayanagara sought to attract Persian talent.[86]

Professors Richard Eaton and Philip Wagoner suggest that Bijapur's assimilation of Chalukya architecture should be seen as an attempt to directly associate Bijapuri kingship with the glory of the Chalukyas. Providing the example of the great hall of the Aravattukhambada temple in Bankapur[87] (incidentally the same Bankapur founded by Bankeya, the general of the long-forgotten ninth-century Vallabha Amoghavarsha), converted by Ali Adil Shah I into the Jami mosque, they compare it to the Ottoman empire's conversion of the Byzantine church of St Sophia to the Hagia Sophia mosque. 'In cases such as these,' they write, 'agents of change used their power not to vandalise or annihilate, but to preserve, and in this way connect themselves with a society and a culture whose architectural achievements they manifestly admired.'[88] An inscription of Someshvara II, placed by a Brahmin in service of the Bijapuri court by the name of Baid Panditji, decorates one of the gates of the city to this day,[89] as do inscriptions of Someshvara II and Vikramaditya VI at the main entrance to Bijapur, set up by Sultan Ibrahim I in the mid-sixteenth century. Ibrahim even created a dramatic colonnade at this entrance, recycling Chalukya pillars in the more geometric metropolitan Kalyana style from an abandoned Narasimha temple of the city. These signify an almost unheard-of position of prominence granted by a Persianate polity to its predecessors, an attempt as clear as Vijayanagara's to present itself as the legitimate successors of the Chalukyas.

Bijapur's sense of wonder at the inherited imperial sovereignty of the Deccan is illustrated by a text from the reign of Ali Adil Shah I, dating to the late sixteenth century. Bijapur was as removed in time from the Kalyana Chalukyas as we are from Bijapur, and its people were well aware of the fact that it was only the latest of many empires that ruled the region. The Bijapuri historian Rafi al'din Shirazi, for example, was thoroughly impressed by the enormous Krishneshvara monolith at Ellora, carved out during the reign of the Rashtrakutas in the eighth century. Reflecting the attitudes of the Persianate world, he described it as being a depiction of a king in his palace, rather than an idol of Shiva. But Shirazi's wonder at this extraordinary edifice shines through:

> The skill of each workshop [that worked on the temple] is cut into rock to such a degree that the human mind cannot imagine it ... One should spend several days at the palace if one wishes to see them all, and to understand them fully a long lifetime would be needed ... So many beautiful and well-wrought things are in those buildings and courtyards that, if one wished to explain them all, he would fail to reach the goal. The listener should prepare for fatigue of the brain![90]

For Shirazi and many other Muslims, whether Deccani or settled in the Deccan, the magnificent temples of the medieval period were to be admired for their beauty and protected as God's works.[91]

The resurgence of north Indian power under the Mughal empire in the late sixteenth century, and the arrival of armies led by Rajput generals and Mughal princes in the Deccan, signalled the final end of the direct legacy of the Vallabhas. The Deccan Sultanates, worn down by generations of warfare, were subsumed within the subcontinent-spanning Mughal empire. The emperor Aurangzeb Alamgir, generally thought of as a compulsive iconoclast, has left us a surprisingly humane testimony of his own visit to Ellora, describing the Kailashanatha monolith in a letter as 'one of the wonders of the true transcendent Artisan [God]'.[92] This fabulous temple, a remnant of an ancient Deccan sovereignty, was left untouched by this mighty north Indian gunpowder empire.

Though the Chalukyas and Rashtrakutas were gradually forgotten, the Deccan at large continued to remain one of the subcontinent's dominant geopolitical regions: the power of the Marathas and Mysore, for example, would prove to be one of the greatest challenges to conquerors, from the Mughals to the British. The Vallabhas' stories would lie dormant until nineteenth- and twentieth-century British efforts to translate and reconstruct images of an 'authentic' Hindu past before the advent of Muslim-led polities in the subcontinent. This reconstructed past would soon be appropriated into regional nationalist narratives while being generally neglected by postcolonial histories of the subcontinent, which were fixated on 'imperial moments' centred on the Gangetic plains and northern India. Indeed, despite its importance in shaping the subcontinent, the medieval Deccan was barely represented in the National Museum in New Delhi up to 2020, whereas the Guptas of fifth-century north India occupied an entire gallery. Today the Chalukyas and Rashtrakutas, and their successors and rivals, are remembered in modern southern Indian states, though their memory pales in comparison to the Marathas and Vijayanagara, and the dynamics they shaped are generally poorly understood.

Politically expedient reclamations are commonplace: twentieth-century Kannada cinema frequently depicted the Vatapi Chalukyas, who in reality pioneered the use of Sanskrit, as proud Kannada speakers. More recently, the region of Hyderabad–Karnataka has been renamed 'Kalyana-Karnataka', though modern Basavakalyan is a relatively minor town and Kalyana Chalukya temples are relatively neglected in the area. Meanwhile, Bijapur (officially renamed Vijayapura) has lost much of its Chalukya legacy to neglect, especially in comparison to Hampi/Vijayanagara. The temples of the Vatapi Chalukyas in Pattadakal are a UNESCO World Heritage Site, and those of the Hoysalas in southern Karnataka are major tourist attractions. The Kakatiyas are revered in Telangana state, serving as the namesake of a major irrigation project and the source of some material for Tollywood films, while Kakatiya architecture features on the state emblem. The Rashtrakutas, however, are barely remembered except for their Gangetic expeditions, while the Seuna Yadavas are almost totally forgotten outside of their entanglements with the armies of Delhi in the thirteenth and fourteenth centuries. In comparison, the Cholas have become one of the most important dynasties in modern Tamil nationalism, with their seafaring expeditions often presented as evidence of Indian 'colonization' of Southeast Asia, and they are the subject of vast quantities of historical fiction as well as a major upcoming film.[93]

Despite all these reclamations and rewritings, the Vallabhas' actual legacy continues in sometimes surprising and subtle ways. The impact they had on urbanism, caste, courtly languages and the religious landscape of southern India continues to shape the way we live today. Many of the sites mentioned in this book – not merely the great capitals, but even minor towns such as Bankapura, Lokkigundi and Sudi – have been continuously inhabited to the present day. The Lingayats, descended from a religious tradition tied to the history of the great city of Kalyana, are among the most politically influential groups in modern-day Karnataka. Jain monasteries which trace their ancestry to the Vallabhas or their vassals continue to thrive in coastal Karnataka. The site of Shravanabelagola – once patronized by the Gangas, allies of the Rashtrakuta Vallabhas – continues to be a major site of Jain pilgrimage not far from modern Bengaluru. The Devanagari script, which is used across India for Hindi and Sanskrit today, is descended from the same family of scripts as the Nagari script, used by the chancellery of the Kalyana Chalukyas from the eleventh to twelfth centuries.[94]

One final example of the Chalukyas' pervasive and surprising influence lies in the Hindu laws of inheritance used during the British Raj. These laws were based on a codification of the *Mitakshara* of Vijnaneshvara, composed during the reign of Vikramaditya VI, and were widely used through the Indian subcontinent (with the exception of Bengal) by British judges.[95] To the British, the conciseness of the text, its popularity with Brahmins across their domains, and its association with 'classical', upper-caste Indian kingship led to the assumption that it laid down the 'traditional' rules by which 'Hindu' society – in reality an inaccurate colonial label applied to a far more heterogeneous populace – should be governed. Thus the application of this single Sanskrit text – written by an elite twelfth-century Deccani Brahmin – to the vast, complex and diverse societies of the nineteenth and twentieth centuries had significant and often damaging effects on the vast majority of South Asians, who had probably never even heard of the *Mitakshara* and instead dealt with inheritance using their own laws and traditions. It was only in 1956, with the introduction of the Hindu Code Bills, that the *Mitakshara*'s reign over India's peoples finally came to an end.[96] But by then it had significantly influenced the application of inheritance law and distribution of property for many generations. Indeed, many of the readers of this book may have grandparents or great-grandparents whose lives were directly impacted by this text composed in the Vallabhas' glittering court nearly a thousand years ago.

This exemplifies the interconnected nature of the history of the subcontinent's peoples, despite all the polities and dynasties that came after, despite all the appropriation and erasures of the history of the Vallabhas. We might wish to forget the complex and sometimes uncomfortable ways in which every region of South Asia has shaped the present we live in today, but the legacies of history are not easily erased.

The story of the Vallabhas who ruled the Deccan, the story of the men who called themselves Fortune's Favourite and Earth's Beloved, is one of constant savagery, brilliant ambition, and horrific loss and injustice. This book has tried to tell it in a way that reveals something of the complicated individuals they were, and allows a glimpse of the teeming, forgotten peoples – our distant ancestors – whom they ruled over. But all this is only one story, one narrative, one region, one period, one group of elite families. The immensity of medieval south India still looms over us, demanding that we continue to tell its stories, and learn from its horrors and glories.

Notes

Introduction

1. Abu Zayd al-Sirafi, *Two Arabic Travel Books: Accounts of India and China*, ed. and trans. Tim Mackintosh-Smith (New York University Press, 2014), 39.
2. Jayashri Mishra, *Social and Economic Conditions Under the Imperial Rashtrakutas* (Commonwealth Publishers, 1992), 190–91. The original text has been edited to improve flow.
3. The origins of the name 'Chalukya' are hotly debated; this is one version presented by Professor Durga Prasad Dikshit. See Durga Prasad Dikshit, *Political History of the Chalukyas of Badami* (Abhinav Publications, 1980), 23–24.

1. Harsha's Laughter

1. The date of the battle between the Chalukya ruler Pulakeshin II and his rival Harsha has relatively recently been conclusively narrowed down to this window. See S.S. Bahulkar and Shilpa Sumant, 'The Bijapur-Mumbai Copperplate Grant of Cālukya Ruler Pulakeśin II, Dated April 04, 619 CE, Mentioning His Triumph over Emperor Harṣavardhana,' *Annals of the Bhandarkar Oriental Research Institute* XCIII (2012): 205–09.
2. This is assuming that Professor Durga Prasad Dikshit is correct in inferring Pulakeshin II was five years old in 597, which would have

made him about twenty-five in 618. See Durga Prasad Dikshit, *Political History of the Chalukyas of Badami* (Abhinav Publications, 1980), 54. However, this is based mostly on his assumption of an 'appropriate' age for Pulakeshin to overthrow his uncle Mangalesha. Meanwhile, Harsha was (according to his court poet Banabhatta) just fifteen when he became the king of Kannauj in 606, which would have made him twenty-seven in 618. This is, again, doubtful, because it would have made Harsha's sister, the widow of the king of Kannauj and one of the main drivers behind his accession to that throne in the *Harshacharita*, just twelve years old at the time. We cannot be absolutely certain of their ages.

3. This book follows Bakker's depiction of this conflict as arising from the two clashing over the control of Gujarat. See Hans Bakker, *The World of the Skandapurāṇa: Northern India in the Sixth and Seventh Centuries*, Groningen Oriental Studies, Supplement, Vol. 4 (Brill, 2014).

4. Alternative translations include 'Lion Maned', this is the translation used by Professor Dikshit. See Dikshit 1980, 33.

5. Prithwis Chandra Chakravarti, *The Art of War in Ancient India* (University of Dacca, 1941), 99–102.

6. Daud Ali, *Courtly Culture and Political Life in Early Medieval India* (Cambridge University Press, 2006), 38–43.

7. Vasudeva S. Agrawala, *The Deeds of Harsha: Being a Cultural Study of Bana's Harshacharita* (Prithivi Prakashan, 1969), 62–63.

8. Chakravarti 1941, 97.

9. Ali 2006, 54. Citing *Epigraphia Indica* VI, 6. Hereafter *EI*.

10. Agrawala 1969, 88. To what extent can the *Harshacharita* be used as a source for the life that Pulakeshin II may have lived? It is probably a useful source, with some caveats. Harsha and Pulakeshin were almost exact contemporaries, and at the time of their birth neither seemed destined for imperial sovereignty. However, both were part of families that were 'royal' and thus likely steeped in the same cultural milieu (Ali 2006) of the Sanskrit cosmopolis. See Sheldon Pollock, *The Language of the Gods in the World of Men: Sanskrit, Culture and Power in Premodern India* (University of California Press, 2006). For Pulakeshin's family this culture would have been only recently adopted.

References to horoscopes being cast, announcements being made, recitals of song and dance, vassals visiting and so on are present in the *Harshacharita*. These are also tropes associated with a royal birth in most Sanskrit courtly literature of the period – which means that the royals of the Deccan were likely well aware of the 'proper' rituals attending the birth of a crown prince. This assumption is further bolstered by the Chalukyas' performance of many major Vedic and Puranic royal sacrifices – aligning themselves with a prestigious foreign culture – for at least two generations by the time of Pulakeshin II and Harsha. As such, allowing for Banabhatta's somewhat hyperbolic writing style and regional differences in practice, the events presented here may serve as a broad-strokes reconstruction of Pulakeshin's early life. Of course, there must have been considerable variation in the details and order of elements between what actually happened and what is presented here, but these speculations are useful and instructive in suggesting the possible outlines of the events of the time.

11. For a detailed study, see Carol Radcliffe Bolon, *Forms of the Goddess Lajja Gauri in Indian Art* (Pennsylvania State University Press, 1992).
12. Agrawala 1969, 88.
13. Ibid., 99.
14. Ronald B. Inden, *Imagining India* (Indiana University Press, 2000), 240.
15. Ibid.
16. The depiction of medieval Indian states as 'imperial formations' which used rituals as a socio-political 'world-ordering mechanism' within more amorphous polities is based on Ronald Inden's work. See Inden 2000, Chapter 6.
17. Agrawala 1969, 88–89.
18. Ali 2006, 36.
19. Ibid., 51–52.
20. Ibid.
21. Ibid., 51.
22. Though the Satavahanas of the first century CE were a powerful polity, they do not seem to have retained a predominant position in South Asian geopolitics for more than a few decades during the reign of Gautamiputra Satakarni, probably *c.* 60–85 CE.

23. Dikshit 1980, 23–24. The clan will hereafter be referred to as the Chalkes, but it is worth noting that there may be many other possible origins for their future dynastic title.

24. Narendra Nath Bhattacharyya, *Ancient Indian Rituals and Their Social Contents* (Manohar, 1975), 1.

25. Ibid., 1–2.

26. Ibid., 2.

27. Ariel Glucklich, *The Strides of Vishnu: Hindu Culture in Historical Perspective* (Oxford University Press, 2008), 111–12.

28. Ibid., 4.

29. Ibid., 3.

30. Ibid., 112.

31. Bhattacharyya 1975, 5–6.

32. Kapila Vatsyayan, *The Square and the Circle of the Indian Arts*, Second Edition (Abhinav, 1997), 24–27.

33. Ibid.

34. Ibid., 27.

35. Ibid., 27–28. They also represented the primal Cosmic Man, thus establishing a correspondence between the microcosm and macrocosm in order to ritually manipulate both.

36. Bhattacharyya 1975, 4.

37. Glucklich 2008, 112–13. Modern Hindu organizations such as the Arya Samaj argue that no animal was actually sacrificed and that the entire ritual is entirely symbolic – but archaeological excavations at ancient sites such as Kaushambi have discovered hundreds of bones of various sacrificed animals. Even if they were not sacrificed for the Ashvamedha itself, the idea that ancient rituals did not involve bloodshed is clearly not borne out by the evidence. As for whether historical performances of the Ashvamedha were indeed performed exactly as described, the evidence does not permit us to make a definitive statement. It should also be noted that other Indian philosophical traditions, such as the empiricist Carvakas, roundly criticized the Ashvamedha and described its creators as 'buffoons'. See Bhattacharyya 1975, 2, footnote 9.

38. Glucklich 2008, 112–13.

39. Ibid., 113.

40. Stephanie W. Jamison, 'Roles for Women in Vedic Srauta Ritual', in *Goddesses and Women in the Indic Religious Tradition*, ed. Arvind Sharma, Brill's Indological Library, Vol. 24 (Brill, 2005), 1–17, 9.

41. Bhattacharyya 1975, 18–22.

42. Glucklich 2008, 113.

43. Bhattacharyya 1975, 5.

44. Glucklich 2008, 113.

45. Vatsyayan 1997, 30.

46. Glucklich 2008, 114.

47. Bhattacharyya 1975, 1.

48. Dikshit 1980, 33.

49. Ibid., 34.

50. Ibid.

51. See John Michael McKnight, 'The Gupta Temple Movement: A Study of the Political Aspects of the Early Hindu Temple', PhD dissertation (McMaster University, 1973).

52. Susan Locher Buchanan, 'Cāḷukya Temples: History and Iconography', PhD dissertation (Ohio State University, 1985).

53. Ibid., 37.

54. Buchanan 1985.

55. Ibid., 22.

56. Ibid., 13.

57. Ronald Inden, 'Hierarchies of Kings in Early Medieval India', *Contributions to Indian Sociology* 15, nos. 1–2 (1981): 99–125, 102, https://doi.org/10.1177/006996678101500108.

58. Buchanan 1985, 13.

59. Ibid.

60. Ali 2006, 49.

61. Malini Adiga, *The Making of Southern Karnataka: Society, Polity and Culture in Early Medieval Period, AD 400–1030* (Orient BlackSwan, 2006), 107.

62. To Pulakeshin as to many later Indians such as the Rajputs and Marathas, ritually attaining high-caste status and militarily establishing their sovereignty went hand in hand, and to conflate the two made great sense in their political circumstances.

63. Adiga 2006, 36.

64. It's almost certain that growing up in the area, Pulakeshin II would have seen dolmens; they were everywhere, and in some cases still modified and used well into the eighth century CE. See Srikumar M. Menon, 'The Curious Case of the Galaganatha Dolmen: Possible Links between Megalithic Monuments and Early Temples at Aihole', *Heritage: Journal of Multidisciplinary Studies in Archaeology* 2 (2014): 54–73.

65. Dilip K. Chakrabarti, *The Geopolitical Orbits of Ancient India: The Geographical Frames of the Ancient Indian Dynasties* (Oxford University Press, 2011), Kindle Edition, Location 1188.

66. Chakrabarti 2011, Location 1633.

67. Ali 2006, 53.

68. Gary Michael Tartakov, 'The Beginning of Dravidian Temple Architecture in Stone', *Artibus Asiae* 42, no. 1 (1980): 39–99.

69. Dikshit 1980, 42.

70. Ibid., 54. It is doubtful that Ereya could have been that young. Assuming his father was alive when the Chalukya capital was moved to Vatapi, he must have been at least fifty-six years old in 597 (especially given that Dikshit depicts him as one of Pulakeshin I's commanders), which seems a rather elderly age to have an oldest child aged five. This is especially so given how prolific and frequent Indian royal marriages were. Professor Dikshit is probably off by a decade or so.

71. Cathleen Ann Cummings, 'A Study of the Iconographic Program of the Lokesvara (Virupaksa) Temple, Pattadakal', PhD dissertation (Ohio State University, 2006), 203.

72. Dikshit 1980, 40.

73. Ibid., 41.

74. Hsüan-tsang, *Buddhist Records of the Western World*, Vol. II, trans. Samuel Beal (London, 1884), 256.

75. Inden 1981, 103.

76. *Manusmriti* 7.96, quoted and translated in Richard H. Davis, 'Indian Art Objects as Loot', *The Journal of Asian Studies* 52, no. 1 (1993): 22–48, 27.

77. This is implied by her triumphant declaration in 601 CE that she

had spent the entire fortune of her birth family, the Kalachuris, in a victory procession to honour her marital family's gods including Shiva Makuteshvara. See R.N. Nandi, *Religious Institutions and Cults in the Deccan (c. A.D. 600–A.D. 1100)* (Motilal Banarsidas, 1973), 12.

78. Dikshit 1980, 56.
79. Ibid., 57.
80. For a similar example, see David Smith, 'One Man and Many Women: Some Notes on the Harem in Mainly Ancient and Medieval India from Sundry Perspectives', *Cracow Indological Studies* 14 (2012): 1–16, 8.
81. Dikshit 1980, 60.
82. Cummings 2006, 203.
83. This trope is ever-present in Indian courtly literature and even in political manuals. See Ali 2006, 53–54.
84. This, at least, is the version that Ereya presents. See *EI* VI, 9.
85. Ibid.
86. *EI* VI, 9. The terms used in the inscription are apparently taken from the *Arthashastra* or a similar manual. 'Power of good counsel' (*mantrashakti*) refers to ministers and councillors, and 'power of energy' (*utsahashakti*) to a rallied population and army.
87. K.V. Ramesh, 'Pulakesin II – His Career and Personality', in *The Chalukyas of Badami: Seminar Papers*, ed. Nagaraja Rao M.S. (The Mythic Society, 1978), 53–65, 56.
88. Chakrabarti 2011, Location 1734.
89. Ibid., Location 1633.
90. Dikshit 1980, 76.
91. The Roman emperors Trajan and Hadrian both used bridges made of boats, as depicted in their victory columns in Rome.
92. Dikshit 1980, 58.
93. Ramesh 1978, 55–56.
94. Dikshit 1980. 73. Professor Dikshit's identification of the two as Rashtrakutas is quite tenuous.
95. *EI* VI, 9.
96. *EI VI, 9*. Though *hamsa* is translated as 'swan', this follows Vogel's argument that the term actually refers to the bar-headed goose, as

swans are not native to the subcontinent. See Jean Phillippe Vogel, *The Goose in Indian Literature and Art* (E.J. Brill, 1962).

97. Ibid., 10.

98. Dikshit 1980, 76.

99. Ghulam Yazdani, *The Early History of the Deccan*, Vol. I (Oxford University Press, 1960), 213. Hereafter *EHD* I.

100. Ramesh 1978, 56.

101. Pius Malekandathil, *Maritime India* (Primus Books, 2010), 4.

102. Ranabir Chakravarti, 'Merchants, Merchandise and Merchantmen in the Western Seaboard of India: A Maritime Profile (500 BCE–1500 CE)', in *The Trading World of the Indian Ocean, 1500–1800*, ed. Om Prakash (Pearson, 2012), 53–116.

103. *EI* VI, 10.

104. While Professor Dikshit thinks this was accomplished by the 'Chalukyan navy' (Dikshit 1980, 77), there is little evidence that any imperial formation based in the interior of the Deccan systematically invested in a state navy until the early modern period.

105. Ibid.

106. Dikshit 1980, 96.

107. For a detailed study, see Kathleen D. Morrison, 'Trade, Urbanism, and Agricultural Expansion: Buddhist Monastic Institutions and the State in the Early Historic Western Deccan', *World Archaeology* 27, no. 2 (1995): 203–21.

108. Carla M. Sinopoli, 'On the Edge of Empire: Form and Substance in the Satavahana Dynasty', in *Empires: Perspectives from Archaeology and History*, eds. Susan E. Alcock et al. (Cambridge University Press, 2001), 155–78.

109. Mirashi 1955, lx.

110. Buchanan 1985, 122.

111. Ibid., 442. Cited in Cummings 2006, 211.

112. Buchanan 1985, 123.

113. Hsüan-tsang 1884 (Vol. II), 256.

114. Ronald M. Davidson, *Indian Esoteric Buddhism: A Social History of the Tantric Movement* (Columbia University Press, 2002), 39.

115. For a reconstruction of the events leading up to Harsha's accession, see Hans Bakker, *The World of the Skandapurāṇa* (Brill, 2014).

116. Bakker 2014, 70–71.

117. See Shankar Goyal, 'Acquisition of the Maukhari Empire by Harsha', *Proceedings of the Indian History Congress* 62 (2001): 1090–91, http://www.jstor.org/stable/44155859. Shankar argues, accurately, that Harsha had no actual claim to the throne of Kannauj either through his sister or in his own right, and that even if he managed to win the sympathies of the city's elite – perhaps through his Buddhist connections – he may have had to conquer the rest of the Maukhari kingdom by force.

118. Hsüan-tsang 1884, 213.

119. Bakker 2014, 108.

120. Dikshit 1980, 78.

121. Bahulkar and Sumant 2017.

122. Banabhatta quoted in Chakravarti 1941, 99. Of course, this was a description of a generic day's march for Harsha's moving court, not a military campaign, so the number of leagues and the composition of the force tasked with punishing Pulakeshin may have been different from what is presented here.

123. Ibid.

124. Ibid., 100.

125. Ibid.

126. Ibid., 101.

127. Daud Ali, 'Aristocratic Body Techniques in Early Medieval India', in *Rethinking a Millennium: Perspectives on Indian History from the Eighth to the Eighteenth Century: Essays for Harbans Mukhia*, ed. Rajat Datta (Aakar, 2008), 69–93.

128. A. Aruna, *State Formation in the Eastern Deccan, 7th Century A.D.– 13th Century A.D.* (Bharatiya Kala Prakashan, 2000), 101.

129. Pradeep P. Barua, *The State at War in South Asia* (University of Nebraska Press, 2005), 7.

130. Ibid., 12.

131. Chakravarti 1941, 52.

132. Konstantin Nossov and Peter Dennis, *War Elephants* (Osprey Publishing, 2008), 18.

133. Ibid., 19.

134. Prashant Srivastava, 'The Harsha-Pulakesin II War', in *Select Battles in Indian History*, Vol. I, eds. K.K. Thapyal and S.N. Mishra (Agama Kala Prakashan, 2002), 126–30.

135. Hsüan-tsang 1884 (Vol. II), 257.

136. Agrawala 1969, 24.

137. Ibid., 50.

138. Pulakeshin himself was unable to do anything further with this victory. Perhaps he realized he would be unable to confront Harsha in a pitched battle on north Indian terrain. In any case, his future campaigns were in the south. So the battle was apparently not as decisive as it is often thought to be, but the outcome was probably very unexpected.

139. Bahulkar and Samant 2017.

2. Pulakeshin's Blood

1. Bakker 2014, 112.

2. Karen C. Lang, 'Candrakirti on the Medieval Military Culture of South India', in *Buddhism in the Krishna River Valley of Andhra*, eds. Sree Padma Holt and A.W. Barber (SUNY Press, 2008), 130. The Vishnukundins of Vengi had to face multiple incursions from the Pallavas of Kanchi at roughly the same time that the Chalukyas under Pulakeshin I first began to establish their kingdom.

3. Dikshit 1980, 92.

4. Ibid., 91.

5. Buchanan 1985, 100.

6. Dikshit 1980, 92.

7. The ensuing discussion, it should be noted, is by necessity a simplistic explanation of a much more complex process of religious change. The rise of Puranic Hinduism and the fading away of south Indian Buddhism is still a matter of considerable scholarly debate.

8. Himanshu Prabha Ray, 'Creating Religious Identity: Archaeology of Early Temples in the Malaprabha Valley', in *Archaeology and Text: The Temple in South Asia*, ed. Himanshu Prabha Ray (Oxford University Press, 2010), 15–37.

9.   See John Michael McKnight, 'The Gupta Temple Movement: A Study
      of the Political Aspects of the Early Hindu Temple', PhD dissertation
      (McMaster University, 1973); Michael D. Willis, *The Archaeology of
      Hindu Ritual: Temples and the Establishment of the Gods* (Cambridge
      University Press, 2009); Nicholas B. Dirks, 'Political Authority and
      Structural Change in Early South Indian History', *Indian Economic
      and Social History Review* 13, no. 2 (1976): 125–57, https://doi.
      org/10.1177/001946468101300201.
10.   Buchanan 1985, 26–27.
11.   Ibid., 22.
12.   Ibid., 22.
13.   Buchanan 1985, 32.
14.   See Part 2, 'Kalyana and the Chalukya Legacy', in Richard M. Eaton
      and Phillip B. Wagoner, *Power, Memory, Architecture: Contested Sites
      on India's Deccan Plateau, 1300–1600* (Oxford University Press, 2014),
      77–161.
15.   Buchanan 1985, 109.
16.   *EHD* I, 205.
17.   Dikshit 1980, 22.
18.   Ibid.
19.   Ibid.
20.   See Vidya Dehejia, *The Body Adorned: Sacred and Profane in Indian Art*
      (Columbia University Press, 2009), specifically Chapter 1.
21.   *EHD* I, 216.
22.   Ibid.
23.   *EHD* II, 472.
24.   Aruna 2000, 101.
25.   Ibid., 102.
26.   Ibid.
27.   *EHD* II, 472.
28.   Lang 2008, 135.
29.   Ibid.
30.   Ibid., 140–42.
31.   Ibid., 138.
32.   Ibid., 128.

33. Karen Pechilis Prentiss, *The Embodiment of Bhakti* (Oxford University Press, 1999), 69.

34. Ibid., 71.

35. Vidya Dehejia, *Slaves of the Lord: The Path of the Tamil Saints* (Munshiram Manoharlal, 2002), 33.

36. Ibid., 56.

37. Prentiss 1999, 62–63.

38. Ibid., 72.

39. Dandin, *Tales of the Ten Princes*, trans. A.N.D. Haksar (Penguin India, 2007), Kindle Edition, Location 1156.

40. Dehejia 2002, 37.

41. Marilyn Hirsh, 'Mahendravarman I Pallava: Artist and Patron of Māmallapuram', *Artibus Asiae* 48, no. 1 (1987): 109–30.

42. Chakrabarti 2011, Location 1669.

43. Mahendravikramavarman, '*Matta-Vilāsa*: A Farce', trans. L.D. Barnett, *Bulletin of the School of Oriental and African Studies* 5, no. 4 (1930): 697–717.

44. Hirsch 1987, 118.

45. Wendy Doniger, *The Hindus: An Alternative History* (Penguin, 2009), 363.

46. Lang 2008, 143.

47. Dikshit 1980, 94.

48. Ibid.

49. *EHD* I, 216.

50. The ensuing description is based on Chalukya inscriptions and information from medieval courtly sources, as studied in Ali 2006.

51. The *Arthashastra* recommends that when the enemy possesses a strategic advantage, *samsraya* or submission is the best policy.

52. Chakrabarti 2011, Location 1672.

53. Dikshit 1980, 95.

54. Chakrabarti 2011, Location 1659.

55. N. Venkataramanayya, *The Eastern Cālukyas of Vēngi* (Vedam Venkataraya Sastry & Bros, 1950), 17.

56. Dikshit 1980, 77.

57. Ibid., 94.

58. *EHD* I, 217.
59. *South Indian Inscriptions*, Vol. I, 152. Hereafter *SII*. It should be noted that the Pallavas might have been conjuring great victories out of indecisive clashes to bolster their military reputation.
60. Dikshit 1980, 95.
61. *EHD* I, 217.
62. Ibid., 219.
63. *SII* II, no. 98: Velurpalaiyam Plates of Vijaya-Nandivarman (III).
64. Buchanan (1985) argues it is more likely that the Pallavas invaded just after Pulakeshin's death, while other authors have presented his death more dramatically.

3. Vikramaditya's Revenge

1. Malini Adiga, 'Of Concubines and Devadasis: Prostitution in Early Medieval Kartataka', *Proceedings of the Indian History Congress* 73 (2012).
2. R.H. Kulkarni, 'Vatapi Ganapati, an art historical revisit', *New Indian Express*, 22 August 2020, https://www.newindianexpress.com/opinions/2020/aug/22/vatapi-ganapati-an-art-historical-revisit-2186817.html
3. The man responsible for this, the Pallava general Paranjothi, supposedly went on to become a Shaiva saint. It should be noted that there is no contemporary evidence supporting this oral legend and it may date to the twelfth century, when the canon of Shaiva saints was being developed. However, it was not unheard of for kings to seize and relocate idols that were politically important to their rivals. See Davis 1993.
4. *EHD* I, 219.
5. *SII* XI Part I, 1.
6. Ibid., As noted in Chapter 1, Vallabharaja was an abbreviation of the title Sri Prithivi-Vallabha-Maharajadhiraja, the full Chalukya imperial title. The fact that their inveterate enemies, the Pallavas, used it to refer to them is a sign of just how widely the title was identified with the Chalukyas.

7. Ali 2006, 55.
8. *EHD* I, 219.
9. Dikshit 1980, 116.
10. Ibid.
11. Adiga 2012.
12. Kumkum Roy, *The Power of Gender and the Gender of Power: Explorations in Early Indian History* (Oxford University Press, 2010), 212.
13. Ali 2006, 51.
14. This book hereafter uses these terms interchangeably; the term 'harem' has Orientalist connotations today and tends to strip these women of their agency.
15. *Arthashastra* 5.3.3, 5.3.7, in Patrick Olivelle, *King, Governance, and Law in Ancient India: Kautilya's Arthaśāstra* (Oxford University Press, 2013), 261.
16. Ali 2006, 52.
17. Ibid., 54.
18. Malini Adiga, 'Dharmasastras, the Dravidian Kinship System and Female Inheritance in Karnataka in the Early Medieval Period (400 A.D. to 1300 A.D.)', *Proceedings of the Indian History Congress* 64 (2003).
19. Dikshit 1980, 121.
20. This is based on the assumption that the 'Ganga-Mahadevi' who requested Vikramaditya's land grant at Gadval in 674 was indeed his 'favourite queen', as portrayed in G.R. Rangaswamaiah, 'Bhuvikrama's Role in the Chalukya–Pallava Conflict (635–679)', *Proceedings of the Indian History Congress* 35 (1974), http://www.jstor.org/stable/44138760.
21. Dikshit 1980, 123.
22. See Ranabir Chakravarti, 'The Pull Towards the Coast: Politics and Polity in India (*c.* 600–1300 CE)', *Presidential Address (Monograph), Indian History Congress, 72nd Session* (2011); Dilip K. Chakrabarti, *The Geopolitical Orbits of Ancient India: The Geographical Frames of the Ancient Indian Dynasties* (Oxford University Press, 2010).
23. Dikshit 1980, 122.
24. Older Chalukya inscriptions also appear in Sanskrit, but it was

Vikramaditya who established a standard *prashasti* format and added the classic '*jayatyāviṣkṛtaṁ viṣṇorvarāhaṁ*' verse to the beginning.

25. Pollock 2006, 145–46.
26. Pollock 2006, 152.
27. Ibid.
28. *EI* XXXII, 175–84.
29. Ibid.
30. Alexis Sanderson, 'The Śaiva Age', in *Genesis and Development of Early Tantrism*, ed. Shingo Einoo (University of Tokyo, 2009), 266.
31. Nandi 1973, 85.
32. Flood 2004, 124.
33. Ibid.
34. Thomas J. Hopkins, *The Hindu Religious Tradition* (Wadsworth Publishing Company, 1971), 98. Cited in Cummings 2006.
35. David Chandler, *A History of Cambodia* (Taylor and Francis, 2018), Kindle Edition. It would seem that it was easier for Pashupatas to use maritime trade networks to reach Cambodia than it was to brave the warlike peoples of the Deccan to reach the Malaprabha river valley – at least until the rise of the Chalukyas made the region much more amenable to Shaiva monastic power.
36. George M. Moraes, *The Kadamba Kula* (B.X. Furtado & Sons, 1931), 250.
37. Nandi 1973, 83.
38. Ibid., 107.
39. Sanderson 2009, 267.
40. Nandi 1973, 104.
41. Sanderson 2009, 256. This is the Pashupata version of the consecration ritual. We cannot be sure this is what Vikramaditya's consecration looked like but it is likely to have been so, considering that the Pashupatas were already quite influential in northern Deccan.
42. Ibid., note 595.
43. Ibid.
44. Ibid.
45. These details may be inferred from Deccan hero stones from the period.
46. Sanderson 2009, 257.

47. Representations of this silk cap, which somewhat resembles a fez without a tassel, can be seen in sculptures of Pallava kings at Mahabalipuram.

48. Michael D. Rabe, 'The Māmallapuram Praśasti: A Panegyric in Figures', *Artibus Asiae* 57, no. 3 (1997): 189. This book follows Doniger (2009) in her conclusion that Rabe's analysis is the most likely explanation for the structure of the work.

49. Ibid., 200.

50. This story is recounted in the Vana Parva of the Mahabharata.

51. A reference to Agastya's two fathers and his slaying of Vatapi can be found in the Sabha and Vana Parvas of the Mahabharata.

52. Rabe 1997.

53. Ibid.

54. Ibid.

55. Dikshit 1980, 124.

56. *EI* X, 105.

57. This is heavily indicated by the appearance of Vikramaditya's horse Chitrakantha in his *prashastis*. The horse is most likely meant to be a sign of wealth, status and martial valour, but it could only have been militarily useful if accompanied by other horses in a cavalry unit.

58. *EHD* I, 222.

59. Romila Thapar, *The Penguin History of Early India: From the Origins to AD 1300* (Penguin UK, 2015), 331.

60. K.A. Nilakanta Sastri, *A History of South India from Prehistoric Times to the Fall of Vijayanagar* (Oxford University Press, 1997), 138. The Gangas would claim quite a record of killing Pallava kings in battle.

61. He was already in Tamilakam by 671, but by 674 he had apparently gained a decisive edge over the Pallavas.

62. Dikshit 1980, 124.

63. Sanderson 2009, 258. The purpose of these multiple consecrations was to repeatedly invest the kings with sacred authority to complement their martial authority, establishing their position at the top of the social hierarchy.

64. Dikshit 1980, 124. Emphasis added.

65. Rabe 1997, 230.

66. Ibid.
67. Ibid.
68. *EHD* I, 222.
69. Ibid., 224.
70. Dikshit 1980, 132.
71. *SII* I, 154.
72. The young Pallava king would claim a tremendous victory (ibid.), and later sources would claim that he had sacked Vatapi, which Sastri (1997) and Thapar (2015) both take at face value. This is debatable given that the Chalukyas make no mention of such a dramatic event. After all, the second sacking of Vatapi within a century would certainly have been worthy of note and have left some material traces. At best, the Pallavas may have succeeded in raiding Chalukya territory before being repelled by Vinayaditya and Vijayaditya.

4. Great Goddess

1. Dikshit 1980, 133.
2. Ibid., 148.
3. On Vinayaditya's visits to river fords, see Subhashini Kaligotla, 'Shiva's Waterfront Temples: Reimagining the Sacred Architecture of India's Deccan Region', PhD dissertation (Columbia University, 2015), https://academiccommons.columbia.edu/doi/10.7916/D83N2B1V/download, 230.
4. Ibid., 231–32.
5. Hemanth Kadambi, 'Sacred Landscapes in Early Medieval South India: The Chalukya State and Society (ca. AD 550–750)', PhD dissertation (University of Michigan, 2011), 230.
6. Dikshit 1980, 148.
7. The princesses were likely still children; the younger of them would give birth to Vikramaditya's son and heir only around 720 CE. They may have had many daughters up to that point, whose names have not survived.
8. Davis 1993, 37.
9. Dikshit 1980, 153.

10. Ibid., 152.
11. The Satavahana king Gautamiputra Satakarni is believed to have done something similar to seize relics of the Buddha, but this is difficult to verify as the only sources claiming this were commissioned by his immediate relatives.
12. Davis 1993, 40.
13. Ibid., 40–41.
14. Inden 2000, 258.
15. Ibid.
16. Kadambi 2011, 88.
17. Himanshu Prabha Ray, 'Creating Religious Identity: Archaeology of Early Temples in the Malaprabha Valley', in *Archaeology and Text: The Temple in South Asia*, ed. Himanshu Prabha Ray (Oxford University Press, 2010), 15–37.
18. Ibid.
19. R. Champakalakshmi, *Trade, Ideology and Urbanisation: South India, 300 BC to AD 1300* (Oxford University Press, 1996), 313.
20. Ibid., 520.
21. Meera Abraham, *Two Medieval Merchant Guilds of South India* (Manohar, 1988), 47.
22. Ibid., 74.
23. Kadambi 2011, 155.
24. Srinivas V. Padigar, 'Craftsmen's Inscriptions from Badami: Their Significance', in *Ellora Caves: Sculpture and Architecture*, eds. Ratan Parimoo, Deepak Kannal and Shivaji Pannikar (Aprant, 2018), Revised Edition, 313.
25. Ibid., 316.
26. Kaligotla 2015, 184–85.
27. Ibid., 183.
28. *Indian Antiquary*, Vol. X, 103. Hereafter *IA*.
29. Buchanan 1985, 344.
30. Ibid.
31. Kaligotla 2015, 174.
32. Ali 2006, 35.
33. Dikshit 1980, 220–21.

34. Ibid., 221.
35. Nandi 1973, 16–17.
36. Ibid., 213.
37. Ibid., 212.
38. Ali 2006, 52.
39. Ibid.
40. Ibid.
41. Ali 2006, 54.
42. Early Chalukya texts make it fairly clear that they were familiar with the vocabulary of texts finalized in the early centuries CE and associated with the 'mortal goals' of *artha* and *dharma*, such as the *Arthashastra* and *Manavadharmashastra*, thus making it highly likely that they were also aware of the *Kamasutra*, dedicated to the goal of *kama* and dating from slightly later than these two. In his seminal work on court culture, Daud Ali (2006) uses it alongside a later Chalukya text, the *Manasollasa*, to develop an understanding of the attitudes of the courtly world.
43. Vatsyayana, *Kama Sutra: A Guide to the Art of Pleasure*, trans. A.N.D. Haksar (Penguin, 2011), 57.
44. Ibid., 58.
45. Ali 2006, 54.
46. Vatsyayana 2011, 110.
47. Ibid.
48. An example is Prince Vikramaditya's aunt Kumkumadevi. See *EI* XXXII, 317–25. Mangalesha's mother also did something similar in her donations to the god Makuteshvara.
49. Buchanan 1985, 352.
50. Ibid.
51. Arguably the most powerful and prominent was the ninth-century Odia queen Tribhuvana-Mahadevi.
52. *EHD* I, 235; *SII* XI, 2.
53. Cummings 2006, 99.
54. Ibid., 97.
55. This idea is explored at length in the second chapter of Cummings 2006.

56. Ibid., 101.

57. *EI* XIV, 189.

58. Ibid.

59. Khalid Yahya Blankinship, *The End of the Jihad State: The Reign of Hisham Ibn' Abd al-Malik and the Collapse of the Umayyads* (SUNY Press, 1994), 131.

60. Dikshit 1980, 160.

61. Robert DeCaroli, 'An Analysis of Daṇḍin's Daśakumāracarita and Its Implications for Both the Vākāṭaka and Pallava Courts', *Journal of the American Oriental Society* 115, no. 4 (1995).

62. Ibid.

63. 'Introduction', in Dandin 2007. For ease of reading, Sarasvati is substituted for 'Vedhas' spouse'.

64. Ibid.

65. Ibid.

66. Ibid.

67. DeCaroli 1995.

68. Dandin 2007, Location 1549.

69. Ibid., Location 1551.

70. Ibid., Location 1569.

71. John Keay, *India: A History. Revised and Updated* (Grove/Atlantic 2011), 180.

72. Hugh Kennedy, *The Armies of the Caliphs: Military and Society in the Early Islamic State* (Routledge, 2013), 6.

73. Ibid., 7.

74. Peter Frankopan, *The Silk Roads: A New History of the World* (Bloomsbury, 2015), 43.

75. Hans Bielenstein, *Diplomacy and Trade in the Chinese World, 589–1276* (Brill, 2005), 75.

76. K.A. Nilakanta Sastri, *Foreign Notices of South India: From Megasthenes to Ma Huan* (University of Madras, 1939), 116.

77. Ibid.

78. Keay 2011, 174.

79. Sastri 1997, 139.

80. Keay 2011, 176.

81. *SII* I, 10.
82. Cummings 2006, 101, Note 167.
83. Assuming Vijayaditya was at least in his twenties in 674 (since Vikramaditya I mentions him commanding armies), he would have been in his eighties by the 630s.
84. Why attack in 731 and not in 728? It may be because the Arab position in western India had suffered a temporary setback and they were already being attacked by other Indian states, so Vikramaditya could signal his strength by leading an attack in another direction. In any case, if Vikramaditya was going to get involved with the Arabs, he would certainly have done it during Junaid's first set of campaigns in Gujarat in the early 720s. That he chose to attack the Pallavas instead and rekindle a conflict that had been at rest for at least forty years suggests that he had only been waiting for the right opportunity. Moreover, the possibility that Paramesvara-Varman II's position was weaker in 731 than in 728 due to domestic factors we know nothing about – thus prompting Vikramaditya to attack him – cannot be ruled out. The fact that he surrendered a ransom apparently without offering serious resistance certainly points to the fact that his position was weaker than one would expect.
85. Adiga 2006, 102.
86. We will see an example of such a lord, the Rashtrakuta king Danti-Durga, in Chapter 5.
87. Dikshit 1980, 160; Sastri 1997, 141.
88. Sastri 1997, 141.
89. Blankinship 1994, 134.
90. Arabs are generally referred to as Tajikas or Parasikas in Indian sources, which according to Jayashri Mishra (1992, 171) is derived from 'Taji', 'an Arabic word meaning Arab country and also Arab horse'. Meanwhile, Brajadulal Chattopadhyaya indicates that the term was 'derived from Arabic tribal or tribal confederation of the Tayy', and, further, that 'an old Parthian formation of the name which by the third century must have been Tāzīg may be envisaged'. See Brajadulal Chattopadhyaya, *Representing the Other: Sanskrit Sources and the Muslims, Eighth to Fourteenth Century* (Primus Books, 1998), Kindle

Edition. This book will use the term 'Tajika' to refer to the Umayyad armies in this chapter, and call them Arabs and Persians elsewhere, in order to bring out the disparate meanings with which the terms are imbued in medieval and modern contexts.

91. Blankinship 1994, 133.
92. Ibid.
93. It should be noted that the Arabs were not exceptional in their involvement in the slave trade: African and Indian rulers also participated in it to various extents through the medieval period.
94. Blankinship 1994, 134.
95. Ibid., 148.
96. Ibid.
97. Ibid., 146.
98. R.C. Majumdar claims that the Rashtrakuta king Danti-Durga was commanded by Vikramaditya II to assist against the Tajikas. See note 109 below. R.C. Majumdar, *The Age of Imperial Kannauj, The History and Culture of the Indian People*, Vol. 4, *Second Edition* (Bharatiya Vidya Bhavan, 1959). There is no evidence provided to support this assertion, and this book will depict Danti-Durga's relationship with the Chalukyas somewhat differently.
99. Ibid., 187.
100. Pulakeshi-Raja was the paternal cousin of Vikramaditya II's grandfather Vinayaditya. Strictly speaking this makes him his first cousin twice removed, but 'distant grand-uncle' has been used as a more intuitive term.
101. Dikshit 1980, 167.
102. *Corpus Inscriptionum Indicarum* IV, 144. Hereafter *CII*.
103. Ibid. Paraphrased to simplify the language.
104. Ibid. Paraphrased to simplify the language.
105. Blankinship 1994, 188.
106. Ibid.
107. It is worth mentioning that though the Arabs hereafter adopted more peaceful policies, they did not speak for the entire Muslim world, and the subcontinent would eventually be invaded by Turks, Afghans, Turco-Mongols and Persians.
108. Blankinship 1994.

109. Majumdar 1959, 18, Note 11: 'This para is based on the inference suggested by the Navsari Plates of Pulakeshin and Ellora Plates of Dantidurga.' In the Navsari Plates, Pulakeshin (Pulakeshi-Raja in the text) mentions no other allies in his battle, and the Rashtrakuta king Danti-Durga in his Ellora Plates similarly makes no claims to this effect. Dr Majumdar may be basing this on a misreading of the Ellora Plates suggesting that Danti-Durga conquered Sind, but this has been dismissed by other scholars. As the editor of the Ellora Plates of Dantidurga puts it: 'there is no question of Dantidurga conquering Sind.' See *EI* XXV, 29.

110. *CII* IV, 143.

111. Ibid.

112. Ibid. Pulakeshi was only the second generation of Chalukyas to have a strong position in Lata and may very well have been seen as a foreigner by his subjects.

113. Ibid.

114. Given the fragmentary nature of the evidence, this is proposed as a much better explanation for Danti-Durga's sudden rise to prominence than Majumdar's (1959) proposal.

115. Chakrabarti 2011, Location 1756.

116. Inden 2000, 244.

117. In later inscriptions of Vikramaditya II, he implies that he went to war with the Pallavas *immediately* after his accession, which does not make sense since he makes no reference to them in inscriptions dedicated in the second year of his reign. Dikshit (1980) argues that this second campaign occurred between 735 and 740 but does not connect it to domestic politics owing to the assumption that Pulakeshi-Raja was acting on Vikramaditya's orders. Though Dikshit mentions Pulakeshi's use of the title Parama-Bhattaraka, he does not connect it to the Pallava campaigns, and seems uncertain about Pulakeshi's intentions. The perspective adopted here is that all these occurrences *are* connected, and that the second campaign may have been prompted by a need to respond to Pulakeshi-Raja's activities in the northern part of the Chalukya domains.

118. He would later claim to have sacked Kanchi, which, given that his

power was concentrated in northern Maharasthra, seems implausible unless he had done it under the authority of the Chalukyas early in his career.

119. Sastri 1997, 139–40.

120. Dikshit 1980, 167.

121. *EI* III, 360.

122. Ibid., 359.

123. Ibid., 360.

124. *SII* I, 146.

125. Kaligotla 2015, 181.

126. Buchanan 1985, 400.

127. It is possible to make this statement with confidence as it is hardly possible that the queen would *not* have interacted with the chief architect of her own temple, given that both of them are explicitly mentioned in inscriptions on it. Given that Loka-Mahadevi also administered territory in her own right, it is also very likely that she was used to speaking and commanding both female and male subordinates and likely had her own court.

128. *IA* X, 164–65. In this inscription, Loka-Mahadevi announces that Gundan had averted the excommunication of his caste by building the temple. As such, it seems reasonable to assume that any issue which led to such an important guild almost being excommunicated would certainly have caused a huge scandal.

129. It is, according to the *Dharmasutras*, illegal to provide any sustenance to one who has been excommunicated from caste. We cannot be certain this was followed uniformly across the subcontinent or even to what degree it was followed if it was.

130. *Gautama Dharmasutra* 21.1, in Patrick Olivelle, *Dharmasutras: The Law Codes of Ancient India* (Oxford University Press, 1999), 114.

131. Cummings 2006, 95.

132. Buchanan 1985, 399.

133. Cummings 2006, 102.

134. Buchanan 1985, 399.

135. Ibid., 400.

136. *IA* X, 166.

137. Ibid., 167.
138. Ibid.
139. M.K. Dhavalikar, 'Sutradhara', *Annals of the Bhandarkar Oriental Research Institute* 52, no. 1 (1971): 218.
140. Cummings 2006, 102.
141. Ibid., 91.
142. Kaligotla 2015, 177.
143. Cummings 2006, 120.
144. Ibid., 125.
145. Ibid., 126–27.
146. Ibid., 127–28.
147. Ibid., 138.

5. The Elephant Fort

1. *EHD* I, 249.
2. The only source directly attesting to this event dates to more than a hundred years after it may have happened, at a time when the Rashtrakutas had an unpleasant relationship with the Chalukyas of Vengi. Its depiction of the marriage as a 'rakshasa' marriage, involving the abduction of the bride, could have been a fabrication or a literary device to reinforce Rashtrakuta virility – especially given that is followed soon after by a verse describing how one of them 'forcefully wrested away the Fortune of the Chalukya family' on the battlefield. See *EI* XVIII, 252.
3. Michaela Soar, 'The Tîrtha at Ellora', in Parimoo, Kannal and Pannikar, eds. 2018, 64.
4. *EI* XIV, 127.
5. There can be little doubt about Danti-Durga's close relationship with his Chalukya mother (though of course his apparent closeness to her may be a propaganda device to establish that he was half Chalukya) considering he would later claim that she donated land in each of the 400,000 villages he ruled over.
6. Chakravarti 1941, 56.
7. Ibid.

8. *Arthashastra* 2.2.15–16, quoted in Thomas R. Trautmann, *Arthashastra: The Science of Wealth* (Penguin, 2016). 'Those from the east, Cedi and Karusha, from the Dasharnas and Aparantas are considered of medium quality among elephants' (80).

9. In *EHD* I, Kosala is depicted as being the last of Danti-Durga's conquests, but no justification is given for this supposition.

10. Thomas R. Trautmann, *Elephants and Kings: An Environmental History* (University of Chicago Press, 2015), 65.

11. Chakravarti 1941, 54.

12. A man with a regnal name meaning 'Elephant Fort' probably made them an integral part of his strategy. In ancient Indian writing, the fort, *durga*, was one of the seven constituent elements of the state. Elephant sculptures are present in large numbers in the great monolithic Krishneshvara temple built by his uncle and successor, and it is difficult not to see a nod to Danti-Durga here.

13. *EHD* I, 254. The authors argue that it is likely Danti-Durga gained the title Prithivi-Vallabha for helping Pulakeshi-Raja against the Tajikas (though he concedes that this narrative is purely conjectural). This book presents an alternative hypothesis that better fits the evidence we have. To reiterate: it is suggested that Pulakeshi-Raja attempted to seize independence, that Vikramaditya's second expedition to Kanchi was a response to this, and that Danti-Durga helped Vikramaditya bring Pulakeshi-Raja into line, being rewarded with the title Prithivi-Vallabha for his services as well as for his conquests in central India and his Chalukya descent. Note that this does not necessarily imply Danti-Durga attacked Pulakeshi-Raja immediately – merely that he had generally won significant victories and may have been acknowledged as an important partner by Vikramaditya. A decade later, Danti-Durga claimed to have completed the conquest of Lata.

14. Soar 2018, 64.

15. Ibid., 64.

16. Ibid., 66.

17. Ibid., 65.

18. Ibid.

19. Ibid., 63.

20. Ibid., 64.

21. Lisa Nadine. Owen, 'Art, Architecture and Devotional Practice at Ellora', in *Living Rock: Buddhist, Hindu and Jain Cave Temples in the Western Deccan*, ed. Pia Brancaccio (Marg Foundation, 2013), 136.

22. Ibid.

23. Though the term 'Kalachuri artists' has been used previously to refer to artisans from here who made some of the early Chalukya temples in Vatapi, perhaps 'Ellora artists' would be a better way to do justice to this influential hub of Deccani sculptural traditions.

24. Soar 2018, 73.

25. Ibid.

26. Ibid., 77.

27. Lisa Nadine Owen, *Carving Devotion in the Jain Caves at Ellora* (Brill, 2012), 132.

28. *EI* XXV, 29.

29. Dikshit 1980, 184.

30. *EHD* I, 254, and footnote 2.

31. Dikshit 1980, 170.

32. There is much debate as to the chronology of Danti-Durga's conquests and some writers prefer to place these early in his reign. I think that performing the Hiranyagarbha before the death of Vikramaditya II would have been a remarkably bold statement for Danti-Durga to make especially against a relatively well-established overlord – and thus I place it after the accession of Kirti-Varman II.

33. Anant Sadashiv Altekar, *The Rashtrakutas and Their Times; being a political, administrative, religious, social, economic and literary history of the Deccan during C. 750 AD to C. 1000 AD* (Oriental Book Agency, 1934), 40.

34. *IA* XI, 114.

35. Kalidasa, *Meghadutam*, trans. Srinivas Reddy (Penguin Random House, 2015), 1:31.

36. *EHD* I, 255.

37. Inden 2000, 247.

38. Ibid., 248. Inden argues that this was meant to replace the Ashvamedha.

39. D.C. Ganguly, 'The "Gurjaras" in the Rastrakuta Inscriptions', *Proceedings of the Indian History Congress* 3, vol. 3 (1939).

40. *Matsya Puranam* 274.65, in B.D. Basu, ed. *The Sacred Books of the Hindus Translated by Various Sanskrit Scholars* (The Indian Press, 1917).

41. *Matsya Puranam* 274.30–32. 'Banners of various colours resembling the complexion of the four Lokapalas should be made.'

42. Inden 2000, 247.

43. Ibid.

44. Bhattacharyya 1975, 72.

45. *Matsya Puranam* 275.25.

46. This reconstruction is conjectural, as are other narratives of the period. However, it seems reasonable to assume that Danti-Durga's attack on Lata was after the accession of Kirti-Varman II, as it was a very direct move against the Chalukyas, no matter Pulakeshi-Raja's disloyalties. Such an attack could have forced Vikramaditya II to take the field to defend his own status as a powerful overlord.

47. *IA* XI, 114.

48. Dikshit 1980, 185.

49. Ibid.

50. Soar 2018, 67.

51. *IA* XI, 114.

52. V.V. Mirashi, 'Manor Plates of Rāshṭrakūta Dantidurga: Śaka Year 671', *Proceedings of the Indian History Congress* 21 (1958).

53. This is, to my mind, the simplest explanation for why the merchant corporation of the Manor plates (ibid.) would acknowledge a Rashtrakuta governor, called Danti-Durga Prithivi-Vallabha, but not acknowledge him as *maharajadhiraja, paramabhattaraka* or the equivalent.

54. Mirashi 1958.

55. Whitney M. Cox, 'Scribe and Script in the Cāḷukya West Deccan', *The Indian Economic and Social History Review* 47, no. 1 (2010): 19.

56. Owen 2012, 135.

57. M.K. Dhavalikar, *Ellora: Monumental Legacy* (Oxford University Press, 2003), 38.

58. Carmel Berkson, '*Daśāvatāra Cave:* Its Importance in the History of World Art', in Parimoo, Kannal and Pannikar eds. 2018, 167.
59. Ibid., 172.
60. Ibid.
61. Cummings 2006, 214.
62. Owen 2012, 133, footnote 8.
63. *EHD* I, 256, quoting a later Rashtrakuta inscription.
64. It cannot be ruled out that some of Danti-Durga's family members, including his much older uncle Krishna and his ambitious sons Dhruva and Govinda, had something to do with this, as they had plenty to gain from this sudden tragic death.
65. According to some sources Danti-Durga had two young sons, but in the absence of a protector they appear to have been unceremoniously murdered and are never mentioned again.
66. *EI* III, 6.
67. Ibid., 7.
68. Cox 2010, 19.
69. Dikshit 1980, 189.
70. Ibid.
71. *EHD* I, 259.
72. This may be an allusion to a practice of abducting or raping women who accompanied a defeated army. *EI* XVIII, 252.
73. Inden 2000, 249.
74. Indeed, this may be the actual conclusion that we are meant to draw from the later Rashtrakuta inscription, which first mentions the abduction over a hundred years after the actual fact. Perhaps this is an assertion of virility or adherence to the Kshatriya dharma this later Rashtrakuta, Amoghavarsha I, wishes to claim on behalf of his ancestors. We cannot even be sure if Bhavanaga was abducted, given the paucity of evidence. All we can say for certain is that she was, indeed, Danti-Durga's mother.
75. *EHD* I, 258.
76. *EI* XIV, 123.
77. Ibid., 128.
78. He was married to a Chalukya princess by the name of Vijaya-

Mahadevi, thus making him Vikramaditya II's brother-in-law and the uncle of Kirti-Varman II.

79. G.R. Rangaswamaiah, 'The Rashtrakuta Relations with the Gangas of Talkad', in *The Rashtrakutas of Malkhed: Studies in Their History and Culture*, ed. B.R. Gopal (The Mythic Society/Geetha Book House, 1994).

80. Adiga 2006, 117.

81. Shivanna 1977.

82. Rohitha Eswar, Vrushab Mahesh and K. Krishnan, '"Iha" to "Para": A Hero's Transitional Journey to the Other World from This World – Reading Veeragals of Hassan', *Heritage: Journal of Multidisciplinary Studies in Archaeology* 2 (2014).

83. Adiga 2006, 325.

84. Ibid., 327–28.

85. Ibid., 325.

86. Shivanna, 'Rashtrakuta Krishna I and Gangavadi (758–774 A.D.)', *Proceedings of the Indian History Congress* 38 (1977); *EHD* I, 259.

87. Divya Shekhar, 'Inscription Stone discovered in Hebbal could be Bengaluru's oldest', *The Economic Times*, 23 June 2018, https://economictimes.indiatimes.com/magazines/panache/inscription-stone-discovered-in-hebbal-could-be-bengalurus-oldest/articleshow/64708042.cms, accessed 17 December 2019.

88. *EI* XIII, 282.

6. To Kailasha

1. Where the capital of the early Rashtrakutas was is a matter of considerable debate. Though inscriptions show us that later Rashtrakuta kings ruled from Manyakheta as well as a host of other royal cities, there is less evidence to show where their power was concentrated immediately after the overthrow of the Vatapi Chalukyas. Considering the scale of the investments made in Cave 16, the Krishneshvara, it is fair to assume that Krishna Rashtrakuta frequently visited Ellora once he had secured his grip over the Deccan.

2. This would be Yashovarman of Kannauj, *c.* 725–52 CE.

3. Deepak Kannal, 'The Regional Lineages and Possible Masters at Kailāśanātha Temple of Ellora', in Parimoo, Kannal and Pannikar eds. 2018, 205.

4. Kannal 2018, 204.

5. M.K. Dhavalikar, 'Kailasa: The Stylistic Development and Chronology', in Gopal ed. 1994.

6. Kannal 2018, 203. Professor Kannal discussed his ideas with the author in Bengaluru in 2019. While the book presents a further developed version, the credit for the reconstruction should go to him.

7. Kannal 2018, 203.

8. H. Goetz, 'The Kailasa of Ellora and the Chronology of Rashtrakuta Art', *Artibus Asiae* 15, no. 1/2 (1952).

9. Kannal 2018, 206.

10. *EI* VI, 212.

11. *EI* X, 84. Some translators present this as 'Beloved of Warriors'.

12. *EI* VI, 212. Though Govinda's inscriptions record that he had led a 'victorious army' into Vengi, they do not detail a military confrontation. It seems likely that if there *had* been such a confrontation, the crown prince would hardly have neglected to mention it.

13. Many historians put the date of the marriage to after Dhruva's accession and supposed attack on Vishnuvardhana IV in 780. This is questionable because it doesn't seem likely the Chalukya princess Shila-Mahadevi would be accepted as Dhruva's chief queen and equal partner *after* he had just defeated her father.

14. These would be Karkka and Stambha. Stambha was old enough to rule as a viceroy in Gangavadi very soon after Dhruva's bid for the throne in 780, which means he would have been a child – at least – in 770. His elder brother, Karkka, predeceased Dhruva.

15. Kannal 2018, 206. Professor Kannal argues that there is no evidence supporting the idea that the *entire* temple was excavated during the reign of Krishna I. This book therefore depicts it as having been completed sometime during the reign of Dhruva.

16. Shivanna, 'An Estimate of Dhruva', in Gopal ed. 1994. This is an excessively rosy estimate of the man given how little evidence of his personality actually survives – what does come across are ambition and ruthlessness, which is how this book portrays him.

17. *EI* IX, 194–97: 'His younger brother … who, on perceiving him to be self-conceited … and even devoid of policy … assumed the royal authority … in order that sovereignty might not deviate from the family.' It is difficult to take this claim at face value given that it was issued by a descendant of Dhruva's, who can hardly be expected to be honest about how his line rose to power. It certainly seems, however, that Dhruva's public explanation for his usurpation was his brother's debauchery.

18. *EI* VI, 212. See also *EI* XXII, 180.

19. *EI* XXII, 99.

20. Ali 2006, 119, footnote 57.

21. Ibid., footnote 56.

22. Ibid., 118–19.

23. Ibid., 119.

24. This may also be a recognition of the role she played in manoeuvring him on to the throne in the first place, perhaps with the support of her father Vishnuvardhana IV of Vengi.

25. Inden 2000, 261.

26. *EHD* I, 263.

27. *EI* XXII, 101.

28. Abridged from *EI* XXII, 104.

29. Ibid., footnote 2.

30. Shivanna 1994.

31. In this matter the book follows the narrative of Altekar (1934). A later date makes sense since: (a) it would have made no strategic sense for Dhruva to head north, far away from his domains, unless he was confident there would be no deadly attacks from the Gangas; (b) Shila-Mahadevi would hardly have neglected to mention something this important in her 786 inscription; and (c) it was only in 788 that Dhruva imprisoned the Ganga king Sivamara II, thus freeing up resources for a northern campaign.

32. Chakravarti 1941, 93–103.

33. Ibid., 122.

34. K.K. Handiqui, *Yaśastilaka and Indian Culture* (Jaina Samskriti Samrakhsana Sangha, 1949), 59.

35. S.K. Bose, *Boots, Hooves, and Wheels: And the Social Dynamics Behind South Asian Warfare* (Vij Books, 2015), Electronic Edition, 'Warfare of the Late First Milennium'.
36. *EI* IV, 347. While the description of Dhruva is likely just poetic licence, its details are nevertheless interesting.
37. *EI* IV, 334–37.
38. Both art historical evidence (in the form of hero stones) and literary evidence (in sources such as the *Arthashastra* and *Nitisara*) depict highly organized formations, though literary sources describe somewhat impractical arrangements of troops.
39. For a study of the experience of battle in the front lines, see John Keegan, *The Face of Battle: A Study of Agincourt, Waterloo and the Somme* (Random House, 2011), and Philip Sabin, 'The Face of Roman Battle', *The Journal of Roman Studies* 90 (2000).
40. See Sabin 2000.
41. If it was a planned retreat, Vatsaraja would not have lost the Pala umbrellas to Dhruva.
42. Davidson 2002, 53.
43. *EHD* I, 264.
44. Davidson 2002, 53.
45. Inden 2000, 250. This is a description of Dhruva's son Govinda III's *pali-dhvaja*, but it should be fairly similar to Dhruva's considering they fought the same enemies.
46. Ibid., 251.
47. M.N. Vahia, A.P. Jamkhedkar and Parag Mahajani, 'Astronomical Orientation of Caves in Ajantha and Ellora', *Journal of Multidisciplinary Studies in Archaeology* 5 (2017).
48. Mishra 1992, 87.
49. Altekar 1934, 263.
50. Ali 2006, 118.
51. Ibid.
52. Betel, as a marker of courtly sophistication, would grow much more important in Deccan in the following centuries, but scattered references to it can be found from earlier.
53. *EI* IV, 334–37.

54. Ali 2006, 116.
55. While it is unclear whether the future emperor Govinda III was Shila-Mahadevi's son or not, it is highly likely. Govinda's selection as heir apparent may have been because he was the grandson and nephew of the present and future kings of Vengi, and thus most likely to be able to control the vast Rashtrakuta political network.
56. Roger Vogler, *The Kailas at Ellora: A New View of a Misunderstood Masterwork* (INTACH Aurangabad and Mapin Publishing 2015), 18.
57. Ibid., 27.
58. Kannal 2018, 208.
59. Vogler 2015, 31.
60. This will be explored in detail later. The ideas come from Inden (2000) and Diana L. Eck, *India: A Sacred Geography* (Harmony, 2012).
61. Sudhir Kakar, *Intimate Relations: Exploring Indian Sexuality* (University of Chicago Press, 1989), 138. Quoted in Vogler 2015, 42–43.
62. K.V. Soundara Rajan, *The Ellora Monoliths* (Gian, 1988), 90. Quoted in Vogler 2015, 31.
63. Benjamin J. Fleming, 'Ellora Cave 16 and the Cult of the Twelve Jyotirlingas', in *Living Rock: Buddhist, Hindu and Jain Cave Temples in the Western Deccan*, ed. Pia Brancaccio (Marg Foundation, 2013), 118.
64. Ibid., 119–20.
65. Ibid., 120–21.
66. Stephen Markel, 'The "Rāmāyaṇa" Cycle on the Kailāsanātha Temple at Ellora', *Ars Orientalis* 30, Supplement 1 (2000).
67. John Stratton Hawley, 'Scenes from the Childhood of Kṛṣṇa on the Kailāsanātha Temple, Ellora', *Archives of Asian Art* 34 (1981).
68. *IA* XII, 228–30.
69. *EI* IV, 334–37.
70. Vogler 2015, 47.
71. *IA* XIII, 228–30.

7. King of Poets

1. *EI* XVIII, 254.
2. This is based on a description from the *Yashastilaka*, a near-contemporary Jain text composed under the patronage of a Rashtrakuta vassal.

3. Govinda III's son Amoghavarsha is generally given credit for completing Manyakheta, but this does not mean he initiated its construction. This decision was probably made by Govinda. See Mishra 1992, 205. Both 'Manya' and 'Kheta' can mean different things, and the name translates roughly to 'Sacred Shield', 'Auspicious Shield' or 'Venerable Shield' or even 'Honoured Weapon' or 'Honoured Field'.

4. While Malkhed is commonly identified with Manyakheta, precious little archaeological work has been done to verify this.

5. Assuming that Govinda was Shila-Mahadevi's son by Dhruva, the earliest possible date for his birth (as depicted in this book) is 772, making him about thirty at this point. *EHD* I instead suggests that Govinda was born after Dhruva's accession in 780, fought alongside him in north India before he was ten, led a series of campaigns and had a son at the age of barely twenty in 800, and yet died of old age in 814.

6. *EI* VI, 250.

7. Davis 1993, 37.

8. Ibid.

9. *EHD* I, 274.

10. Ali 2006, 70.

11. Ibid., 71.

12. Ibid., 87–88.

13. Ibid., 73.

14. Ibid., 124.

15. Ibid., 132.

16. Ibid.

17. Ibid., 133.

18. Ibid., 132.

19. Ibid., 133.

20. Ibid., 134.

21. *EI* XVIII, 254.

22. This was Vijayaditya II, son of Vishnuvardhana IV and brother of Shila-Mahadevi. He was an inveterate enemy of the Rashtrakutas, having earlier been dethroned by Govinda III and replaced by his younger brother before managing to crown himself.

23. Though Vijayaditya is recorded as having frequently battled the Gangas, these probably date to the earlier part of his career while he was Govinda III's vassal, since they both had a common enemy in the Rashtrakutas after Govinda's death and it seems unlikely they would fight each other at that point. Of course, hostilities may have broken out again after the Vengi Chalukyas and Rashtrakutas reached an arrangement in 821.

24. Chakrabarti 2011, Location 1797.

25. G.R. Rangaswamaiah, 'The Rashtrakuta Relations with Gangas of Talkad', in Gopal ed. 1994, 206.

26. *EI* XVIII, 254–55.

27. Ibid.

28. Karkka was the son of Indra Rashtrakuta, Govinda's younger brother and right-hand man. He is often portrayed as having been Amoghavarsha's regent, but there is little to no evidence attesting to this. See V.V. Mirashi, 'The Javakheḍa Plates of Amoghavarsha I: Śaka 742: A Critical Examination of Some Problems', *Proceedings of the Indian History Congress* 23 (1960): 31–36, http://www.jstor.org/stable/44304005.

29. *EHD* I, 274.

30. Sastri 1994, 173.

31. Inden 1981, 105.

32. It may be worth pointing out the irony in an individual who depended on the direct and indirect labour of hundreds, if not thousands, for his day-to-day activities and consumption saying this.

33. These quotes are from the *Prasnōttararatnamālika*, 'The Jewel-Garland of Questions and Answers', attributed to Amoghavarsha. See Mishra 1992, 117–18.

34. *EI* XVIII, 254.

35. Was Amoghavarsha himself truly as introspective as presented here? His inscriptions certainly seem to have somewhat different priorities than those of his contemporaries, detailing the control of the senses, the vagaries and duties of kingship, repeated betrayals and abdications, and so on. It is certainly probable that the various difficulties of his early life had an impact on his psyche.

36. This is the general conclusion reached by Professor Shonaleeka Kaul in *Imagining the Urban: Sanskrit and the City in Early India* (Seagull Books, 2011).

37. Ibid., 206.

38. Paul Dundas, *The Jains*, Second Edition (Routledge, 2002), 119.

39. Nandi 1973, 47.

40. Mukund Lath, 'Somadeva Suri and the Question of Jain Identity', in *The Assembly of Listeners: Jains in Society*, eds. Michael Carrithers and Caroline Humphrey (Cambridge University Press, 1991), 19–30, 29.

41. Nandi 1973, 59.

42. Ibid., 61.

43. Ibid., 2.

44. Ibid., 52.

45. *EHD* I, 279.

46. Dundas 2002, 120.

47. Though Mahalakshmi is also worshipped in Jainism, the sacrifice of a finger suggests that Amoghavarsha was approaching this from the ritual practice of left-hand tantra, generally associated with Shaivism and Shaktism at this time.

48. R.V.S. Sundaram, *Śrīvijaya's Kavirājāmārgaṁ*, trans. Deven M. Patel (Manohar, 2017), 18.

49. Kalinga is generally thought of as a name for premodern Odisha, but the area corresponding to Odisha actually consisted of a number of smaller kingdoms, including Kalinga, Kongoda, Dakshina Kosala, and Uttara and Dakshina Tosali.

50. Handiqui 1949, 26–27. 'Charger' has been changed to 'horse' for readability.

51. These are mentioned as important towns in his *Kavirajamargam*. See Sundaram 2017, 29.

52. 'The Helgo Treasure: A Viking Age Buddha', *Irish Archaeology* (28 December 2013), http://irisharchaeology.ie/2013/12/the-helgo-treasure-a-viking-age-buddha/. The article cites peer-reviewed chapters and archaeological surveys.

53. Edward Pollard and Okeny Charles Kinyera, 'The Swahili Coast and the Indian Ocean Trade Patterns in the 7th–10th Centuries CE,' *Journal of Southern African Studies* 43, no. 5 (2017): 1–21, 7.

54. S.A.M. Adshead, *T'ang China: The Rise of the East in World History* (Palgrave Macmillan, 2004), 68.

55. Tansen Sen, *Buddhism, Diplomacy and Trade: The Realignment of Sino-Indian Relations, 600–1400* (University of Hawai'i Press, 2004), 152.

56. Ramendra Nath Nandi, *State Formation, Agrarian Growth and Social Change in Feudal South India c. AD 600–1200* (Manohar, 2000), 114.

57. Ibid., 126.

58. Mishra 1992, 45.

59. Ibid., 50.

60. Ibid., 25.

61. Ibid., 26.

62. Malekandathil 2010, 9.

63. This can be seen in the Quilon copper plates of Sthanu Ravi, where the Syrian Mar Sapir Iso is mentioned as having founded a town. Witnesses include members of the Manigramam as well as the chief of Venad and a local militia group. See Y. Subbarayalu, *South India Under the Cholas* (Oxford University Press, 2012), 177–78.

64. Amira K. Bennison, *The Great Caliphs: The Golden Age of the 'Abbasid Empire* (Yale University Press, 2009), 140.

65. Ibid., 140.

66. Malekandathil 2010, 21.

67. Chakravarti 2012, 84.

68. Malekandathil 2010, 21.

69. Sastri 1939, 124.

70. Elizabeth Lambourn, 'Describing a Lost Camel: Clues for West Asian Mercantile Networks in South Asian Maritime Trade (Tenth–Twelfth Centuries CE),' in *Ports of the Ancient Indian Ocean: Proceedings of the Kolkata Colloquium 2011 (Median Project)*, eds. M.-F. Boussac, J.-F. Salles and J.-.B. Yon (Primus Books, 2016), 366.

71. Ibid.

72. *EI XXXII*, 47.

73. Lambourn 2016, 368.

74. *EI XXXII*, 47.

75. Ranabir Chakravarti, 'Merchants, Merchandise and Merchantmen in the Western Seaboard of India: A Maritime Profile (*c.* 500 BCE–1500

CE),' in *The Trading World of the Indian Ocean, 1500–1800*, eds. Om Prakash and D.P. Chattopadhyaya (Pearson Education, 2012), 99.

76. For a discussion on how this was circumvented, see Lambourn 2016.

77. Gautam Jantakal, Bhushan Kapadia and Prakash Jinjuvadiya, *History and Coinage of the Rashtrakutas* (IIRNS Publications LLP, 2019), 34–35.

78. This mostly involved various small-scale boiling and refinement.

79. Sen 2004, 150.

80. Adshead 2004, 81.

81. Mishra 1992, 147.

82. Ibid., 152.

83. Ibid., 170.

84. Chakravarti 2012, 97.

85. Ibid., 86.

86. Kurush F. Dalal, 'Sanjan: Digging Deep Into History', *Live History India*, 22 September 2019, https://www.livehistoryindia.com/story/cover-story/sanjan-digging-deep-into-history/.

87. Rhea Mitra and Kurush F. Dalal, 'A Report on the Glass Vessels from Sanjan, 2002', *Journal of Indian Ocean Archaeology* 2 (2005).

88. S.P. Gupta et al., 'Preliminary Report on the Excavations at Sanjan (2002)', *Puratattva* 32 (n.d.).

89. Mishra 1992, 172.

90. Bennison 2009, 145.

91. Mishra 1992, 170.

92. Burjor Avari, *Islamic Civilization in South Asia: A History of Muslim Power and Presence in the Indian Subcontinent* (Routledge, 2019), 30.

93. Alberuni, *Alberuni's India*, trans. Edward C. Sachau (Kegan Paul, Trench, Trubner & Co., 1910), xxxi–xxxii. See also Avari 2019, 32.

94. Gopal Stavig, 'Congruencies Between Indian and Islamic Philosophy', *Annals of the Bhandarkar Oriental Research Institute* 81, no. 1/4 (2000), http://www.jstor.org/stable/41694615.

95. Devices known as 'yantras' are mentioned in the *Yashastilaka* of Somadeva, a Jain ascetic writing in the tenth century who appears to have modelled his description of a royal court on that of Manyakheta. In the eleventh century, these 'yantras', corresponding to much better-

attested automata in the courts of Constantinople and Baghdad, are mentioned in literature produced by the Malwan ruler Bhoja of Dhara. All these hint at Indian courts importing Abbasid technology. See Daud Ali, 'Bhoja's Mechanical Garden: Translating Wonder across the Indian Ocean, circa 800–1100 CE', *History of Religions* 55, no. 4 (2016).

96. Ibid., 171.
97. Chakravarti 2012, 99.
98. Ibid., 92–93.
99. Ibid.
100. Sastri 1939, 125.
101. Ibid.
102. Mishra 1992, 205.
103. Ibid., 206.
104. Mishra 1992, 190–91.
105. Pollock 2006, 343.
106. Ibid., 330.
107. Ibid., 343.
108. Ibid., 344.
109. Sundaram 2017, 28.
110. Pollock 2006, 349.
111. Sundaram 2017, 31.
112. Ibid., 32.
113. Ibid., 35.
114. Ibid., 45.
115. Pollock 2006, 344.
116. Ibid., 342.
117. Ibid., 332.
118. Ibid., 339.
119. Ibid., 341.
120. Ibid., 337.
121. Suryanath U. Kamath, 'Amoghavarsha I: An Appraisal,' in Gopal ed., 84.
122. Rangaswamaiah in Gopal ed. 1994, 206.
123. Sastri 1939, 123. This claim was based on a misunderstanding of

Rashtrakuta territories as extending all the way to China, so it should be taken with a pinch of salt. Interestingly, the Arabs claim that this is a classification that originated in India and China.

124. *EI* VI, 35.
125. Ibid., 35.
126. Mishra 1992, 107–08.
127. *EI* VI, 35–36.
128. Ibid.
129. Vedam Venkataraya Sastry, 'The Rashtrakutas and Vengi and Cultural Contacts', in Gopal 1994, 173.
130. Ibid. It is quite possible that given Vijayaditya III's later activities he was nowhere near as crushed by this Rashtrakuta victory as the Rashtrakutas make him out to be.
131. Rangaswamaiah in Gopal ed. 1994, 207.
132. *EHD* I, 260.
133. *EI* VI, 35.

8. King of Kings

1.   *EI* IV, 289.
2.   This was at Rameshvaram, not Kanyakumari.
3.   *EI* IV, 290.
4.   Marasimha was the son of the Ganga king Butuga II, Krishna III's brother-in-law. He was Butuga's son by another wife, but retained a close bond to the Rashtrakuta emperor.
5.   Pollock 2006, 335.
6.   Ibid., 334.
7.   Paraphrasing *EHD* I, 296.
8.   Altekar 1934, 122.
9.   *EI* XXII, 43–44.
10. Chakrabarti 2011, Location 2050.
11. Altekar 1934, 121.
12. *EI* XXII, 43–44.
13. *EHD* I, 297.

14. Archaeological and literary evidence from medieval India strongly suggests that most royal cities, such as Dvarasamudra in the southern Deccan, were organized along a central axis.

15. This is based on descriptions from Somadeva's *Yashastilaka*, completed in 959 in the court of a Rashtrakuta vassal, filled with details apparently inspired by the composer's time in Manyakheta. See Mishra 1992, 83.

16. Ibid., 89.

17. *The Inscriptions of Nagai*, Hyderabad Archaeological Series, No. 8 (The Nizam's Government, 1928), 18. This refers to the Chalukya ruler Jayasimha II, but is an example of medieval attitudes to captured women more generally – similar examples can be found across India at this time.

18. Altekar 1934, 155.

19. Ibid.

20. Early medieval *prashastis*, Rashtrakuta *prashastis* specifically, frequently mention this; for a more detailed discussion. See Ali 2006.

21. Inscriptions of Siyaka's successor Vakpati, made on the blank sides of copper plates stored in Manyakheta's land record offices, have been found. *EI* XXIII, 101.

22. This is based on descriptions from Somadeva's *Yashastilaka*, as well as the work of Daud Ali. See Ali 2006.

23. Somadeva mentions these in his *Yashastilaka*. See Mishra 1992, 89.

24. Marasimha II defeated some unnamed enemy at Manyakheta. See *EI* V, 177–80. This was almost certainly Siyaka, as there is no other enemy he would have had to fight there.

25. Altekar 1934, 131–32.

26. *EHD* I, 319.

27. Ibid., 320. The authors of *EHD* I suggest that this wife was from the imperial line, but her father, Bhammaha Ratta, is not found in other Rashtrakuta inscriptions, suggesting they were from a minor branch.

28. We know that Marasimha II recaptured Manyakheta from Siyaka, and given that Taila's landholdings were close to the city, it seems reasonable to assume that the man played some sort of role in this incident. Soon after, Marasimha returned to Gangavadi. In later years, Taila is known

to have been active in the Konkan and the northern and southern
Deccan but never claims conquest of Manyakheta, suggesting it was
already under his control.

29. *EHD* I, 205.
30. Pollock 2006, 154.
31. *Epigraphia Carnatica*, Vol. II, lxxxiv. Hereafter *EC*.
32. Arvind K. Singh, 'Interpreting the History of the Paramāras', *Journal of the Royal Asiatic Society* 22, no. 1 (2012). This may have been a deliberate move either to claim the mantle of Amoghavarsha Rashtrakuta or to establish himself as rewarding loyal followers, or both.
33. Merutungācārya, *The Prabandhacintāmaṇi, or Wishing-Stone of Narratives*, trans. C.H. Tawney (The Asiatic Society, 1901). These raids are also depicted as originating in the Deccan, with Vakpati being a righteous monarch who only defended his territory. Given the titles he claimed and his father's activities in the Deccan, this depiction is clearly disingenuous or based on a misremembering of historical events.
34. This was Karkka II, *EHD* I, 299.
35. *EHD* I, 321.
36. Ibid.
37. V.R. Deoras, 'Fresh Light on the Southern Campaigns of the Rāshṭrakūṭa Emperor Kṛishṇa III', *Proceedings of the Indian History Congress* 20 (1957).
38. This 'futile war' is referenced in *EHD* I, 320 and in Marasimha II's inscription. See *EI* V, 179–80.
39. *EI* V, 180.
40. Ibid. Verse abridged for readability.
41. *EHD* I, 321. 'Gangavadi' by this time also included much of Banavasi as a result of Krishna's gratitude towards his powerful brother-in-law.
42. *EHD* I, 321.
43. Taila died in 997/98, and Vakpati was still alive and spending his loot on patronizing poets in 993/94 going by dedications to him. This leaves a date of 994–96 for his death. See Merutungācārya 1901, ix.
44. Merutungācārya 1901, 30–36.
45. Who, in the story, is named after an actual historical figure attested to

in inscriptions: Vakpati's minister Rudraditya, whose story the poet respun with all the appropriate compositional elements, turning him into an archetypal ideal minister.

46. Patron–client relationships in medieval India could range from intense bonds, with death being sworn by the subordinate party if they failed their duties to manipulative, cynical, extortionate equations not dissimilar to those in modern boardrooms.

47. *EHD* I, 322.

48. *EI* XVIII, 252.

49. *EHD* I, 322, citing *EI* II, 215.

50. Ibid.

51. This, according to Merutunga, happened after an ill-fated seduction of Taila's sister Mrinalavati who was apparently deputed to serve food to Vakpati, but this can safely be dismissed given what we know of courtly protocol and other aspects of the chronology.

52. At least this is the fate of Vakpati in Merutunga's tale. Merutungācārya 1901, 35.

53. Ibid., 36.

54. Hugh Kennedy, *The Prophet and the Age of the Caliphates*, Second Edition (Pearson Longman, 2004), 313.

55. Ibid., 316.

56. Ibid., 317.

57. Ibid., 319.

58. For a detailed discussion, see Raoul McLaughlin, *Rome and the Distant East: Trade Routes to the Ancient Lands of Arabia, India and China* (Continuum, 2010).

59. S.A.M. Adshead and Reshmi Dutta-Flanders, *China in World History* (Palgrave Macmillan, 1988), 109.

60. Ibid.

61. See Tonio Andrade, *The Gunpowder Age: China, Military Innovation, and the Rise of the West in World History* (Princeton University Press, 2017).

62. Tansen Sen, 'The Military Campaigns of Rajendra Chola and the Chola-Srivijaya-China Triangle', in *Nagapattinam to Suvarnadwipa: Reflections on the Chola Naval Expeditions to Southeast Asia*, eds.

Hermann Kulke, K. Kesavapany and Vijay Sakhuja (Manohar, 2019) Reprint.

63. Ibid.

64. Ibid.

65. Ibid., 62.

66. Ibid., 63.

67. Sen 2019, 63.

68. Hermann Kulke, 'The Naval Expeditions of the Cholas in the Context of Asian History', in Kulke, Kesavapany and Sakhuja, eds. 2019, 5.

69. Whitney Cox, *Politics, Kingship, and Poetry in Medieval South India: Moonset on Sunrise Mountain* (Cambridge University Press, 2016), 42.

70. Ibid., 42–44.

71. *SII* III, 29. Rajaraja was supposed to have been a 'tender youth' when he ordered the burning of the Chera fleet.

72. Robert Sewell, *Historical Inscriptions of Southern India (Collected till 1923)*, ed. Krishnaswami S. Aiyangar (Madras University, 1932), 55. There is some debate over whether Kandalur was a port or a military school; the evidence seems to indicate the former.

73. Mamata Chaudhuri, 'Ship-Building in the Yuktikalpataru and Samarangana Sutradhara', *Indian Journal of the History of Science* 11 (1975): 143.

74. Wilhelm Geiger and Mabel C. Rickmers trans., *Cūlavaṃsa: Being the More Recent Part of the Mahāvaṃsa* (Asian Educational Services, 1992), 186.

75. Ibid., 187.

76. Ibid., 188.

77. K.A. Nilakanta Sastri, *The Cōḷas* (University of Madras, 1955), 173.

78. George W. Spencer, 'The Politics of Plunder: The Cholas in Eleventh-Century Ceylon', *The Journal of Asian Studies* 35, no. 3 (1976).

79. Geiger and Rickmers 1992, 188.

80. Sastri 1955, 174.

81. *EHD* I, 323.

82. K.G. Krishnan, *Karandai Tamil Sangam Plates of Rajendrachola I* (Archaeological Survey of India, 1984), 198–99.

83. Usha R. Vijailakshmi, 'Tamilian Migration into Karnataka (The Period

of Chola Conquest of Southern Karnataka and the Consolidation of Power from 850–1279 AD)', *Proceedings of the Indian History Congress* 66 (2006).

84. J. Durga Prasad, 'The Chalukyas of Vengi', in *Comprehensive History and Culture of Andhra Pradesh, Volume III: Early Medieval Andhra Pradesh AD 624–1000*, ed. B. Rajendra Prasad (Tulika, 2009).

85. Cox 2016, 36.

86. Geeta Vasudevan, *The Royal Temple of Rajaraja: An Instrument of Chola Imperial Power* (Abhinav, 2003), 44.

87. Adam Hardy, *Theory and Practice of Temple Architecture in Medieval India: Bhoja's Samarāṅgaṇasūtradhāra and the Bhojpur Line Drawings* (Indira Gandhi National Centre for the Arts, 2015), 4.

88. Vasudevan 2003, 44.

89. These are all enumerated at great length in *SII* II.

90. Vasudevan 2003, 44.

91. Ibid., 46.

92. See, for example, *SII* XIV.

93. Richard H. Davis, *Ritual in an Oscillating Universe: Worshipping Śiva in Medieval India* (Princeton University Press, 2014), 5.

94. Ranna, *Gadāyuddham: The Duel of the Maces*, ed. Akkamahadevi, trans. R.V.S. Sundaram and Ammel Sharon (Manohar, 2019), 19.

95. Ibid., xvi.

96. Ibid., xvii. The technical term is *rasa*, which means 'essence'.

97. Ibid., 11.

98. Pollock 2006, 155.

99. This process was started by Vikramaditya V.

100. Pollock 2006, 159.

101. Ibid.

102. Ibid., 156.

103. Ibid.

104. *IA* XVI, 21.

105. Pollock 2006, 158.

106. Ibid., 156.

107. Ibid., 157.

108. Ali 2006, 82.

109. Pollock 2006, 160.
110. *EHD* I, 324. The grand old stupa itself was not damaged.
111. An extensive discussion can be found in Spencer 1976.
112. *EHD* I, 324.
113. *EI* XVI, 75.
114. Sastri 1955, 176.
115. Death while defending 'women's honour' is quite frequently celebrated in hero stones. See S. Settar and Gunther D. Sontheimer, eds. *Memorial Stones* (Institute of Indian Art, 1982).
116. *SII* II, 13.
117. *EHD* I, 327. This was Jayasimha II.
118. Ibid., 325.
119. Pollock 2006, 179, citing a Paramara period source.
120. *EHD* I, 326. If Bhoja Paramara was celebrating the conquest of the Konkan with Brahmins from Manyakheta and Vatapi in 1020, it must have taken him some time to establish enough of a permanent presence to do this. It may be that he took advantage of Rajendra's invasion, or that Rajendra took advantage of his, or even that these attacks were coordinated in some way. See note below.
121. Professor Sastri is of the opinion that this event happened before 1008, because in Rajendra's first claim to have captured 'Mannaikkadakam' (Manyakheta) he mentions Satyasraya as the Chalukya king, and this man died in 1008. See also *SII* III, 18. However, the Karandai plates of Rajendra I (Krishnan 1984), issued in his eighth regnal year (1021–22), explicitly say that Rajendra was only able to capture Manyakheta after his father's death, which was in 1014. In addition, Jayasimha II, Satyasraya's son, is known to have used Kalyana as his capital in 1033. The destruction of Manyakheta must thus have happened during 1014–33. In the 1020s, Rajendra was occupied with organizing raids along the eastern coast and the second set of raids on Kedah. (He sent out one raid in 1017.) In 1018–19, Chola armies were busy in Sri Lanka, as per the *Mahāvaṃsa* and *Cūlavaṃsa*. At a strategic level, the likeliest date for the burning of Manyakheta is therefore in the late 1010s, when Jayasimha was preoccupied with Bhoja's invasion attempt to his north. This leads us to the conclusion that Rajendra's earlier

claim of having captured Manyakheta in 1008 was intended to portray his early career in Karnataka as successful to his domestic audience; it was most likely a limited raid on its suburbs that was repelled by Chalukya armies.

122. Krishnan 1984, 199. Of course, the inscription only describes Manyakheta, and does not specify that the army actually encamped in the *sal* orchards, but it seems likely.

123. Ibid.

124. Ibid. The poet is quite clear about the fact that Rajendra himself was at his capital when this act happened.

125. Ibid.

126. Ibid. The poet's name was Narayana, son of Samkararya and a resident of Parshvagrama. I have simplified the language for readability.

127. Ibid. I have simplified the language for readability.

128. This would be Akkadevi, the sister of Jayasimha II, the formidable aunt of Someshvara I, who will appear in the next chapter.

129. *IA* VI, 54 and *EI* XVIII, 321 via *EHD* I, 326.

130. Krishnan 1984, 199.

131. Spencer 1976.

132. See Noboru Karashima, 'Medieval Commercial Activities in the Indian Ocean Region as Revealed from Chinese Ceramic-Sherds and South Indian and Sri Lankan Inscriptions', in Kulke, Kesavapany and Sakhuja eds. 2019.

133. Geraldine Heng, 'An Ordinary Ship and Its Stories of Early Globalism', *Journal of Medieval Worlds* 1, no. 1 (2019): 13, https://doi.org/10.1525/jmw.2019.100003.

134. Ibid., 42–43.

135. Ibid., 49–50.

136. Sen 2019, 63.

137. Ibid., 17.

138. Subbarayalu 2012, 40.

139. Ibid., 190.

140. R. Champakalakshmi, *Trade, Ideology and Urbanisation: South India 300 BC to AD 1300* (Oxford University Press, 1996), 317. See also Noboru Karashima, 'South Indian Merchant Guilds in the Indian

Ocean and Southeast Asia', in Kulke, Kesavapany and Sakhuja eds. 2019, 151.

141. Sen 2004, 156–58.

142. Karashima 2019, 141.

143. Subbarayalu 2012, 177–78.

144. Ibid., 178.

145. Sen 2019, 69.

146. Noboru Karashima and Tansen Sen, 'Chinese Texts Describing or Referring to the Chola Kingdom as Zhu-nian', in Kulke, Kesavapany and Sakhuja eds. 2019, 297–98.

147. Hans Bielenstein, *Diplomacy and Trade in the Chinese World, 589–1276* (Brill, 2005), 77.

148. Ibid. Emphasis added.

149. Karashima and Sen 2019, 299.

150. Ibid., 77–78.

151. For a detailed discussion, see Tansen Sen, 'The Military Campaigns of Rajendra Chola and the Chola-Srivijaya-China Triangle', in Kulke, Kesavapany and Sakhuja eds. 2019.

152. Krishnan 1984, 200.

153. Kulke 2019, 6.

154. *EHD* I, 327.

155. This ended at the inconclusive battle of Maski (Musangi). See *EHD* I, 327–28.

156. Sastri 1955, 205–06.

157. *EHD* I, 328.

158. Hermann Kulke, 'Śrīvijaya Revisited: Reflections on State Formation of a Southeast Asian Thalassocracy', *Bulletin de l'Ecole Française d'Extrême-Orient* 102, no. 1 (2016): 62–63.

159. Nitish Sengupta, *Land of Two Rivers: A History of Bengal from the Mahabharata to Mujib* (Penguin, 2011).

160. *EI* IX, 233.

161. Sastri 1955, 209–10.

162. The lords of the Deccan played a significant role in the politics of east-central India: both the Kalyana Chalukyas and Rashtrakutas intermarried with the Kalachuris of Chedi, and in the later part of the

Chola–Chalukya wars, the Kalyana Chalukyas even attempted to seize forts such as Chakrakuta in Chhattisgarh. See Sastri 1955, 206.

163. Ibid., 255.

164. Ali 2006, 99.

165. *The Inscriptions of Nagai*, 19.

166. Ibid.

167. Nalini Sadhale and Y.L. Nene, 'Sarameyavinōda in Mānasollāsa: Dogs for Recreation and Hunting', *Asian Agri-History* 14, no. 3 (2010), https://www.asianagrihistory.org/pdf/articles/8_Sarameyavinoda.pdf.

168. Ali 2006, 100.

169. Subbarayulu 2012, 214.

170. Daud Ali, 'The Service Retinues of the Chola Court: A Study of the Term Veḷam in Tamil Inscriptions', *Bulletin of the School of Oriental and African Studies* 70, no. 3 (2007).

171. B. Arunachalam, *Chola Navigation Package* (Maritime History Society, 2004), 53.

172. Noboru Karashima and Y. Subbarayulu, 'Ancient and Medieval Tamil Sanskrit Inscriptions Relating to Southeast Asia and China', in Kulke, Kesavapany and Sakhuja eds. 2019, 279–80.

173. *SII* II, 28.

174. Karashima and Subbarayulu 2019.

175. *SII* II, 28.

176. Kulke 2019, 64.

177. Ibid.

178. Ibid.

179. *SII* II, 28.

180. *EHD* I, 330. Jayasimha II does not seem to have issued inscriptions from Kalyana.

181. Kulke 2016, 68.

182. Ibid.

183. Karashima and Sen 2019, 299–300.

184. Sen 2004, 156.

185. Kulke 2019, 10. See also Karashima and Subbarayulu 2019.

186. Kulke 2019, 43.

187. See P. Shanmugam, 'India and Southeast Asia: South Indian Cultural Links with Indonesia', in Kulke, Kesavapany and Sakhuja eds. 2019.

188. See Hema Devare, 'Cultural Implications of the Chola Maritime Fabric Trade with Southeast Asia', in Kulke, Kesavapany, and Sakhuja eds. 2019.
189. Risha Lee, 'Rethinking Community: The Indic Carvings of Quanzhou', in Kulke, Kesavapany and Sakhuja eds. 2019.
190. Davis 1993, 42.
191. Ibid.
192. Ibid.

9. Lord of the Moon

1. Pattadakal became the site of the imperial coronation once again after the establishment of the Kalyana Chalukyas. See *EHD* I, 382.
2. The illustration was based on Prasanna Kumar Acharya, *Architecture of Mānasāra: Illustrations of Architectural and Sculptural Objects with a Synopsis*, Mānasāra Series, Vol. 5 (Oxford University Press, 1934), Plate No. 138. The Mānasāra is a medieval Deccan text, and the illustration is based on a Chalukya sculpture.
3. Sastri 1955, 221.
4. *SII* III, 56. I have tweaked it to improve readability.
5. Ibid.
6. Ibid.
7. Ibid.
8. *EHD* I, 333.
9. The Chalukya general Nagavarma was already claiming this in 1047, and it seems to make sense that this had happened by the events of the 1045 campaign. See also Shrinivas Ritti and G.C. Shelke eds. *Inscriptions of Nanded District* (Yashwant Mahavidyalaya, 1968), xxiii.
10. Cox 2010, 5, footnote 9.
11. *EHD* I, 334.
12. *EI* XXIX, 62–63.
13. *EHD* I, 335. The authors suggest this was Prince Vikramaditya, Someshvara's second son. This seems a little doubtful as he died in 1126. Assuming this Vikki is indeed Vikramaditya, he must have been nearing twenty if he was a commander, thus making him over a hundred years old at the time of his death.

14. *EHD* I, 335.
15. Ibid.
16. Sastri 1955, 249–51.
17. Pollock 2006, 109.
18. Michael Willis, 'Dhār, Bhoja and Sarasvatī: From Indology to Political Mythology and Back', *Journal of the Royal Asiatic Society* 22, no. 1 (2012): 130.
19. Srinivas Reddy, *Raya: Krishnadevaraya of Vijayanagara* (Juggernaut Books, 2020).
20. Ibid.
21. K.N. Seth, *The Growth of the Paramara Power in Malwa* (Progress Publishers, 1978), 153.
22. Ibid., 154.
23. Arvind K. Singh, 'Interpreting the History of the Paramāras', *Journal of the Royal Asiatic Society* 22, no. 1 (2012): 21.
24. Pollock 2006, 180.
25. Ibid.
26. Seth 1978, 152.
27. Venkataraya V. Sastri, 'The Latter Days of Bhoja "The Great"', *Proceedings of the Indian History Congress* 10 (1947): 263.
28. Ritti and Shelke eds. 1968, xxiii–xxiv.
29. *EI* XVII, 123.
30. *SII* III, 56.
31. *EHD* I, 336.
32. *SII* III, 57.
33. *EHD* I, 336.
34. Ibid.
35. Ibid.
36. Ibid.
37. Ibid.
38. These might be exaggerations.
39. The extent of this evacuation is unknown, but it seems inconceivable that Someshvara would sit around and allow Kalyana and its people to burn, when Rajadhiraja's burning of Kampili and Pundur had given him so much advance warning. It also helps explain how the

Chalukyas were able to bounce back from the destruction of their
capital so quickly.

40. *EHD* I, 336.

41. Ibid.

42. Davis 1993, 34.

43. Ibid., 32.

44. Though we do not know the details of these parades, Rajadhiraja's
youngest brother Vira-Rajendra would perform similar spectacles
with loot from the Chalukyas. See Davis 1993.

45. This is speculation, but buttermilk was a prescribed drink for medieval
Deccan kings. See G.K. Shrigondekar, ed. *Mānasollāsa of King
Someśvara*, Vol. II (Oriental Institute, 1939), 22.

46. The Kakatiyas were present at the sacking of Kanchi that followed
soon after. See *EHD* I, 333.

47. In 1050, Sudi, further west from Rajadhiraja's 1047 campaign trail, was
granted 'a renewal of their corporate constitution which had partly
broken down in the stress of the war with the Cholas'. See *SII* XI-I,
84.

48. *EC* VIII, 56.

49. Ibid.

50. *SII* III, 57.

51. *EHD* I, 337.

52. *SII* XI-I, 75.

53. Ibid., 256.

54. Sastri 1955, 255.

55. Richard M. Eaton, *A Social History of the Deccan, 1300–1761: Eight
Indian Lives*, The New Cambridge History of India (Cambridge
University Press, 2005), 99.

56. *EHD* I (330) suggests that 'Someshvara 'made' the city 'not in the sense
of having founded it for the first time, but in that of having adopted
it as capital of his empire, adorned it with many new buildings, and
added to the amenities of life available there'. Of course Kalyana was
already an ancient site, but the authors may have neglected to consider
the alternative presented here: namely that Someshvara *rebuilt* Kalyana
after Rajadhiraja's burning.

57. Prasanna Kumar Acharya, *Architecture of Mānasāra: Translated from Original Sanskrit*, Mānasāra Series, Vol. 4 (Munshiram Manoharlal, 1934), 65, 83.
58. This, at least, is how vastu experts see it (and thus perhaps how Someshvara's *sthapatis* saw it as well). See Sashikala Ananth, *The Penguin Guide to Vaastu: The Classical Indian Science of Architecture and Design* (Penguin Books, 1998), 115.
59. Acharya 1934, 70–71.
60. Katherine E. Kasdorf, 'Forming Dōrasamudra: Temples of the Hoysaḷa Capital in Context', PhD dissertation (Columbia University, 2013), 73.
61. Ibid., 74.
62. Acharya 1934 (Vol. 4), 79.
63. Eaton and Wagoner 2014, 7.
64. These details can be inferred from texts composed in Kalyana a little later, such as the *Vikramankadevacharitam*, as well as Chalukya *prashastis* and sculptures.
65. *SII* XI-I, 100.
66. Adiga 2003, 178.
67. Nandi 2000, 118.
68. *EHD* I, 340.
69. Ibid.
70. See *Gazetteer of the Bombay Presidency, Volume I Part II: History of the Konkan Dakhan and Southern Maratha Country* (Government Central Press, 1896), 435, 439.
71. Ibid.
72. *IA* XVIII, 274.
73. *SII* XI, 84, 87.
74. Ibid.
75. Om Prakash Prasad, 'Trade in the Growth of Towns: A Case Study of Karnataka (c. 600–1200 A.D.)', *Proceedings of the Indian History Congress* 41 (1980).
76. Cox 2010, 9.
77. Ibid., 10.
78. Ibid., 11.

79. Ibid., 10.
80. Ibid., 19.
81. Nandi 2000, 111.
82. Ibid., 108.
83. Ibid., 109.
84. Ibid., 109–10.
85. Ibid., 113.
86. Ibid., 117.
87. Ibid.
88. James McHugh, 'The Incense Trees of the Land of Emeralds: The Exotic Material Culture of *Kāmaśāstra*', *Journal of Indian Philosophy* 39, no. 1 (2011).
89. Gerard Foekema, *Architecture Decorated with Architecture: Late Medieval Temples of Karnataka, 1000–1300* (Munshiram Manoharlal, 2003), 49.
90. Adam Hardy, 'Tradition and Transformation Continuity and Ingenuity in the Temples of Karnataka', *Journal of the Society of Architectural Historians* 60, no. 2 (2001).
91. Foekema 2003, 52.
92. Ibid.
93. Ibid., 82.
94. Eaton and Wagoner 2014, 80.
95. Ibid., 79.
96. Ibid., 80–81.
97. Ibid., 82.
98. Ibid., 79.
99. Hardy 2001, 194.
100. *EHD* I, 338.
101. Ibid., 336.
102. Davis 1993, 34.
103. *SII* III, 63.
104. Ibid.
105. *EHD* I, 338.
106. Handiqui 1949, 60. This might not be an accurate description of all the Tamil soldiers at Koppam in 1054, but it likely holds true for at least a proportion of them.

107. Ibid.
108. Karashima and Sen 2019, 296. Chinese sources describe elephants advancing at the forefront of the Chola army.
109. Ibid., 303. The titles can be seen in vols I–III of *SII*.
110. *SII* III, 63.
111. Shrigondekar 1939, 27.
112. Ibid.
113. Ali 2000, 264. Medieval courtly texts such as the *Manasollasa* recommend this for men of the court.
114. Ibid.
115. Bilhana, *Vikramankadeva Caritam: Glimpses of the History of the Cāḷukyas of Kalyana*, trans. Sures Chandra Banerji (Sambodhi Publications, 1965), 266.
116. *EHD* I, 339. It is not explicitly stated that these two set out to kill the emperor; that is, however, what the evidence suggests.
117. *SII* III, 63. Someshvara's generals get the credit for this, but given the lack of concrete detail about the battle, it is equally possible that Rajadhiraja died ignominiously at the hands of anonymous archers. That said, his death is depicted as coming at the hands of Someshvara's generals since that is what the fragmentary sources attest to.
118. Shrigondekar 1939, 27.
119. Ibid., 30.
120. *SII* III, 63.
121. Ibid.
122. *EHD* I, 338.
123. Sastri 1955, 258.
124. Ibid., 257.
125. *SII* III, 63.
126. The translation provided in *EHD* I, 339 has been merged with that provided in *EI* XV, 345.
127. *SII* XI-I, 92.
128. *EHD* I, 339, and *The Inscriptions of Nagai*, 20.

10. Fortune's Favourites

1.   Cox 2016, 36.
2.   *SII* XI-I, 77.
3.   *EHD* I, 341.
4.   Cox 2016, 36.
5.   He is referred to as 'Rajiga' in Chalukya sources, likely an insulting diminutive comparable to 'Vikki' (see *EHD* I, 335). His original name was likely Rajendra; he would use that name later in his career, as we will see. I refer to him as 'Rajiga' in this formative period, following the precedent of Cox 2016, and for ease of reading; there are otherwise too many Rajendras in this royal drama.
6.   Cox 2016, 38.
7.   Velcheru Narayana Rao and David Shulman, *Classical Telugu Poetry: An Anthology* (University of California Press, 2002), 59.
8.   Ibid., 56.
9.   See Velcheru Narayana Rao and David Shulman, *Symbols of Substance: Court and State in Nāyāka Period Tamil Nadu* (Oxford University Press, 1992).
10. Merutungācārya 1901, 30–36.
11. Singh 2012, 21.
12. Ibid.
13. Pollock 2006, 179–80.
14. *EHD* I, 341–42. The authors claim that the campaigns in Vengi were a prelude to this battle, but this book presents an alternative explanation of the evidence – namely that the battle of Kudala-Sangama was a minor skirmish embellished by later Chola propaganda (following Cox 2016), and that the main thrust of the Chola–Chalukya wars of 1061–62 was Vengi, which led to the death of Vijayaditya's son Shaktivarman II.
15. *EHD* I, 342.
16. For a detailed discussion, see Malini Adiga, 'Rape in Early Medieval Karnataka: Inter-Village Warfare and Opportunities for Male Heroism', *Proceedings of the Indian History Congress* 78 (2017).
17. Ryali plates of Vijayaditya VII, quoted in N. Venkataramanayya, *The*

Eastern Cāḷukyas of Vengi (Vedam Venkataraya Sastry & Bros, 1950), 39–40.

18. Ibid.
19. Cox 2016, 42.
20. Sastri 1955, 271–72.
21. Bilhana, *The Vikramânkadevacharita, A Life of King Vikramâditya-Tribhuvanamalla of Kalyana*, ed. Georg Bühler (Central Book Depot, 1875), 32.
22. *SII* III, 68.
23. Ibid.
24. Ibid.
25. Sastri 1955, 290.
26. Cox 2016, 67.
27. Ibid., 64.
28. Ibid., 74.
29. Cox 2016, 67.
30. Ibid., 68.
31. This book uses Professor Sastri's depiction of this 'diplomatic revolution'. See Sastri 1955, 290.
32. As mentioned in the previous chapter, the authors of *EHD* think he was present in the 1044 campaign in Vengi. At the very least he would have had to be approaching his twenties if he was one of the Chalukya commanders that Rajadhiraja Chola mentions in his inscriptions. This means he was probably born sometime in the late 1020s. However, Vikramaditya VI only died in 1126 – which would have made him an improbable hundred and ten years of age at the time of his death.
33. Bilhana 1875, 30.
34. Shrigondekar 1939, 25–26. This was not specifically said about Vikramaditya but is prescribed as standard for Chalukya kings by his son Someshvara III, making it quite likely that it was something that Vikramaditya did.
35. Ibid.
36. *EHD* I, 347.
37. Whitney Cox, 'Sharing a Single Seat: The Poetics and Politics of Male Intimacy in the Vikramāṅkakāvya,' *Journal of Indian Philosophy* 38, no. 5 (2010).

38. Sastri 1955, 269.
39. Bilhana's *Vikramankadevacharitam* makes it clear that the court accompanied Someshvara and that he walked into the waters. See Cox 2016, 126.
40. This is also from Bilhana. See ibid.
41. Cox 2016, 127.
42. *EHD* I, 349.
43. Vira-Rajendra did actually fight a limited war with Someshvara II, which may or may not have been responsible for Vikramaditya's appointment as governor of Gangavadi. See *EHD* I, 350.
44. Cox 2016, 73.
45. Ibid.
46. Ibid., 75.
47. Ibid., 94.
48. Ibid.
49. Ibid., 114.
50. *EHD* I, 351.
51. Ibid., 351–52.
52. Ibid., 353.
53. Ibid., 352.
54. Ibid., 354.
55. This, at least, is the version depicted in the *Vikramankadevacharitam*.
56. *EHD* I, 355.
57. Ibid.
58. Ibid., 366.
59. Ibid., 364–65.
60. Eaton and Wagoner 2014, 6.
61. Donald R. Davis and David Brick, 'Social and Literary History of Dharmaśāstra: Commentaries and Legal Digests', in Patrick Olivelle and Donald R. Davis, Jr., eds. *The Oxford History of Hinduism: Hindu Law: A New History of Dharmaśāstra* (Oxford University Press, 2018), 40.
62. These are all described as aspects of the emperor's schedule in the *Manasollasa* of Someshvara III.
63. *EHD* I, 367.

64. K.A. Nilakanta Sastri, *The Cōḷas*, Volume II (Part I) (University of Madras, 1937), 15–16.

65. Ibid., 49.

66. Ibid., 36–37. According to Professor Sastri, the powerful Anantavarman Codaganga, ruler of much of twelfth-century Kalinga, Utkala and Tosali (corresponding to modern-day Odisha), was the son of Rajiga-Kulottunga's daughter.

67. Ibid., 48.

68. For a brief account, see *EHD* I, 359–64. While this claims that the 'Chalukya empire managed to fairly easily weather the storm', this explanation seems to fit the evidence better: Hoysala Vishnuvardhana very clearly had imperial ambitions and all but declared them openly with his enormous Vira-Narayana (now the Chennakeshava) temple at Belur.

69. Sastri 1937, 42.

70. Ibid., 44.

71. Ibid., 179. The course of events is much more complex than the brief summary presented here. Indeed, on multiple occasions, the Hoysalas actually came to the aid of the Cholas to maintain the balance of power against the Pandyas.

72. Ibid., 208.

73. It is worth pointing out that the Vijayanarayana and the Gondeshvara display architectural influences from North India, probably due to the pan-subcontinental imperial ambitions of their ruling dynasties, and their historical involvement with Malwa. The Ramappa is more Deccano-Dravidian.

74. There would be one last Chalukya ruler, Someshvara IV, after Bijjala, but for all intents and purposes the dynasty's power came to an end with Bijjala's coup.

75. H.S. Shivaprakash, *I Keep Vigil of Rudra: The Vachanas* (Penguin Random House, 2010).

76. O.L. Nagabhushana Swamy, ed. *The Sign: Vachanas of 12th Century* (Prasaranga Kannada University, 2007).

77. Eaton and Wagoner 2014, 14.

78. Prithvi Datta Chandra Shobhi, 'Kalyāṇa is Wrecked: The Remaking of

a Medieval Capital in Popular Imagination', *South Asian Studies* 32, no. 1 (2016).

79. Shivaprakash 2010, xii.

80. A detailed discussion may be found in Richard M. Eaton and Phillip B. Wagoner, 'Warfare on the Deccan Plateau, 1450–1600: A Military Revolution in Early Modern India?' *Journal of World History* 25, no. 1 (2014).

81. Srinivas Reddy, 'Stallions of the Indian Ocean', in *Exploring Materiality and Connectivity in Anthropology and Beyond*, eds. Philipp Schorch, Martin Saxer and Marlen Elders (UCL Press, 2020).

82. Eaton and Wagoner 2014, 98–106.

83. Ibid., 96–97.

84. Ibid., 106–13.

85. Ibid., 89.

86. Ibid., 128.

87. Ibid., 139–45.

88. Ibid., 156.

89. Ibid., 137–38.

90. Carl W. Ernst, 'Admiring the Works of the Ancients: The Ellora Temples as Viewed by Indo-Muslim Authors', in David Gilmartin and Bruce B. Lawrence, eds. *Beyond Turk and Hindu: Rethinking Religious Identities in Islamicate South Asia* (University of Florida Press, 2000), 108.

91. Ibid., 107.

92. Ibid., 109.

93. This would be *Ponniyin Selvan*.

94. This is a claim made by Whitney Cox in the 2010 paper 'Scribe and Script in the Cālukya West Deccan' (p. 19) and repeated by Eaton and Wagoner in their 2014 book, *Power, Memory, Architecture* (p. 8).

95. Ludo Rocher, 'Inheritance: Dāyabhāga', in Olivelle and Davis, Jr., 2018.

96. Ibid., 178.

Bibliography

List of Abbreviations

CII	Corpus Inscriptionum Indicarum
EC	Epigraphia Carnatica
EHD	Early History of the Deccan
EI	Epigraphia Indica
IA	Indian Antiquary
SII	South Indian Inscriptions

Primary Sources

Alberuni. *Alberuni's India*. Edited and translated by Edward C. Sachau. Kegan Paul, Trench, Trubner & Co, 1910.

al-Sirafi, Abu Zayd. *Two Arabic Travel Books: Accounts of India and China*. Edited and translated by Tim Mackintosh-Smith. New York University Press, 2014.

Bilhana. *The Vikramânkadevacharita, a Life of King Vikramâditya-Tribhuvanamalla of Kalyâṇa*. Edited by George Bühler. Bombay: Central Book Depot, 1875.

Bilhana. *Vikramānkadeva Caritam: Glimpses of the History of the Cāḷukyas of Kalyāṇa*. Translated by Sures Chandra Banerji. Sambodhi Publications, 1965.

Cūlavaṃsa: Being the More Recent Part of the Mahāvaṃsa. Geiger, Wilhelm, and Mabel C. Rickmers. Asian Educational Services, 1992.

Dandin. *Tales of the Ten Princes*. Translated by A.N.D. Haksar. Penguin India, 2007. Kindle Edition.

Gazetteer of the Bombay Presidency, Volume I Part II: History of the Konkan Dakhan and Southern Maratha Country. Government Central Press, 1896.

Hsüan-tsang. *Buddhist Records of the Western World*. Translated by Samuel Beal. 2 volumes. Trübner, 1884.

Kalidasa. *Meghadutam*. Translated by Srinivas Reddy. Penguin Random House India, 2015.

Karashima, Noboru, and Tansen Sen. 'Chinese Texts Describing or Referring to the Chola Kingdom as Zhu-Nian'. In *Nagapattinam to Suvarnadwipa: Reflections on the Chola Naval Expeditions to Southeast Asia*, edited by Hermann Kulke, K. Kesavapany and Vijay Sakhuja, 292–315. Manohar, 2019.

Karashima, Noboru, and Y. Subbarayulu. 'Ancient and Medieval Tamil Sanskrit Inscriptions Relating to Southeast Asia and China'. In *Nagapattinam to Suvarnadwipa: Reflections on the Chola Naval Expeditions to Southeast Asia*, edited by Hermann Kulke, K. Kesavapany and Vijay Sakhuja, 271–91. Manohar, 2019.

Krishnan, K.G. *Karandai Tamil Sangam Plates of Rajendrachola I.* Archaeological Survey of India, 1984.

Mackintosh-Smith, Tim, James E. Montgomery, Philip F. Kennedy and Shawkat M. Toorawa, eds. *Two Arabic Travel Books: Accounts of China and India and Mission to the Volga*. New York University Press, 2014.

Mahendravikramavarman. '*Matta-vilāsa*: A Farce'. Translated by L.D. Barnett. *Bulletin of the School of Oriental Studies*, 5, no. 4 (1930): 697–717.

Matsya Puranam. The Sacred Books of the Hindus Translated by Various Sanskrit Scholars, edited by B.D. Basu. Allahabad: The Panini Office, 1917.

Merutungācārya. *The Prabandhacintāmaṇi, or Wishing-Stone of Narratives*. Translated by C.H. Tawney. The Asiatic Society, 1901.

Mirashi, Vasudev Vishnu. *Corpus Inscriptionum Indicarum*. Vol. IV, part I. Government Epigraphist for India, 1955.

Olivelle, Patrick. *Dharmasutras: The Law Codes of Ancient India*. Oxford University Press, 1999.

Olivelle, Patrick, trans. *King, Governance, and Law in Ancient India: Kautilya's Arthaśāstra*. Oxford University Press, 2013.

Ranna. *Gadāyuddham: The Duel of the Maces*. Edited by Akkamahadevi. Translated by R.V.S. Sundaram and Ammel Sharon. Manohar, 2019.

Sewell, Robert. *Historical Inscriptions of Southern India (Collected till 1923)*. Edited by Krishnaswami S. Aiyangar. Madras University, 1932.

Shrigondekar, G.K., ed. *Mānasollāsa of King Someśvara*. Vol. 2. Oriental Institute, 1939.

Shrinivas, Ritti, and G.C. Shelke, eds. *Inscriptions of Nanded District*. Yashwant Mahavidyalaya, 1968.

Sundaram, R.V.S., and Deven M. Patel, trans. Śrīvijaya's *Kavirājāmārgaṁ*. Manohar, 2017.

The Inscriptions of Nagai. Hyderabad Archaeological Series, No. 8. The Nizam's Government, 1928.

Various Editors. *Epigraphia Carnatica*. Vols II, VIII. Mysore Archaeological Department, University of Mysore.

Various Editors. *Epigraphia Indica*. Vols III, IV, V, VI, X, XIII, XIV, XV, XVI, XVIII, XIX, XXV, XXIX, XXXII. Archaeological Survey of India.

Various Editors. *Indian Antiquary*. Vols VI, X, XI, XII. Swati Publications.

Various Editors. *South Indian Inscriptions*. Vols I, II, III. Archaeological Survey of India.

Vatsyayana. *Kama Sutra: A Guide to the Art of Pleasure*. Translated by A.N.D. Haksar. New Delhi: Penguin Books, 2011.

Secondary Sources

Abraham, Meera. *Two Medieval Merchant Guilds of South India*. Manohar, 1988.

Acharya, Prasanna Kumar. *Architecture of Mānasāra: Translated from the Original Sanskrit*. Mānasāra Series, Vol. 4. Munshiram Manoharlal, 1934.

———. *Architecture of Mānasāra: Illustrations of Architectural and Sculptural Objects with a Synopsis*. Mānasāra Series, Vol. 5. Oxford University Press, 1934.

Adiga, Malini. 'Dharmasastras, the Dravidian Kinship System and Female

Inheritance in Karantaka in the Early Medieval Period (400 A.D. to 1300 A.D.)'. *Proceedings of the Indian History Congress* 64 (2003): 173–84.

———. *The Making of Southern Karnataka: Society, Polity and Culture in Early Medieval Period, AD 400-1030*. Orient BlackSwan, 2006.

———. 'Of Concubines and Devadasis: Prostitution in Early Medieval Kartataka'. *Proceedings of the Indian History Congress* 73 (2012): 144–54.

———. 'Rape in Early Medieval Karnataka: Inter-Village Warfare and Opportunities for Male Heroism'. *Proceedings of the Indian History Congress* 78 (2017): 207–19.

Adshead, S.A.M. *T'ang China: The Rise of the East in World History*. Palgrave Macmillan, 2004.

Adshead, S.A.M., and Reshmi Dutta-Flanders. *China in World History*. Palgrave Macmillan, 1988.

Agrawala, Vasudeva S. *The Deeds of Harsha: Being a Cultural Study of Bana's Harshacharita*. Prithvi Prakashan, 1969.

Alcock, Susan E., Terence N. D'Altroy, Kathleen D. Morrison and Carla M. Sinopoli, eds. *Empires: Perspectives from Archaeology and History*. Cambridge University Press, 2001.

Ali, Daud. 'Violence, Gastronomy and the Meanings of War in Medieval South India.' *The Medieval History Journal* 3, no. 2 (2000): 261–89. https://doi.org/10.1177/097194580000300204.

———. *Courtly Culture and Political Life in Early Medieval India*. Cambridge University Press, 2006.

———. 'The Service Retinues of the Chola Court: A Study of the Term Velam in Tamil Inscriptions'. *Bulletin of School of Oriental and African Studies* 70, no. 3 (2007): 487–509.

———. 'Aristocratic Body Techniques in Early Medieval India'. In *Rethinking a Millennium – Perspectives on Indian History from the Eighth to the Eighteenth Century: Essays for Harbans Mukhia*, edited by Rajat Datta, 69–93. Aakar, 2008.

———. 'Bhoja's Mechanical Garden: Translating Wonder across the Indian Ocean, circa 800–1100 CE'. *History of Religions* 55, no. 4 (2016): 460–93.

Altekar, Anant Sadashiv. *The Rashtrakutas and Their Times; Being a Political, Administrative, Religious, Social, Economic and Literary History of the*

Deccan during C. 750 AD to C. 1000 AD. Oriental Book Agency, 1934.

Andrade, Tonio. *The Gunpowder Age: China, Military Innovation, and the Rise of the West in World History*. Princeton University Press, 2017.

Ariel, Glucklich. *The Strides of Vishnu: Hindu Culture in Historical Perspective*. Oxford University Press, 2008.

Aruna, A. *State Formation in the Eastern Deccan (7th Century AD–13th Century AD)*. Bhartiya Kala Prakashan, 2000.

Arunachalam, B. *Chola Navigation Package*. Maritime History Society, 2004.

Bahulkar, S.S., and Shilpa Sumant, eds. 'The Bijapur–Mumbai Copperplate Grant of the Cālukya Ruler Pulakeśin II, Dated April 04, 619 CE, Mentioning His Triumph over Emperor Harṣavardhana'. *Annals of the Bhandarkar Oriental Research Institute* XCII (2012): 205–09.

Bakker, Hans. *The World of the Skandapurāṇa: Northern India in the Sixth and Seventh Centuries*. Groningen Oriental Studies, Vol. 4, Supplement. Brill Academic Publishers, 2014.

Barua, Pradeep P. *The State at War in South Asia*. University of Nebraska Press, 2009.

Bennison, Amira K. *The Great Caliphs: The Golden Age of the ʿAbbasid Empire*. Yale University Press, 2009.

Berkson, Carmel. *Ellora: Concept and Style*. Second Edition. Abhinav Publications, 2004.

———. 'Daśāvatāra Cave: Its Importance in the History of World Art'. In *Ellora Caves: Sculpture and Architecture*, edited by Ratna Parimoo, Deepak Kannal and Shivaji Panniker, Revised Edition, 166–82. Aprant, 2018.

Bhattacharyya, Narendra Nath. *Ancient Indian Rituals and Their Social Contents*. Manohar, 1975.

Bielenstein, Hans. *Diplomacy and Trade in the Chinese World, 589–1276*. Brill, 2005.

Blankinship, Khalid Yahya. *The End of the Jihad State: The Reign of Hisham Ibn'Abd al-Malik and the Collapse of the Umayyads*. SUNY Press, 1994.

Bolon, Carol Radcliffe. *Forms of the Goddess Lajja Gauri in Indian Art*. Pennsylvania State University Press, 1992.

Bose, S.K. *Boot, Hooves, and Wheels: And the Social Dynamics Behind South Asian Warfare*. Vij Books India, 2015.

Buchanan, Susan Locher. 'Cāḷukya Temples: History and Iconography'. PhD dissertation. Ohio State University, 1985.

Burjor, Avari. *Islamic Civilization in South Asia: A History of Muslim Power and Presence in the Indian Subcontinent*. Routledge, 2019.

Chakrabarti, Dilip K. *The Geopolitical Orbits of Ancient India: The Geographical Frames of the Ancient Indian Dynasties*. Oxford University Press, 2011.

Chakravarti, Prithwis Chandra. *The Art of War in Ancient India*. University of Dacca, 1941.

Chakravarti, Ranabir. 'The Pull Towards the Coast: Politics and Polity in India (c. 600–1300 CE)'. *Presidential Address Indian History Congress*, 2011, 1–48.

———. 'Merchants, Merchandise and Merchantmen in the Western Seaboard of India: A Maritime Profile (500 BCE–1500 CE)'. In *The Trading World of Indian Ocean, 1500–1800*, edited by Om Prakash and D.P. Chattopadhyaya, 53–116. Pearson Education, 2012.

Champakalakshmi, R. *Trade, Ideology and Urbanisation: South India 300 BC to AD 1300*. Oxford University Press, 1996.

Chandler, David. *A History of Cambodia*. Taylor and Francis, 2018.

Chattopadhyaya, Brajadulal. *Representing the Other: Sanskrit Sources and the Muslims, Eighth to Fourteenth Century*. Primus Books, 1998.

Chaudhuri, Mamata. 'Ship-Building in the Yuktikalpataru and Samarangana Sutradhara'. *Indian Journal of the History of Science* (1975): 137–47.

Cousens, Henry. *The Chalukya Architecture of the Kanarese Districts*. Central Government of India, 1926.

Cox, Whitney. 'Scribe and Script in the Cāḷukya West Deccan'. *The Indian Economic and Social History Review* 47, no. 1 (2010): 1–28.

———. 'Sharing a Single Seat: The Poetics and Politics of Male Intimacy in the Vikrāmaṅkakāvya.' *Journal of Indian Philosophy* 38, no. 5 (2010): 485–501.

———. 'Politics, Kingship, and Poetry in Medieval South India: Moonset on Sunrise Mountain.* Cambridge University Press, 2016.

Cummings, Cathleen Ann. 'A Study of the Iconographic Program of the Lokesvara (Virupaksa) Temple, Pattadakal'. PhD dissertation. Ohio State University, 2006.

Dalal, Kurush. 'Sanjan: Digging Deep Into History'. *Live History India*, 22 September 2019. https://www.livehistoryindia.com/story/cover-story/ sanjan-digging-deep-into-history/.

Davidson, Ronald M. *Indian Esoteric Buddhism: A Social History of the Tantric Movement*. Columbia University Press, 2002.

Davis, Jr., Donald R., and David Brick. 'Social and Literary History of Dharmaśāstra: Commentaries and Legal Digests'. In *The Oxford History of Hinduism: Hindu Law: A New History of Dharmaśāstra*, edited by Patrick Olivelle and Donald R. Davis, Jr., 30–48. Oxford University Press, 2018.

Davis, Richard H. 'Indian Art Objects as Loot'. *The Journal of Asian Studies* 52, no. 1 (1993): 22–48.

———. *Ritual in an Oscillating Universe: Worshipping Śiva in Medieval India*. Princeton University Press, 2014.

DeCaroli, Robert. 'An Analysis of Daṇḍin's Daśakumāracarita and Its Implications for Both the Vākāṭaka and Pallava Courts.' *Journal of the American Oriental Society* 115, no. 4 (1995): 671–78.

Dehejia, Vidya. *Slaves of the Lord: The Path of the Tamil Saints*. Munshiram Manoharlal, 2002.

———. *The Body Adorned: Sacred and Profane in Indian Art*. Columbia University Press, 2009.

Deoras, V.R. 'Fresh Light on the Southern Campaigns of the Rāshṭrakūṭa Emperor Kṛishṇa III.' *Proceedings of the Indian History Congress* 20 (1957): 133–40.

Devare, Hema. 'Cultural Implications of the Chola Maritime Fabric Trade with Southeast Asia.' In *Nagapattinam to Suvarnadwipa: Reflections on the Chola Naval Expeditions to Southeast Asia*, edited by Hermann Kulke, K. Kesavapany and Vijay Sakhuja, 178–92. Manohar, 2019.

Dhavalikar, M.K. 'Kailasa: The Stylistic Development and Chronology'. In *The Rashtrakutas of Malkhed: Studies in Their History and Culture*, edited by B.R. Gopal, 254–64. The Mythic Society/Geetha Book House, 1994.

———. *Ellora: Monumental Legacy*. Oxford University Press, 2003.

———. 'Sutradhar'. *Annals of the Bhandarkar Oriental Research Institute*, no. 52 (1971): 215–20.

Dikshit, Durga Prasad. *Political History of the Chalukyas of Badami*. Abhinav Publications, 1980.

Dirks, Nicholas B. 'Political Authority and Structural Change in Early South Indian History'. *Indian Economic and Social History Review* 13, no. 2 (1976): 125–57. https://doi.org/10.1177/001946468101300201.

Doniger, Wendy. *The Hindus: An Alternative History*. Penguin, 2009.

Dundas, Paul. *The Jains*. Second Edition. Routledge, 2002.

Durga Prasad, J. 'The Chalukyas of Vengi'. In *Comprehensive History and Culture of Andhra Pradesh, Vol. 3: Early Medieval Andhra Pradesh AD 624–1000*, edited by B. Rajendra Prasad, 32–46. Tulika Books, 2009.

Eaton, Richard M. *A Social History of the Deccan, 1300–1761: Eight Indian Lives*. The New Cambridge History of India. Cambridge University Press, 2005.

Eaton, Richard M., and Phillip B. Wagoner. *Power, Memory, Architecture: Contested Sites on India's Deccan Plateau, 1300–1600*. Oxford University Press, 2014.

———. 'Warfare on the Deccan Plateau, 1450–1600: A Military Revolution in Early Modern India?' *Journal of World History* 25, no. 1 (2014): 5–50.

Eck, Diana L. *India: A Sacred Geography*. Harmony, 2012.

Ernst, Carl W. 'Admiring the Works of the Ancients: The Ellora Temples as Viewed by Indo-Muslim Authors'. In *Beyond Turk and Hindu: Rethinking Religious Identities in Islamicate South Asia*, edited by David Gilmartin and Bruce B. Lawrence, 98–120. University of Florida Press, 2000.

Eswar, Rohitha, Vrushab Mahesh and K. Krishnan. '"Iha" to "Para": A Hero's Transitional Journey to the Other World from This World – Reading Veeragals of Hassan'. *Heritage: Journal of Multidisciplinary Studies in Archaeology* 2 (2014): 108–24.

Fleming, Benjamin J. 'Ellora Cave 16 and the Cult of the Twelve Jyotirlingas.' In *Living Rock: Buddhist, Hindu and Jain Cave Temples in the Western Deccan*, edited by Pia Brancaccio. Marg Foundation, 2013.

Flood, Gavin. *The Blackwell Companion to Hinduism*. Wiley, 2003.

Foekema, Gerard. *Architecture Decorated with Architecture: Late Medieval Temples of Karnataka, 1000–1300*. Munshiram Manoharlal, 2003.

Frankopan, Peter. *The Silk Roads: A New History of the World*. Bloomsbury, 2015.

Ganguly, D.C. 'The "Gurjaras" in the Rastrakuta Inscriptions'. *Proceedings of the Indian History Congress* 3 (1939): 513–15.

Goetz, H. 'The Kailasa of Ellora and the Chronology of Rashtrakuta Art'. *Artibus Asiae* 15, no. 1/2 (1952): 84–107.

Goyal, Shankar. 'Acquisition of the Maukhari Empire by Harsha'. *Proceedings of the Indian History Congress* 62 (2001): 1090–91.

Gupta, S.P., Kurush Dalal, R. Nanji and Abhijit Dandekar. 'Preliminary Report on the Excavations at Sanjan (2002)'. *Purattatva* 32 (n.d.): 182–244.

Handiqui, Krishna Kanta. *Yaśastilaka and Indian Culture*. Jain Samskriti Samraksha Sangha, 1949.

Hardy, Adam. 'Tradition and Transformation: Continuity and Ingenuity in the Temples of Karnataka'. *Journal of the Society of Architectural Historians* 60, no. 2 (2001): 180–99.

———. *Theory and Practice of Temple Architecture in Medieval India: Bhoja's Samarāṅgaṇasūtradhāra and the Bhojpur Line Drawings*. Indira Gandhi National Centre for Arts, 2015.

Hawley, John Stratton. 'Scenes from the Childhood of Kṛṣṇa on the Kailāsanātha Temple, Ellora'. *Archives of Asian Art* 34 (1981): 74–90.

Heng, Geraldine. 'An Ordinary Ship and Its Stories of Early Globalism'. *Journal of Medieval Worlds* 1, no. 1 (2019): 11–54. https://doi.org/10.1525/jmw.2019.100003.

Hirsh, Marilyn. 'Mahendravarman I Pallava: Artist and Patron of Māmallapuram'. *Artibus Asiae* 48, no. 1 (1987): 109–30.

Hopkins, Thomas J. *The Hindu Religious Tradition*. Wadsworth Publishing Company, 1971.

Inden, Ronald. 'Hierarchies of Kings in Early Medieval India'. *Contributions to Indian Sociology* 15, no. 1–2 (1981): 99–125. https://doi.org/10.1177/006996678101500108.

———. *Imagining India*. Indiana State University, 2000.

Jamison, Stephanie W. 'Roles for Women in Vedic Srauta Ritual'. In *Goddesses and Women in the Indic Religious Tradition*, edited by Arvind Sharma, 1–17. Brill's Indological Library 24. Brill, 2005.

Jantakal, Gautam, Bhushan Kapadia and Prakash Jinjuvadiya. *History and Coinage of the Rashtrakutas*. IIRNS Publications LLP, 2019.

Kadambi, Hemanth. 'Sacred Landscapes in Early Medieval South India: The Chalukya State and Society (ca. AD 550-750)'. PhD dissertation. University of Michigan, 2011.

Kakar, Sudhir. *Intimate Relations: Exploring Indian Sexuality*. University of Chicago Press, 1989.

Kaligotla, Subhashini. 'Shiva's Waterfront Temples: Reimagining the Sacred Architecture of India's Deccan Region'. PhD dissertation. Columbia University, 2015. https:/academiccommons.columbia.edu/doi/10.7916/D83N2B1V/download.

Kamath, Suryanath U. 'Amoghavarsha I: An Appraisal'. In *The Rashtrakutas of Malkhed: Studies in Their History and Culture*, edited by B.R. Gopal, 82–88. The Mythic Society, 1994.

Kannal, Deepak. 'The Regional Lineages and Possible Masters at Kailāśanātha Temple of Ellora'. In *Ellora Caves: Sculpture and Architecture*, edited by Ratan Parimoo, Deepak Kannal and Shivaji Panniker, Revised Edition. Aprant, 2018.

Karashima, Noboru. 'Medieval Commercial Activities in the Indian Ocean Region as Revealed from Chinese Ceramic-Sherds and South Indian and Sri Lankan Inscriptions'. In *Nagapattinam to Suvarnadwipa: Reflections on the Chola Naval Expeditions to Southeast Asia*, edited by Hermann Kulke, K. Kesavapany and Vijay Sakhuja, 20–60. Manohar, 2019.

———. 'South Indian Merchant Guilds in the Indian Ocean and Southeast Asia'. In *Nagapattinam to Suvarnadwipa: Reflections on the Chola Naval Expeditions to Southeast Asia*, edited by Hermann Kulke, K. Kesavapany and Vijay Sakhuja, 135–57. Manohar, 2019.

Kasdorf, Katherine E. 'Forming Dōrasamudra: Temples of the Hoysaḷa Capital in Context'. PhD dissertation. Columbia University, 2013.

Kaul, Shonaleeka. *Imagining the Urban: Sanskrit and the City in Early India*. Seagull Books, 2011.

Keay, John. *India: A History*. Revised and Updated. Grove/Atlantic Inc., 2011.

Keegan, John. *The Face of Battle: A Study of Agincourt, Waterloo and the Somme*. Random House, 2011.

Kennedy, Hugh. *Prophet and the Age of the Caliphates*. Second Edition Pearson Longman, 2004.

———. *The Armies of the Caliphs: Military and Society in the Early Islamic State*. Routledge, 2013.

Konstantin, Nossov, and Peter Dennis. *War Elephants*. Osprey Publishing, 2008.

Kulkarni, R.H. 'Vatapi Ganapati, an art historical revisit'. *New Indian Express*, 22 August 2020. https://www.newindianexpress.com/opinions/2020/aug/22/vatapi-ganapati-an-art-historical-revisit-2186817.html

Kulke, Hermann. 'Śrīvijaya Revisited: Reflections on State Formation of a Southeast Asian Thalassocracy'. *Bulletin de l'Ecole Française d'Extrême-Orient* 102, no. 1 (2016): 45–95.

———. 'The Naval Expeditions of the Cholas in the Context of Asian History'. In *Nagapattinam to Suvarnadwipa: Reflections on the Chola Naval Expeditions to Southeast Asia*, edited by Hermann Kulke, K. Kesavapany and Vijay Sakhuja, 1–20. Manohar, 2019.

Lambourn, Elizabeth. 'Describing a Lost Camel: Clues for West Asian Mercantile Networks in South Asian Maritime Trade (Tenth–Twelfth Centuries CE)'. In *Ports of the Ancient Indian Ocean: Proceedings of the Kolkata Colloquium 2011 (Median Project)*, edited by M.F. Boussac, J.F. Salles and J.B. Yon, 351–407. Primus Books, 2016.

Lang, Karen C. 'Candrakirti on the Medieval Military Culture of South India'. In *Buddhism in the Krishna River Valley of Andhra*, edited by Sree Padma Holt and A.W. Barber, 127–50. SUNY Press, 2008.

Lath, Mukund. 'Somadeva Suri and the Question of Jain Identity'. In *The Assembly of Listeners: Jains in Society*, edited by Michael Carrithers and Caroline Humphrey, 19–30. Cambridge University Press, 1991.

Lee, Risha. 'Rethinking Community: The Indic Carvings of Quanzhou'. In *Nagapattinam to Suvarnadwipa: Reflections on the Chola Naval Expeditions to Southeast Asia*, edited by Hermann Kulke, K. Kesavapany and Vijay Sakhuja, 240–70. Manohar, 2019.

Majumdar, R.C. *The Age of Imperial Kannauj*. The History and Culture of the Indian People, Vol. 4. Second Edition. Bharatiya Vidya Bhavan, 1959.

Malekandathil, Pius. *Maritime India*. Primus Books, 2010.

Markel, Stephen. 'The "Rāmāyaṇa" Cycle on the Kailāsanātha Temple at Ellora'. *Ars Orientalis* 30, Supplement 1 (2000): 59–71.

McHugh, James. 'The Incense Trees of the Land of Emeralds: The Exotic

Material Culture of *Kāmaśāstra'*. *Journal of Indian Philosophy* 39, no. 1 (2011): 63–100.

McKnight, John Michael. 'The Gupta Temple Movement: A Study of Political Aspects of the Early Hindu Temple'. PhD dissertation. McMaster University, 1973.

McLaughlin, Raoul. *Rome and the Distant East: Trade Routes to the Ancient Lands of Arabia, India and China.* Continuum, 2010.

Menon, Srikumar M. 'The Curious Case of the Galaganatha Dolmen: Possible Links Between Megalithic Monuments and Early Temples at Aihole'. *Heritage: Journal of Multidisciplinary Studies in Archaeology* 2 (2014): 54–73.

Mirashi, Vasudev Vishnu. 'Manor Plates of Rāshṭrakūta Dantidurga: Śaka Year 671'. *Proceedings of the Indian History Congress* 21 (1958).

———. 'The Javakheḍa Plates of Amoghavarsha I: Śaka 742: A Critical Examination of Some Problems'. *Proceedings of the Indian History Congress* 23 (1960): 31–36.

Mishra, Jayashri. *Social and Economic Conditions Under the Imperial Rashtrakutas.* Commonwealth Publishers, 1992.

Mitra, Rhea, and Kurush Dalal. 'A Report on the Glass Vessels from Sanjan, 2002'. *Journal of Indian Ocean Archaeology* 2 (2005): 62–68.

Moraes, George M. *The Kadamba Kula.* B.X. Furtado & Sons, 1931.

Morrison, Kathleen D. 'Trade, Urbanism, and Agricultural Expansion: Buddhist Monastic Institutions and the State in the Early Historic Western Deccan'. *World Archaeology* 27, no. 2 (1995): 203–21.

Nandi, Ramendra Nath. *Religious Institutions and Cults in the Deccan (c. A.D. 600–A.D. 1100).* Motilal Banarsidass, 1973.

———. *State Formation, Agrarian Growth and Social Change in Feudal South India c. AD 600–1200.* Manohar, 2000.

Owen, Lisa Nadine. *Carving Devotion in the Jain Caves at Ellora.* Brill, 2012.

Brancaccio, Pia, ed. 'Art, Architecture and Devotional Practice at Ellora'. In *Living Rock: Buddhist, Hindu and Jain Cave Temples in the Western Deccan*, edited by Pia Brancaccio, Marg Foundation, 2013.

Padigar, Srinivas V. 'Craftsmen's Inscriptions from Badami: Their Significance'. In *Ellora Caves: Sculpture and Architecture*, edited by Ratan Parimoo, Deepak Kannal and Shivaji Panniker, Revised Edition, 313–19. Aprant, 2018.

Pollard, Edward, and Okeny Charles Kinyera. 'The Swahili Coast and the Indian Ocean Trade Patterns in the 7th–10th Centuries CE'. *Journal of Southern African Studies* 43, no. 5 (2017): 927–47. https://doi.org/10.10 80/03057070.2017.1345266.

Pollock, Sheldon. *The Language of the Gods in the World of Men: Sanskrit, Culture and Power in Premodern India*. University of California Press, 2006.

Prasad, Om Prakash. 'Trade in the Growth of Towns: A Case Study of Karnataka (c. 600–1200 A.D.)'. *Proceedings of the Indian History Congress* 41 (1980): 152–60.

Prentiss, Karen Pechilis. *The Embodiment of Bhakti*. Oxford University Press, 1999.

Rabe, Michael D. 'The Māmallapuram Praśasti: A Panegyric in Figures'. *Artibus Asiae* 57, no. 3 (1997): 189–241.

Ramesh K.V. 'Pulakesin II – His Career and Personality'. In *The Chalukyas of Badami: Seminar Papers*, edited by M.S. Nagaraja Rao, 53–65. The Mythic Society, 1978.

Rangaswamaiah, G.R. 'Bhuvikrama's Role in the Chalukya–Pallava Conflict (635–679)'. *Proceedings of the Indian History Congress* 35 (1974): 60–63. http://www.jstor.org/stable/44138760.

———. 'The Rashtrakuta Relations with the Gangas of Talkad'. In *The Rashtrakutas of Malkhed: Studies in Their History and Culture*, edited by B.R. Gopal, 204–10. The Mythic Society, 1994.

Ray, Himanshu Prabha. 'Creating Religious Identity: Archaeology of Early Temples in the Malaprabha Valley'. In *The Temple in South Asia*, edited by Himanshu Prabha Ray, 15–37. Oxford University Press, 2010.

Reddy, Srinivas. 'Stallions of the Indian Ocean'. In *Exploring Materiality and Connectivity in Anthropology and Beyond,* edited by Philipp Schorch, Martin Saxer and Marlen Elders, 98–115. UCL Press, 2010.

———. *Raya: Krishnadevaraya of Vijayanagara*. Juggernaut Books, 2020.

Ritti, Shrinivas, and G.C. Shelke. *Inscriptions of Nanded District*. Yashwant Mahavidyalaya, 1968.

Rocher, Ludo. 'Inheritance: Dāyabhāga'. In *The Oxford History of Hinduism: Hindu Law: A New History of Dharmaśāstra*, edited by Patrick Olivelle and Donald R. Davis, Jr., 164–78. Oxford University Press, 2018.

Roy, Kumkum. *The Power of Gender and the Gender of Power: Explorations in Early Indian History*. Oxford University Press, 2010.

Sabin, Philip. 'The Face of Roman Battle'. *The Journal of Roman Studies* 90 (2000): 1–17.

Sadhale, Nalini, and Y.L. Nene. 'Sarameyavinōda in Mānasollāsa: Dogs for Recreation and Hunting.' *Asian Agrarian History* 14, no. 3 (2010): 273–83.

Sanderson, Alexis. 'The Śaiva Age: The Rise and Dominance of Śaivism During the Early Medieval Period'. In *Genesis and Development of Early Tantrism*, edited by Shingo Einoo, 41–349. University of Tokyo, 2009.

Sashikala, Ananth. *The Penguin Guide to Vaastu: The Classical Indian Science of Architecture and Design*. Penguin Books, 1998.

Sastri, K.A. Nilakanta, *The Cōḷas, Volume II (Part I)*. University of Madras, 1937.

———. *Foreign Notices of South India: From Megasthenes to Ma Huan*. University of Madras, 1939.

———. *The Cōḷas, Volume I*. University of Madras, 1955.

———. *A History of South India from Prehistoric Times to the Fall of Vijayanagar*. Oxford University Press, 1997.

Sastri, V. Venkataraya. 'The Latter Days of Bhoja "The Great"'. *Proceedings of the Indian History Congress* 10 (1947): 260–68.

———. 'The Rashtrakutas and Vengi and Cultural Contacts'. In *The Rashtrakutas of Malkhed: Studies in Their History and Culture*, edited by B.R. Gopal, 171–80. The Mythic Society, 1994.

Sen, Tansen. *Buddhism, Diplomacy and Trade: The Realignment of Sino-Indian Relations, 600–1400*. University of Hawai'i Press, 2004.

———. 'The Military Campaigns of Rajendra Chola and the Chola–Srivijaya–China Triangle'. In *Nagapattinam to Suvarnadwipa: Reflections on the Chola Naval Expeditions to Southeast Asia*, edited by Hermann Kulke, K. Kesavapany and Vijay Sakhuja, 61–74. Manohar, 2019.

Sengupta, Nitish. *Land of Two Rivers: A History of Bengal from the Mahabharata to Mujib*. Penguin Books, 2011.

Seth, K.N. *The Growth of the Paramara Power in Malwa*. Progress Publishers, 1978.

Settar, S., and Gunther D. Sontheimer, eds. *Memorial Stones*. Institute of Indian Art, 1982.

Shanmugam, P. 'India and Southeast Asia: South Indian Cultural Links with Indonesia'. In *Nagapattinam to Suvarnadwipa: Reflections on the Chola Naval Expeditions to Southeast Asia*, edited by Hermann Kulke, K. Kesavapany and Vijay Sakhuja, 208–27. Manohar, 2019.

Shekhar, Divya. 'Inscription Stone Discovered in Hebbal Could Be Bengaluru's Oldest'. *The Economic Times*, 23 June 2018. https://economictimes.indiatimes.com/magazines/panache/inscription-stone-discovered-in-hebbal-could-be-bengalurus-oldest/articleshow/64708042.cms.

Shivanna. 'Rashtrakuta Krishna I and Gangavadi (758–774 A.D.).' *Proceedings of the Indian History Congress* 38 (1977): 65–70.

———. 'An Estimate of Dhruva'. In *The Rashtrakutas of Malkhed: Studies in Their History and Culture*, edited by B.R. Gopal, 73–81. The Mythic Society, 1994.

Shivaprakash, H.S. *I Keep Vigil of Rudra: The Vachanas*. Penguin Random House India, 2010.

Shobhi, Prithvi Chandra Datta. 'Kalyāṇa Is Wrecked: The Remaking of a Medieval Capital in Popular Imagination'. *South Asian Studies* 32, no. 1 (2016): 90–98.

Singh, Arvind K. 'Interpreting the History of the Paramāras'. *Journal of the Royal Asiatic Society* 22, no. 1 (2012): 13–28.

Sinopoli, Carla M. 'On the Edge of Empire: Form and Substance in the Satavahana Dynasty'. In *Empires: Perspectives from Archaeology and History*, edited by Susan E. Alcock, Terence N. D'Altroy, Kathleen D. Morrison and Carla M. Sinopoli, 155–78. Cambridge University Press, 2001.

Smith, David. 'One Man and Many Women: Some Notes on the Harem in Mainly Ancient and Medieval India from Sundry Perspectives'. *Cracow Indological Studies* XIV (2012): 1–16.

Soar, Michaela. 'The Tīrtha at Ellora'. In *Ellora Caves: Sculpture and Architecture*, edited by Ratan Parimoo, Deepak Kannal and Shivaji Panniker, Revised Edition, 63–79. Aprant, 2018.

Soundara Rajan, K.V. *The Ellora Monoliths*. Gian, 1988.

Spencer, George W. 'The Politics of Plunder: The Cholas in Eleventh-Century Ceylon'. *The Journal of Asian Studies* 35, no. 3 (1976): 405–19.

Srivastava, Prashant. 'The Harsha–Pulakeshin II War'. In *Select Battles in Indian History*, edited by K.K. Thapyal and S.N. Mishra, 126–30. Agama Kala Prakashan, 2002.

Stavig, Gopal. 'Congruencies between Indian and Islamic Philosophy'. *Annals of the Bhandarkar Oriental Research Institute* 81, no. 1/4 (1994): 213–26. http://www.jstor.org/stable/41694615.

Subbarayalu, Y. *South India Under the Cholas*. Oxford University Press, 2012.

Sundaram, R.V.S., ed. *Śrīvijaya's Kavirājāmārgaṃ*. Translated by Deven M. Patel. Manohar, 2017.

Swamy, O.L. Nagabhushana, ed. *The Sign: Vachanas of 12th Century*. Prasaranga Kannada University, 2007.

Tartakov, Gary Michael. 'The Beginning of Dravidian Temple Architecture in Stone'. *Artibus Asiae* 42, no. 1 (1980): 39–99.

Thapar, Romila. *The Penguin History of Early India: From the Origins to AD 1300*. Penguin UK, 2015.

'The Helgo Treasure: A Viking Age Buddha'. *Irish Archaeology*, 28 December 2013. http://irisharchaeology.ie/2013/12/the-helgo-treasure-a-viking-age-buddha.

Trautmann, Thomas R. *Elephants and Kings: An Environmental History*. University of Chicago Press, 2015.

———. *Arthashastra: The Science of Wealth*. Penguin, 2016.

Vahia, M.N., A.P. Jamkhedkar and Parag Mahajani. 'Astronomical Orientation of Caves in Ajantha and Ellora'. *Journal of Multidisciplinary Studies in Archaeology* 5 (2017): 806–12.

Vasudevan, Geeta. *The Royal Temple of Rajaraja: An Instrument of Chola Imperial Power*. Abhinav, 2003.

Vatsyayan, Kapila. *The Square and the Circle of the Indian Arts*. Second Edition. Abhinav, 1997.

Velcheru, Narayana Rao, and David Shulman. *Classical Telugu Poetry: An Anthology*. University of California Press, 2002.

Venkataramanayya, N. *The Eastern Cālukyas of Vēngi*. Vedam Venkataraya Sastry and Bros, 1950.

Vijailakshmi, Usha R. 'Tamilian Migration into Karnataka (The Period of Chola Conquest of Southern Karnataka and the Consolidation of Power from 850–1279 A.D.' *Proceedings of the Indian History Congress* 66 (2006): 239–51.

Vogel, Jean Phillippe. *The Goose in Indian Literature and Art*. E.J. Brill, 1962.

Vogler, Roger. *The Kailas at Ellora: A New View of a Misunderstood Masterwork*. INTACH Aurangabad and Mapin Publishing, 2015.

Willis, Michael D. *The Archaeology of Hindu Ritual: Temples and the Establishment of the Gods*. Cambridge University Press, 2009.

——. 'Dhār, Bhoja and Sarasvatī: From Indology to Political Mythology and Back'. *Journal of the Royal Asiatic Society* 22, no. 1 (2012): 129–53.

Yazdani, Ghulam, ed. *The Early History of Deccan*. Vol. I. Oxford University Press, 1960.

Acknowledgements

Lords of the Deccan has been three years in the making – three years in which the manuscript and my understanding of the world evolved and transformed alongside so many friends, mentors, loved ones and kind strangers.

I do not know the names of these strangers, but this book would not have been possible without their unthinking generosity to a young man in awe of a history that they hold in trust for us all. Writing a book about such a distant past is a journey in solitude, but I will never forget the people whom I met in my travels through the Deccan. Their kindness added so much humanity to the images that were taking shape through my research. Thank you to the bus conductor who advised me on the best routes to take from Pattadakal to Aihole; to the drivers and passengers of shared autos at Aurangabad and Ellora; to the kind old gentleman at the Mythic Society in Bengaluru, who was more than happy to look up an out-of-print publication for me; to the brilliant and thoughtful scholars, photographers and government officers who have made knowledge available online in priceless archives for anyone to read. To everyone who has taken time out to email, tweet or message me on social media and otherwise, inquiring about the progress of my work. To the bravehearts who have defied lobbies and interest groups to keep Library Genesis alive – *Lords of the Deccan,* and hundreds of other such books, would not exist but for you. You are truly among the unsung heroes of our generation.

To my parents and my sister, whose love has taught me so much; and to my aunts, uncles and cousins; to Jasman Preet Randhawa, who was there through my darkest times; to P., who entered and left my life so suddenly, but filled it with such love in the brief time we had. To the Amazing Humbug (S.G.), Kevin Fernandes, Sujata Shukla, Anand Ganapathy and Aishwarya Narayanan. Your bottomless faith in me and your encouragement to learn more, teach more and grow to be better has shaped me profoundly. To Aditya Ramanathan and Parul Shanker, whose warm home and enthusiasm for history taught me so much. To Arjun Ullas, Keshav Rajendran, Karthik Nair, Krishna P. Unny, Jajwalya Karajgikar, Mahathi G., Tejas A.P., Karthik Malli and Ashwitha Jayakumar, who so unexpectedly became some of my dearest friends, and whose kindness, humour and knowledge have inspired me deeply.

To my research assistant Sarthak Sharma – you are among the brightest and smartest young scholars I know. Thank you for your keen attention to detail, critical mind, eclectic online presence, for your friendship and for all your hard work. Thank you for following your deepest passion and for living your life. To Nakshatra Soni and Shaaz Sheikh, two gifted young artists whom I very serendipitously met on Instagram and who made such marvelous cover art for this book. To Chiki Sarkar, Parth Mehrotra and their team at Juggernaut. I could not have asked for a smarter group of people to bring *Lords of the Deccan* to life.

To the good folk at the Takshashila Institution – Lt. Gen. Prakash Menon, Pranay Kotasthane, Nitin Pai, Manoj Kewalramani, Shambhavi Naik, Rohan Seth, Suyash Desai, Anupam Manur, Prateek Waghre, Sowmya Prabhakar, Shivakumar, Sridevi and Lakshman. To the friends I made there – Ram Ganesh Kamatham, Ganesh Chakravarthi, Madhav Chandavarkar, Antara Krishnamurthy, Nidhi Gupta, Shibani Mehta, Hamsini Hariharan, Manasa Venkatraman,

Asawari Ghatage and Yazad Jal. I have learned so much from all of you over the years, and I am most grateful for your encouragement.

To everyone I have worked with at IVM Podcasts – Vinay Joshi, Jalasmi Hathi, Tejas Shringarpure, Ekta Valecha, Alika Gupta, Abbas Momin, Karthik Mohan, and of course, Amit Doshi. Your investment in my work has allowed me to follow my deepest intellectual passions. It has led me to meet so many people who have transformed me over the years.

To Dr. Deepthi Murali, Professor Daud Ali, Professor Srinivas Reddy, Professor Cathleen Ann Cummings, Dr. Devika Rangachari, Professor Gil Ben-Herut, Professor Kurush F. Dalal and Dr. Namita Sugandhi. As an outsider to the academic world of history and historiography, your kind words and selfless sharing of your thoughts has inspired me in my efforts to bring the work of scholars such as yourselves to young people across the world. Thanks especially to Dr. Deepthi Murali for her endless encouragement and warm advice; to Professor Srinivas Reddy for our discussions on Vijayanagara; to Professor Daud Ali for his kind words on my work as a public history writer; and to Professors Cathleen Ann Cummings and Kurush F. Dalal for generously sharing their photographs of medieval artifacts and architecture with me.

Special thanks are due to Manu S. Pillai for making *Lords of the Deccan* happen. I am grateful to him for introducing me to Parth Mehrotra at Juggernaut; for his kind words on my many projects and for his feedback on this manuscript. To Rana Safvi, Ira Mukhoty, Ambassador T.C.A. Raghavan and William Dalrymple. Your gracious comments and encouragement on this book mean the world to me. I am exhilarated to have received them, and I earnestly hope that my work can live up to yours in the future.

And most crucially, thank you, Parth Mehrotra. As my friend and editor, you have constantly encouraged me to make *Lords of the Deccan* the book that I've always dreamt of writing. You have taught me so much over the last few years, and I feel tremendously lucky to have had your frankness and critical mind helping make this book, this labour of my heart and mind, something that I can be proud of forever.

Anirudh Kanisetti
January 2022

Index

1

CRAFTED
FOR MOBILE
READING

*Thought you would never read a book
on mobile? Let us prove you wrong.*

juggernaut.in

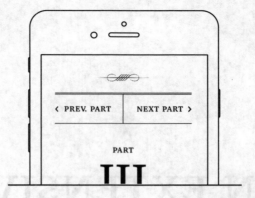

Beautiful Typography

The quality of print transferred
to your mobile. Forget ugly PDFs.

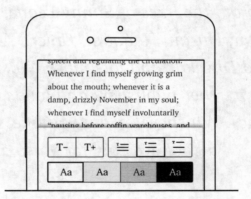

Customizable Reading

Read in the font size, spacing
and background of your liking.

AN EXTENSIVE LIBRARY

Including fresh, new, original Juggernaut books from the likes of Sunny Leone, Praveen Swami, Husain Haqqani, Umera Ahmed, Rujuta Diwekar and lots more. Plus, books from partner publishers and loads of free classics. Whichever genre you like, there's a book waiting for you.

juggernaut.in

juggernaut.in

3

DON'T JUST READ; INTERACT

We're changing the reading experience from passive to active.

juggernaut.in

Ask authors questions

Get all your answers from the horse's mouth. Juggernaut authors actually reply to every question they can.

Rate and review

Let everyone know of your favourite reads or critique the finer points of a book – you will be heard in a community of like-minded readers.

Gift books to friends

For a book-lover, there's no nicer gift than a book personally picked. You can even do it anonymously if you like.

Enjoy new book formats

Discover serials released in parts over time, picture books including comics, and story-bundles at discounted rates. And coming soon, audiobooks.

4

LOWEST PRICES & ONE-TAP BUYING

Books start at ₹10 with regular discounts and free previews.

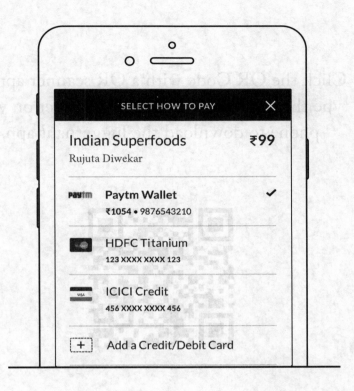

Paytm Wallet, Cards & Apple Payments

On Android, just add a Paytm Wallet once and buy any book with one tap. On iOS, pay with one tap with your iTunes-linked debit/credit card.

Click the QR Code with a QR scanner app or type the link into the Internet browser on your phone to download the Juggernaut app.

For our complete catalogue, visit www.juggernaut.in
To submit your book, send a synopsis and two
sample chapters to books@juggernaut.in
For all other queries, write to contact@juggernaut.in